Matthew

Matthew

CHARLES H. TALBERT

Baker Academic
a division of Baker Publishing Group
Grand Rapids, Michigan

Published by Baker Academic
a division of Baker Publishing Group
PO Box 6287, Grand Rapids, MI 49516-6287
www.bakeracademic.com

Printed in the United States of America

Library of Congress Cataloging-in-Publication Data

Talbert, Charles H.
   Matthew / Charles H. Talbert.
      p.   cm. — (Paideia)
   Includes bibliographical references (p.   ) and indexes.
   ISBN 978-0-8010-3192-2 (pbk.)
     1. Bible. N.T. Matthew—Commentaries. I. Title.
BS2575.53.T36 2010
226.2'07—dc22

2010010556

10 11 12 13 14 15 16   7 6 5 4 3 2 1

To
colleagues in the department of religion
at Baylor University
friends and fellow learners

Contents

Figures and Tables

Foreword

Paideia: Commentaries on the New Testament is a series that sets out to comment on the final form of the New Testament text in a way that pays due attention both to the cultural, literary, and theological settings in which the text took form and to the interests of the contemporary readers to whom the commentaries are addressed. This series is aimed squarely at students—including MA students in religious and theological studies programs, seminarians, and upper-divisional undergraduates—who have theological interests in the biblical text. Thus, the didactic aim of the series is to enable students to understand each book of the New Testament as a literary whole rooted in a particular ancient setting and related to its context within the New Testament.

The name "Paideia" reflects (1) the instructional aim of the series—giving contemporary students a basic grounding in academic New Testament studies by guiding their engagement with New Testament texts; (2) the fact that the New Testament texts as literary unities are shaped by the educational categories and ideas (rhetorical, narratological, etc.) of their ancient writers and readers; and (3) the pedagogical aims of the texts themselves—their central aim being not simply to impart information but to form the theological convictions and moral habits of their readers.

Each commentary deals with the text in terms of larger rhetorical units; these are not verse-by-verse commentaries. This series thus stands within the stream of recent commentaries that attend to the final form of the text. Such reader-centered literary approaches are inherently more accessible to liberal arts students without extensive linguistic and historical-critical preparation than older exegetical approaches, but within the reader-centered world the sanest practitioners have paid careful attention to the extratext of the original readers, including not only these readers' knowledge of the geography, history, and other context elements reflected in the text but also their ability to respond correctly to the literary and rhetorical conventions used in the text. Paideia commentaries pay deliberate attention to this extratextual repertoire in order to highlight the ways in which the text is designed to persuade and move its readers. Each rhetorical unit is explored from three angles: (1) introductory matters; (2) tracing the train of thought or narrative or rhetorical flow of the argument; and (3) theological issues raised by the text that are of interest to the contemporary Christian. Thus, the primary focus remains on the text and not its historical context or its interpretation in the secondary literature.

Our authors represent a variety of confessional points of view: Protestant, Roman Catholic, and Greek Orthodox. What they share, beyond being New Testament scholars of national and international repute, is a commitment to reading the biblical text as theological documents within their ancient contexts. Working within the broad parameters described here, each author brings his or her own considerable exegetical talents and deep theological commitments to the task of laying bare the interpretation of scripture for the faith and practice of God's people everywhere.

Mikeal C. Parsons
Charles H. Talbert

Preface

What! Another commentary on Matthew? After decades of relative neglect, the First Gospel has in recent times been the object of intense scrutiny. Numerous very good commentaries have appeared: Davies and Allison (1988–97), Luz (1989–2005), Hagner (1993–95), Gundry (1982), Harrington (1991), Boring (1995), Carter (2000), Nolland (2005), Schnackenburg (2002), Gnilka (1986–88), Bonnard (1963), and Turner (2008), to mention only a few. When I reluctantly accepted the invitation from Baker Academic to do the volume on Matthew in the new Paideia series and began to read the recent commentaries and other secondary source materials, I wondered, Why does another need to be done? The level of accomplishment in these recent commentaries is very high. When I started through the Greek text of the First Gospel and tried to make systematic sense of Matthew's narrative world, however, I found myself arriving at what seemed to be a "fresh" approach in nearly every section of the Gospel. It was then that I finally felt another commentary might be in order. What is offered here is an attempt at a fresh reading of the First Gospel, done hopefully with lucid brevity, that is accessible to upper-level undergraduates, seminarians, graduate students, pastors, and teachers.

The secondary literature on Matthew is enormous. A person could spend a career trying to master it. I am very grateful both to Baylor graduate students who in two seminars on Matthew did in-depth histories of research on key segments of the Gospel and to a couple of advanced undergraduate classes at Baylor that did similar surveys of periodical literature for me. Special thanks must go to several graduate assistants who did summer research assignments on ancient parables, miracle stories, conflict stories, and yes, the collection of even more periodical bibliography. Jim McConnell, Alicia Myers, Kalvin Budiman, and especially Jesse Robertson and Julien Smith, thank you for your indispensable efforts on behalf of this project. Thanks must also go to

David Oakley, my graduate assistant for 2008–9, who did the work for the abbreviations, and to Tim Brookins, my current graduate assistant, who prepared the subject index. I also owe a lasting debt to my former colleague, Dr. Sharyn Dowd, who allowed me to teach her doctoral seminar on the Synoptic Gospels twice while she accepted responsibility for my Pauline seminar. It was but another of her gracious efforts on my behalf. It is not possible to express the depth of my appreciation to Dr. Stephen von Wyrick of the University of Mary Hardin-Baylor for his generous act of making available images for this volume from his large collection of pictures of biblical lands. Because recent commentaries by John Nolland (2005) and Craig Keener (1999) contain extensive bibliographies and because of the cumulative bibliography on Matthew and Q edited by F. Neirynck, J. Verheyden, and R. Corstjens (1998), I have chosen to include only a limited bibliography and to document in a representative, rather than an exhaustive, way. I hope my documentation and bibliography are enough to indicate my grounding in current research and to give an interested reader a lead into further study.

Gratitude must also be expressed to *Biblica* for permission to use material from my article "Indicative and Imperative in Matthean Soteriology," 82 (2001): 515–38; to T&T Clark International for permission to use material from my article "Is It with Ethics That the Sermon on the Mount Is Concerned?" in *Literary Encounters with the Reign of God*, edited by Sharon Ringe and Paul Kim (New York: T&T Clark, 2004), 45–63; to the University of South Carolina Press for permission to use material from my book *Reading the Sermon on the Mount: Character Formation and Decision Making in Matthew 5–7* (Columbia: University of South Carolina Press, 2004); and to Princeton University Press for permission to use material from my article "Miraculous Conceptions and Births in Mediterranean Antiquity," in *The Historical Jesus in Context*, edited by A. J. Levine, Dale C. Allison Jr., and John D. Crossan (Princeton, NJ: Princeton University Press, 2006), 79–86. Quotations from the Old Testament Pseudepigrapha are from James M. Charlesworth, ed., *The Old Testament Pseudepigrapha*, 2 vols. (Garden City, NY: Doubleday, 1983–85); and quotations from the Qumran documents are from Florentino García Martínez, *The Dead Sea Scrolls Translated*, 2nd ed. (Leiden: Brill; Grand Rapids: Eerdmans, 1996).

I am deeply indebted to my wife, Dr. Betty W. Talbert, director of spiritual formation at George W. Truett Seminary of Baylor University, for graciously allowing me to withdraw from family responsibilities for three successive summers and to think of one thing only: Matthew. Without her usual generosity, this project would never have reached completion.

Charles H. Talbert
Easter 2009

Abbreviations

General

art.	article	NT	New Testament
b.	Babylonian Talmud	OT	Old Testament
chap(s).	chapter(s)	pl.	plural
col.	column	pt.	part
Eng.	English Bible versification	sg.	singular
		sp.	spurious
frag.	fragment	*t.*	Tosefta
Heb.	Hebrew	*tg.*	Targum
m.	Mishnah	*y.*	Jerusalem Talmud
marg.	marginal reading		

Bible Texts and Versions

ESV	English Standard Version
JB	Jerusalem Bible
KJV	King James Version
LXX	Septuagint
MT	Masoretic Text
NA[27]	*Novum Testamentum Graece*. Edited by [E. and E. Nestle,] B. Aland et al. 27th rev. ed. Stuttgart: Deutsche Bibelgesellschaft, 1993.
NAB	New American Bible
NASB	New American Standard Bible
NIV	New International Version
NJB	New Jerusalem Bible
NRSV	New Revised Standard Version

REB	Revised English Bible
RSV	Revised Standard Version
TEV	Today's English Version
UBS[4]	*The Greek New Testament*. Edited by B. Aland et al. 4th rev. ed. Stuttgart: Deutsche Bibelgesellschaft and United Bible Societies, 1994.

Ancient Corpora

OLD TESTAMENT

Amos	Amos
1–2 Chron.	1–2 Chronicles
Dan.	Daniel
Deut.	Deuteronomy
Eccles.	Ecclesiastes
Esther	Esther
Exod.	Exodus
Ezek.	Ezekiel
Ezra	Ezra
Gen.	Genesis
Hab.	Habakkuk
Hag.	Haggai
Hosea	Hosea
Isa.	Isaiah
Jer.	Jeremiah
Job	Job
Joel	Joel
Jon.	Jonah
Josh.	Joshua
Judg.	Judges
1–2 Kings	1–2 Kings
Lam.	Lamentations
Lev.	Leviticus
Mal.	Malachi
Mic.	Micah
Nah.	Nahum
Neh.	Nehemiah
Num.	Numbers
Obad.	Obadiah
Prov.	Proverbs
Ps./Pss.	Psalms
Ruth	Ruth
1–2 Sam.	1–2 Samuel
Song	Song of Songs
Zech.	Zechariah
Zeph.	Zephaniah

DEUTEROCANONICAL BOOKS

Bar.	Baruch
1–2 Esd.	1–2 Esdras
1–4 Macc.	1–4 Maccabees
Sir.	Sirach
Sus.	Susanna
Tob.	Tobit
Wis.	Wisdom of Solomon

NEW TESTAMENT

Acts	Acts
Col.	Colossians
1–2 Cor.	1–2 Corinthians
Eph.	Ephesians
Gal.	Galatians
Heb.	Hebrews
James	James
John	John
1–3 John	1–3 John
Jude	Jude
Luke	Luke
Mark	Mark
Matt.	Matthew
1–2 Pet.	1–2 Peter
Phil.	Philippians
Philem.	Philemon
Rev.	Revelation
Rom.	Romans
1–2 Thess.	1–2 Thessalonians
1–2 Tim.	1–2 Timothy
Titus	Titus

DEAD SEA SCROLLS AND RELATED WRITINGS

CD	*Damascus Document*
1QapGen ar	*Genesis Apocryphon*
1QH[a]	*Thanksgiving Hymns[a]*
1QM	*War Scroll*

1QpHab	Pesher on Habakkuk	Pesah.	Pesahim
1QS	Rule of the Community	Pesiq. Rab.	Pesiqta Rabbati
1QSa	Rule of the Congregation	Pirqe R. El.	Pirqe Rabbi Eliezer
4QFlor	Florilegium	Qidd.	Qiddushin
4QpIsa	Pesher on Isaiah	Rosh HaSh.	Rosh HaShanah
4QpPs37	Pesher on Psalm 37	Sanh.	Sanhedrin
4QPrNab ar	Prayer of Nabonidus in	Shabb.	Shabbat
	Aramaic	Sheqal.	Sheqalim
11QApPs^a	Apocryphal Psalms^a	Shev.	Shevi'it
11QT^a	Temple Scroll^a	Shevu.	Shevu'ot
		Songs Rab.	Song of Songs Rabbah

TARGUMIC TEXTS

Tg. Isa.	Targum Isaiah
Tg. Onq.	Targum Onqelos
Tg. Ps.	Targum Psalms
Tg. Ps-J.	Targum Pseudo-Jonathan

RABBINIC LITERATURE

Ag. Ber.	Aggadat Bereshit
Avod. Zar.	Avodah Zarah
Avot R. Nat.	Avot of Rabbi Nathan
B. Bat.	Bava Batra
Bek.	Bekhorot
Ber.	Berakhot
B. Metzi'a	Bava Metzi'a
B. Qam.	Bava Qamma
Deut. Rab.	Deuteronomy Rabbah
Eccles. Rab.	Ecclesiastes Rabbah
Eruv.	Eruvin
Exod. Rab.	Exodus Rabbah
Gen. Rab.	Genesis Rabbah
Git.	Gittin
Hag.	Hagigah
Hul.	Hullin
Ker.	Keritot
Lam. Rab.	Lamentations Rabbah
Lev. Rab.	Leviticus Rabbah
Meg.	Megillah
Me'il.	Me'ilah
Mek.	Mekilta
Menah.	Menahot
Midr. Teh.	Midrash Tehillim (Psalms)
Ned.	Nedarim
Num. Rab.	Numbers Rabbah
Ohol.	Oholot

Ta'an.	Ta'anit
Tem.	Temurah
Yevam.	Yevamot

OLD TESTAMENT PSEUDEPIGRAPHA

Apoc. Ab.	Apocalypse of Abraham
Apoc. El.	Apocalypse of Elijah
2 Bar.	2 Baruch (Syriac Apocalypse)
1 En.	1 Enoch (Ethiopic Apocalypse)
2 En.	2 Enoch (Slavonic Apocalypse)
Jub.	Jubilees
L.A.B.	Liber antiquitatum biblicarum (Pseudo-Philo)
L.A.E.	Life of Adam and Eve
Let. Aris.	Letter of Aristeas
Liv. Pro.	Lives of the Prophets
Pss. Sol.	Psalms of Solomon
Sib. Or.	Sibylline Oracles
Syr. Men.	Sentences of the Syriac Menander
T. Ab.	Testament of Abraham
T. Ash.	Testament of Asher
T. Benj.	Testament of Benjamin
T. Dan	Testament of Dan
T. Gad	Testament of Gad
T. Iss.	Testament of Issachar
T. Jos.	Testament of Joseph
T. Jud.	Testament of Judah
T. Levi	Testament of Levi
T. Mos.	Testament of Moses
T. Naph.	Testament of Naphtali
T. Reu.	Testament of Reuben

T. Sim.	Testament of Simeon
T. Sol.	Testament of Solomon
T. Zeb.	Testament of Zebulun

APOSTOLIC FATHERS

Barn.	Barnabas
1–2 Clem.	1–2 Clement
Did.	Didache
Diogn.	Diognetus
Herm. Mand.	Shepherd of Hermas, Mandate
Herm. Vis.	Shepherd of Hermas, Vision
Ign. Eph.	Ignatius, To the Ephesians
Ign. Pol.	Ignatius, To Polycarp
Ign. Rom.	Ignatius, To the Romans

| Ign. Smyrn. | Ignatius, To the Smyrnaeans |
| Mart. Pol. | Martyrdom of Polycarp |

NEW TESTAMENT APOCRYPHA AND PSEUDEPIGRAPHA

Acts Andr.	Acts of Andrew
Acts John	Acts of John
Acts Paul	Acts of Paul
Acts Thom.	Acts of Thomas
Apoc. Pet.	Apocalypse of Peter
Ep. Apos.	Epistle to the Apostles
Gos. Pet.	Gospel of Peter
Prot. Jas.	Protevangelium of James
Ps.-Clem.	Pseudo-Clementine Writings

Ancient and Medieval Authors

ABELARD

| Comm. Rom. | Commentary on Romans |

ACHILLES TATIUS

| Leuc. Clit. | Leucippe et Clitophon (The Adventures of Leucippe and Cleitophon) |

AELIAN

| Var. hist. | Varia historia |

AELIUS THEON

| Progym. | Progymnasmata |

AESCHYLUS

| Eum. | Eumenides |
| Prom. | Prometheus vinctus (Prometheus Bound) |

ANAXIMENES OF LAMPSACUS

| Rhet. Alex. | Rhetorica ad Alexandrum (Ars rhetorica) |

APOLLODORUS

| Bibl. | Bibliotheca (Library) |

APOLLONIUS OF RHODES

| Argon. | Argonautica |

ARISTOPHANES

| Nub. | Nubes (Clouds) |

ARISTOTLE

| Rhet. | Rhetorica (Rhetoric) |

ARRIAN

| Anab. | Anabasis (Going Up [from the coast]) |

ARTEMIDORUS DALDIANUS

| Onir. | Onirocritica |

ATHANASIUS

| Vit. Ant. | Vita Antonii (Life of Antony) |

ATHENAEUS

| Deipn. | Deipnosophistae |

ATHENAGORAS

Leg.   *Legatio pro Christianis*

AUGUSTINE

Civ.   *De civitate Dei (The City of God)*

Cons.   *De consensu evangelistarum (Harmony of the Gospels)*

AULUS GELLIUS

Noct. att.   *Noctes atticae (Attic Nights)*

BONAVENTURE

Leg. maior   *Legenda maior*

CICERO

Att.   *Epistulae ad Atticum*

De or.   *De oratore*

Div.   *De divinatione*

Inv.   *De inventione rhetorica*

Leg.   *De legibus*

Nat. d.   *De natura deorum*

Rep.   *De republica*

Top.   *Topica*

Tusc.   *Tusculanae disputationes*

CLEMENT OF ALEXANDRIA

Exc.   *Excerpta ex Theodoto (Excerpts from Theodotus)*

Paed.   *Paedagogus (Christ the Educator)*

Strom.   *Stromata (Miscellanies)*

CORNUTUS

Nat. d.   *De natura deorum*

CYPRIAN

Idol.   *Quod idola dii non sint*

DEMETRIUS OF PHALERON

Eloc.   *De elocutione (On Style)*

DIO CASSIUS

Rom. Hist.   *Roman History*

DIO CHRYSOSTOM

Or.   *Orationes*

DIODORUS SICULUS

Bib. hist.   *Bibliotheca historica*

DIOGENES LAERTIUS

Vit. phil.   *Vitae philosophorum (Lives of the Philosophers)*

DIONYSIUS OF HALICARNASSUS

Ant. rom.   *Antiquitates romanae*

EPICTETUS

Diatr.   *Diatribai (Dissertationes)*

Ench.   *Enchiridion*

EPIPHANIUS

Pan.   *Panarion* or *Adversus haereses (Refutation of All Heresies)*

EURIPIDES

Bacch.   *Bacchae*

Hel.   *Helena*

Hipp.   *Hippolytus*

EUSEBIUS

Dem. ev.   *Demonstratio evangelica (Demonstration of the Gospel)*

Hist. eccl.   *Historia ecclesiastica (Ecclesiastical History)*

Praep. ev.   *Praeparatio evangelica (Preparation for the Gospel)*

GREGORY OF NYSSA

Or. cat.   *Oratio catechetica magna (Catechetical Oration)*

HELIODORUS

Aeth.   *Aethiopica*

HERMOGENES

Progym.   *Progymnasmata*

Abbreviations

HERODOTUS

Hist.   Historiae (Histories)

HESIOD

Theog.   Theogonia (Theogony)

HILARY OF POITIERS

Hom. Ps.   Homilies on the Psalms

HIPPOLYTUS

Contra Jud.   Contra Judaeos (Against the Jews)

HOMER

Il.   Ilias (Iliad)
Od.   Odyssea (Odyssey)

HORACE

Sat.   Satirae (Satires)

HYGNIUS

Astronom.   Poetica astronomica

IAMBLICHUS

Vit. Pyth.   Vita Pythagorae (Life of Pythagoras)

IRENAEUS

Haer.   Adversus haereses (Against Heresies)

ISOCRATES

Nic.   Nicocles

JEROME

Comm. Am.   Commentariorum in Amos
Comm. Isa.   Commentariorum in Isaiam
Pelag.   Adversus Pelagianos
Vir. ill.   De viris illustribus

JOHN CHRYSOSTOM

Hom. Matt.   Homiliae in Matthaeum

JOSEPHUS

Ag. Ap.   Against Apion
Ant.   Jewish Antiquities

J.W.   Jewish War
Life   The Life

JUSTIN MARTYR

1 Apol.   Apologia i
Dial.   Dialogus cum Tryphone (Dialogue with Trypho)

LIVY

Hist.   Historiae (Ab urbe condita)

LUCIAN

Alex.   Alexander or Pseudomantis (Alexander the False Prophet)
Demon.   Demonax
Deor. conc.   Deorum concilium (Parliament of the Gods)
Nigr.   Nigrinus
Peregr.   De morte Peregrini (The Passing of Peregrinus)
Philops.   Philopseudes (The Lover of Lies)
Syr. d.   De syria dea (The Goddess of Syria)
Ver. hist.   Vera historia (A True Story)
Vit. auct.   Vitarum auctio (Philosophies for Sale)

MARINOS

Vit. Proc.   Life of Proclus

MELITO

Pascha   Peri pascha (On the Passover)

ORIGEN

Cels.   Contra Celsum (Against Celsus)
Comm. Matt.   Commentarium in evangelium Matthaei (Commentary on the Gospel of Matthew)
Comm. Rom.   Commentarii in Romanos (Commentary on Romans)

OVID

Metam.   Metamorphoses

PAUSANIAS

Descr.   Graeciae descriptio (Description of Greece)

PETRONIUS

Sat.   Satyrica

PHILO

Abr.   De Abrahamo (On the Life of Abraham)

Cher.   De cherubim (On the Cherubim)

Conf.   De confusione linguarum (On the Confusion of Tongues)

Congr.   De congressu eruditionis gratia (On the Preliminary Studies)

Contempl.   De vita contemplativa (On the Contemplative Life)

Decal.   De decalogo (On the Decalogue)

Flacc.   In Flaccum (Against Flaccus)

Frag.   Fragments

Fug.   De fuga et inventione (On Flight and Finding)

Hypoth.   Hypothetica

Legat.   Legatio ad Gaium (On the Embassy to Gaius)

Migr.   De migratione Abrahami (On the Migration of Abraham)

Mos.   De vita Mosis (On the Life of Moses)

Praem.   De praemiis et poenis (On Rewards and Punishments)

Prob.   Quod omnis probus liber sit (That Every Good Person Is Free)

Prov.   De providentia (On Providence)

Sacr.   De sacrificiis Abelis et Caini (On the Sacrifices of Cain and Abel)

Somn.   De somniis (On Dreams)

Spec.   De specialibus legibus (On the Special Laws)

Virt.   De virtutibus (On the Virtues)

PHILOSTRATUS

Ep.   Epistolae (Love Letters)

Vit. Apoll.   Vita Apollonii (Life of Apollonius of Tyana)

Vit. soph.   Vitae sophistarum (Lives of the Sophists)

PLATO

Apol.   Apologia (Apology of Socrates)

Phaedr.   Phaedrus

Resp.   Respublica (Republic)

PLINY THE ELDER

Nat.   Naturalis historia (Natural History)

PLUTARCH

Aem.   Aemilius Paullus

Alc.   Alcibiades

Alex.   Alexander

Alex. fort.   De Alexandri magni fortuna aut virtute

Apoph. lac.   Apophthegmata laconica

Arist.   Aristides

Brut.   Brutus

Cat. Maj.   Cato Major (Cato the Elder)

Cons. Apoll.   Consolatio ad Apollonium

Cor.   Marcius Coriolanus

Cupid. divit.   De cupiditate divitiarum

Inim. util.   De capienda ex inimicis utilitate

Is. Os.   De Iside et Osiride (On Isis and Osiris)

Abbreviations

Lyc.	Lycurgus
Mor.	Moralia
Num.	Numa
Pel.	Pelopidas
Per.	Pericles
Princ. iner.	Ad principem ineruditum
Pyrrh.	Pyrrhus
Quaest. rom.	Quaestiones romanae et graecae, or Aetia romana et graeca
Rom.	Romulus
Sera	De sera numinis vindicta
Sull.	Sulla
Them.	Themistocles
Virt. prof.	Quomodo quis suos in virtute sentiat profectus

PORPHYRY

Marc.	Ad Marcellam
Vit. Pyth.	Vita Pythagorae

QUINTILIAN

Inst.	Institutio oratoria

SENECA THE ELDER

Con.	Controversiae

SENECA THE YOUNGER

Apoc.	Apocolocyntosis (The Pumpkinification of Claudius)
Ben.	De beneficiis
Clem.	De clementia
Ep.	Epistulae morales
Ira	De ira
Tranq.	De tranquillitate animi

SILIUS ITALICUS

Pun.	Punica (On the Punic Wars)

STATIUS

Silv.	Silvae

STRABO

Geogr.	Geographica (Geography)

SUETONIUS

Aug.	Divus Augustus
Dom.	Domitianus
Galb.	Galba
Jul.	Divus Julius
Vesp.	Vespasianus
Vit.	Vitellius

TACITUS

Agr.	Agricola
Ann.	Annales
Hist.	Historiae

TATIAN

Orat.	Oration against the Greeks

TERTULLIAN

An.	De anima (The Soul)
Apol.	Apologeticus (Apology)
Carn. Chr.	De carne Christi (The Flesh of Christ)
Marc.	Adversus Marcionem (Against Marcion)
Mon.	De monogamia (Monogamy)
Praescr.	De praescriptione haereticorum (Prescription against Heresies)
Virg.	De virginibus velandis (The Veiling of Virgins)

THOMAS AQUINAS

Summa	Summa Theologica

VIRGIL

Aen.	Aeneid
Ecl.	Eclogae
Georg.	Georgica

XENOPHON

Cyr.	Cyropaedia
Mem.	Memorabilia
Symp.	Symposium

Ancient Collections and Anonymous Works

Corp. herm.   *Corpus hermeticum*

Modern Works, Editions, Series, and Collections

ANF   *The Ante-Nicene Fathers*. Edited by Alexander Roberts and James Donaldson. 10 vols. New York: Christian Literature Co., 1885–96. Repr., Grand Rapids: Eerdmans, 1950–51.

BDAG   Bauer, W., F. W. Danker, W. F. Arndt, and F. W. Gingrich. *A Greek-English Lexicon of the New Testament and Other Early Christian Literature*. 3rd ed. Chicago: University of Chicago Press, 2000.

NPNF   *A Select Library of Nicene and Post-Nicene Fathers of the Christian Church*. Edited by Philip Schaff. 1st series. 14 vols. New York: Christian Literature Co., 1887–1900. Repr., Grand Rapids: Eerdmans, 1956.

OTP   *Old Testament Pseudepigrapha*. Edited by J. H. Charlesworth. 2 vols. Garden City, NY: Doubleday, 1983–85.

P.Oxy.   *The Oxyrhynchus Papyri*. Edited by B. P. Grenfell et al. 73 vols. London: Egypt Exploration Society, 1898–2009.

Matthew

Introduction

This introduction will consist of three main sections: first, a brief survey of the type of historical questions usually associated with such introductions; second, a discussion of Matthean soteriology that provides the lens through which to read the First Gospel correctly; and third, a clarification of the commentary's methodological assumptions.

Literary Issues

Authorship

Who wrote the Gospel of Matthew? The external evidence links the First Gospel and Matthew, one of the Twelve. Near the middle of the second century, Papias told what he thought about the authorship of Mark. It was followed by this statement: "Matthew composed the Sayings [*logia*] in the Hebrew language, and everyone translated them as he was able" (Eusebius, *Hist. eccl.* 3.39.16, author trans.). At the end of the second century, Pantaenus of Alexandria gave his opinion. When he went to India, he found the Gospel of Matthew had preceded him. Bartholomew, one of the apostles, he says, had preached there and had left the Gospel of Matthew in Hebrew (Eusebius, *Hist. eccl.* 5.10.3). Irenaeus, near AD 180, says that Matthew wrote "a gospel . . . for the Hebrews in their own language" (*Haer.* 3.1.1, author trans.). Jerome wrote: "Matthew, also called Levi, . . . was the first in Judea to write a Gospel of Christ in Hebrew for those of the circumcision who believed; who translated it later into Greek, no one knows for sure" (*Vir. ill.* 3, author trans.). Ancient tradition was unanimous. Modern historical scholarship is dubious. The Greek Gospel of Matthew does not appear to be a translation from Hebrew or Aramaic. If, as most think, it uses the Gospel of Mark and Q as sources, then it did not come from an eyewitness. The Gospel itself makes no claim about authorship (as John 21:24 does). Modern scholars regard it properly as an anonymous writing. One recent debate over whether its author was a Christian Jew (most scholars) or a Christian gentile (e.g., Nepper-Christensen 1954; Strecker 1962; Meier 1979; Sato 2001) has pretty well been settled in favor of the former claim. Another current argument over whether there was one author or the Gospel was produced by a group, as a school product (e.g., Stendahl 1968; Gale 2005), remains undecided.

Date

When was the First Gospel written? There have been recent arguments for a pre-70 date (e.g., Hagner 1995; Gamba 1998; Nolland 2005). Despite their claims, the general consensus is that Matthew was written after 70, most likely between 80 and 100.

Locale

Where was Matthew written? It "was situated in an urban environment, perhaps in Galilee or perhaps more toward the north in Syria but, in any case, not necessarily Antioch" (the words of J. Kingsbury, in Balch 1991, 264). Although Antioch of Syria has long been the preferred locale, it could have been Sepphoris, Caesarea Maritima, Tiberius, Tyre, Sidon, Damascus, or less likely Pella across the Jordan (Viviano 2007, 4). Alexandria and Edessa are also improbable options.

Recipients

For whom was this Gospel produced? The long-standing consensus is that Matthew was produced for a community (a cluster of like-minded congregations in a limited geographical area; e.g., Stendahl 1968; Gale 2005; Riches and Sim 2005). Recently, some have recommended that we see the four canonical Gospels as written, not each for its own community, but for all Christians (e.g., Bauckham 1998). Richard Bauckham's thesis is most plausible for Luke-Acts, impossible for the Fourth Gospel (because of the evidence of the Johannine Epistles), and less likely for Matthew. Even if it were written in the context of a specific community, however, it would not likely have been designed for that locale only. The Shepherd of Hermas (Herm. *Vis.* 2.4.3) indicates that by the time Matthew was written, even if one copy of a Christian writing was designed for a church in a local area, other copies would be sent to sister churches abroad for their edification.

Numerous efforts have been made to describe the Matthean community. In 1991, the volume edited by David Balch yielded the following descriptors: in an urban location, including gentiles but mostly Jews, considering itself a sect within Judaism, whose biblical interpretation reflects scribal culture.

A description of its social location has been attempted by Evert-Jan Vledder (1997), who discerns the following strata in advanced agrarian societies:

Urban elite: The top layer (possessing land and office), e.g., the Roman governor, Jewish chief priest, and Sanhedrin

Retainer class: Those who serve the political elite, e.g., tax collectors, Pharisees, and scribes

Urban nonelite: Merchants and artisans, e.g., Joseph the carpenter and fishermen like Peter, Andrew, James, and John

The degraded and expendable classes (outside the city walls): E.g., tanners, lepers, beggars, and robbers

Peasants: E.g., slaves and tenants

Matthew's community was composed mostly of the nonelite. The author(s) of the First Gospel belonged to the retainer class (scribes), as did the community's leaders. The community's opponents were mostly from the ruling and retainer classes. Matthew's community regarded itself as Jewish. It was a Christian Judaism, one species of the genus Judaism (Boccaccini 1991). Since Matthew's community was still within Judaism, the conflicts reflected in Matthew's Gospel were real and intense. Another front on which the Gospel fought was against Roman imperial ideology and power (Riches and Sim 2005). Though the Gospel may be understood within two contexts (Jewish and Roman), it is difficult to see the Roman imperial setting as equally central to Matthew's concerns.

Sources

What sources did the First Evangelist use? Although its dominance has been challenged, the two-source theory continues to be the preferred explanation for Matthew's sources. Mark and Q plus oral tradition, M, provide material for the First Evangelist to interpret. Of late, this source theory has been seen through fresh eyes. Gerad Genette (1982) provides one new perspective, using the categories "hypertext" and "pretext" or "hypotext." A hypertext is a secondary text that is written entirely on the basis of a preceding pretext/hypotext but without being a formal commentary on its pretext/hypotext. For example, Virgil's *Aeneid* is a hypertext to Homer's *Odyssey*. Viewed through this lens, Mark is a pretext/hypotext for Matthew's hypertext. Matthew is a secondary text written on the basis of its predecessor Mark but not as a commentary on Mark. Another new perspective for viewing the two-source theory is voiced by John Riches (2000, 304–5): Matthew retold the story found in Mark in a way analogous to the retelling of Genesis by *Jubilees*, Josephus (*Ant.*), Pseudo-Philo (*L.A.B.*), and the *Genesis Apocryphon* (1QapGen ar). The First Gospel, then, belongs to a category like rewritten Bible.

Genre

To what genre does Matthew belong? The preponderance of recent opinion places the canonical Gospels within the genre of ancient biography (Burridge 1992; Talbert 1977). Within that larger circle, Matthew seems to be an encomiastic biography (written to praise its hero; Neyrey 1998; Shuler 1982) that also aims to defend its hero against attack. A gospel, then, is not a unique literary type but a Christian version of an ancient Mediterranean genre that focused on an individual's life with the aim of exposing what was essential to that person's being.

Plot

What is the plot of Matthew? While arguments about what exactly is meant by "plot" continue (e.g., Merenlahti 2002), of the three main efforts to describe the First Gospel's plot (Matera 1987; Kingsbury 1992; Powell 1992), Mark Powell's suggestion has found the greatest support (e.g., Branden 2006, 90–114). He argues that Matthew's narrative embodies one main plot and at least two subplots. The main plot is God's plan to save his people from their sins. This effort is opposed by Satan. Subplot one, derivative of the main plot, involves Jesus's activity and its opposition at every turn by the religious leaders. Subplot two, also derivative of the main plot, consists of Jesus's efforts in relation to his disciples. They assist in the accomplishment of the first part of God's plan but hinder the accomplishment of the second part. Matthew's plot, then, concerns the saving activity of God enacted through the narrative's main character, Jesus. Only the main plot is resolved favorably. After the resurrection, Jewish opposition continues and some disciples continue to doubt.

Arrangement

How is the First Gospel organized? The obvious answer is that Matthew follows a rough chronological sequence: birth, baptism, Galilean ministry, journey to Jerusalem, and Jerusalem ministry leading to Jesus's death and resurrection. This was one of the ways to structure an encomiastic biography (Neyrey 1998, citing Quintilian, *Inst*. 3.7.15). Beyond this fact, various options have been proposed.

1. Matthew consists of five discourses (5:1–7:29; 9:36–11:1; 13:1–52; 17:25–18:35; 24:3–26:1), each preceded by a narrative section that is linked to the subsequent sayings and each closed by a similar refrain ("and when Jesus had finished"). Birth narratives open the Gospel (chaps. 1–2), and the passion and resurrection narratives close it (chaps. 26–28). (Bacon 1930, e.g., associated this structure with a theory that it paralleled the five books of Moses and constituted a new law. This association has been widely critiqued.)

2. The First Gospel is arranged in a chiastic pattern (e.g., Lohr 1961; Fenton 1959): (A) chaps. 1–4; (B) chaps. 5–7; (C) chaps. 8–9; (D) chap. 10; (E) chaps. 11–12; (F) chap. 13; (E′) chaps. 14–17; (D′) chap. 18; (C′) chaps. 19–22; (B′) chaps. 23–25; (A′) chaps. 26–28. (Cf. M. Thompson 1982 for a critique.)

3. Matthew is divided into three segments (1:1–4:16—the person of Jesus; 4:17–16:20—the proclamation of Jesus; and 16:21–28:20—the suffering, death, and resurrection of Jesus) signaled by the repetition of the phrase *apo tote ērxato ho Iēsous* (from then Jesus began) in 4:17 and 16:21. (See Kingsbury 1989; cf. Neirynck 1988 for a critique.)

4. The Gospel consists of six units: 1:1–4:16 (God initiates the story of Jesus); 4:17–11:1 (Jesus manifests God's saving presence in his public ministry of preaching and healing); 11:2–16:20 (Jesus's action reveals his identity, necessitating a response from humans); 16:21–20:34 (Jesus teaches his disciples that God's purposes involve his death and resurrection); 21:1–27:66 (in Jerusalem, Jesus is rejected by Jewish leaders and dies at their hands); 28:1–20 (God's saving purposes are not thwarted). (So Carter 1992; as far as I know, no one else has yet supported this proposal.)

5. The arrangement consists of an overture (1:1–4:11) plus a hinge (4:12–17), followed by the corpus (4:18–25:46) plus a hinge (26:1–16), followed by the finale (26:17–28:20). The corpus itself consists of two main parts (4:18–16:12 and 17:1–25:46) connected by a hinge (16:13–28). Each of these two main parts breaks into two subunits connected by hinges: 4:18–16:12 divides into 4:18–11:1 and 12:1–16:12 connected by 11:2–30; 17:1–25:46 divides into 17:1–20:34 and 21:18–25:46 connected by 21:1–17. (So Weren 2006; this proposal is too recent to have received much response.)

6. The First Evangelist did not think in terms of any fixed arrangement. There is no grand scheme to be found. The Gospel is structurally mixed (so Gundry 1982, 10–11; Hagner 1993, 1:liii).

W. D. Davies and Dale Allison (1988, 1:61) conclude their survey of the structural options: "The alternation in Matthew between narrative and discourse is firmly established, as is the number of major discourses, five. . . . These two certainties constitute the foundation stone upon which all further discussion must build." Recent commentaries reflect this view (e.g., Fiedler 2006; Turner 2008). It is therefore upon these two certainties that this commentary's reading of the First Gospel will build.

This volume's understanding of the First Gospel's organization is represented in the accompanying outline. One distinctive here is the recognition of two places where the narratives are divided into two parts. Also, as the second part of this introduction will show, this recognition of five discourses is not associated with the claim that the First Gospel is a new Pentateuch and Jesus's teaching a new law. There is, however, throughout the Gospel a Mosaic typology (Allison 1993). This typology is a part of Matthew's focus on the typological fulfillment of sacred history, not a contention that Jesus brings a new law.

Would the ancient auditor have been aware of compositional arrangements in a text such as Matthew's (assuming that they are present in the Gospel)? Cicero gives his opinion:

> Everybody is able to discriminate between what is right and wrong in matters of art and proportion by a sort of subconscious instinct, without having any theory of art and proportion of their own . . . because these are rooted deep in the general sensibility, and nature has decreed that nobody shall be entirely devoid of these faculties. . . . It is remarkable how little difference there is between the expert and the plain man as critics. (*De or.* 3.50.195, 197, trans. Sutton and Rackham 1942)

This commentary will assume, with Cicero, that the auditors of the Gospel would indeed have been conscious of the patterning of the narrative and the discourses, even if these auditors were uneducated in a classical sense.

Purpose

What is the purpose of the Gospel? As long as a redactional-critical method held sway in NT studies, the general method of scholarship was to look for various tendencies and motifs in a Gospel and then to infer that some problem in the editor's milieu was a catalyst for each tendency and motif. In that case, if one isolated a dozen tendencies/motifs in Matthew, then the Gospel could be said to have a dozen purposes. This eventually was recognized as so absurd that perspective shifted. Given our limited knowledge, there would be no way to sort out such a mixture. These days the four canonical Gospels are viewed not as occasional writings responding to current problems but as foundation documents that might reflect awareness of problems past, present, and (potentially) future. A foundation document would provide the basic values upon which the readers' lives would be based and by which their lives would be evaluated. It would provide them their identity as followers of Jesus. In this light, the Gospel of Matthew's purpose is to form the Christian identity and character of its readers. If so, then *how* does it do that? This question leads to the second part of this introduction: Matthean soteriology.

Matthean Soteriology

In virtually all NT scholarship it is believed that, at least to some degree, the relation of the indicative (gift) and imperative (demand) in Matthew constitutes a theological problem for Christians. A spectrum of representative opinion will indicate some of the shades of judgment about this issue. (For what follows, cf. Talbert 2001.)

The Perceived Problem

Some scholars contend that Matthew is legalistic. Willi Marxsen (1993) is typical. He contrasts two types of ethics. On the one hand, if God is conceived of as one who sets requirements and makes his relationship with people dependent on their fulfilling these requirements, then the practice of ethics promises realization of the relationship. It is assumed that humans are capable of meeting the admission requirements. On the other hand, if God is conceived of as one who has already come to humans with love—without any precondition—then the relationship already exists and humans can act (ethics), out of gratitude. It is assumed that humans can act rightly only if they are enabled by God's prior act. The former type (God sets requirements), Marxsen thinks, is a Pharisaic ethic; the latter (God comes with love) is a Christian ethic. Marxsen believes, moreover, that Matthew represents the first type of ethic. Matthew's imperative, then, consists of admission requirements for entering the kingdom of heaven. Marxsen says, further, that to avoid this conclusion, one must demonstrate that Matthew undergirds the imperatives with an indicative that enables the doer to follow the imperatives. He does not believe this can be done. That is, Matthew's demand/imperative constitutes God's requirement of humans if they are to attain a relationship with him. There is no prior indicative/gift/grace that bestows a relation, unconditionally, quite apart from human performance and to which human performance can respond.

Marxsen's position is problematic on two counts. On the one hand, Matthew clearly sees a person's entering into Jesus's community as due to divine initiative. The disciples are called (4:18–22) before Jesus gives the Sermon on the Mount. Matthew 28:19–20 specifies that the nations are to be made disciples and baptized before they are taught to observe all that Jesus commanded. That the kingdom has been inaugurated in Jesus's ministry (12:28) means that repentance (4:17) is a response to a prior act of God. Matthew is clearly not legalism. A divine indicative enables one's entry into the community of Jesus's disciples. On the other hand, Marxsen represents a perspective on Pharisaic Judaism that is pre–E. P. Sanders, or for that matter pre–G. F. Moore. Most modern scholars would regard a Pharisaic ethic not as legalism (in which one gets into the covenant relation by works of law) but as covenantal nomism (in which one gets into the covenant by grace and obeys the law thereafter out of gratitude). To such scholars, Marxsen's description of the second type of ethic (his Christian one) sounds much like the covenantal nomism many modern scholars associate with Pharisaic Judaism.

The issue of Matthew's ethic is better focused by certain other scholars (e.g., Eskola 1997; Laato 1995) as to whether or not Matthew represents legalistic covenantal nomism (in which one enters the covenant relation by grace and then stays in it and enters the age to come by works of law). This legalistic covenantal nomism is seen in contrast to a new covenant piety, in which God or Christ or the Holy Spirit enables one to be obedient in an ongoing way after one is in the covenant relation. That is, in new covenant piety one enters the relation by grace, stays in the relation by grace, and enters the age to come by grace. In this view, the life of a disciple is by grace from start to finish. This grace is not a substitute for obedience to God's will but enables it. The question must be refined beyond Marxsen's statement of it. Properly put, the issue is this: does Matthew see the imperative as admissions requirements, either initially into Jesus's community or ultimately into the age to come, that humans must meet in order to gain either or both of these benefits? For the reasons cited above, most scholars today believe that entry into Jesus's community is by grace. The current debate is over what follows in the disciple's life. Is there an indicative that underlies and enables fulfillment of the imperative in disciples' lives after their entry into the community of Jesus?

Other scholars believe that Matthew reflects covenantal nomism. That is, Matthew employs an indicative/grace for the disciple to enter the relationship but has no developed notion of grace for staying in or entering the age to come. Petri Luomanen (1998b) represents this stance. He speaks of Matthew as reflecting a defective covenantal nomism. He contends that Matthew wanted to understand Jesus's proclamation within the framework of traditional covenantal nomism and so pass it on to his Jewish contemporaries. There are differences, of course, between Matthew's content and that of non-Christian Judaism, but from a structural point of view, Matthew has much in common with covenantal nomism. God's election forms the starting point. This grace enables one to join the people of God. It remains a presupposition, however, that is not spelled out. Jesus's atonement, which is restricted to enabling one to stay in the people of God rather than to initial inclusion, functions very much as sacrifice did in non-Christian Jewish covenantal nomism. This is an aid to one's staying in. It is part of the synergism of staying in the people of God and entering the age to come. This position is subject to the criticisms of people like Timo Eskola (1997) and Timo Laato (1995), who regard synergism in the postentry period as legalistic covenantal nomism. If Matthew represents covenantal nomism, then the indicative allows one to join the people of God but is not solely responsible for one's staying in, or for entering the age to come.

Another group of scholars believe that Matthew has both an indicative and an imperative but that the former does not control the latter. At least three shades of opinion must be noted:

1. Some see the imperative as explicit in Matthew but the indicative as only implicit. Roger Mohrlang (1984) is representative of this opinion. He is concerned with the question of how the concept of grace enters into Matthew's understanding of ethics. He summarizes:

   > Matthew does not exploit this assumed structure of grace, and does not build his ethics explicitly upon it (rarely is ethical behavior motivated by considerations of grace); for the most part, it remains in the background, simply taken for granted—the largely unspoken context in which the Gospel is set. (80)

   Subsequent summary statements add clarification. "The concept of Jesus's continuing presence with the community is as little explicitly integrated with the evangelist's ethics as his view of the Spirit" (112). Further, Matthew's Gospel, with its emphasis on demand and obedience, results in a Gospel "almost totally devoid of explicit reference to God's aid in the moral-ethical realm" (114). For scholars who hold this view, only the imperative is explicit; the indicative is merely implicit.

2. Others believe that both indicative and imperative are present in Matthew but that the link between them is not clearly spelled out (e.g., Luz 1995). The miracle stories, for example, have a central function of announcing salvation (the indicative) in the earthly career of Jesus. It is not the kerygma of the death and resurrection of Jesus that conveys the indicative in Matthew, however; it is the abiding presence of Jesus in the community. Jesus's ethics constitute the imperative. Both components, indicative and imperative, stand together, but their relationship is not clearly defined. It is not apparent how demand and gift belong together. This is a weakness in Matthew's theology.

3. David Seeley (1994, 21–52) argues that Matthew contains multiple perspectives that cannot be blended into a smooth unity. On the one hand, there is the claim that Jesus's atoning death provides salvation: Jesus is the one who brings salvation. On the other hand, there is a focus on Jesus as the spokesperson who describes a way of life to be followed. In this perspective, salvation does not involve Jesus. It takes place between a person and God the Father. Whether it occurs or not depends on the person's own initiative. There is no need for Jesus's atoning death. Jesus is, however, the end-time judge who decides on the basis of a person's deeds in this life. There is nothing that would lead one to see the first perspective as the underlying structure embracing all else. So in Matthew, the emphasis on the law is very much at odds with the parts of Matthew that focus on Jesus as redeemer. Matthew never consolidates these two portraits of Jesus presented by the building blocks he has used. "We can see Matthew wrestling with his traditions, and we can see them wrestling back. In this case, they seem to have won the match" (52). Matthew never quite brings the two, the indicative and the imperative, together. "They are . . . there, like an unharmonious choir demanding to be heard" (52).

Yet another group of scholars see indicative and imperative as present in Matthew and attempt to explain how the indicative has priority. Hubert Frankemölle (1997, 2:552–60) and David Kupp (1996) represent this stance. Both affirm that the concept of Jesus's presence with the disciples, rooted in the OT view of God's compassionate and caring presence among his people, is Matthew's leading idea. Out of the God-with-us theme, Matthew's entire plot is constituted. The expressions "with us/you" and "in your midst" are synonyms both in the OT and in Matthew. Over one hundred occurrences of this formula are found in the OT, mostly in the historical books and with individuals, though sometimes with the whole people. It mostly drops out of use in postbiblical Judaism. The formula signals empowerment of God's people. This expression applied to Jesus (1:23; 18:20; 28:19–20) is part of Matthew's Christology and makes possible his soteriology. This is a significant advance toward understanding the relation of indicative and imperative in Matthew. It enables one to see how God is present in Jesus; how Jesus is present with the disciples or in their midst; how this presence enables both church discipline (18:20) and mission (28:20). On at least these two fronts, the indicative is clearly prior to the imperative, and God's grace explicitly enables his people's obedient response in the period subsequent to their entry into Jesus's community. In the form in which it is presented, however, the proposed quilt is too small to cover the whole Matthean bed. Where, for example, is the indicative that covers ethical activity of the disciple? More work needs to be done in the direction in which these scholars are pointing.

It is usually thought, then, that Matthew emphasizes the imperative at the expense of the indicative, demand over gift. If one wanted to falsify this perception, what would be necessary? Two things at least. First, one would need to identify Matthew's indicative, if there is one. Second, one would need to show how this indicative controls Matthew's imperative. In the pages that follow, these two points will be pursued.

Identifying Matthew's Indicative

How would one recognize Matthew's indicative, if there is one? It seems obvious that Matthew does not operate in the Pauline conceptual world (e.g., divine indwelling). Could it be that there are other conceptual worlds besides those used by Paul for speaking about divine enablement of human activity? If so, then the failure to recognize Matthew's indicative may be due to the reader's failure to recognize the First Evangelist's conceptual repertoire. It is my contention that Matthew has a strong indicative if one knows where to look. An attempt to clarify Matthew's conceptual world needs to indicate both (1) the type of narrative approach he uses and (2) at least some of the techniques employed in such an approach. We begin with the type of narrative approach used.

Matthew begins and ends his Gospel with narratives that attest repeated divine inbreaks into human affairs. Here God very much has the initiative, and humans respond. For example, the birth narratives begin with a miraculous conception of Jesus (1:18), about which Joseph is reassured by an angel of the Lord (1:20–21). The wise men from the East are directed to Jesus by a miraculous star (2:2) and are sent on their way by a warning in a dream (2:12). Joseph is warned by an angel of the Lord to flee to Egypt (2:13). After Herod's death, an angel tells Joseph it is safe to return to Israel (2:19–20). At the end of the Gospel, when Jesus dies, the earth shakes, rocks split, and bodies of saints are raised and appear to many in Jerusalem (27:51–53). In connection with the stories of Jesus's resurrection, there is a great earthquake, and an angel descends from heaven, rolls back the stone from before the tomb (28:2), frightens the soldiers nearly to death (28:4), and tells the women that Jesus has been raised (28:6). The beginning and ending of the First Gospel are full of explicit divine interventions into human affairs. The main body of the Gospel, which contains the five big teaching sections (Matt. 5–25), is narrated in a very different way. Especially when the text concerns disciples' obedience to the teachings of Jesus, divine intervention appears to be either absent or well hidden in the background. Hence the problem about the indicative and the imperative in the First Gospel.

There are different ways to explain such shifts in the narrative. Gerhard von Rad (1962, 1:52–53) tries to understand the different approaches to God's action in history in OT narrative by setting up a dichotomy between an early view and a later one. The older idea of God's action in history involves Yahweh's immediate visible and audible intervention (e.g., Gen. 28:17; similar to the beginning and ending of Matthew's Gospel). A later idea dispenses with any outwardly perceptible influence of Yahweh on history. God's guidance comes in hidden ways (e.g., the narrative of the wooing of Rebecca, the Joseph stories, Ruth, the history of the succession to David; more like Matt. 5–25). A new way of picturing Yahweh's action in history led to a new technique in narrative.

> An era which no longer experienced Yahweh's working mainly in the sacral form of miracles . . . could therefore no longer satisfactorily express its faith in a sacral narrative-form. . . . Nature and History . . . became secularized, and was as it were, overnight released from the sacral orders sheltering it. In consequence, the figures in stories now move in a completely demythologized and secular world. . . . In order to show Yahweh at work, these story-tellers have no need of wonders or the appearance of charismatic leaders—events develop apparently in complete accord with their own inherent character. (von Rad 1962, 1:56)

Psychological processes (e.g., Saul's love-hate relation with David) dominate in a world that has slipped into the habit of looking on human affairs in such a secular way.

Meir Sternberg (1985, 106) is surely right, however, when he notes that in the Hebrew Bible the books mix overt and implicit guidance by God. The difference in style is due not to a historical development in the way God's activity in the world was seen but to a "compositional alternative of treatment, in the interests of plotting and variety" (106). Take Genesis, for example. Genesis starts out with "God said, and it was so." This has a long-range effect on one's perceptual set.

> It develops a first impression of a world controlled by a prime mover and coherent to the exclusion of accident. Reinforced at strategic junctures by later paradigms and variants, it also enables the narrative to dispense with the continual enactment of divine intervention that would hamper suspense and overschematize the whole plot. (105)

This way of dealing with the divine activity (indicative) he calls "omnipotence behind the scenes." It is seen at work in the stories about Joseph and about David's accession to the throne. In the NT, other scholars have seen the same technique in the activities of Paul in Acts 23–28, for example. I suggest, then, that we look for techniques appropriate to a narrative style that often deals in "omnipotence behind the scenes." It is this type of narrative that one encounters in Matt. 5–25, insofar as disciples are concerned. It is, therefore, for techniques that allow the evangelist to speak in terms of "omnipotence behind the scenes" that one should search.

At least four techniques in Matthew fit such a method of narration: (1) I am with you/in your midst; (2) invoking the divine name; (3) it has been revealed to you/you have been given to know; and (4) being with Jesus. Each of these devices will be examined in order.

God with us. Let us begin with the formula "with you" or "in your midst," a technique of speaking about divine enablement that has been the subject of some discussion in NT circles. The definitive work on the formula is by W. C. van Unnik (1959, 270–305). He examined the more than one hundred passages using this formula in the LXX and grouped them in about six categories. He noted that the formula is found rarely in Psalms and Prophets but frequently in the Historical Books (i.e., in narrative). It is used mostly with individuals but sometimes with the nation. It involves the empowering or enabling of someone or some group involved in a divine task. Certain early Christian writers also used the formula (e.g., Luke 1:28; Acts 7:9–10; 10:38; 18:9–10; John 3:2; 8:29; 14:16–17; 16:32; Rom. 15:33; 2 Cor. 13:11; Phil. 4:9; 2 Thess. 3:16; 1 Cor. 14:25; 2 Tim. 4:22; Matt. 1:23; 28:20; 18:20). Josephus and Philo, however, do not retain the formula. Later Jewish exegetical material, moreover, does not use the phrase as the OT did. One of the most interesting observations made by van Unnik is about the connection between this formula and the Spirit. The relation between God's "being with" someone and the Spirit's involvement is too frequent to be accidental. Consider these examples:

Joseph	God was with Joseph (Gen. 39:23).
	God's Spirit was in Joseph (Gen. 41:38).
Moses	God will be with Moses (Exod. 3:12).
	The Spirit is on Moses (Num. 11:17).
Joshua	God will be with Joshua (Josh. 3:7).
	Joshua was full of the Spirit (Deut. 34:9).
Gideon	God is with Gideon (Judg. 6:12).
	The Spirit of the Lord took possession of Gideon (Judg. 6:34).
Saul	God is with you (1 Sam. 10:7).
	The Spirit came upon you (1 Sam. 10:6).
David	The Lord was with David (1 Sam. 18:12, 14).
	The Spirit came upon David (1 Sam. 16:13).
Israel	I am with you (Hag. 2:4).
	My Spirit abides among you (Hag. 2:5).
Jesus	God was with him (Acts 10:38b).
	God anointed him with the Spirit (Acts 10:38a).
Mary	The Lord is with you (Luke 1:28).
	The Holy Spirit will come upon you (Luke 1:35).
Jesus's disciples	to be with you (John 14:16)
	The Spirit will dwell with/in you (John 14:17).
church at Corinth	One convicted declares that God is among them because of prophecy, which is a manifestation of the Spirit (1 Cor. 14:24–25).

Van Unnik concludes that the expression "with you" refers to the dynamic activity of God's Spirit enabling people to do God's work by protecting, assisting, and blessing them. Given this background, one would have to conclude that when Matthew uses the formula "with you" or "in your midst," he is speaking of God's prior enabling activity (the indicative), activity that empowers individuals to do the tasks set before them. It also may explain why Matthew's discussion of the Spirit is so underdeveloped. This formula (with you/in your midst) was an alternative, but less explicit, way of speaking of God's activity among his people.

In Matthew scholars have frequently noted the use of the phrase "with you" or "in your midst" in three texts: 1:23; 18:20; and 28:20. The first (1:23) says the name of the one to be born will be called Emmanuel (which means, God with us). This is Matthew's controlling image when speaking of the divine presence in Jesus. The ripple effect of this statement is seen throughout the Gospel:

3:17	the voice from heaven at the baptism
8:23–27	What sort of man is this?
12:6	Something greater than the temple is here.
12:18	I will put my Spirit upon him.
14:32–33	Those in the boat worshiped him.
9:8; 15:29–31	After Jesus's acts, God is glorified.
17:5	the voice from heaven at the transfiguration
21:9; 23:39	the one who comes in the name of the Lord
28:9, 17	worshiped him

The auditor is never allowed to forget that when Jesus is active, God is present. What Jesus does and says, God is doing and saying through him. In Matthew, Jesus mediates the divine presence; he is God with us.

There are more "with us" phrases in Matthew than the remaining two (18:20 and 28:20). They may be grouped in terms of where they fit on a time line in salvation history. Regarding Jesus's earthly life, consider the following:

9:15	Can the wedding guests fast while the bridegroom is with them?
17:17	How long am I to be with you?
26:11	You do not always have me [with you].
26:18	I will keep the Passover with my disciples.
26:20	He sat at table with the twelve disciples.
26:36	Jesus went with them to Gethsemane.

For the period between Jesus's resurrection and parousia, there are the oft-noticed duo 18:20 ("Where two or three are gathered in my name, I am there among them" [NRSV]) and 28:20 ("I am with you always, to the end of the age" [NRSV]). For the period of the age to come, there is 26:29 ("I will never again drink . . . until that day when I drink it new with you in my Father's kingdom" [NRSV]). In Matthew's schema, when Jesus is with the disciples, God is present with them. Moreover, in most cases the presence is obviously an enabling one. This is one way that the First Evangelist speaks about divine enablement of the disciples. It is subtle and can be easily missed if one has not first been sensitized by the evidence from the OT background.

"The name." A second technique employed by the First Evangelist to speak about divine enablement of disciples (the indicative) is associated with "the name." In the Scriptures of Israel, the name was considered part of the personality (Bietenhard 1967). So the name is used interchangeably with the person (Pss. 7:17; 9:10; 18:49; 68:4 [68:5 MT]; 74:18; 86:12; 92:1 [92:2 MT]; Isa. 25:1; 26:8; 30:27–28; 56:6; Mal. 3:16; also in the NT: Acts 1:15; 5:41; 18:15; Rev. 3:4; 11:13; 3 John 7; Matt. 6:9). Furthermore, the OT uses the name as a way of speaking about the presence of God involved with humans. For example, when one swears (1 Sam. 20:42; Lev. 19:12), curses (2 Kings 2:24), or blesses (2 Sam. 6:18), invoking the name of Yahweh, the name thus pronounced evokes Yahweh's presence, attention, and active intervention. Or again, the name of Yahweh is said to assist humans (Ps. 54:1 [54:3 MT]: in response to prayer, where name is used in synonymous parallelism with might/power [cf. Jer. 10:6]; Ps. 89:24 [89:25 MT]: where God's steadfast love's being with him is used in synonymous parallelism with "in my name shall his horn be exalted"; Ps. 20:1 [20:2 MT]: in response to prayer, where name is used together with God's protection [cf. Prov. 18:10]). The same motif of divine assistance is found in the NT related to the name of Jesus:

1 Cor. 6:11	The name of the Lord Jesus is used in parallelism with the Spirit of God, and the two are credited with the converts' being washed, sanctified, and justified.
Acts 4:12	We are saved only through the name of Jesus.
Acts 10:43	Forgiveness comes in his name.
1 John 5:13	Eternal life comes through his name.
Mark 9:39	Mighty works are in his name.
Acts 3:6	The lame man is told to walk, in the name of Jesus.
Acts 9:34	The language is Jesus Christ heals you, so walk, indicating the interchangeability of name and person.
Acts 4:7	By what name or power do you do this?
Rom. 10:13	Those who call on the name of the Lord [Christ] will be saved.

In the NT, one meets the phrase "to be baptized in the name of." Three different prepositions are used in such phrases for "in": *epi* (Acts 2:38), *en* (Acts 10:48), and *eis* (Acts 8:16; 19:5; 1 Cor. 1:13, 15; Matt. 28:19). Although W. Heitmüller (1903) thought there was a difference between *en* and *epi* on the one hand and *eis* on the other, the three prepositions do not seem to offer significantly different meanings (e.g., Justin Martyr, *1 Apol.* 61, who uses *epi onomatos* with his trinitarian formula whereas Matthew uses *eis*). Generally speaking, "in the name of" conveys the meaning "under the authority of," or "with the invocation of." Given its background, however, it can also carry the connotations of "in the presence of" ("name" and "presence" are interchangeable concepts; cf. Ps. 89:24; 1 Cor. 6:11) and/or "in the power of" ("name" and "power" are parallel concepts; cf. Ps. 54:1; Acts 4:7). Since name and person are interchangeable (cf. Acts 3:6 with 9:34), moreover, there does not seem to be any significant difference between being baptized in (*en*)/into (*epi*) the name of Christ and being baptized into (*eis*) Christ.

Matthew 28:19–20 indicates that evangelization involves baptizing new disciples into the name of the Father, the Son, and the Holy Spirit. At least three inferences may be drawn. First, such a one is in a relation of belonging to/being under the authority of the Father, Son, and Holy Spirit. This bonding is reflected in Matt. 10:40 ("Whoever welcomes you welcomes me, and whoever welcomes me welcomes the one who sent me" [NRSV]); 18:5 ("Whoever welcomes one such child in my name welcomes me" [NRSV]); and 25:31–46 ("As you did it to the least of these followers of Christ, you did it to me"). This is not all that is implied, however. Second, Matt. 18:20 shows that the invocation of Jesus's name evokes his presence among the disciples. By extension, whenever the disciples pray the "Our Father" (6:9–13), the invocation of the name of the Father would evoke his presence in and provision for the disciples' lives (including leading not into temptation and delivering from the evil one). To invoke the name of God unleashes the power that makes intelligible the words "With God nothing is impossible" (19:26). Third, it is at least possible and perhaps probable that the First Evangelist understood Christian baptism in terms of Matt. 3:11 (He will baptize you with the Holy Spirit). If so, then the Spirit's presence is presumed by Matthew to be a part of the disciples' lives to enable them. To be baptized into the triune name, therefore, is to enter into a bonded relationship that will provide one with the divine resources to enable following the guidance of what comes next (all that I have commanded you).

Revelation. A third technique employed by the First Evangelist to indicate the divine indicative in the lives of Jesus's disciples is associated with revelation by the Father and/or Jesus to them. In Matt. 11:25–27, in a context of chapters 11–13, where the focus is on revelation and concealment, the Matthean Jesus offers thanks to his Father, who has revealed "these things" to babes rather than to the wise. In light of the previous paragraph (11:20–24), "these things" must refer to the kingdom's breaking in through the ministry of Jesus (so eschatological secrets having to do with the divine plan of salvation for the world). The larger context would indicate, moreover, that the "babes" are Jesus's disciples. Then Jesus states, "No one knows the Son except the

Father, and no one knows the Father except the Son and anyone to whom the Son chooses to reveal him" (11:27b–c NRSV). The second part of this statement portrays Jesus as the one with a knowledge of heavenly mysteries who can reveal them to others. Two backgrounds have been proposed as an aid to understanding this text. The first is wisdom. Just as God knows wisdom (Job 28:12–27; Sir. 1:6–9; Bar. 3:32), so also the Father knows the Son. Just as wisdom knows God (Wis. 8:4; 9:1–18), so the Son knows the Father. Just as wisdom makes known the divine mysteries (Wis. 9:1–18; 10:10), so also Jesus reveals God's hidden truth. Just as wisdom calls people to take up her yoke and find rest (Sir. 51:23–30), so Jesus extends a similar invitation. The second background is the Teacher of Righteousness. The similarity with the Teacher of Righteousness at Qumran has been noted since at least the 1950s. God has disclosed the mysteries to the Teacher of Righteousness (1QpHab 7.4–5; 1QH^a 4.27–28), and he has disclosed them to many others (1QH^a 4.27–28 [col. 12]; 2.13–18 [col. 10]). In both cases the revelation has to do with the proper understanding of the eschatological moment. The Matthean Jesus's disciples have been given this revelation by the Son. Both sets of comparative materials enable one to read the Matthean text in light of ancient Jewish thought. The two sides of the revelatory focus are treated in Matthew in other texts.

This theme of revelation comes up again in chapter 13. Here the focus is on the revelatory function of the Son. In 13:10–17 Jesus tells his disciples: "To you it has been given to know the secrets of the kingdom of heaven [cf. 13:16–17]. . . . For to those who have, more will be given, and they will have an abundance" (vv. 11–12b NRSV). The latter part of the statement surely points to a post-Easter setting, when the revelation will continue. In 13:16–17 Jesus says to them: "Blessed are your eyes, for they see, and your ears, for they hear. Truly I tell you, many prophets and righteous people longed to see what you see, but did not see it, and to hear what you hear, but did not hear it" (NRSV). The disciples are recipients of revelation. In 13:23 the good soil is interpreted to mean the one "who hears the word and understands it . . . [and] bears fruit." (Note: Mark 4:20 has "hear the word and accept it"; Luke 8:15 has "hold it fast in an honest and good heart"; only Matt. 13:23 has "understands it.") So the understanding is given by Jesus to the disciples, and it produces fruit. That is, the revelation is empowering, enabling in their daily lives. The emphasis on "understanding" continues to the end of the section on parables. In 13:51, only in Matthew does Jesus ask the disciples: "Have you understood all this?" They answer: "Yes." The Son has made his revelation to them, and it has been effective to enable and empower. They will yield fruit as good soil.

That the Father knows the Son was the first part of the sentence in 11:27b. The Son's revelation to the disciples has been confirmed in chapter 13. Now several passages indicate the Father's role in the revelatory process as well.

15:13	Jesus says: "Every plant that my heavenly Father has not planted will be uprooted. Let them alone; they are blind guides" (NRSV). The reference is to scribes and Pharisees. The language contrasts these "wise ones" with the disciples/babes. There are echoes of the parable of the weeds among the wheat (13:24–30). The blind ones are planted not by the Father but the enemy. They are to be left alone until the judgment. They have not been given the revelation.
16:16–17	Peter makes his confession: "You are the messiah, the son of the living God." Jesus responds: "Blessed are you [cf. 13:16]. . . . Flesh and blood has not revealed this to you, but my Father in heaven" (NRSV). The Father knows the Son and has revealed his identity to Peter.
17:5–6	On the mount of transfiguration, a voice comes from heaven to the three disciples: "This is my beloved son, with whom I am well pleased; listen to him." This echoes an earlier declaration (to John the Baptist at least) at the baptism in 3:17: "This is my beloved Son, with whom I am well pleased" (RSV).
7:1–12	We find a thought unit that makes two main points. First, 7:1–5 contends that one should not judge others until having first judged oneself. Second, 7:6–12 affirms that it is necessary to discern between good and bad (7:6), that this may be done with wisdom gained from God through prayer (7:7–11), and that any judgments made as a result should be in line with the golden rule (7:12). In this text, moral discernment is the result of prayer to the disciples' Father in heaven. One should remember that Matthew considered such insight empowering, as also the invocation of the Father's name.

In sum: a third technique used by the First Evangelist to indicate God's omnipotence behind the scenes for enabling Jesus's disciples is the concept of revelation—from Jesus and from the Father.

Being with Jesus. The fourth technique employed by Matthew to point to the divine indicative in the lives of Jesus's followers involves the notion of being "with Jesus." Writings of this period speak of four types of teachers with adult followers: (1) philosophers (e.g., Socrates); (2) sages (e.g., Sirach); (3) interpreters of Jewish law (e.g., scribes, Pharisees, Essenes); (4) prophets or seers (e.g., John the Baptist; the Egyptian Jew mentioned by Josephus, *J.W.* 2.261–73; *Ant.* 20.169–72; Acts 21:38). When auditors of Matthew's Gospel heard the story of Jesus and his followers, into which of these categories would they have unconsciously slotted Jesus and the disciples?

The overall picture of Jesus and his disciples in Matthew can be sketched with four stokes of a brush.

1. Jesus gathers followers, through either a summons (4:18–22; 9:9) or attraction (4:23–25).
2. They follow him (4:20, 22, 25; 9:9).
3. They are with him.
      The Twelve: 17:1, Jesus took with him Peter and James and John; 26:51, one of those with Jesus; 26:69, you were with Jesus; 26:71, this man was with Jesus.
      The crowds: 15:32, they have been with Jesus for three days.

4. They derive benefit from his company.

> The Twelve: 8:23–27, safety in a storm; 19:27–29, eschatological benefits promised; 17:1–8, vision of Jesus and message from heaven
>
> The crowds: 4:23–25, healings; 8:1–4, healing; 9:10, tax collectors and sinners accepted; 14:13–21, feeding; 19:2, healing

For a Mediterranean auditor of this Gospel, the closest analogy would have been a philosopher and his disciples. The four strokes with which the Gospel paints Jesus and his followers would have seemed familiar from depictions of philosophers in antiquity (Robbins 1984, 89–105).

1. Philosophers gathered disciples either by summons (e.g., Aristophanes, *Nub.* 505, has Socrates tell Strepsiades to "follow me"; Diogenes Laertius, *Vit. phil.* 2.48, tells of Socrates meeting Xenophon and saying "follow me" and learn) or by attraction (Philostratus, *Vit. Apoll.* 1.19, says Damis was drawn to Apollonius).
2. A philosopher's disciples followed him (e.g., Philostratus, *Vit. Apoll.* 1.19, has Damis say to Apollonius: "Let us depart, . . . you following God, and I you"; 4.25 has Demetrius of Corinth follow Apollonius as a disciple; Josephus, *Ant.* 8.354, influenced by the philosophical schools, depicts the Elijah-Elisha relation as that of philosopher-teacher and disciple).
3. The disciples are with him (e.g., Philostratus, *Vit. Apoll.* 1.19, has Damis stay with the philosopher and commit to memory whatever he learned; Josephus, *Ant.* 8.354, says that Elisha was Elijah's disciple and attendant as long as Elijah was on earth).
4. The disciples receive benefit from being in the company of the philosopher (see the sidebar).

These statements about the benefits that disciples received from "being with" a philosopher do not refer to the disciples' imitation of their teacher but rather to their being enabled by their association with him. This is a philosophic variation on the general Mediterranean belief that being in the presence of a deity causes transformation of the self. Pythagoras, for example, declared that "our souls experience a change when we enter a temple and behold the images of the gods face to face" (Seneca the Younger, *Ep.* 94.42). This conviction was widespread in antiquity (e.g., *Corp. herm.* 10.6; 13.3; Philo, *Mos.* 1.158–59; 2.69; *Legat.* 1.5; *Contempl.* 2.11, 13, 18; 4.34; *Congr.* 56; *Praem.* 114; 2 Cor. 3:18; 1 John 3:6; *Diogn.* 2.5). All such cases involve human transformation by vision. In the case of the philosopher, the vision is not of a god but of a godlike man. The effects are the same: human transformation.

The benefits, it was believed, were not limited to being with the philosopher in person. First of all, recollection had its impact. Xenophon, *Mem.* 4.1.1, speaks about the recollection of Socrates by his disciples when they were separated as an aid to virtue. "The constant recollection of him in absence brought no small good to his constant companions and followers" (trans. Marchant and Todd 1923). Furthermore, books and the use of the imagination also played a part. Seneca, *Ep.* 52.7 and 11.8–10, advocates looking to the ancients for models with whom to associate. In *Ep.* 25.6, he says that if one cannot be in a philosopher's presence, one should come to know him through books, acting as if he were constantly at one's side. Epistles 25.5; 11.10; and 11.8 advocate using the imagination to picture the teacher as ever before one and oneself as ever in the teacher's presence. The presence of the disciples with their master through books and imagination was regarded, however, as second best. Seneca, *Ep.* 6.5, writes: "The living voice and the intimacy of a

---

Benefits to Philosopher's Disciples

Xenophon, *Mem.* 4.1.1, says of Socrates:

> "Socrates was so useful in all circumstances and in all ways, that any observer gifted with ordinary perception can see that nothing was more useful than the companionship [syneinai] of Socrates, and time spent with him [met' ekeinou] in any place and in any circumstances." (trans. Marchant and Todd 1923)

In *Mem.* 1.2.24–28, Xenophon says: "So long as they were with [synēstēn] Socrates, they found him an ally who gave them strength [edynasthēn] to conquer their evil passions" (ibid.). Seneca the Younger, *Ep.* 6.5–6, says in the same vein:

> "Cleanthes could not have been the express image of Zeno, if he had merely heard his lectures; he also shared his life, saw into his hidden purposes, and watched him to see whether he lived according to his own rules. Plato, Aristotle, and the whole throng of sages who were destined to go each his different way, derived more benefit from the character than from the words of Socrates. It was not the classroom of Epicurus, but living together under the same roof, that made great men of Metrodorus, Hermarchus, and Polyaenus." (trans. Gummere 1970–79)

In *Ep.* 94.40–42, Seneca says association with good men is an aid to virtue. "We are indeed uplifted by meeting wise men; and one can be helped by a great man even when he is silent." In the *Cynic Epistles* he says, "It is not the country that makes good men, nor the city bad ones, but rather time spent with good men and bad. Consequently, if you want your sons to become good men and not bad, send them . . . to a philosopher's school" ("The Epistles of Crates," 12, trans. Malherbe 1977). It was the association with the teacher that gave the disciples their benefits and made them better people.

common life will help you more than the written word" (trans. Gummere 1970–79). The point is that disciples' being with their teacher was an aid to personal transformation. Being with him conveyed benefits in their moral progress. Being with him enabled them to do good and to be better people. Plutarch captured part of why that is so. In *Virt. prof.* 84d, he says that being in the presence of a good and perfect man has this effect on a person: "Great is his craving all but to merge his own identity in that of the good man" (trans. Perrin 1914–26).

Matthew used the idea of disciples being with their teacher to convey part of his indicative. During Jesus's earthly career his disciples were with him. They heard him teach and saw him act. They saw the correspondence between his life and teaching. They could ask him questions and hear his answers. Ancient auditors would have assumed that this common life enabled the disciples' progress in their formation by Jesus. In the Sermon on the Mount, for example, Jesus says to his disciples that they are salt and light (5:13–14) and are sound trees that bear good fruit (7:17–18). That is, Jesus assumes that transformation of the disciples' characters has begun to take place. From the Gospel's plot, the only thing so far that could explain their transformation is the fact that, having been called, they followed Jesus (4:20, 22). That is, they were with him, and this association had a transforming quality.

If being in a philosopher's presence was regarded as transforming in a way that was more than disciples' imitation of their master, so likewise the disciples' being with Jesus in Matthew speaks of more than their imitation of him. Transformation by vision is heightened in the First Gospel by the fact that Jesus is depicted as divine. In Matthew, God is present in Jesus (1:23). The evangelist, as a consequence, speaks of the worship of Jesus before his resurrection (e.g., 2:11; 8:2; 9:18; 14:33; 15:25; 20:20, all unique to Matthew) as well as after it (28:9, 17, also unique to Matthew). Since in 4:10 Jesus says that worship belongs to God alone and since Jesus does not reject the worship, he must be viewed as Emmanuel, the one in whom and through whom God is present (1:23). By presenting Jesus as an appropriate object of worship, the evangelist "does, for all practical purposes, portray Jesus as divine" (Powell 1995b, 58). Hence, the disciples' being "with him" has not only the philosophic frame of reference but also the overtones of being changed by beholding deity. In Matthew, then, for the disciples to be "with Jesus" is for them to be transformed by their vision of God-with-us.

After Jesus's departure, they could have been with him early on, in part, through their memory and recollection of him. Later it would have been through their reading of the First Gospel. They were with Jesus as they moved through the narrative plot with him. The being with him made possible by the story powered their transformation.

The power of the story to enable change is captured in an old Hasidic tale:

When the Baal Shem had a difficult task before him, he would go to a certain place in the woods, light a fire and meditate in prayer—and what he set out to perform was done. When a generation later the "Maggid" of Meseritz was faced with the same task he would go to the same place in the woods and say: We can no longer light the fire, but we can still speak the prayers—and what he wanted done became reality. Again a generation later Rabbi Moshe Leib of Sassov had to perform this task. And he too went into the woods and said: We can no longer light the fire, nor do we know the secret meditations belonging to the prayer, but we do know the place in the woods to which it all belongs—and that would be sufficient; and sufficient it was. But when another generation had passed and Rabbi Israel of Rishin was called upon to perform the task, he sat down on his golden chair in his castle and said: We cannot light the fire, we cannot speak the prayers, we do not know the place, but we can tell the story of how it was done. And the story-teller adds, the story which he had told had the same effect as the actions of the other three. (Scholem 1995, 349–50)

Being with him and experiencing the vision of God-with-us—in person, by means of recollection, or by means of the book (the First Gospel)—powerfully assisted their life of obedience.

How Matthew's Indicative Controls His Imperative

The four techniques discussed above function in the Gospel of Matthew to provide an indicative of divine enablement that underlies the imperative in an ongoing way. This section will show how this is so.

We begin with Matt. 28:19–20. On the basis of all power being given (by God) to him (cf. Matt. 11:27; Dan. 7:13–14), the Matthean Jesus issues a command to his followers. As you go, make disciples, baptizing them and teaching them (28:19–20a). A promise follows: "I am with you always, to the end of the age" (28:20b NRSV). Jesus's promise is that he will empower them so they can fulfill the mission he has just commanded them to undertake. How else could the work of Jesus be accomplished if he did not enable it? (Indeed, 13:37 says that it is the son of man who sows the seed!) There is a widespread consensus that 28:18–20 is the key to understanding the whole Gospel. For this reason some have sought to use 28:20 as the indicative underlying the imperative throughout the First Gospel. This seems impossible, however. Matthew 28:19–20 limits the presence of Jesus with the disciples to their mission. Jesus is with those evangelizing. What about those being evangelized (baptized and then taught to observe all that Jesus commanded)? Matthew 28:19–20 is silent about this dimension. Surely the general answer to this question is Matt. 19:26, all things are possible with God. The issue is this: how does Matthew see this divine enablement being worked out?

The four techniques that speak of divine activity behind the scenes are relevant here:

1. Revelation enables both the confession of Jesus (16:17) and the bearing of abundant fruit (13:23, which surely includes ethical living).

2. Baptism in the name of the Father, Son, and Holy Spirit opens the door to divine assistance. For example, when two or three are gathered in Jesus's name, then he is present in their midst (18:20). This logion, which seems to be a Christian variant of a non-Christian Jewish saying about the Shekinah's presence in the midst of two or three who discuss torah (*m. Avot* 3.2b [3]; *Avot R. Nat.* [B] 34), is set in the context of church discipline. It indicates that when Christians are involved in the task of settling disputes among church members, the presence of Jesus is with them to empower their decisions. Or when disciples are brought before hostile authorities, "what you are to say will be given to you at that time; for it is not you who speak, but the Spirit of your Father speaking through you" (10:19–20 NRSV). Here a revelation given to disciples is combined with the activity of the Spirit, in whose name one has been baptized (cf. 3:11). Or again, when disciples invoke the name of their heavenly Father (6:9–13; 7:7–11), this evokes his answering response (e.g., leading us not into temptation, delivering us from the evil one, giving us discernment about the difference between good and evil).

3. Jesus's being with his disciples affects the way they behave (9:15 NRSV: "The wedding guests cannot mourn as long as the bridegroom is with them, can they?") and provides them aid when their faith is weak (17:17, 19–20).

4. When the disciples are with Jesus, their character is shaped for the better. The Gospel assumes one's actions arise out of one's character (12:35 NRSV: "The good person brings good things out of a good treasure, and the evil person brings evil things out of an evil treasure"; 15:18–19 NRSV: "What comes out of the mouth proceeds from the heart, and this is what defiles. For out of the heart come evil intentions, murder, adultery, fornication, theft, false witness, slander"). The Sermon on the Mount assumes that Jesus's disciples have been transformed (5:13, 14: "You are the salt of the earth"; "You are the light of the world"; 6:22; 7:17–18). How is this possible (in the plot of the First Gospel)? All that has gone before is their call and their following Jesus, that is, being with him (4:18–22). Being with him, it is implied, has changed their character. As one moves through the Gospel, it is not difficult to see how this takes place. When Jesus teaches with a "focal instance" (e.g., 5:38–42; see Tannehill 1975, 67–77), it requires the reorientation of the hearer's values; when he teaches in certain parables that shatter one's old world (e.g., 20:1–15) and help form a new one, it necessitates reorienting one's life. When Jesus's proverbs jolt their hearers out of the continuity of their lives (e.g., Matt. 5:44; 16:25; 19:24), it demands a reorientation. When Jesus behaves in certain provocative ways (e.g., 8:2–3; 9:10–13; 12:1–14), it forces disciples to reorient their lives. When the disciples encounter Jesus's healing as visual teaching (e.g., 15:29–30), they join the crowds in glorifying the God of Israel (15:31).

Being with Jesus is a constant aid to transcending one's old ways, to being transformed by the renewing of one's mind (Rom. 12:2). No area of life is left untouched by one or more of Matthew's four techniques for alluding to divine assistance in a disciple's experience.

Another angle from which to view the four techniques is to look at how they relate to the five major teaching sections of the First Gospel ("all that I have commanded you," i.e., Matthew's imperative). (1) The link with Matt. 18 is explicit. Both the name of Jesus and Jesus's presence in the disciples' midst are employed. (2) A connection with chapter 13 is seen in Jesus's revelation to the disciples of the eschatological plan of God. (3) Matthew 10 is covered under 28:20's "with you" in the disciples' mission and by the invocation of the name of the Spirit of the Father, who speaks through the disciples. (4) The Sermon on the Mount utilizes the invocation of the name in prayer to the Father and speaks of discernment being given to those who ask. The disciples' being with Jesus explains how their character could be salt and light. (5) In the eschatological chapters of the fifth teaching section, 26:29 comes into play. Jesus will be with his disciples even beyond the resurrection/judgment, when they share the messianic banquet together. There is no big teaching section that is not linked to Matthew's techniques for speaking about the enabling presence of God in the disciples' lives.

Two reminders are helpful at this point. First, one should remember that functionally these techniques are virtually interchangeable in a biblical context. (a) The presence of God "with you" is virtually synonymous with "assistance by God's name" (Ps. 89:24 [89:25 MT]: "My faithfulness and steadfast love shall be with him; and in my name his horn shall be exalted"; cf. Matt. 18:20). (b) The presence of God "with you" is an alternative way of saying "God's Spirit is in your midst" (Hag 2:4–5: "Take courage, all you people of the land, says the LORD; work, for I am with you, says the LORD of hosts, according to the promise that I made you when you came out of Egypt. My spirit abides among you; do not fear"; cf. Luke 1:28, 35). (c) The presence of God "with you" is closely associated with revelation given to one (1 Kings 1:37: the Lord will be with Solomon; 4:29: God gave Solomon wisdom and understanding; cf. John 14:16–17, 26). (d) "In the name of" and Spirit are closely linked (1 Cor. 6:11: in the name of the Lord Jesus Christ and in the Spirit, you were washed, sanctified, justified). Anyone familiar with this biblical way of speaking would have been sensitive to Matthew's use of his conceptual repertoire. Second, one should remember that in the First Evangelist's scheme of things, when the narrative speaks of Jesus's presence, it is God who is with us in Emmanuel (Matt. 1:23).

At every point in a disciple's life and at every stage of salvation history, therefore, Matthew speaks of the divine indicative, divine enablement for the whole of a disciple's existence from its beginning to the messianic banquet. Granted, all of this is unobtrusive, almost invisible to the eye that is focused on the surface of the plot of the Gospel. That is as it should be, given that in Matt. 5–25, as far as disciples are concerned, the evangelist is telling his story in terms of omnipotence-behind-the-scenes. This is not the way Paul or the Fourth Evangelist would tell the story, but it is Matthew's way. Matthew's way, moreover, is neither soteriological legalism nor legalistic covenantal nomism. Like Paul, his soteriology is by grace from start to finish. Matthew just uses a different conceptual repertoire. Surely he cannot be faulted for that!

When the reader proceeds to a reading of the First Gospel and to a reading of this commentary, it should be with a recognition that Matthean soteriology is grace-oriented from start to finish. Read in this way, Matthew comes across as a soteriological ally of Paul and the Fourth Gospel, not their antithesis.

Methodological Assumptions

The first presupposition of this volume is that its purpose is to interpret the final form of the First Gospel. It is Matthew's narrative world with which we are engaged. While the tradition behind the redaction is a legitimate historical question, it is not the same thing as interpreting the Gospel of Matthew. Volumes that try to pursue both tasks at the same time usually slight one or the other of the objectives (e.g., Blomberg 1992, whose concern to validate the historicity of Matthew's tradition results in a less-than-adequate engagement with Matthew's narrative world). To do Matthew's theological project justice, no effort will be expended in this volume on the question of the historicity of the tradition. This is not a denial of such historicity but a methodological decision to bracket that question for the moment.

A second presupposition is that interpretation is best done by reading with the authorial audience (Rabinowitz 1977; 1987; 1989). The final form of the text is given a close reading, and then the question is asked, how would an ancient auditor have heard Matthew's narrative? This move, of course, requires some knowledge of the cultural repertoire of ancient Mediterranean peoples. This explains the use of a variety of "parallels," Jewish and Greco-Roman, throughout the volume. When the modern reader encounters such parallels, it does not mean that this commentary assumes that the biblical author(s) borrowed the material, with the result that Christianity is a syncretistic religion. Rather, it is assumed that the Christian movement has its own religious integrity. The question is, how would a communication by the Jesus movement, with its own identity derived from its unique relation to the one God—Father, Son, and Holy Spirit—have been heard by Jews and pagans alike?

Matthew 1:1–2:23

Birth Narratives

Introductory Matters

Several questions of structure call for discussion before we trace the flow of the narrative in the first two chapters of Matthew's Gospel.

Why Separate Matthew 1–2 from 3–4?

First, the question arises, Why separate 1:1–2:23 from 3:1–4:17? For those who regard the phrase *apo tote ērxato* (from then [Jesus] began) in 4:17 and 16:21 as the marker of Matthew's three major divisions (e.g., Krentz 1964; Kingsbury 1989, 7–25), 1:1–2:23 belongs with 3:1–4:17, making up the first division of the First Gospel.

Moreover, there is a significant link between 2:22–23 and 4:12–14.

When he heard (2:22/4:12)
he withdrew (2:22/4:12)
to/into Galilee (2:22/4:12)
to/from Nazareth (2:23/4:13)
the word fulfilled (2:23/4:14)

There are weighty reasons, however, to see a significant break between 2:23 and 3:1 (Davies and Allison 1988, 1:287). First, *apo tote ērxato* (from then he began) is not a reliable guide to Matthew's division of his narrative. In 26:16 we find *apo tote* (from then) and in 11:20 *tote ērxato* (then he began) without any sign of their being significant markers. The two uses of the full three-word formula, furthermore, do not compare with the fivefold repetition of *kai egeneto hote etelesen ho Iēsous* (and when Jesus had finished: 7:28; 11:1; 13:53; 19:1; 26:1) as narrative markers. Second, the story in 1:1–2:23 deals with the birth and infancy of Jesus while that in 3:1–4:17 focuses on Jesus as a young adult. There is a twenty- to thirty-year gap between the two. Third, 3:1–12 shifts to a new subject: the Baptist. Fourth, except for son of God, the christological designations of 1:1–2:23 (e.g., son of Abraham, Emmanuel, son of David, king of the Jews, one like Moses) fade into the background in 3:1–4:17. Fifth, the narratives in 1:1–2:23 and in 3:1–4:17 draw on different sources for their material and constitute different genres. If Matt. 3:1–17 draws material from Mark and Q, the genre is theologically interpreted tradition with ties to biography. If 1:1–2:23 is theologically interpreted tradition, its genre is a matter of debate: history? haggadah? midrash? Of the three options only haggadah (edifying narratives that graphically elaborate events associated with and meaningful to faith) comes close (Soares Prabhu 1976, 13–14). Sixth, 1:1–2:23 and 3:1–4:17 each has its own structural organization. Structure divides rather than joins the two segments of narrative. For these reasons, this commentary will treat 1:1–2:23 as a self-contained section of the Gospel.

Sources of Matthew 1–2

A second matter concerns sources. Although attempts have been made to argue for a pre-Matthean source or sources behind chapters 1–2 (e.g., Davies and Allison 1988, 1:190–95, who claim three stages of development), none has produced a consensus among scholars. That there was tradition from which the First Evangelist worked, however, is indicated by the independent use of similar material in Luke (Brown 1977, 34–35). Their common material includes: (1) Joseph is of Davidic descent (Matt. 1:16, 20; Luke 1:27, 32; 2:4); (2) Joseph and Mary, though betrothed, do not yet live together (Matt. 1:18; Luke 1:27, 34); (3) an angel announces the coming birth (Matt. 1:20–23; Luke 1:30–35); (4) the conception is not through intercourse of Mary with Joseph (Matt. 1:20, 23, 25; Luke 1:34) but through the Holy Spirit (Matt. 1:18, 20; Luke 1:35); (5) the angel instructs that the name of the child be Jesus (Matt. 1:21; Luke 1:31); (6) an angel says Jesus is to be Savior (Matt. 1:21; Luke 2:11); (7) the birth of the child takes place after Joseph and Mary have come to live together (Matt. 1:24–25; Luke 2:5–6); (8) the birth is in Bethlehem (Matt. 2:1; Luke 2:4–6); (9) the birth is during the reign of Herod the Great (Matt. 2:1; Luke 1:5); (10) the child is reared at Nazareth (Matt. 2:23; Luke 2:39). Each evangelist, while using this common tradition, has developed it very differently. Our task will be to discern Matthew's distinctive development of the tradition.

The Components and Arrangement of Matthew 1–2

The third introductory matter concerns the components of the Matthean narrative of Jesus's origins and their organization and development in chapters 1–2. Matthew 1:1–17 has a genealogy. In 1:18–2:23 are five scenes, each with the same components, though the order varies:

1. 1:18–25: Dream command, fulfillment of Scripture, obedience to the command
2. 2:1–12: Fulfillment of Scripture, dream command, obedience to the command
3. 2:13–15: Dream command, obedience, fulfillment of Scripture
4. 2:16–21: Fulfillment of Scripture, dream command, obedience
5. 2:22–23: Dream warning, obedience, fulfillment of Scripture

Three of the pericopes have dream reports (1:18–25; 2:13–15; 2:16–21); two contain references to dreams (2:12; 2:22; Dodson 2002).

Matthew 1:1–2:23 in the Narrative Flow

Birth narratives (1:1–2:23)
Genealogy and birth (1:1–25)
  Heading (1:1)
  Genealogy (1:2–16)
  Concluding summary (1:17)
  A dream and a birth (1:18–25)
Dreams and commands (2:1–23)
  The magi (2:1–12)
  Flight to Egypt (2:13–15)
  Return to Israel (2:16–21)
  Removal to Nazareth (2:22–23)

At one level, the genealogy (1:1–17) and the first dream report (1:18–25) go together logically while the final four pericopes with dreams logically belong together. This yields a twofold division that corresponds roughly to the current chapter divisions. It will be in these terms that the following section, the rhetorical development and function of Matt. 1–2, will initially unfold.

Tracing the Narrative Flow

Genealogy and Birth (1:1–25)

Matthew 1:1–25 is the first component of chapters 1–2. It consists of four main units: a heading (1:1), the genealogy (1:2–16), a concluding summary (1:17), and a dream and a birth (1:18–25).

1:1. The heading (1:1) reads: **Book of the genesis of Jesus Christ, son of David, son of Abraham** (cf. Gen. 5:1 LXX, the book of the genesis of humans). The major question regarding 1:1 is whether this heading refers to the genealogy only (Garland 2001, 15), to 1:2–25 (Brown 1977, 59), to 1:2–2:23, to 1:2–4:17 (Bauer 1990), or to the entire Gospel (Davies and Allison 1988, 1:153–54; Boring 1995, 125). For our purposes here, it is sufficient to say that verse 1 covers at least the first chapter of Matthew (the genealogy and first dream report).

1:2–16. The genealogy itself (1:2–16) consists of three subunits (1:2–6a, 6b–11, 12–16) specified by the concluding summary in 1:17. It unfolds in reverse order from that of the heading (1:1: Jesus Christ, son of David, son of Abraham): Abraham, David, the Christ (1:17). It was not uncommon in Israel's scriptures to have a genealogy open a narrative (cf. Gen. 5–9: a genealogy and the story of Noah; Gen. 11:10–25:11: a genealogy and the story of Abraham). Hellenistic biographies also often opened with genealogies or accounts of a hero's ancestors (e.g., Plutarch, *Alex.* 2; *Brut.* 1; Suetonius, *Jul.* 6; Tacitus, *Agr.* 4; Josephus, *Life* 1–6).

To refer to Jesus as "son of Abraham" would have evoked certain connections. Three seem relevant here. First, *T. Levi* 8.14–15 ("from Judah a king will arise, . . . a descendant of Abraham, our father") connects the messianic king with Abrahamic lineage (cf. Gal. 3:16; Gen. 17:6). Second, Abraham, the gentile who became the father of the Jews, signals the First Gospel's interest in gentiles (cf. Gen. 17:6; 1 Macc. 12:21; Matt. 3:9; 8:11–12; Gal. 3:8; Rom. 15:8–12). Indeed, Josephus (*Ant.* 1.162–68) portrays Abraham as a missionary going down to Egypt. Third, *Jubilees* portrays Abraham as one who resisted evil spirits and the devil (12.20: "Save me from the hands of evil spirits which rule over the thought of the heart of man, and do not let them lead me astray from following you, O my God" [*OTP* 2:81]; 17.15–18.19: Abraham's willingness to sacrifice Isaac is depicted in the context of a test by Prince Mastema to determine Abraham's faithfulness).

To refer to Jesus as "son of David" would have evoked at least two connections in the auditors of Matthew. First, "son of David" had become a messianic reference by Matthew's time (cf. *Pss. Sol.* 17; 4QFlor 1.11–13; 4QpIsa, frags. 8–10, col. 3.11–25; 2 Esd. [*4 Ezra*] 12:32; Rom. 1:3–4). Second, in the OT (with the exception of 2 Sam. 13:1), "son of David" refers to Solomon, through whom Matthew's genealogy traces the royal line (unlike Luke 3:31, which traces the line through David's otherwise insignificant son Nathan; Bohler 1998). Solomon had become associated with healing and exorcism (*L.A.B.* 60.3; Josephus, *Ant.* 8.45–49; *T. Sol*; *b. Git.* 68a–b). Quite apart from Solomon, however, the Davidic messiah was expected to feed the sheep, strengthen the weak, heal the sick, bind up the crippled, bring back the straying, and seek the lost (Ezek. 34). In Matthew's references to Jesus as son of David (1:1; 9:27; 12:23; 15:22; 20:30, 31; 21:9, 15), both messianic and healing overtones are found. A son of David was expected by some Jews to be a messianic shepherd for God's people. The historical David was to be shepherd over Israel (2 Sam. 5:1–2; 1 Chron. 11:1–2; Ps. 2:9 LXX; *Tg. Ps.* 2.9; Ps. 78:70–71; 4Q504, frags. 1–2, col. 4.6–8). The ideal Davidic figure of the future was also expected to shepherd the people (Mic. 5:4; Ezek. 34:23–24; 37:24; *Pss. Sol.* 17.40–41: the Davidic Messiah will shepherd the Lord's flock). Later, in Matt. 2:6, a composite quotation from Mic. 5:1–2 and 2 Sam. 5:2 speaks of an eschatological ruler who will shepherd God's people; 26:31, in a composite quotation from

Zech. 13:7 and Ezek. 34:31, speaks about striking the shepherd and the sheep being scattered; 9:36, echoing 1 Kings 22:17, says Jesus had compassion on the crowds because they were like sheep without a shepherd (Willitts 2007).

To refer to Jesus as "the Christ" (1:17) would have been only to focus the implications of "son of Abraham" and "son of David." To speak of Jesus as messiah at the end of this genealogy would be to insert him into a history and a people. God gave promises to Abraham (Gen. 12:2–3; 18:18) and to David (2 Sam. 7:12–14). In Jesus, the climax of the list, the genealogy says, these promises have been fulfilled. This establishes the point of view in terms of which the following narrative about Jesus is to be understood (Bauer 1990, 464). Jesus brings to realization all that was implicit in the events, persons, and declarations of Israel's history.

That God has brought Israel's history to its fulfillment in Jesus was not without its challenges. On the one hand, God's redemptive activity has had to

The Women in Matthew's Genealogy

Explanations for the presence of women in Matthew's genealogy follow two trajectories. If emphasis is on similarities among the women, the argument runs like this: The first four women were probably all gentiles. Tamar (Gen. 38) and Rahab (Josh. 2, 6) were Canaanites. Ruth (Ruth 1–4) was a Moabite. Bathsheba (2 Sam. 11–12), who was married to Uriah the Hittite, was also probably a gentile. So gentiles were a part of God's plan from early on. Also, all four were involved in sexual activity that outsiders might view negatively. Tamar tricked her father-in-law into having sex with her (though levirate marriage was acceptable by Jewish standards); Rahab was a prostitute; Ruth seduced her kinsman Boaz; Bathsheba committed adultery with David. Although the rabbis regard some of them as righteous gentiles (e.g., Rahab and Ruth in *Eccles. Rab.* 5.11.1), one would have to conclude that God worked through unconventional women. That a young, betrayed, pregnant girl would be the mother of Israel's messiah continues the theme (Nowell 2008).

If differences among the five women are taken seriously, the argument runs like this. Rahab and Ruth were non-Jews, the former a Canaanite and the latter a Moabite, who were people of faith (cf. Josh. 2:9, "I know that the LORD has given you the land"; Ruth 1:16, "Your God [will be] my God"; 4:11, "like Rachel and Leah"). These two women reinforce the universalistic dimension of the promise to Abraham (Gen. 12:3, through Abraham all nations will be blessed). Tamar, a non-Canaanite (Gen. 38 does not say so, but *T. Jud.* 10 and *Jub.* 42.1–7 say she was Jewish), by her association with Judah reveals the sinfulness of the Davidic line beginning with Judah (Gen. 38:26). The wife of Uriah, by her association with David, reveals once again the sinfulness of the Davidic line from it origins. The fifth woman, Mary, gives birth to the messiah who will reverse the sinfulness of the Davidic line (e.g., Matt. 3:14–15, Jesus is better than John, but they both fulfill all righteousness) and fulfill the universalistic promise to Abraham (e.g., Matt. 15:21–28; Heil 1991b).

deal with the unexpected, the unrespectable, the unconventional as agents in salvation history (cf. Judah, 1:3; Tamar, 1:3; Rahab, 1:5a; Ruth, 1:5b; David, 1:6; the wife of Uriah, 1:6; other kings starting with Solomon, 1:7; Mary, 1:16; Schnackenburg 2002, 17; Mattila 2002, 81) and with catastrophes (like the exile, 1:11–12). On the other hand, the genealogy itself presents a problem. It is Joseph's genealogy. It is he who is of the lineage of David. He, however, is not said to be the father of Jesus, only **the husband of Mary, of whom Jesus, the one called Christ, was born** (1:16). How then can Joseph's genealogy locate Jesus within the Davidic line?

1:17. **Therefore all the generations from Abraham until David were fourteen generations, and from David until the Babylonian exile were fourteen generations, and from the Babylonian exile until the Christ were fourteen generations.** The number fourteen was conventional in genealogies. In 1 Chron. 1–2 are fourteen generations from Abraham to David; in *2 Bar.* 53–74 world history is divided into fourteen periods from Adam to the messiah; in *m. Avot* 1.1–12 are fourteen links in the chain of tradition between Moses and the last of the pairs of teachers. So Matthew's auditors would have experienced nothing out of the ordinary in this opening of his narrative.

1:18–25. What follows, Matt. 1:18–25, answers the question raised by 1:16: how is Joseph's genealogy significant if Joseph is not the father of Jesus? It also answers the question, how can Mary be Jesus's mother if not by Joseph? The initial sentence says it clearly: **Concerning Jesus Christ, his genesis was thus** (1:18). The *geneseōs* of 1:1 and the *genesis* of 1:18 tie the two pericopes together. The latter is more specific than the former. The latter tries to explain the ambiguities of verse 16 regarding the connection of Joseph and Mary to Jesus. The pericope (1:18–25) has four parts alternating between direct address to the reader and the narration of the story (Kingsbury 2001).

A Direct address to the reader (1:18a)
  B Narration of the story (1:18b–21)
A' Direct address to the reader (1:22–23)
  B' Narration of the story (1:24–25)

Each section of narration ends with the name of Jesus (1:21a: **You shall call his name Jesus**; 1:25: **He called his name Jesus**).

How is Mary linked to Jesus? Before a sexual relationship with Joseph began, she became pregnant. **That which is begotten in her is by the Holy Spirit** (1:20). Mary is said to be Jesus's mother because of a miraculous conception (not by Joseph). If Joseph is not the father, how then can his genealogy apply to Jesus? Joseph's naming of the baby constituted legal recognition of the child as his own (*m. B. Bat.* 8.6: "If a man said, 'This is my son,' he may be believed" [trans. Danby 1933, 377]). Hence, 1:18–25 say that Jesus is not only legally a son of Joseph and hence of David's line but also Emmanuel (God with us,

1:23) through the action of the Holy Spirit. Verses 22–23 address the auditors directly. The miraculous conception of Mary fulfills Isa. 7:14: **Behold, the virgin** (*parthenos*) **will conceive and bear a son, and they will call his name Emmanuel** (1:23). This text from Isaiah originally was addressed to King Ahaz of Judah when he was threatened by Syria and Israel to the north (Isa. 7:1–2; 2 Kings 16). The prophet Isaiah assures Ahaz that their plans to conquer Judah will not succeed. As encouragement, Yahweh offers the king a sign. A child to be named Emmanuel will be born. During that child's early life, the lands of Syria and Israel will be wasted and will be a threat to Judah no more (Isa. 7:1–17). The Hebrew text refers to a young woman of marriageable age (*almah*, not *betulah*, which means "virgin") and indicates that she was pregnant without anything unusual being associated with her pregnancy. The LXX and Matt. 1:23 translate *almah* (young woman) by *parthenos* (virgin; Bratcher 1958). That the First Evangelist intended for Isa. 7:14 to be understood this way is clarified by 1:25: **and he did not know her** (have sexual relations with her) **until she brought forth a son.** In this way the questions raised in 1:16 are answered. Did Mary have sexual relations with Joseph after Jesus's birth? Among the earliest witnesses, Tertullian (*Marc.* 4.19) and Irenaeus (*Haer.* 3.16, 21, 22) say yes. The *Protevangelium of James* says no.

The genealogy and the first dream report (1:2–17; 1:18–25) say that Jesus is on the one hand legally the son of Abraham and son of David through Joseph and on the other Emmanuel (God with us) through the Holy Spirit. Matthew 1 speaks about *who* Jesus is and *how* he became such (Stendahl 1960). This is how in chapter 1 the First Evangelist has developed his tradition rhetorically. How has he developed his material in chapter 2?

Dreams and Commands (2:1–23)

Matthew 2:1–23 is composed of four units built around dream commands (2:1–12; 2:13–15; 2:16–21; 2:22–23). These four units answer the questions *from where* does Jesus come and *where* does he then go? They all center upon the theme of God's protection of the one born king

Figure 1. The Church of the Nativity in Bethlehem, with doorway requiring a person to stoop to enter. The first church was dedicated by Queen Helena in AD 339. The Emperor Justinian in the early sixth century ordered the fourth-century structure to be torn down and a new church built to replace it. This building has remained in use to the present day.

The Meaning of "to Fulfill" in Matthew 1:23

That Jesus is said to fulfill the Jewish scriptures can be understood in at least two ways: predictive fulfillment and typological fulfillment. On the one hand, predictive fulfillment requires that the prophet was speaking specifically of the coming of the messiah in the distant future. On the other hand, typological fulfillment refers to an event in Jesus's career as the fullest expression of a divinely intended significant pattern of events (a type). Isaiah 7:14 predicts a child to be born *during* rather than *after* Ahaz's lifetime, as a sign of God's promise of deliverance. Matthew 1:23 uses Isa. 7:14 as a guarantee that the birth of the child signals a deliverance from sins. This is not predictive fulfillment. Rather, Jesus's birth is a fulfillment of the Jewish scriptures in a typological sense. His birth is the fullest expression of a type of God's activity, namely, the birth of a child functioning as a guarantee of God's promised deliverance of his people (Hamilton 2008). Matthew lays the basis for Christians' typological reading of the OT. What has happened or is happening is a replaying of sacred history—in Jesus's case, fulfillment (Riches 2000, 234).

of the Jews. Dreams function to give protection to the child, just as they sometimes did in the larger environment (Josephus, *Ant.* 11.326–35; Plutarch, *Them.* 26.2–4; 30.1–3).

2:1–12. In 2:1–12 magi (gentiles who are able to recognize signs and foretell events, including the rise of kings) come to Jerusalem, alerted by a star, asking, **Where is the one born king of the Jews? We have seen his star in the east, and we have come to worship him** (2:2).

When Herod asks the chief priests and scribes where the messiah was to be born, they answer "Bethlehem" and cite Mic. 5:2 as proof, an example of predictive fulfillment (Hamilton 2008): **And you, Bethlehem, in the land of Judah, you are in no way least among the princes of Judah, for**

Figure 2. Matthew's account of the magi who journeyed from the East to visit the infant Jesus has inspired many works of art. This woodcut by Albrecht Dürer dates to 1511.

First-Century Hopes

In the West, Virgil (*Ecl.* 4) sang expectantly of a new beginning when justice would return. This new time was associated with the birth of a boy by whom the golden age would arise. This child was deemed Apollo come down from heaven. In the East, there was a similar longing. Josephus (*J.W.* 6.312) says that there was "an ambiguous oracle, likewise found in their [the Jews'] sacred scriptures that at that time one from their country would become ruler of the world. This they understood to mean someone of their own race, and many of their wise men went astray in their interpretation of it" (Thackeray 1927–28). Tacitus (*Hist.* 5.13) tells a comparable story. He says that the "majority [of Jews] were convinced that the ancient scriptures of their priests alluded to the present as the very time when the Orient would triumph and from Judea would go forth men destined to rule the world" (C. Moore 1925–31). Suetonius (*Vesp.* 4) relates a similar expectation. Both Josephus (*J.W.* 6.313) and Tacitus (*Hist.* 5.13) claim that this prophecy was fulfilled in Vespasian and Titus.

Writing at the end of the first century, the First Evangelist claimed that the Scriptures were fulfilled not in Roman emperors but in Jesus.

out of you will come forth a prince who will shepherd my people Israel (2:6). Herod asks the magi to go and locate the child and to return afterward to tell him where the child may be found so that he too can go and worship him.

The star then leads the magi to the place where the child is. They worship him, giving gifts as appropriate. When they are warned in a dream not to return to Herod, they go home by another route. This pericope uses *where* Jesus was born to establish further his Davidic, messianic roots. It also provides a competitive portrait of two kings (Herod and Jesus). Even though Herod was an Idumean, he liked to call himself king of the Jews (Josephus, *Ant.* 15.373; 16.311). It is as well a picture of two kinds of response to Jesus as king (Herod and the magi; Bauer 1995).

Figure 3. Flight into Egypt. Another Dürer woodcut, this one dating to around 1504. Joseph and Mary are depicted in the garb of German peasants. The head of the young Jesus appears between Mary and the horn of the ox.

2:13–15. This and the following two subunits (2:16–21 and 2:22–23) focus on travels: *where* Jesus went. The first subunit says the family fled to Egypt (the traditional refuge for Palestinian Jews seeking asylum: cf. 1 Kings 11:40; 2 Kings 25:26; Josephus, *Ant.* 12.387; *J.W.* 7.409–10) to escape the wrath of Herod.

2:16–21. The second subunit says that the family returned to the land of Israel after Herod had died.

2:22–23. The third subunit tells us that the family moved to Nazareth in Galilee when they heard that Archelaus reigned over Judea. (Josephus, *Ant.* 17.213–18; *J.W.* 2.1–13 tells how Archelaus ordered a massacre immediately after the death of his father, sufficient reason for Joseph to be cautious about living in the region Archelaus controlled.)

Functions of the Unit as a Whole

The unit 1:1–2:23 as a whole points to the Jesus-Moses parallels, launches an encomium of Jesus, and sets up Jesus as a challenge to the imperial power of Rome. If at one level 1:18–2:23 is arranged to answer the questions of *who* Jesus is, *how* that can be established, *where* he comes from, and *where* he went after his birth, at another level the narrative flow is controlled by a typology of Moses and Jesus (Allison 1993). Consider the similarities between the tradition about Moses and those about Jesus in Matt. 1–2.

Table 1
Parallels between Jesus and Moses

Moses	Jesus
A genealogy locates Moses within the line that runs from the patriarchs (Exod. 1:1–5; 6:14–20).	A genealogy places Jesus within the lineage coming from Abraham (Matt. 1:2–16).
In a dream, an angel prophesied of Moses that he would save the people (*L.A.B.* 9.10: a dream of Miriam; Josephus, *Ant.* 2.210–16: a dream of Moses's father).	In a dream, an angel told Joseph that Jesus would save his people (Matt. 1:21).
At the time of Moses's birth, Pharaoh gave orders to do away with every male Hebrew child (Exod. 1:15–22).	The birth of Jesus was accompanied by Herod's slaughter of the infants (Matt. 2:16–18).
Pharaoh decided to kill the male Hebrew babies because he learned about the birth of the future liberator of Israel (Josephus, *Ant.* 2.205–9).	Herod killed the infants because he learned about the birth of the king of the Jews (Matt. 2:2–18).
Pharaoh learned of the future deliverer from the sacred scribes (Josephus, *Ant.* 2.205, 234).	Herod learned of the coming savior from the chief priests and scribes (Matt. 2:4–6).
When Moses was a young man, he was forced to leave his homeland because Pharaoh wanted to kill him (Exod. 2:15).	As a child, Jesus was providentially taken from the land of his birth because Herod wanted to kill him (Matt. 2:13–14).

Moses	Jesus
After the death of Pharaoh, Moses was commanded by God to return to Egypt (Exod. 4:19).	After the death of Herod, Joseph was commanded by an angel to return to Israel (Matt. 2:19–20).
Moses took his wife and sons and returned to Egypt (Exod. 4:20).	Joseph took his wife and son and returned to Israel (Matt. 2:21).

For anyone who knew the Moses legends in antiquity, it would have been impossible to miss the remarkable similarities between them and Matthew's story of Jesus's origins. If chapters 1–2 have a strong Davidic emphasis, they also have a decided Mosaic focus. Since, however, Moses was regarded as a king in Jewish tradition (e.g., Philo, *Mos.* 1.334; *Mek.* on Exod. 18:14) and since Philo (in *Mos.* 1) presents Moses "as the perfect representation of the ideal of kingly character" (Feldman 2002, 258), this Mosaic typology in no way detracts from the focus on Jesus's royal role. Davidic kingship and Mosaic kingship merge. In fact, in Matt. 1–2 three lines merge: son of Abraham, son of David, and second Moses (cf. *T. Levi* 8.14–15: from Judah a king will arise, a prophet of the Most High, a descendant of Abraham). The future greatness of the child would be difficult to miss.

On yet another level of narrative flow, therefore, one must consider how the narrative functions as an encomium (praise of the hero; Neyrey 1998). Ancient biographies were often structured according to the formal criteria for praise. The *progymnasmata* (schoolbooks instructing students about how to write well) and other books on rhetoric give precise rules for writing an

Celestial Phenomena as Signs

In antiquity, stars, comets, and constellations were believed to signal the birth of a ruler. Cicero (*Div.* 1.47) says that on the night of Alexander the Great's birth, magi prophesied on the basis of a brilliant constellation that the destroyer of Asia had been born. Tacitus (*Ann.* 14.22) asserts that it is the general belief that the appearance of a comet means a change of emperors. So when a comet appeared during Nero's reign, people speculated about Nero's successor as though Nero were already deceased. In *T. Levi* 18.3, it is said about the priestly Messiah: "His star will rise in the heaven as of a king." Eusebius (*Dem. ev.* 9.1) reflects the cultural assumptions. He says that in "the case of remarkable and famous men we know that strange stars have appeared, what some call comets, or meteors, or tails of fire, or similar phenomena that are seen in connection with great or unusual events" (Gifford 1981). In the Jewish scriptures Num. 24:17 says: "A star shall come out of Jacob, and a scepter shall rise out of Israel." To seek the identity of a new king on the basis of a star's appearance, then, would fit common Mediterranean assumptions.

encomium. Relating the beginning of a figure's life, an encomium spoke of his race, country, ancestors, and parents (e.g., Menander Rhetor 2.369.18–3.370.5). Matthew does just that. Jesus is of the seed of Abraham (i.e., a Jew); he was born in Israel in the city of kings, Bethlehem; and his human father was of the line of David. Jesus had a great family heritage. An encomium also spoke of marvelous occurrences at the individual's birth, such as dreams (e.g., Hermogenes, *Progym.* 7.22–24). In Matt. 1–2 are five accounts of dreams that control the plot. Among the marvels were also oracles announcing the hero's birth and early life (Quintilian, *Inst.* 3.7.11). Matthew has a series of fulfillment texts interspersed throughout the birth narrative (Isa. 7:14 at 1:23; Mic. 5:2 at 2:6; Hosea 11:1 at 2:15; Jer. 31:15 at 2:18; and possibly Judg. 13:5–7 at 2:23). Furthermore, celestial phenomena were believed to communicate the approval of the heavens (Cicero, *Top.* 20.76–77). Matthew's story of the star that alerted and guided the wise men from the east would also be an appropriate part of an encomium on Jesus's birth. The First Evangelist follows the conventional rules for an encomium in Mediterranean antiquity, and in so doing he uses the items honored as part of the Jewish context within which the Gospel was written. This, in fact, was what Aristotle (*Rhet.* 1.9.30) advised: "One should speak of whatever is honored among each people."

One final function of Matthew's birth narrative demands attention. By beginning his narrative with 1:23 ("They shall call his name Emmanuel, which means 'God with us'") and ending with 28:18 ("All authority in heaven and upon the earth has been given to me"), the First Evangelist has put the question sharply, To whom does the world belong? (Carter 1998; 2005). Roman imperial propaganda claimed, for example, that Domitian's very being manifested the divine presence (Statius, *Silv.* 5.2.170; cf. Matt. 1:23) and that Jupiter commanded Domitian to rule the world and thereby bless it (Statius, *Silv.* 4.3.128–29, 139–40; cf. Matt. 28:18–20). When the birth narrative says, "You shall call his name Jesus, for he will save his people from their sins" (1:21), the evangelist has raised the question, To whom do we look for salvation? In the Priene inscription of about AD 9, the Decree of the Asian League lauds Augustus as "a Savior who has made war to cease and who shall put everything in peaceful order." The inscription continues by saying that "the birthday of our God [i.e., Augustus] signaled the beginning of Good News for the world because of him" (Danker 1982, 217). Whether or not the evangelist intended it to be such a challenge to imperial theology, auditors in the Mediterranean world at the end of the first century could hardly have heard it otherwise. The claims for the king of the Jews compete with those for the Roman emperor. Who owns the world, who manifests God's presence, and who is the savior? There are competing confessions! Matthew's view is that it is Jesus.

Theological Issues

Miraculous Conceptions and Births

The first theological issue to be considered is related to the miraculous conception of Jesus in Matt. 1:20. Two canonical Gospels, Matthew and Luke, contain infancy narratives. Within these two infancy narratives is a tradition that says Jesus was conceived by the Spirit in a miraculous way. In Matt. 1:20 the angel says to Joseph, "Joseph, son of David, do not be afraid to take Mary as your wife, for the one begotten in her is from the Holy Spirit." In Luke 1:34 Mary asks the angel who has told her that she will bear the Son of the Most High: "How can this be, since I am a virgin?" The angel answers: "The Holy Spirit will come upon you, and the power of the Most High will overshadow you; therefore the child to be born will be holy; he will be called Son of God" (1:35). Witherington (2006, 52) is representative of a number of scholars when he says, "This story of the conception of the Messiah through the agency of the Holy Spirit is without any real precedent in Old Testament, early Jewish, or pagan literature of the period." A clarifying question to be asked is, how would the authorial audience have heard this material in Matthew and Luke? What cultural assumptions did auditors bring to a hearing of these Gospels?

Greco-Roman precedents. Ancient Mediterranean peoples told stories of miraculous conceptions and births that occurred both in heroic time and in the historical past (the following translations are the author's). In the *mythical past* were accounts of individuals born of a divine mother and a human father: for example, Achilles (born of the divine Thetis and the human Peleus [Homer, *Il.* 20.206–7; 24.59]), Aeneas (born of Aphrodite and the mortal Anchises [*Il.* 2.819–22; 5.247–48; also Ovid, *Metam.* 14.588]), and Persephone (born of Demeter and Iasion [Homer, *Od.* 5.116–28]).

In Homer, *Il.* 20.199–209, for example, Aeneas and Achilles meet in battle. As custom dictated, they taunt one another before fighting.

> Aeneas said: "Son of Peleus, do not try to frighten me with words, as if I were a child, since I too know how to taunt. We know each other's parents and lineage for we have heard the ancient stories. . . . They say that you [Achilles] are the son of Peleus and that your mother was Thetis, a daughter of the sea. I am the son of Anchises and my mother is Aphrodite." (trans. Murray 1924–25)

In the mythical past there were also those believed to be the offspring of a god and a human mother: for example, Asclepius (son of Apollo and the mortal Coronis [Diodorus Siculus, *Bib. hist.* 4.71.1]); Hercules (son of Zeus and the human Alcmene [*Il.* 14.315–28; Diodorus Siculus, *Bib. hist.* 4.9.1, 3; Apollodorus, *Epitome* 2.5.8]); Dionysus (son of Zeus and Semele [Homer, *Il.* 14.315–28]); Perseus (son of Zeus and Danae [Homer, *Il.* 14.315–28]); Aristaeus (son of Apollo and Cyrene [Diodorus Siculus, *Bib. hist.* 4.81.1–3]); Romulus (son of Mars and the mortal Ilia, or Rhea, or Silvia [so Cicero, *Rep.* 1.41; 2.2; also Plutarch, *Rom.* 2.3–6]).

Diodorus Siculus (first century BC) relates what the Greeks say about the birth of Dionysus. Cadmus was sent from Phoenicia to search for the maiden Europa. During his travels, in obedience to an oracle, he founded the city of Thebes and settled there. He married Harmonia and had a number of offspring, one of whom was Semele.

> Now with Semele, because of her beauty, Zeus had intercourse, doing it without speaking. . . . Whereupon she asked him to treat her as he did Hera. Zeus, therefore, encountered her as a god with thunder and lightning, making himself manifest as they came together. Semele, who was pregnant, was not able to bear the god's power. So she gave birth prematurely and was herself killed by the fire. (*Bib. hist.* 4.2.1–4, trans. C. Oldfather 1933–67)

Diodorus also tells how the god Apollo was attracted to a maiden named Cyrene, daughter of Hypseus, son of Peneius (*Bib. hist.* 4.81.1). He carried her off to Libya, where he later founded a city named after her. She gave birth to a son, Aristaeus, whom he gave to the nymphs to raise (*Bib. hist.* 4.81.2). Again, the first-century BC historian Dionysius of Halicarnassus tells of a vestal virgin, Ilia or Rhea (*Ant. rom.* 1.76.3–4), who went to a grove consecrated to Mars to fetch pure water for use in the sacrifices and was "ravished by someone in the sacred area . . . whose appearance was much more marvelous than the size and beauty of humans" (*Ant. rom.* 1.77.1–2).

Sometimes ancient authors would give two traditions: one miraculous and the other nonmiraculous. Plutarch, from the end of the first and the beginning of the second century AD, provides this example from Promathion's history of Italy:

> Tarchetius, king of the Albans, . . . encountered a strange phantom at home. A phallus rising up out of the hearth remained for many days. An oracle of Tethys was in Tuscany. From it an interpretation of the phenomenon was brought to Tarchetius. A virgin should mate with the phantom. From her a son would be born who would have great valor, good fortune, and great strength. Tarchetius, therefore, told the prophecy to one of his daughters and instructed her to mate with the phantom. She resisted and sent a handmaid instead. . . . When the handmaid bore twins by the phantom, Tarchetius gave them to Teratius to destroy. He carried them to the riverside. There a she-wolf came to them and nursed them. Birds brought bits of food to them. A cowherd found the twins and took them home with him. In this way they were saved. (*Rom.* 2.3–6, trans. Perrin 1914–26)

41

In *Rom.* 3.1–3, Plutarch says the story that has the greatest credence is the one given by Diocles of Peparethus and Fabius Pictor. It focuses on a vestal virgin, Ilia or Rhea or Silvia, who was found to be pregnant, contrary to the established law for vestals. She was saved from death, however, by the intercession of the king's daughter, Antho. The vestal virgin gave birth to two boys, large and beautiful. Plutarch says it was the boys' mother who claimed that Mars was the father. It was said by others, however, that the girl was deceived into doing this by Amulius, who came to her dressed in armor (*Rom.* 4.2).

In *historical time* it was especially of rulers and philosophers that stories were told about miraculous conceptions and births. Among the philosophers, Pythagoras was said to be the offspring of Apollo and the human Pythais, the most beautiful of the Samians (Porphyry, *Vit. Pyth.* 2); Plato was believed to be the son of Apollo and Amphictione (Diogenes Laertius, *Vit. phil.* 3.1–2, 45); Apollonius of Tyana was thought to be the son of Proteus, a divinity of Egypt, or Zeus (Philostratus, *Vit. Apoll.* 1.4.5–9; 1.6).

Diogenes Laertius, in the third century AD but citing early sources, says of Plato:

> Plato was the son of Ariston and Perictione. . . . Speusippus in the work titled *Plato's Funeral Feast*, Clearchus in the *Encomium on Plato*, and Anaxilaides in the second book *Concerning Philosophers*, tell how at Athens there was a story . . . that Apollo appeared to Ariston in a dream; whereupon he did not touch Perictione until the child's birth. (*Vit. phil.* 3.1–2, trans. R. Hicks 1925)

The early-third-century church father Origen offers a supplement to Laertius's account:

> It is not absurd to employ Greek stories to talk with Greeks, to show we Christians are not the only people who use a miraculous story like this one [i.e., about Jesus's conception]. For some [Greeks] think it proper . . . to relate even of recent events that Plato was the son of Amphictione, while Ariston was prevented from having sexual intercourse with his wife until she gave birth to the one sired by Apollo. (*Cels.* 1.37; cf. *ANF* 4:412)

Writing in the third century AD about the first-century philosopher Apollonius, Philostratus says:

> To his mother, before his birth, came a divinity of Egypt, Proteus. . . . She was not frightened but asked him: "What will I bear?" He said: "Me!" She asked: "Who are you?" He said: "Proteus, the god of Egypt." (*Vit. Apoll.* 1.4.5–9, trans. Conybeare 1912)

Among the rulers spoken of in terms of a miraculous conception and birth, Alexander the Great and Augustus Caesar stand out. At the end of the first or the beginning of the second century AD, Plutarch contains this account:

> Philip, after the vision [in a dream, he saw himself putting a lion-shaped seal on his wife's womb, 2.4], sent Chavion of Megalopolis to Delphi. Chavion then brought Philip a word from the god [Apollo], telling him to sacrifice to Ammon and to reverence this god greatly. He also told Philip that he would lose his sight in the eye with which he had spied on the god, who in the form of a snake had shared the bed of his wife. Also Olympias, as Eratosthenes says, when Alexander was sent upon his expedition, told him alone the secret about his begetting. She challenged him to behave worthily of his origins. Others, however, say she rejected the idea and said: "Alexander must stop slandering me to Hera." (*Alex.* 3.1–4, trans. Perrin 1914–26)

In the second century AD, Aulus Gellius has this to say about Alexander's origins:

> Olympias, wife of Philip, sent a witty response to her son, Alexander, when he wrote to her: "King Alexander, son of Jupiter Hammon, to his mother Olympias, sends greeting." Olympias responded in this manner: "Please, my son, be quiet, neither slandering nor accusing me before Juno. She will be vengeful toward me if you say in your letters that I am her husband's lover." (*Noct. att.* 13.4.1–2, trans. Rolfe 1927)

Gellius comments that in this way Olympias urged Alexander to give up the foolish idea he had formed from his incredible success, namely, that he was the son of Jupiter (*Noct. att.* 13.4.3).

In the early second century AD, Suetonius wrote:

> In the books of Asclepias of Mendes, *Theologumena*, I read: Atia came to the solemn service of Apollo in the middle of the night. Her litter was set down in the temple and she went to sleep. A snake crawled up to her, then went away. Upon awakening she purified herself as she would after sexual relations with her husband. There then appeared on her body a mark colored like a snake. She could not rid herself of it, so she stopped going to public baths. Augustus was born ten months after and therefore was thought to be the son of Apollo. (*Aug.* 94.4, trans. Rolfe 1997–98)

In most of these stories the liaisons between gods and humans involved sexual relations, either with the deity's identity known (as with Zeus and Semele [Diodorus Siculus, *Bib. hist.* 4.2.1–4] or Proteus and the mother of Apollonius of Tyana [Philostratus, *Vit. Apoll.* 1.4.5–9]) or with the deity taking another form (for example, when Zeus could not overcome Alcmene's chastity, he assumed the form of her husband [Diodorus Siculus, *Bib. hist.* 4.9.3], or in a number of cases, the deity took the form of a snake [Plutarch, *Alex.* 3.1–4; Suetonius, *Aug.* 94.4]).

There was, however, another tradition that was averse to thinking of physical sexual contact between deity and humanity. These authors sought some type of begetting that did not involve physical sexual contact. Aeschylus is an early example. In *Suppliants* 17–19, Io is said to be impregnated by Zeus in the form of "the on-breathing of his love." In *Prom.* 848–52, Aeschylus says that at Canobus near the mouth of the Nile, Io will be restored to her senses by Zeus through "the touch of his unterrifying hand." The offspring will be Epaphus (touch-born), named from the touch (*epaphsis*) of the hand of Zeus.

Plutarch gives fullest exposition of this point of view in two of his writings. In "Table Talk" 8, question 1.2 (*Mor.* 9.114–19), the first speaker, Florus, refers to those who attribute Plato's parentage to Apollo and the vision to Ariston, Plato's father, in his sleep, which forbade him to have intercourse with his wife for ten months. The second speaker, Tyndares, replies that it is fitting to celebrate Plato with the line: "He seemed the child not of a mortal man but of a god." When, however, Plato himself speaks of the uncreated and eternal god as father and maker of the cosmos, "it happened not through semen but by another *power of God* [*dynamei tou theou*] that God begot in matter the principle of generation, under whose influence it became receptive and was changed." Thus Tyndares says he does not think it strange *if* "it is not by a physical approach, like a man's, but by some other kind of contact or *touch* that a god alters mortal nature and makes it pregnant with a more-divine offspring." Tyndares continues: "The Egyptians say that Apis [the sacred bull, the earthly incarnation of Osiris] is begotten by the *touch* [*epaphē*] of the moon."

In *Num.* 4.1–4, Plutarch begins by speaking of the story that Numa forsook the life of the city to live in the country because, it was said, he had a marriage with a goddess, Egeria. Such a tale, Plutarch says, is like stories from the Phrygians, Bithynians, and Arcadians. He concludes that it is not impossible to think that deity should be willing to consort with men of superlative goodness, wisdom, and holiness. Yet he says, "It is difficult to believe that a god or phantom would take carnal pleasure in a human body and its beauty" (4.3). Plutarch continues: "Nevertheless the Egyptians make a plausible distinction in such a matter. A woman can be made pregnant by a *spirit* [*pneuma*] of a god, but for a human there is no physical intercourse with a god" (4.4). This trajectory shows that it was possible in Mediterranean antiquity to think of a miraculous conception without conceiving of it in terms of sexual intercourse between a deity and a human. It would be no surprise, then, for ancient auditors to hear that Jesus's conception was via "spirit" or "power" and involved "overshadowing" (touch). (For other examples, see Mussies 1988.)

There were two main reasons the ancients spoke of miraculous conceptions and descent from a deity. The first was an attempt to *explain an individual's superiority* to other mortals. Generally, Mediterranean peoples looked at one's birth or parentage to explain a person's character and behavior. In Plutarch, Remus has been brought before Numitor for punishment. When Numitor sees the youth, he is

> amazed at the youth's surpassing greatness of body and strength, and noting from his face the unsubdued boldness and vitality of his psyche despite the present circumstances, and hearing that his works and acts were like his appearance, . . . he asked who he was and what were the circumstances of his birth. (*Rom.* 7.3–4, trans. Perrin 1914–26)

Birth is believed to explain later deeds and character.

If it was believed to be true in general, then a truly superior person could only be explained by a divine origin. For example, the story of Ilia related above continues by reporting that her ravisher told her not to grieve, since "out of her being ravished, she would give birth to two sons [i.e., Romulus and Remus] whose deeds would excel all others." A divine begetting results in superior deeds! Diodorus Siculus says,

> When Zeus had sexual relations with Alcmene he made the night three times longer than usual and by the length of time given to making the child he foreshadowed the superior nature of the one begotten. (*Bib. hist.* 4.9.2, trans. C. Oldfather 1933–67)

The second-century AD writer Arrian says of Alexander the Great, "And so not even I can suppose that a man quite beyond all other men was born without some divine influence" (*Anab.* 7.30). As in the story of Alexander, great success implies a divine origin. Again, Philostratus explains that Apollonius would excel in wisdom because he had been begotten by the deity Proteus, who also excelled in wisdom (*Vit. Apoll.* 1.4.5–9). Origen says that Greek stories like that of Apollo's begetting Plato

> are really fables. They have been invented about a man they think has greater wisdom and power than others. Their claim, then, is that he received the beginning of his physical existence from a better, diviner sperm, something that is fitting for persons who are greater than ordinary humans. (*Cels.* 1.37; cf. *ANF* 4:412)

Diogenes Laertius quotes an epitaph:

> And how, if Phoebus [Apollo] did not cause Plato to be born in Greece, did he [Plato] heal human minds with letters? For even as the divinely begotten Asclepios is a healer of the body, so Plato is of the immortal soul. (*Vit. phil.* 3.45, trans. R. Hicks 1925)

In other words, Plato could not do what he did if he had not been the offspring of a god. Thus the ancients used stories of miraculous conceptions and births as an explanation of the superiority of the individual.

The second function of such stories of miraculous conceptions in antiquity was the *veneration of a benefactor*. In the first century BC, Cicero quotes Ennius regarding Romulus: "O father, O sire, O one whose blood comes from gods" (*Rep.* 1.41). Cicero says that Romulus

> was born of father Mars (we concede this to the popular tradition, preserved from ancient times, handed down by our ancestors who thought that those who merited good from the community should be regarded as descendents of the gods and endowed with divine qualities). (*Rep.* 2.2, trans. Keyes 1928)

Here the tradition of Romulus's supernatural conception is part of the ancient Roman veneration of benefactors. Diodorus Siculus concludes his story about the begetting of Dionysus by Zeus and Semele by saying that after Semele had been consumed by the fire, Zeus gave the premature child to the nymphs to raise (*Bib. hist.* 4.2.4). As a result, Dionysus discovered wine and taught humans to cultivate the vines. He became one of the gods whose benefaction (the most pleasing drink) is most approved by humans, just as with Demeter (wheat). Similarly, Diodorus Siculus reports that Apollo and Cyrene's son Aristaeus learned from the nymphs

> how to make cheese, how to make beehives, and how to cultivate olives. He was the first to teach humans these things. . . . Those who received the benefits gave Aristaeus honors like those given to gods, as had been done for Dionysus. (*Bib. hist.* 4.81.3, trans. C. Oldfather 1933–67)

Ovid tells of Venus approaching Jupiter with a request on behalf of Aeneas, her son and Jupiter's grandson (*Metam.* 14.581–608). Based on Aeneas's worthiness, Jupiter grants Venus's wish. So Aeneas, the legendary ancestor of the Romans, is honored by the Roman populace with temple and sacrifice. Pliny the Elder says that to enroll rulers among the deities is the most ancient method of showing gratitude for their benefactions (*Nat.* 2.19). It was part of the Roman mentality to venerate benefactors by ascribing divinity to them. This sometimes included stories of their miraculous conception and birth.

Would such a way of thinking have been possible for ancient Jews? Many have denied it. In *2 En.* 23, however, Melchizedek is conceived without human intervention but with no mention of his mother's having had sexual intercourse with a god. This shows that a begetting by God in a way that did not involve a woman's sexual intercourse with a deity was accepted by at least some Jews in antiquity (Nolan 1979, 70; Nickelsburg 2006, 104–8).

Christian meaning. Early Christian auditors of Matthew and Luke would have assumed that the stories of Jesus's divine begetting were needed to explain

How Should Parallels Be Understood?

There are two different ways that non-Christian parallels to Christian writings have been interpreted. One is characteristic of the history-of-religions school. This approach interprets such parallels as borrowing by Christians from non-Christian sources. This leads to the conclusion that Christianity is a syncretistic religion. Like stew in the kitchen, it consists of a bit of this and a bit of that all stirred up together. A recent example of this approach to Matt. 1–2 is Roger Aus (2004). He finds parallels to Matt. 1–2 in ancient Jewish traditions and concludes that the First Evangelist knew and appropriated these sources in order to construct haggadic embellishments on Jesus's birth. The other perspective involves reading with the authorial audience (Rabinowitz 1977; 1987; 1989). The question this approach asks is, what would the ancient auditors of this text have heard when it was read to them? To answer this question, one must have a knowledge of the cultural ethos within which the text circulates. This approach does not assume borrowing by Christians from non-Christians. That issue is held in abeyance. It does assume that Christians would communicate in terms that would be meaningful to auditors.

his marvelous life. If they were Christian auditors, they would have felt that a divine origin for Jesus was appropriate for their chief benefactor and founder. This much the Greco-Roman materials make clear. These auditors, however, were heir not only to the Greco-Roman traditions but also to the Christian traditions before and contemporary with them. Two aspects of this Christian tradition call for attention.

First, the Gospel of Mark, which most think was earlier than Matthew and Luke, did not have a birth narrative. It begins with the baptism practiced by John the Baptist and with Jesus as a full-grown man.

Second, some Christians believed that their relation with God depended on their taking the initiative and performing acceptably so that God would respond approvingly (e.g., Gal. 2:15–16; 3:1–5). The church father Irenaeus (late second century) speaks of Cerinthus, a semignostic Jewish Christian from the late first century, who believed that

> Jesus was not born of a virgin, but was the son of Joseph and Mary according to the usual manner of begetting. *Because* he was more righteous, more prudent, and wiser than other humans, after his baptism the Christ descended upon him in the form of a dove. Then he preached the unknown Father and performed miracles. (*Haer.* 1.26)

The Gospel of Mark, without a miraculous birth narrative, was susceptible of such an interpretation: a meritorious Jesus who is rewarded by God. If Jesus is the model for disciples, then in this line of reasoning Christians too must be

---

Exaltation/Deification in Antiquity

Both pagans and some Jews regarded exaltation (Jews) and deification (pagans) to be based on the prior merit of the one so elevated. Cicero says deification for merit was a Stoic topos (*Nat. d.* 1.15.38–39; 2.24.62). Plutarch says that Isis and Osiris were translated into gods because of their virtues (*Is. Os.* 27), as were Heracles and Dionysus later. Philo says that God appointed Moses as ruler on account of his goodness and his nobility of conduct (*Mos.* 1.148) and that the kingly office was bestowed on Moses by God because of Moses's righteousness (*Mos.* 1.154).

---

meritorious. Ever since Paul, at least, this was not what mainstream Christians believed. Rather, the relation with God was based on God's gracious initiative, to which humans responded in trust and obedience (faith).

When Matthew and Luke added birth narratives with a miraculous conception as part of their editing or rewriting of Mark, they were saying that the type of life seen in Jesus can only be produced by God's prior, gracious, creative act. If it is so for Jesus, then it is likewise true for his followers. The tradition of miraculous conceptions and births is thereby refined in its Christian Jewish context. In this context, the Greco-Roman conviction that a human's superiority can only be explained by a divine creative act is used to establish the prevenience of divine grace in the divine-human relation. Given the Greco-Roman and early Christian contexts, this is what an ancient auditor would have heard (Jesus's superiority and benefactions, all of which were due to prevenient divine grace).

Genre and Revelation

A second, if related, issue concerns the implications of the genre of the Infancy Narrative. If the genre of Matt. 1–2 is basically haggadah (edifying narrative), a theological question follows: is divine revelation possible through genres other than history? A cursory survey of biblical materials leads to an obvious answer. Yes, divine revelation can and does take place through psalms, proverbs, short stories, parables, epistles, apocalypses, prophetic oracles, and other genres as well. Revelation is not limited to the genre "history." One should not, therefore, be put off by designating the genre of Matt. 1–2 as haggadah. This genre designation in no way precludes Matt. 1–2's functioning as a medium through which divine revelation occurs. As an inference from this observation, moreover, one may then say that the occurrence of revelation experienced through a segment of biblical material does not guarantee its historicity since revelation may occur through the medium of multiple genres (cf. Brown 1977, 562).

PART 1

Matthew 3:1–8:1

Jesus's Ministry Begins

After the infancy narrative of 1:1–2:23 comes 3:1–8:1, the first of five large cycles that constitute the bulk of the First Gospel. This cycle falls into two parts: narrative (3:1–4:17) and discourse (4:18–8:1). The two parts are linked by an emphasis on righteousness. For example, Jesus fulfills all righteousness (3:15) before he calls on his disciples to seek first God's righteousness (6:33).

Matthew 3:1–8:1 in Context

Birth narratives (1:1–2:23)

▶ **Jesus's ministry begins (3:1–8:1)**

Narrative: Jesus begins to fulfill all righteousness (3:1–4:17)

Discourse: Jesus calls disciples to seek God's righteousness (4:18–8:1)

Jesus's authority is revealed (8:2–11:1)

Jesus's ministry creates division (11:2–13:53)

Jesus focuses on his disciples (13:54–19:2)

Jesus and judgment (19:3–26:1a)

Passion and resurrection narrative (26:1b–28:20)

49

Matthew 3:1–4:17

Narrative 1:
Jesus Begins to Fulfill All Righteousness

Introductory Matters

What sets Matt. 3:1–4:17 off as a distinct unit? Its principle of organization. This segment of narrative is held together by an inclusio beginning at 3:2 (John says, "Repent for the kingdom of heaven is at hand") and ending at 4:17 (Jesus says, "Repent for the kingdom of heaven is at hand"). The unit is, moreover, arranged in a chiastic pattern, ABCDED′C′B′A′. In outline form it looks like this:

> A John the Baptist preaches, "Repent for the kingdom is at hand" (3:1–2)
>> B John fulfills the Scriptures (3:3; cf. Isa. 40:3)
>>> C John is Elijah (3:4; cf. Matt. 11:14; 17:12–13; cf. also 2 Kings 1:8)
>>>> D Various responses to John's baptism and John's responses to them, first positive (vv. 5–6) and then negative (vv. 7–10) (3:5–10)
>>>>> E John compares himself with the Mightier One. John is the lesser (3:11–12)
>>>> D′ Jesus's response to John's baptism and John's response to him (3:13–17)

C′ Jesus is the son of God, who reverses Israel's failures in the wilderness (i.e., hunger [cf. Exod. 16]; testing God [cf. Exod. 17]; and idolatry [cf. Exod. 32]) (4:1–11)

B′ Jesus fulfills the Scriptures (4:12–16; cf. Isa. 9:1–2)

A′ Jesus preaches, "Repent, for the kingdom is at hand" (4:17)

Matthew 3:1–4:17 in the Narrative Flow

Birth narratives (1:1–2:23)

Jesus's ministry begins (3:1–8:1)

▶ *Narrative*: Jesus begins to fulfill all righteousness (3:1–4:17)

  The preaching of John the Baptist (3:1–12)

    "Repent, the kingdom is at hand" (3:1–2)

    John fulfills the Scriptures (3:3)

    John is Elijah (3:4)

    Responses to John's baptism (3:5–10)

    John is less than the Mightier One (3:11–12)

  Jesus's response to John's baptism (3:13–17)

  Testing in the wilderness (4:1–11)

  To Galilee to preach (4:12–17)

    Jesus fulfills the Scriptures (4:12–16)

    "Repent, the kingdom is at hand" (4:17)

The flow within the pattern focuses first on John separately, then on the Baptist's relation to Jesus, and finally primarily on Jesus. We will read the text in terms of this chiastic pattern, but since some of the John sections of the chiastic structure are quite brief and some of the Jesus sections much longer, not all elements in the chiasm are on the same level in the accompanying outline.

Tracing the Narrative Flow

The Preaching of John the Baptist (3:1–12)

(A) **3:1–2.** Section A focuses on John's *message*: "Repent, for the kingdom of the heavens has drawn near" (3:2). This is also Jesus's message in 4:17. What does it mean? In the near future, God will demonstrate his faithfulness to the promises of Scripture by the final transformation of the present order into a radically new age wherein the righteous will finally be blessed and the wicked judged.

(B) **3:3.** Section B speaks about John's *role*; he fulfills Isa. 40:3: **A voice crying in the wilderness, "Prepare the way of the Lord, make straight his paths."** This quotation does not follow the MT ("A voice crying, 'In the wilderness prepare the way'") but rather the LXX ("A voice crying in the wilderness, 'Prepare the way'"). The LXX fits better with Matt. 3:1: "In those days, John the Baptist appeared, preaching in the wilderness of Judea." The entirety of 3:1–12 is about John's role of preparation for the imminent arrival of the Lord. In Matthew's reading, John's *identity* is that of Elijah who was to come (11:14; 17:12–13; contrast John 1:23, where the Baptist also identifies himself as the voice crying in Isa. 40:3 but denies in 1:21 that he is Elijah).

Figure 4. The Jordan River flows out of the Sea of Galilee in the north and into the Dead Sea in the south. It was in this river, probably near the Dead Sea, that John the Baptist baptized.

(C) **3:4.** Section C says that **John had his clothing from the hairs of a camel and a leather belt around his waist.** This echoes 2 Kings 1:8, where the messengers describe the man who came to meet them. He was "a hairy man, with a leather belt around his waist." Upon hearing this, the king said, "It is Elijah." According to Mal. 4:5–6 and Sir. 48:10, Elijah was to return with the task of changing the hearts of the people before the day of the Lord's arrival. This the Baptist was endeavoring to do.

(D) **3:5–10.** Section D tells of the mixed responses John received. On the one hand, in 3:5–6 the ordinary people went out to him, and **they were being baptized in the Jordan River by him, confessing their sins.** On the other hand, **many of the Pharisees and Sadducees were coming against** (*epi*) **his baptism** (3:7). They came not to observe only but to oppose John's ministry. They felt no need of repentance (cf. 3:9; 21:32; Carter 2000, 96–97). To them John said, **Every tree that does not produce good fruit will be cut down and cast into fire** (3:10b). In John's opinion, they are not true children of Abraham (3:9).

(E) **3:11–12.** The center point of the chiastic pattern, section E, is an evaluative comparison (a *synkrisis*) of John and the Mightier One. **I am baptizing you in water for repentance. Now the one coming after me is mightier than I, of whom I am not worthy to carry his shoes. He will baptize you in holy wind and fire** (3:11). *Ruach* in Hebrew and *pneuma* in Greek can mean either wind/breath or spirit. The context here (3:10) is that of judgment. There are

Jewish texts that use the combination of wind/breath and fire to speak of God's judgment (e.g., Isa. 4:4; 30:27–28; 2 Esd. [*4 Ezra*] 13:8–11). So here the translation should be wind and fire (judgment), not Holy Spirit and fire (cf. Acts 2:2–3). In this comparison, John, as Elijah who prepares the way for the coming of the Lord, is the lesser (cf. Matt. 11:11–14), though a prominent figure in God's salvific plan. After this comparison, the movement of the narrative focuses on Jesus.

Jesus's Response to John's Baptism (3:13–17)

In section D′ we find Jesus's response to John's baptism. Because of the difficulty in reading it aright, it is necessary to examine this pericope in some detail. In form it consists of the following:

The narrative occasion (3:13)

A defense of Jesus's sinlessness (3:14–15)

An anointing of Jesus for his messianic mission and a divine acknowledgment of Jesus's sonship (3:16–17)

The episode is initiated by Jesus. **Then Jesus came from Galilee to the Jordan to John for the purpose of being baptized by him** (3:13). This is the occasion. It is the way a son of Abraham behaves (1:1–2; 3:9). The first main component of the pericope comes in 3:14–15. In these verses there is material not found in Mark 1:9–11. **But John resisted him, saying, "I have a need to be baptized by you, and are you coming to me?" But Jesus, answering, said to him, "Let it be so now. For in this way it is fitting for *us* to fulfill all righteousness." Then he acquiesced** (3:14–15). It is clear from 3:14 that Jesus is not to be baptized because he is a sinner. Given the context, the Baptist must be assuming that Jesus is the Mightier One who will baptize in holy wind and fire (3:11). Again an evaluative comparison is evident. The sinlessness of Jesus was apparently an issue at the time of and in the geographical area of the First Gospel. A fragment of the *Gospel according to the Hebrews*, written near the time and in the region of Matthew, is preserved by Jerome and gives this tradition:

> Behold, the mother of the Lord and his brethren said unto him: John Baptist baptizeth unto the remission of sins; let us go and be baptized of him. But he said unto them: Wherein (what) have I sinned, that I should go and be baptized of him? Unless peradventure this very thing that I have said is a sin of ignorance. (*Pelag.* 3.2; in James 1924, 6)

Both the *Gospel of the Hebrews* and Matthew reflect a similar concern to show that Jesus's baptism by the Baptist was not an acknowledgment of Jesus's sinfulness.

If the purpose of Jesus's baptism was not "for repentance" (3:11), then why was Jesus baptized by John? Jesus says, "**It is fitting in this way for *us* to fulfill all righteousness**" (3:15). To whom does **us** refer? Unless it is a royal "we," the fulfillment is not by Jesus only. The most likely other candidate is John. For John to baptize Jesus allows both to fulfill all righteousness. In Matthew's plot, since neither is a real candidate for personal repentance, it must be that such an act in their *roles* would fulfill righteousness (facilitate God's saving activity; cf. 21:32; Meier 1980, 391–92; Hagner 1993, 1:56). Jesus's baptism does not fall under the particular emphases of "the higher righteousness" in Matt. 5–7. It is rather part of the process by which the kingdom is to be inaugurated. As such, it is not something that can be repeated. It is not an example of kingdom conduct except insofar as it, like the particular emphases of Matt. 5–7, reflects faithfulness to the covenant relationship (i.e., righteousness; cf. Riches 2000, 191). Who is Jesus, ac-

> ### Sons of God/gods and of a Human Father
>
> In 1 Chron. 22:9–10 Solomon is called both David's son and God's son. Homer (*Il.* 10.144) says Odysseus was sired by Zeus but was heir to the throne of Ithaca because of his father, Laertes. Plutarch (*Alex.* 2.1–3.2) summarizes the genealogy of Alexander that runs through his father, Philip, and then relates the story of Alexander's divine descent. Suetonius (*Aug.* 3.1; 94.4) tells of Augustus's earthly father and then later relates a story of Augustus's divine descent. So the narrative in Matt. 1 portrays Jesus as son of Joseph (David) and as son of God. Such stories of dual paternity occur internationally and tend to have common characteristics.

cording to the narrative so far? He is the messiah (1:17), both the king of the Jews (2:1–12) and a son of David (1:1–16), on the one hand, and God's son begotten by the Spirit (1:20, 25; 2:15), on the other.

Who is John, according to the Matthean narrative so far? He is Elijah (3:4), who is looking for the coming one (3:11) and whose role is preparation for the Lord's coming (3:3). How do these two portraits function as a context for reading Matt. 3:15? The one who is son of David and son of God presents himself to the one who is Elijah in order that together they may prepare for the divine arrival. In this way both function in their roles in a way that is faithful to their covenant relationship with God (fulfillment of righteousness). One should not think, however, that this act that fulfills all righteousness is meant to be exhaustive. It is rather a beginning. Matthew 21:32 indicates that righteousness is not a moment but a way. Hence the aorist verb should properly be translated "begin to fulfill all righteousness" (an ingressive aorist). The involvement of John and Jesus in the latter's baptism "is action which is part of the process whereby the kingdom of heaven is to be inaugurated." It is not an example of kingdom conduct (the higher righteousness) expected of disciples generally and so something to be imitated.

Some Other Versions of Jesus's Baptism

Jerome says that in the Gospel written in Hebrew, read by the Nazarenes, he found this version:

> "And it came to pass when the Lord was come up out of the water, the whole fount of the Holy Spirit descended and rested upon him, and said unto him: My son, in all the prophets was I waiting for thee that thou shouldest come, and I might rest in thee. For thou art my rest, thou art my first begotten son, that reignest forever." (Comm. Isa. 11.2, trans. James 1924, 5)

Epiphanius quotes what the *Gospel of the Ebionites* says about Jesus's baptism.

> "After the people were baptized, Jesus also came and was baptized by John; and as he came up from the water, the heavens were opened, and he saw the Holy Ghost in the likeness of a dove that descended and entered into him: and a voice from heaven saying: Thou art my beloved Son, in thee I am well pleased: and again: This day have I begotten thee. And straightway there shone about the place a great light. Which when John saw he saith unto him: Who art thou, Lord? And again there was a voice from heaven saying unto him: This is my beloved Son in whom I am well pleased. And then John knelt down before him and said: I beseech thee, Lord, baptize thou me. But he prevented him saying: Suffer it: for thus it behoveth that all things should be fulfilled." (Pan. 30, trans. James 1924, 9)

Ignatius says, "Our God, Jesus the Christ, was conceived by Mary by the dispensation of God, 'as well as the seed of David' as of the Holy Spirit: he was born, and was baptized, that by himself submitting he might purify the water" (Ign. *Eph.* 18.2, trans. Lake 1975, 1:190–93).

Justin Martyr says about Jesus's baptism:

> "When Jesus had gone to the river Jordan, where John was baptizing, and when He had stepped into the water, a fire was kindled in the Jordan; and when He came out of the water, the Holy Ghost lighted on Him like a dove.... Now we know that he did not go to the river because He stood in need of baptism ... [but] because of the human race, which from Adam had fallen under the power of death and the guile of the serpent." (Dial. 88, ANF 1:243)

Rather, it is a onetime event that is a necessary condition of the fulfillment of God's purposes (Riches 2000, 191).

Having been baptized, Jesus immediately went up out of the water (3:16a). This introduces the second main component of the episode, Jesus's anointing and God's acknowledgment of his son. This component consists of two parts, each introduced by **and behold** (3:16; 3:17). The first is a vision seen by Jesus

Discerning God's Will through the Flight of Birds

The philosopher Pythagoras tells his disciples about bird omens, symbols, and signs. Birds, he says, are messengers from the gods sent to those whom the gods truly love (Iamblichus, *Vit. Pyth.* 61). Plutarch says that before Numa would accept the kingship, he insisted that it be ratified by heaven (*Num.* 7). This was done by a flight of birds (probably doves). Then he put on the royal robes and was acclaimed "most beloved of the gods." In this case, the birds signaled divine selection. According to the *Protevangelium of James*, "Joseph received the last rod, and behold, a dove came out of the rod and flew on to Joseph's head. And the priest said to Joseph, 'Joseph, to you has fallen the good fortune to receive the virgin of the Lord'" (*Prot. Jas.* 9.1, trans. Schneemelcher 1991–92, 1:429–30). Here the dove signals divine selection. These examples are representative.

alone (3:16b). **And behold, the heavens were opened and he** (Jesus) **saw the Spirit of God descending as a dove, coming upon him.**

In Matthew's plot, the Spirit descends upon the son of David as it did upon David himself when he was anointed king by Samuel (1 Sam. 16:13). That is, God has anointed and empowered Jesus as messianic king. Although Matthew's narrative does not say so, this would have been regarded as fulfilling conventional expectations about the close connection between the messiah and the Spirit (Isa. 11:2; *Pss. Sol.* 17.37; 4Q161 3.11–25; *1 En.* 49.3; 62.2). Also part of conventional expectation would have been the recognition that there would be an interval between Jesus's anointing as messiah and the beginning of his reign (Matt. 28:18–20), as was the case with David (anointed in 1 Sam. 16; beginning to reign over Judah in 2 Sam. 2:4, 7 and over Israel in 2 Sam. 5:3–4).

The second part (3:17) is heard by Jesus and John. **And behold, a voice out of the heavens, saying, "This is my son, the beloved, in whom I take delight."** Whereas in Mark 1:11 and Luke 3:22 the voice from heaven says, "You are my son," in Matt. 3:17 it says, "This is my son." Matthew's version makes it a public address rather than a personal communication to Jesus alone. The most natural way to take "this" is as an announcement at least to Jesus and John. (In John 1:33–34 the Baptist comes to recognize Jesus as God's Son in connection with the Spirit's descent on Jesus.) The content of the voice seems best taken as a conflation of Ps. 2:7, a coronation psalm ("you are my son"), and Isa. 42:1 in the form found in Matt. 12:18 ("my beloved, in whom I take delight"). Just as Joseph had acknowledged Jesus as his son by naming him (1:25) and thereby making the Davidic genealogy Jesus's own, so now God acknowledges Jesus, who was conceived by the Holy Spirit (1:20–23), as his son and servant/child (cf. Neh. 13:26, where Solomon was beloved by God and God made him king over Israel).

The second component (3:16–17) of the baptism pericope should be seen as a visionary experience of Jesus and an auditory experience for Jesus and John. Similarities with the transfiguration narrative, which is a story about a vision and audition for three disciples (17:9), make this apparent (Davies and Allison 1988, 1:320), as shown in table 2.

Table 2
Parallels between Jesus's Baptism and Transfiguration

Baptism	Parallel	Transfiguration
3:13–16a	Setting	17:1–2
3:16b	And behold	17:3a
3:16c	Vision	17:3b
3:17a	And behold	17:5b
3:17	Heavenly voice	17:5c

In the baptism the Matthean Jesus receives his anointing-empowerment as messianic king, and John can testify with Jesus that God himself has recognized Jesus as his own son (cf. the need of two witnesses as in Deut. 19:15).

Why would the First Evangelist associate this anointing and declaration with the Baptist? In Justin Martyr's *Dial.* 8.4, the Jew Trypho says that the messiah is unknown and has no power until Elijah comes to anoint him and make him manifest to all. In 49.1, Trypho says that when Elijah comes, he will anoint the messiah. Because of the absence of early rabbinic evidence of such a belief, many scholars tend to doubt whether the material in Justin is really a Jewish opinion of this early period (Faierstein 1981). Others, however, who see the early Christian movement as a species of the genus Middle Judaism, think that the NT offers valuable data about Judaism that is unavailable from anywhere else for the period before the Mishnah (ca. AD 200; Segal 1990, xv). Matthew's story of Jesus's baptism demands such a conventional belief for a reader to make sense of the plot. We may, therefore, read the Matthean story as a statement that John has faithfully carried out his role of preparation as Elijah (fulfilling all righteousness) by being associated with the messiah's anointing and empowering and by participating in the messiah's public manifestation. In all of Matt. 3:1–17, therefore, the focus is on John's role of

---

Divine Testimony

Cicero says that when the gods give their testimony on a matter, it comes in one or both of two ways: utterances of the gods and works of the gods (*Top.* 20.76–77). Among the works of the gods he mentions the flight of birds in the air. In the visionary experience of Jesus and John, there are both a divine work (the descent of the Holy Spirit as a dove) and a divine utterance ("This is my Son"). An ancient auditor would have heard the two together as God's testimony legitimating Jesus in his role.

Auspicious Beginnings

It was a cultural convention that a king often underwent an initial divine launching of his career. For example, in Plutarch's *Parallel Lives* are two biographies with material that functions similarly to that of Matthew's story of Jesus's baptism. In *Lyc.* 5, Plutarch says Lycurgus's mission to institute good laws and a constitution was preceded by the Delphic Oracle's (Apollo's) address to him as "beloved of the gods and rather god than man" (*Lyc.* 5.3). Thus encouraged, Lycurgus set out on his mission (*Lyc.* 5.4). In *Num.* 7, Plutarch says that before Numa would accept the kingship, he insisted that it be ratified by heaven. This was done by the flight of auspicious birds (in this case, doves). Only then did he put on the royal robes and was acclaimed the "most beloved of the gods." It was said of Numa that he was inclined to the practice of every virtue (*pasan aretēn; Num.* 3.5).

---

preparation for the Lord's coming. When Jesus, moreover, comes to "Elijah," who was supposed to anoint the messiah and make him known, he comes as a "son of David" to make possible his anointing, empowering, and legitimation as son by his Father in heaven, if that is what heaven desires. In so doing, Jesus is acting righteously (i.e., faithful to his relation to God and to God's salvific plan). This vision and audition enable Jesus to begin to fulfill all righteousness in his ministry that follows. To summarize: The Matthean pericope about the baptism of Jesus functions in a twofold way in the First Gospel. It serves both to defend Jesus's sinlessness and to describe his anointing, empowering, and legitimation as God's son.

In Matthew's plot, this episode marks a shift from one stage to another in God's salvific plan. John's role as Elijah is to prepare the way for the coming one (11:10–11); Jesus's role as the messianic king, God's son, is to manifest the gracious coming of God through his earthly ministry (e.g., 12:28) and only later to come as messianic judge (25:31–46) who would baptize with holy wind and fire (3:11). That is why when John said that Jesus should be baptizing him, Jesus said "Allow it *now*" (3:15). This was now; the baptism of wind and fire would be later.

Testing in the Wilderness (4:1–11)

After Jesus's anointing, empowering, and legitimation as God's son, section C′ tells the story of Jesus's testing (*peirasthēnai*) in the wilderness (a place believed to be inhabited by evil spirits; cf., e.g., 4 Macc. 18:8; *1 En.* 10.4–5). Why would this story follow Jesus's baptism? Sirach 2:1 states the principle plainly: "My child, when you come to serve the Lord, prepare yourself for testing [*peirasmon*]." This principle was illustrated in the lives of both Abraham and Job. *Jubilees* 17.15–18.19 depicts the tradition of Abraham's willingness to sacrifice Isaac as a test from Prince Mastema to determine whether or not Abraham was really faithful to God. Job 1–2 likewise presents Job's trials as a test from Satan of his faith in God. As a son of Abraham, Jesus also undergoes testing by the devil. A closer, specific parallel would be Israel's emergence from the water of the sea and its wanderings in the wilderness. Deuteronomy interprets the events: "Remember the long way that the LORD your God has led you these forty years in the wilderness . . . testing [*ekpeirasē*] you to know what was in your heart. . . . Know then in your heart that as a parent disciplines a child so the LORD your God disciplines [*paideusei*] you" (Deut. 8:2, 5 LXX). Generally, testing follows commitment. Specifically, the testing in the wilderness followed the passing through the waters (cf. 1 Cor. 10:1–18 for a similar use of the Israelite experiences of water and wilderness). This is likely the reason why 4:1–11 directly follows 3:13–17.

What is the form of Matthew's story of Jesus's testing in the wilderness? Mark 1:12–13 has a very brief narrative that is unlike Matthew's. Luke 4:1–13 has a longer story, one that involves the same three temptations found in Matthew, but in a different order. Luke's order is: change stones to bread, worship the devil, and throw yourself from the temple's pinnacle. In Matthew the order runs: change stones to bread, throw yourself from the pinnacle of the temple, worship the devil. Whereas Luke's order likely reflects the temptation in the garden (Gen. 3:6: the tree was good for food, a delight to the eyes, and desired to make one wise), Matthew's sequence reflects that of Israel's experiences in the wilderness as narrated by Exodus (Exod. 16: doubting God because of hunger; Exod. 17: testing God; Exod. 32: idolatry or forsaking God). In Matthew there is also a movement from lower (desert) to higher (pinnacle of the temple) to highest (a high mountain). Moreover, the long narrative of Jesus's testing in the wilderness consists of three temptations that involve the use of Scripture in the struggle. In *b. Sanh.* 89b a story of a similar threefold contest between Abraham and the devil involves quotation of Scripture by both sides as a part of the testing of Abraham. The longer temptation narrative, then, appears to reflect a haggadic (story) rabbinic form of the son of Abraham being tested by the devil.

What is the focus of the testing in Matt. 4:1–11? The issue is not whether Jesus is son of God. The devil's questions in verses 3 and 6 that begin "If you are the son of God" would better be translated "Since you are the son of God." If so, then the issue is what it means for Jesus to be the son of God (Boring 1995, 163). The question is, what would the Son's faithfulness (fulfillment of righteousness) look like?

The episode opens with a reference to the Spirit (4:1). **Then Jesus was led into the wilderness by the Spirit to be tempted by the devil.** It is the Spirit that leads Jesus into the contest. Remember Deut. 8:2: "The LORD your God has led you these forty years in the wilderness, . . . testing you to know what was in your heart." There follow three tests presented by Satan (cf. Job 1–2,

---

Matthew 4 and the Shema

Birger Gerhardsson (1966) contends that Matt. 4:1–11 is a haggadic midrash (a commentary on Scripture given in story form) on the Shema (i.e., Deut. 6:4–5). This form of interpretation may be contrasted with a different type of midrash. In *m. Ber.* 9.5 is a non-narrative interpretation of the Shema. It begins, *And thou shalt love the Lord thy God with all thy heart and with all thy soul and with all thy might.* The interpretation follows: *with all thy heart*—with both thy divine impulses, thy good impulse and thine evil impulse; *and with all thy soul*—even if he take away thy soul; *and with all thy might*—with all thy wealth" (trans. Danby 1933, 10). In Matt. 4:1–11, the aim is to show the Son's love of the Father (obedience to the Shema) by depicting his victorious dealing with the same type of temptations that Israel experienced in the wilderness. What does it mean to keep the Shema? It means to act as Jesus did in his three tests in the wilderness when he reversed Israel's disobedience. It is interpretation by means of a story.

---

where Satan is God's instrument to test Job's faithfulness). The first comes in 4:2–4. After forty days of fasting, Jesus is hungry. **And coming to him, the tempter said to him, "Since you are the son of God, tell these stones to become bread"** (4:3). The question is posed: Is sonship a privilege to be exploited? Jesus responds, **It is written, "Not by bread alone will a person live, but by every word proceeding from the mouth of God"** (4:4; Deut. 8:3). Out of this experience the Matthean Jesus is able to speak about such matters in 6:33.

The second test comes in 4:5–7. **Then the devil takes him to the holy city and places him on the pinnacle of the temple** (4:5). (Josephus, *Ant.* 15.411–12, says that from the *stoa basilikē* one could barely see the bottom of the valley below. To look down made one giddy. The pinnacle was south of the outer court.) The devil says to Jesus, **Since you are the son of God, throw yourself down. For it is written, "To his angels God will issue a command about you, and upon their hands they will carry you lest you stub your foot against a stone"** (4:6; Ps. 91:11–12 [90:11–12 LXX]). Here the devil quotes Scripture that speaks of God's promises of protection for the godly. There was certainly divine protection of Jesus in Matt. 2, involving angels (2:13, 19). The Matthean Jesus apparently believes angelic help is something he can request (Matt. 26:53–54). The question then is posed: Is God a servant to do a human's bidding, especially if it is God's son who does the bidding? This test Jesus will face again (16:1; 27:40). Jesus answers, **Again it is written, "You shall not put the Lord your God to a test"** (4:7; Deut. 6:16). Trust in God cannot be turned into presumption.

The third test comes in 4:8–10. **Again the devil takes him into an exceedingly high mountain and shows to him all the kingdoms of the world and their glory. And he said to him, "All these things I will give to you if you fall down**

Prostration, Worship, and Receipt of Kingship

Augustus, Tiberius, and Claudius avoided having others prostrate before them because of its pretentious connotations. Gaius Caligula and Nero were of a different mind. Caligula introduced prostration into his court and associated it with his deification (Philo, *Legat.* 116–17, 352–53; Seneca the Younger, *Ben.* 2.12.1–2; Suetonius, *Vit.* 2). When Tiridates of Armenia came to receive his kingship from Nero, he prostrated himself before the emperor and addressed Nero as a god (Dio Cassius, *Rom. Hist.* 63.5.3). The Matthean Jesus will not fall down before a false god in order to receive kingship from the devil. His kingship has other origins.

and worship me" (4:8–9). The question is posed: Will you become an idolater to get all this? Jesus answers, **Go away, Satan, for it is written, "The Lord your God you shall worship and to him only shall you give service"** (4:10; Deut. 6:13). Jesus's authority over things in heaven and earth will come from God but only after his enthronement (28:18). In all three tests the issue concerns power and how it will be used. The episode comes to a conclusion with 4:11. **Then the devil left him** (*T. Naph.* 8.4), **and behold angels came and served him** (as they did for Elijah after his contest with the prophets of Baal in 1 Kings 19:5–8; cf. also *T. Naph.* 8.4).

To Galilee to Preach (4:12–17)

(B′) **4:12–16.** In section B′ is a highly compressed narrative about Jesus's movements, followed by an indication that they are a fulfillment of Scripture. The narrative comes in 4:12–13. **Now when he heard that John was arrested, he withdrew into Galilee. And leaving Nazareth, when he came to Capernaum by the sea in the regions of Zebulun and Naphtali, he settled there.** As in chapter 2, when faced with danger, Jesus withdraws (cf. 12:15; 14:13; 15:21). Verses 14–16 focus on fulfillment of Scripture (Isa. 9:1–2). **In order that the word through Isaiah the prophet might be fulfilled, saying, "Land of Zebulun and land of Naphtali, way of the sea, beyond the Jordan, Galilee of the gentiles: the people who sit in darkness have seen a great light, and those sitting in the region and shadow of death, light has dawned upon them."** The quotation gives scriptural justification for the geographical location of Jesus's ministry. For Matthew, geography matters (cf. 2:1, 5–6). In this instance, he may well have been defending against charges that the messiah was not expected to come from Galilee (cf. John 1:46; 7:41–42). Since Galilee was often associated with the "nations" (cf. 2 Kings 15:29; 17:24–27; 1 Macc. 5; Strabo, *Geogr.* 16.2.34), the quotation may be offering scriptural warrant to foreshadow the inclusion of the gentiles associated with the son of Abraham (Tisera 1993, 79–100).

(A′) **4:17.** Section A′ concludes this unit of the Gospel. **From then Jesus began to preach and to say, "Repent, for the kingdom of the heavens has drawn near."** At this stage, Jesus's preaching echoes that of the Baptist (3:2).

The Recurring Temptations of Jesus in Matthew

The First Gospel depicts temptations not only as opening Jesus's career but also as a phe-nomenon throughout his ministry. In the heart of his mission, Jesus faces the temptation "Show us a sign" (Matt. 12:38–39; 16:1). In 16:21–23 Satan again confronts him, this time through Peter. At the end of his ministry, he faces temptation in Gethsemane (26:39–44) and again when he is being arrested (26:51–54, 56). As he hangs on the cross, his enemies taunt him with "If you are the son of God, come down from the cross" (27:39–44). The temptations come from Satan, but in most instances they have a human face: religious leaders, disciples, those crucified with him (cf. Gibson 1995).

In Matthew, "kingdom of heaven" and "kingdom of God" are synonyms (cf. Matt. 19:23–24). The terms are used in this Gospel with two connotations and two tenses.

1. A passive connotation and a future tense:
   a future hope, the new age beyond the resurrection (8:11; 26:29)
   whose coming is near at hand (3:2; 4:17; 10:7)
   for which Jesus's disciples are to pray (6:10)
   into which only some will enter (5:20; 7:21; 18:3; 19:23–24; 21:31)
   within which there are degrees of status (5:19; 11:11; 18:1, 4)
2. An active connotation and present tense:
   the present kingly activity of God in Jesus (12:28; cf. 13:16–17)

So in Matthew, kingdom of heaven/God stands both for the ultimate blessing and for the activity of God that causes that blessing to come (Talbert 2004b, 50–51). The evangelist seems to believe that the kingdom (the kingly rule of God) enters the stage of history one step at a time (as in *Jub.* 23; *1 En.* 93 + 91.12–17; Davies and Allison 1988, 1:390; Eloff 2008). So the Baptist's activity of preparation represents one stage (cf. 3:15; 11:11–15), Jesus's ministry of preaching and healing another (12:28), Jesus's exaltation another (28:18), and the son of man's coming as judge yet another (25:31–46). This is a pro-tracted process.

Functions of the Unit as a Whole

When one surveys Matt. 3:1–4:17 as a whole, what functions does it have in the unfolding narrative? It seems on the one hand to continue the encomiastic function already found in Matt. 1–2. Several features in chapters 3–4 are the same as in chapters 1–2. For example, there are oracles, both written (4:15–16) and audible (3:17), that speak about Jesus, as well as visions (3:16) that provide the testimony of God (cf. Cicero, *Top.* 20.76–77). As a part of Jesus's vision in 3:16, there is the perceived flight of a bird, a dove, signifying in Mediterranean culture that a person was beloved of God (Goodenough 1953–68, 8:40–41). There is also a *synkrisis* (an evaluative comparison) between the Baptist and Jesus (3:11, 14), in which John says first that he is not worthy even to carry the Mightier One's shoes and second that he should be baptized by Jesus. Hermogenes says that the best source of argument in encomia (praise) is from comparisons (*Progym.* 17). In Aelius Theon's treatment of encomia, another topic to be covered is important ethical virtues like being just and courageous (*Progym.* 110). In Jesus's dialogue with John before his baptism, he states the need to fulfill all righteousness (be just; 3:15). In Jesus's contest with the devil (4:1–11), he shows himself to be courageous in a test of strength, as well as wise (the latter trait prized by Hermogenes, *Progym.* 16). The overall ethos of the narrative is that of the praise of Jesus.

On the other hand, Matt. 3:1–4:17 also continues the defense of Jesus against real or potential charges that was noted in Matt. 1–2. The baptism narrative clearly defends Jesus's sinlessness (3:14–15). In 4:15–16, moreover, the fulfillment text from Isa. 9:1–2 justifies Jesus's Galilean base of operation against charges that the messiah does not come from Galilee (cf. John 7:41).

Theological Issues

Practicing What One Preaches

What is the religious reason for the depiction of Jesus fulfilling all righteousness (Matt. 3:14–15) before he speaks at length about righteousness in the lives of his disciples (e.g., 5:20; 6:1, 33) in the Sermon on the Mount? The background lies in the Mediterranean ideal of a unity of life and teaching. In Greco-Roman paganism, a number of examples may be cited. The conviction is rooted in Aristotle's *Rhetoric.* He says, "Persuasion is achieved by the speaker's personal character. . . . We believe good men more fully and readily than others. . . . It is not true, as some writers assume in their treatises on rhetoric, that the personal goodness revealed by the speaker contributes nothing to his power of persuasion. On the contrary, his character may almost be called the most effective means of persuasion that he possesses" (*Rhet.* 1.2, trans. Freese 1975). Musonius Rufus says that pupils benefit not so much by meeting with their teacher in the city and listening to formal lectures and discussions as by seeing him at work in the fields, demonstrating by his own labor the lessons that philosophy inculcates (*What Means of Livelihood Is Appropriate for a Philosopher?* 11). In fragment 32, he says, "Do not expect to enjoin right-doing upon men who are conscious of your own wrong-doing" (trans. Lutz 1947). Seneca the Younger says that one's teacher should be someone who will teach by his life, who will tell us what we ought to do and then prove it by practice, who shows us what we should avoid, and then is never caught doing what he has ordered us to avoid (*Ep.* 52.8). Dio Chrysostom says that the word alone, when unaccompanied by the act, is both "invalid and untrustworthy," but that the act alone is "both trustworthy and true, even if no word precedes it" (*Or.* 70.6, trans. H. Crosby 1951). Porphyry contends, "It is a man's actions that naturally afford demonstrations of his opinions, and whoever holds a belief must live in accordance with it, in order that he may be a faithful witness to the hearers of his words" (*Marc.* 8, trans. Zimmern 1986).

Ancient Judaism provides examples of the same belief. Philo reflects the same mind-set: "I know, indeed, that he who is to obtain excellence as a legislator should possess all the virtues fully and completely" (*Mos.* 2.2, trans. Colson 1929–62). In his *That Every Good Person Is Free*, Philo tells of the Indian philosopher Calanus, who was threatened by Alexander the Great. The philosopher responded, "There is no king, no ruler, who will compel us to do what we do not freely wish to do. We are not like those philosophers of the Greeks who practice words for a festal assembly. With us deeds accord with words and words with deeds" (*Prob.* 14.92–96, trans. Colson 1929–62).

Early Christian writings outside the NT echo the same sentiment. The *Didache* says, "Not everyone who speaks in the Spirit is a prophet, but only if he has the ways of the Lord. So the false prophet and the prophet will be known by their ways" (*Did.* 11.8, trans. Lake 1975, 1:327). In *Did.* 11.10 we read, "Every prophet who teaches the truth, if he does not do what he teaches, is a false prophet" (ibid.). Ignatius of Antioch says, "Teaching is good, if the teacher does what he says" (Ign. *Eph.* 15.1, trans. Lake 1975, 1:189).

The cultural repertoire of the ancient Mediterranean world included the conviction that a teacher's words were only to be believed if and when he lived them out in his daily existence. When Matthew's auditors heard that Jesus has begun to fulfill all righteousness before he speaks to his disciples about seeking a righteousness that surpasses other models, they would have inferred the legitimacy of Jesus's teachings and would have accorded him the authority due a true teacher. Why? Because Jesus practices what he teaches. This is true even if Jesus's fulfillment of all righteousness has to do with his role in God's salvific plan, a different arena from that of his disciples.

Ways to Speak about Jesus

Is Matthew's Christology a son-of-God Christology (Kingsbury 1989), a son-of-David Christology (Strecker 1962, 118–20), a wisdom Christology (Deutsch 1996), a prophetic Christology (Stanley 1956), a Mosaic Christology (Bacon 1930), a *kyrios* Christology (Trilling 1959, 21–51), a servant Christology (Hill 1980), or a son-of-man Christology (Blair 1960, 83)? Since L. E. Keck's critique (1986), title-based Christologies have become suspect. Focus is now on the final form of the text, treated as a unified narrative, which is to be understood in a sequential fashion. The narrative controls the meaning of the so-called titles. How is Matthew's use of the various titles to be evaluated? The answer must pay attention to two tendencies: first, the tendency to use many names for one figure, and second, that of employing one designation for multiple figures.

1. In Mediterranean antiquity there is a tendency to use many names for one figure. In Matt. 1:1–4:17 are numerous ways of designating who Jesus is. The most obvious is through titles: for example, son of David, the Christ, son of God, king of the Jews/Israel. These titles are used for Jesus throughout the First Gospel:

son of David	1:1; 9:27; 12:23; 15:22; 20:30–31; 21:9, 15
the Christ	1:17; 2:4–6; 11:2; 16:16
king of the Jews/Israel	2:2; 21:5; 27:11, 29, 37, 42
son of God/my son/the son	2:15; 3:17; 4:3, 6; 8:29; 11:27; 14:33; 24:36; 26:63; 27:43

Matthew uses these titles as synonyms: son of David = the Christ (22:42); the Christ = son of God (16:16; 26:63); the Christ = king of the Jews (2:2, 4–6); son of David = your king (21:5, 9). Hence, when reading the Matthean narrative, one must assume that these titles all refer to one figure, Jesus. The First Gospel assumes that all of the hopes associated with this array of titles are fulfilled in one man, Jesus.

Beyond the use of titles for Jesus, one also encounters a Mosaic typology (chaps. 1–2), allusions to Jesus as servant (3:17: "my beloved, in whom I am well pleased"), and Abrahamic foreshadowings of gentile inclusion (1:1; 2:1, 11; 4:15–16). All of these will, moreover, be met later in the Gospel as well. The Mosaic typology continues throughout the Gospel (Allison 1993). Jesus as servant crops up again (12:17–21). The motif of Jesus as a messiah for the gentiles is shot through the narrative in a variety of foreshadowings and explicit statements (8:5–13, 28–34; 12:17–21; 15:21–28; 24:14; 25:31–46; 28:19–20). These hopes of Israel, Matthew contends, are found fulfilled in this one man, Jesus.

To laud one figure with many names was a common practice in non-Jewish Mediterranean antiquity. For example, Cleanthes' *Hymn to Zeus* begins, "Thou, O Zeus, art praised above all gods: many are thy names and thine is all power for ever" (Barrett 1987, 67). A third-century BC inscription by Artemidorus of Perga, who settled on the island of Thera, speaks of "this Hecate, of many names." Tacitus says the god Serapis was identified by some as Asclepius, by others as Osiris, by still others as Jupiter, but by most as Pluto (*Hist.* 4.84). According to Diogenes Laertius, Stoics hold that "God is one and the same with Reason, Fate, and Zeus; he is also called by many other names" (*Vit. phil.* 7.135, trans. R. Hicks 1925). This practice was rooted in the Jewish scriptures (e.g., Isa. 9:6 uses multiple names for the expected ideal Davidic ruler). It was also embraced by Jews like Philo. In *On the Confusion of Tongues*, for example, he speaks about "God's firstborn, the Word, who holds the eldership among the angels, their Archangel as it were. And many other names are his, for he is called 'the Beginning,' and the Name of God, and His Word, and the Man after His Image, and 'He that sees,' that is Israel" (*Conf.* 146–47, trans. Colson 1929–62). In 4Q246 the names "son of the Most High" and "son of God" are understood as an interpretation of Dan. 7's "one like a son of man." In *1 En.* 45.3 the Elect One will sit on the seat of glory; in *1 En.* 46.3 it is the son of man who does so. In *1 En.* 48.2, 5 the son of man is interchangeable with the Chosen One. In *1 En.* 62.1 the Elect One is synonymous with the son of man mentioned in 62.7. In 2 Esd. (*4 Ezra*) 13:3 one like the figure of a man who flies with the clouds of heaven is identical with "my son" in 13:32, 37, 52. Jews and Greco-Roman peoples alike designated a single figure with many names. In a similar way, Matthew uses a multiplicity of names for Jesus and ties him to still other figures through devices such as typological writing and foreshadowing.

The conflation of names and hopes to describe the one figure is at the heart of Matthew's agenda. Methodologically, this means that the reader does not start with a variety of Jewish figures and hopes and then try to figure out which one of these controls the First Gospel's narrative. It means instead that the reader starts with the Matthean narrative and allows that to control how the various names and hopes function in the First Gospel. Following this latter course, one sees that in the First Gospel there is a single figure with many names. The one figure, moreover, determines how the various labels are to be understood.

2. In Matthew's milieu, there is also a tendency to use one designation for multiple figures. Take, for example, the designation "son of man." In Ps. 8:4 (8:5 LXX: "What is man [*anthrōpos*] that you remember him, or the son of man [*huios anthrōpou*] that you care for him?" [trans. Brenton 1906]), son of man merely refers to a human being. In Ezek. 25:1–2 LXX ("And a word of the Lord came to me, saying, son of man [*huie anthrōpou*] set your face against the sons of Ammon, and prophesy against them" [ibid.]), son of man clearly refers to a prophet. In Ps. 80:17 (79:16 LXX: "Let your hand be upon the man of your right hand, and upon the son of man [*huion anthrōpou*] whom you have made strong for yourself" [ibid.]), son of man obviously refers to the king (cf. Ps. 110:1). In Dan. 7:13–14 LXX ("I beheld in a vision of the night, and behold with the clouds of heaven, coming as a son of man [*huios anthrōpou*], he came to the Ancient of Days" [ibid.]), son of man refers to a heavenly figure who would be involved in the last judgment (7:10, 26). Here is a clear example of how one designation can refer to multiple figures. "Son of man" is not really a title in the Jewish milieu. It is a designation that could be used for multiple figures. It is so used in the First Gospel.

In Matthew, "son of man" seems to carry a number of meanings. In 12:8 son of man refers to the weak, frail human who is the object of God's care; in 12:32 to a human being. In neither of these instances is Jesus making a reference to himself. In Matthew, "son of man" on the lips of Jesus is not always self-referential. At other times son of man refers to a prophetic figure to whom the word of the Lord has come (9:6; 10:23; 11:19; 13:37; 16:13–14; cf. Ezek. 6:1–2; 7:1–2); who is rejected, suffers, and is killed as prophets often were (12:40; 17:12, 22; 20:18, 28; 26:24; cf. 2 Chron. 36:15–16); and who will be raised (17:9, 23). Sometimes it is identified with the messiah/son-of-God tradition (16:13, 16; 25:31, 34; cf. 2 Esd. [4 Ezra] 13:32, 52), and sometimes son of man refers to the king (Matt. 25:31, 34) who will come as judge at the end time (13:41; 16:27, 28; 19:28; 25:31; 26:64; cf. 2 Esd. [4 Ezra] 13:37–38). In Matthew, therefore, when self-referential by Jesus, "son of man" is not a title but rather a single, fluid self-designation of a variety of roles that Jesus plays in God's salvific plan, the two primary ones being prophet and judge (Luz 1992; 1995, 113–14). At the same time, there are links between the son-of-man designation and the titles "messiah" and "son of God." Once again, then, in the First Gospel there is a conflation of roles that apply to the one figure, Jesus. Once again, it is not labels that control the Matthean narrative. It is rather the First Gospel's narrative that determines the meaning of various titles and labels.

The Matthean Jesus as the Ideal King

The First Gospel begins with a focus on Jesus as son of David, king of the Jews. It ends with an ironic depiction of Jesus's crucifixion as his enthronement as king of the Jews. Throughout the narrative, Jesus is described as the Davidic messianic shepherd who feeds and heals his sheep. Non-Jewish auditors of this narrative would have been able to appreciate Jesus's role in it because of its similarities to the picture of the ideal king in contemporary Mediterranean culture. Consider the following dimensions of such a portrait:

1. The ideal king holds an office ordained by Zeus (Dio Chrysostom, Or. 1.11–13; cf. Matt. 3:17); he came as a heaven-sent mediator for the whole world (Plutarch, Alex. fort. 6 [329c–d]; Matt. 28:18–20).
2. The ideal king is characterized by dikaiosynē (righteousness; cf. Matt. 3:14–15) and courage (Dio Chrysostom, Or. 2.54; 62.3–4; cf. Matt. 4:1–11).
3. The ideal king does not use his office to gratify his own desires (Xenophon, Mem. 2.1.2–9; Matt. 26:53–54; 27:40, 42–43); he shuns avarice, hedonism (cf. Matt. 4:3–4), and ambition (cf. Matt. 4:8–10; Dio Chrysostom, Or. 1.82–139); he gains control of himself first before trying to guide others (Dio Chrysostom, Or. 62.1; Plutarch, Princ. iner. 2 [780b]; Matt. 4:1–11).
4. The ideal king is savior (Matt. 1:21), deliverer (cf. 11:4–5), protector (8:25–26; 14:30–31), shepherd (cf. 9:36; 14:14), benefactor of humanity (Dio Chrysostom, Or. 1.11–13, 23–24, 84; 3.6; Plutarch, Alex. 39.1–2; 59.1–5).

5. The ideal king is one who dons a slave's tunic (Dio Chrysostom, *Or.* 4.66; cf. Matt. 20:28).
6. The ideal king effects harmony (*homonoia*; Plutarch, *Alex. fort.* 6 [329c–d]; cf. Matt. 17:24–19:1).
7. The ideal king has the ability to transform his subjects by vision (Plutarch, *Num.* 20.1–8) and by his words and presence (Dio Chrysostom, *Or.* 1.6–8, 24–25; 3.7–9; cf. Matt. *passim*).

Since for some of these ideal kings (e.g., Romulus, Augustus) there were claims of a miraculous birth to begin the career (Plutarch, *Rom.* 2, for Romulus; Dio Cassius, *Rom. Hist.* 45, for Augustus) and an apotheosis (exaltation to heaven) to end it (Plutarch, *Rom.* 28.2–3, for Romulus; Dio Cassius, *Rom. Hist.* 56, for Augustus), a gentile auditor would have heard Matthew's narrative about the son of David with a significant degree of understanding. This narrative is a biographical encomium (praise) of the ideal king as the non-Jewish world saw him. A Jewish auditor would have heard Matthew's narrative in the same way but in terms of the ideal king of Jewish tradition. The First Gospel communicates with both Jewish and gentile audiences.

Matthew 4:18–8:1

Discourse 1:
Jesus Calls Disciples to Seek God's Righteousness

Introductory Matters

Matthew 4:18–8:1 gives the context for and the content of the Sermon on the Mount. The first introductory matter is to note how the Sermon on the Mount parallels similar material in the Gospel of Luke.

Comparing Matthew 5–7 and Luke 6:17–49

Matthew's Sermon on the Mount has a partial parallel in Luke 6:17–49. (What follows is an adaptation of Lambrecht 1985, 36–37.) If one uses the Lukan sermon as a point of comparison, the parallels appear in table 3.

Table 3
Sermon Parallels between Luke and Matthew

Luke	Parallel	Matthew
6:20a	Introduction	5:1–2
6:20b–23	Beatitudes	5:3–12
6:24–26	Woes	
6:27–36	Love of enemy	5:38–48
6:31	Golden rule	7:12
6:37–38	Judging	7:1–2

Luke	Parallel	Matthew
6:39	Blind leader	15:14
6:40	Master/disciple	10:24
6:41–42	Splinter/beam	7:3–5
6:43–45	Tree/fruit	7:16–20
6:46	Lord, Lord	7:21–23
6:47–49	House/storm	7:24–27

If one uses the Matthean sermon as a point of reference, the parallels are as in table 4.

Table 4
Sermon Parallels between Matthew and Luke

Matthew	Parallel	Luke
5:1–2	Introduction	6:20a
5:3–12	Beatitudes	6:20b–23
5:13, 14–16	Salt and light	14:34–35; 11:33
5:17–20	Law	
5:18	Not one dot	16:17
5:21–26	Murder	
5:25–26	Going to judge	12:57–59
5:27–30	Adultery	
5:31–32	Divorce	16:18
5:33–37	Oaths	
5:38–42	Retaliation	6:29–30
5:43–48	Love enemy	6:27–28, 32–36
6:1–4	Almsgiving	
6:5–15	Prayer	
6:16–18	Fasting	
6:19–34	Treasures/cares	12:22–34
7:1–2	Judging	6:37–38
7:3–5	Splinter/beam	6:41–42
7:6	Holy things	
7:7–11	Prayer heard	11:9–13
7:12	Golden rule	6:31
7:13–14	Narrow gate	13:23–24
7:21–23	Lord, Lord	6:46
7:22–23	Don't know you	13:26–27
7:24–27	House/storm	6:47–49

From this survey, assuming the independence of Matthew and Luke, one may conclude that the two Gospels share a common tradition, but each uses it in a different way for their respective purposes.

The Function of the Language in Matthew 5–7

How does the language of the Matthean Jesus function in the Sermon on the Mount? The alternatives are basically two. On the one hand, nearly all interpreters have regarded the sermon as a source of law that is binding on some or all. The sermon provides norms for decision making. The differences among interpreters usually depend on whether it is assumed that the reader is able to obey the commands or is not. For those who believe that humans are not capable of obeying the commands, (1) the repentance view says that the stringent commands function to reduce one to helplessness in the face of one's sin so that one must cast oneself on God's grace for forgiveness and help. (2) The consistent eschatological view, which holds that the demands are emergency measures designed for the brief interim before the end, simply says that since the end did not come, these emergency measures are not possible to perform over the long haul, and so they are irrelevant today. (3) The unconditioned-divine-will view, recognizing that in a fallen world one is incapable of actualizing the unconditioned divine will apart from any human conditioning factors, argues that the individual must then take responsibility for negotiating the closest approximation to the ideal that is humanly possible. For those who believe that humans are capable of doing what the sermon calls for, an absolutist view is typical (e.g., Anabaptists, Tolstoy). The commands of the sermon were given to be obeyed and they remain an obligation upon all who bear the name "Christian" (e.g., Garland 2001, 51). The early church took for granted that the sermon's demands were to be obeyed and could be obeyed. On the other hand, it is possible to view the sermon as performative language that does something to and for the auditor to whom it is addressed. Simply put, the language of the sermon may function as a catalyst for character formation, altering one's perceptions, dispositions, and intentions.

Ethicists draw a distinction between character formation and decision making (Birch and Rasmussen 1976). Character formation concerns *who we are*. Character includes our perceptions (how we see things), dispositions, intentions, and motivations. Decision making and the resultant action concern *what we do*. Making a decision involves an analysis of the situation, a method for arriving at the right choice, and the character of the decision maker. Hence, who we are conditions what we do. Nevertheless, most ethical thought tends to focus on decision making instead of on the moral agent who makes the decision. For example, virtually all approaches to a reading of the Sermon on the Mount regard it as directed to ethical decision making. This has been the thrust of the history of interpretation since the time of the early church (Grant 1978; McArthur 1960, 105–48). Only rarely is there an attempt to treat the sermon as a shaper of character (virtue ethics; e.g., Harrington 1998; Harrington and Keenan 2002). In this commentary, the sayings in the sermon will be understood as aimed at the transformation of the auditors' character by means of changing their perceptions (ways of seeing).

The Organization of Matthew 5–7

How is the Sermon on the Mount organized? Numerous suggestions have been offered: the beatitudes are expounded by what follows (Goulder 1974, 269), the sermon follows a chiastic pattern with the Lord's Prayer at the center (Luz 1989, 1:212), Matt. 5–7 reflects the response of the Gospel to Judaism at Jamnia's three pillars (Davies 1966, 315), or the sermon coheres around a theological theme such as the greater righteousness (Kingsbury 1987). None of these proposals has been able to produce a consensus. It is interesting, however, that all of these approaches manifest broad agreement about the major units that make up the sermon. Usually there is a recognition that 5:3–12 and 5:13–16 are subunits of 5:3–16. Matthew 5:17–20 is recognized as a subunit, even if there is disagreement about whether it is the introduction to 5:21–7:12; 5:21–7:27; or only 5:21–48. Most scholars agree that 5:21–48 and 6:1–18 are distinct units. There is disagreement about 6:19–7:12: should it be taken as a whole, or should 6:19–34 be separated from 7:1–12? There is widespread agreement that 7:13 begins the final segment of the sermon. The accompanying outline is intended to represent the majority reading of its arrangement.

Tracing the Narrative Flow

For what follows, see Talbert 2004b.

Gathering Disciples and Preparing to Teach (4:18–5:2)

Matthew 4:18–5:2 provides the context for the sermon (5:2–7:28). It consists of three segments: 4:18–22; 4:23–25; and 5:1–2. The first two consist of two types of stories about gathering disciples (4:18–22 [summons]; 4:23–25 [attraction]) followed by Jesus's preparation for teaching disciples.

Matthew 4:18–8:1 in the Narrative Flow

Birth narratives (1:1–2:23)

Jesus's ministry begins (3:1–8:1)

Narrative: Jesus begins to fulfill all righteousness (3:1–4:17)

▶ *Discourse:* Jesus calls disciples to seek God's righteousness (4:18–8:1)

Gathering disciples and preparing to teach (4:18–5:2)

Discipleship: Promises and expectations (5:3–16)

Six antitheses: Deficient and surpassing righteousness (5:17–48)

Outward and inward piety (6:1–18)

Possessions: Priorities and trust (6:19–34)

Judging: Condemnation and discernment (7:1–12)

Warnings of catastrophe (7:13–27)

Conclusion: Effects of Jesus's teaching (7:28–8:1)

> ### An Outline
> ### of Matthew 4:18–5:2
>
> **Gathering disciples and preparing to teach (4:18–5:2)**
>
>   "Follow me" (4:18–22)
>
>   Magnetic attraction (4:23–25)
>
>   Sitting to teach (5:1–2)

4:18–22. Some circles understood the gathering of disciples in terms of a summons and a response. Diogenes Laertius, for example, tells of Socrates' call of Xenophon (*Vit. phil.* 2.48). Socrates met Xenophon in a narrow passage and stretched out his stick to bar the way while he inquired where every kind of food was sold. Upon receiving a reply, Socrates put another question: "And where do men become good and honorable?" Xenophon was puzzled. "Then follow me," said Socrates, "and learn." From that time onward, Xenophon was a disciple of Socrates. The reader of the canonical Gospels will recognize this type of call story in Mark 1:16–20 (Matt. 4:18–22); 2:14; Luke 5:1–11; 19:5; John 1:43. In Matt. 4:18–22, therefore, the ancient auditor would have recognized as a conventional type the story of Jesus's summons of Peter, Andrew, James, and John and their following him.

4:23–25. By contrast, others in antiquity viewed gathering disciples as attraction by magnetism. Epictetus (*Diatr.* 3.23.27), for example, asks, "Does a philosopher invite people to a lecture?—Is it not rather the case that, as the sun draws its own sustenance to itself, so he also draws to himself those to whom he is to do good? What physician ever invites a patient to come and be healed by him?" (trans. W. Oldfather 1925–28). When Eliezer desires to study with Johanan ben Zakkai, it is because of the fame of the rabbi (*Avot R. Nat.* [B] 13). Indeed, it is characteristic of the rabbinic tradition to locate the initiative with the person wanting to study with the rabbi. The reader of the Gospels will recognize the attraction type of story in John 1:36–39, 40–42, 45–49, and also here in Matt. 4:23–25.

There is admittedly some debate about whether the crowds in Matt. 4:23–25 are to be regarded as Jesus's disciples even if they follow him (4:25). Two strands of evidence seem decisive. First, the context demands it. In 5:1–2 we are told that Jesus's disciples come to him and he teaches them. In 7:28 we are told that when Jesus has finished his teaching, the crowds are astonished. These two framing texts make it sound as though the sermon is directed to disciples. Second, the larger Gospel context makes it possible. The verb *akolouthein* (to follow) in Matthew is used in both a strictly literal sense of "coming or going after a person" and in a metaphorical/theological sense of discipleship. The crowds in Matthew can sometimes be regarded as Jesus's disciples (8:19–20; 9:27–29; 14:13; 20:29–34; 21:9–11). In these instances, the crowds are part of the larger circle of Jesus's followers (e.g., 10:24, 25, 42; 27:57). Here in Matt. 4:23–25, the crowd that follows Jesus is best understood as part of that wider circle of disciples. They have been attracted to Jesus by the magnetism of his proclamation and healing. It is these disciples, as well as those representative of the circle of the Twelve, that are the audience to whom the sermon is given (Gundry 1982, 65).

5:1–2. With his disciples around him, the Matthean Jesus sits (the posture of a teacher) and begins to speak.

Discipleship: Promises and Expectations (5:3–16)

Matthew 5:3–16, the first thought unit, offers a portrait of disciples together with promises and expectations. There are two subunits: 5:3–12, consisting of nine be-atitudes, and 5:13–16, consisting of two metaphors. The accompanying outline clarifies the structure of this section.

5:3–12. The first subunit is composed of nine beatitudes. These fall into two sub-groupings. (1) The first four deal with the disciples' vertical relationship. (2) The last five focus on horizontal relationships. Of the last five, the first three address relationships in which disciples have the initiative; the last two pertain to relationships in which disciples are acted upon. The beatitudes give a portrait of and promises to disciples (see table 5).

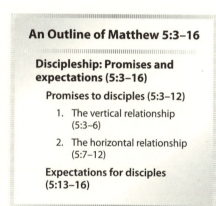

An Outline of Matthew 5:3–16

Discipleship: Promises and expectations (5:3–16)

Promises to disciples (5:3–12)

1. The vertical relationship (5:3–6)
2. The horizontal relationship (5:7–12)

Expectations for disciples (5:13–16)

Table 5
Nine Beatitudes (Matt. 5:3–12)

Portrait	Promises
1. Vertical (5:3–6)	
Blessed . . . poor in spirit	theirs is the kingdom of heaven
Blessed . . . those who mourn	they shall be comforted
Blessed . . . the meek	they shall inherit the earth
Blessed . . . those who hunger and thirst for righteousness	they shall be satisfied
2. Horizontal (5:7–12)	
a. active	
Blessed . . . the merciful	they shall receive mercy
Blessed . . . the pure in heart	they shall see God
Blessed . . . the peacemakers	they . . . called children of God
b. passive	
Blessed . . . those persecuted for righteousness' sake	theirs is the kingdom of heaven
Blessed are you when reviled, persecuted, and defamed	your heavenly reward is great

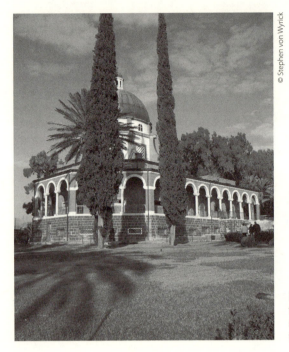

© Stephen von Wyrick

Figure 5. The Mount of Beatitudes Chapel overlooks the Sea of Galilee from the northwest. The lovely structure located in a beautiful spot commemorates the sermon in Matt. 5–7.

1. The first four beatitudes focus on a disciple's relation to God. What does it mean to be **poor in spirit** (5:3a)? The exact phrase is found at Qumran (1QM 14.7). It uses "poor in spirit" in contrast to those with a "hardened heart" (so, the humble before God). In 4Q427 7.1–2, the poor are the opposite of those with a haughty heart. A fragmentary text, a Messianic Vision 6, equates the poor and the faithful to God. This Qumranic usage has roots in Israel's scriptures (e.g., Isa. 61:1–2: the poor are the brokenhearted, those who mourn; Isa. 11:4; 29:19: the poor are synonymous with the meek; Isa. 66:2: the poor are the contrite in spirit). Matthew uses **poor in spirit** as a religious designation. They are the humble before God (Ratzinger 2007, 74–77). To these individuals with the right disposition toward God, the promise is given: the blessing, **the kingdom of the heavens is theirs** (5:3b). Remember that in Matthew the kingdom of heaven/God refers both to the ultimate blessing of the age to come and to the activity of God in the present that causes that blessing to come.

What is meant by **those who mourn** (5:4a)? Isaiah 61:2–3 uses "to comfort all who mourn" to refer to the returned exiles who are facing abundant troubles that grieve them greatly. They are those who need God's help, who lament that the kingdom has not come and God's will is not yet done (cf. Ezek. 9:4). How should one understand **they shall be comforted** (5:4b)? Isaiah 61:2 equates comfort and salvation; 57:18 associates comfort with healing; 40:1–2 associates comfort with pardon for iniquity; Jer. 31:13 equates comfort and redemption. To be comforted, then, is to experience God's salvation. This is the promise to those grieve over the brokenness of this world.

Who are the **meek** (5:5a)? The order of the first three beatitudes is that of Isa. 61: poor, mourners, meek. The third is a virtual replica of Ps. 37:11 (36:11 LXX): "The meek shall inherit the earth" (KJV). Zephaniah 3:12–13 LXX speaks of "a people meek and lowly," those who seek refuge in the name of the Lord. In the LXX, *praüs* (meek) is used to translate three different Hebrew terms, one of which is *'ani*. *Ptōchos* (poor) is also used in the LXX to translate three different Hebrew terms, one of which is *'ani*. Hence "poor" and "meek" are virtual synonyms. They were so used at Qumran (cf. 4QpPs37). The first and third beatitudes, therefore, are virtual synonyms. To **inherit the earth** (5:5b) in Ps. 37 means to gain possession of the land of Canaan. By the NT period, however, "the land" had taken on eschatological connotations (e.g., *2 En.* 50.2). Qumran interprets Ps. 37 as referring to the end-time vindication (4QpPs37 [a]). In Rom. 4, Paul shares this eschatological view of the land/earth. The promise, then, is a virtual synonym of the promise in the first beatitude.

The meaning of **those who hunger and thirst for righteousness** (5:6a) depends on how one understands the evangelist's use of righteousness elsewhere in the Gospel. On the one hand, some have viewed righteousness in all Matthean passages as the conduct expected by God (as in *T. Levi* 13.5: "Do righteousness on earth, in order that you might find it in heaven" [*OTP* 1:793]). On the other hand, others have taken righteousness, at least in some passages in Matthew, as the activity of God that establishes justice (e.g., Isa. 51:5 RSV: "My deliverance draws near speedily, my salvation has gone forth"). Scholarly opinion is divided. In Matt. 5:6 it is likely that the second option is appropriate. The hunger and thirst is the longing for the future kingdom and God's vindication of the right. The blessing for such people is that **they shall be satisfied** (5:6b; cf. Ps. 107:9: "[The LORD] satisfies the thirsty, and the hungry he fills with good things"). Those who long for God's saving activity will find their hunger and thirst satisfied by that very saving activity. All of the first four beatitudes focus on the proper attitude of disciples before God and promise appropriate blessings on those who relate to the Lord in such a way.

2. The next three beatitudes focus on relationships with others in which the disciples have the initiative. Who are the **merciful** (5:7a)? Simply put, they are those who show mercy to other humans. It was a Jewish conviction that God showed mercy to those who were merciful (Ps. 18:25–26 MT: "With the merciful you show yourself merciful" [ESV]; Matt. 6:14–15; 18:23–35). How should **shall obtain mercy** (5:7b) be understood? In this context, it is surely eschatological mercy.

Who are the **pure in heart** (5:8a)? Psalm 24:3–4 says, "Who shall ascend the hill of the LORD? And who shall stand in his holy place? Those who have clean hands and pure hearts." A similar view is found in Ps. 73:1: "the upright, . . . those who are pure in heart." Clean hands and a pure heart are the outer and inner ethical stance of a person. The concern, therefore, is with ethical horizontal relationships. **They shall see God** (5:8b) is a reference to the eschatological vision of the Lord (cf. 2 Esd. [*4 Ezra*] 7:98: the righteous will one day "see the face of him whom they served in life").

The **peacemakers** (5:9a) are the third in the series of beatitudes focused on horizontal relations in which disciples have the initiative. Who are they? Proverbs 10:10 LXX says, "The one who reproves boldly is a peacemaker" (cf. Matt. 18:15; James 5:19–20). Mishnah text *Pe'ah* 1.1 describes another dimension of peacemaking ("These are the things whose fruits a man enjoys in this world while the capital is laid up for him in the world to come: . . . making peace between a man and his fellow" [trans. Danby 1933, 10–11]). The blessing that such people will receive is being **called the children of God** (5:9b). Wisdom 12:19 says that the righteous are God's children. Philo says, "Not every Israelite is God's child, but only the doer of good" (*Spec.* 1.318, trans. Colson 1929–62). Matthew 5:48 points the way. God's children are those who act like God. Who will acknowledge them as children? It is God!

The final two beatitudes direct their attention to disciples' relations with others when they are being acted upon hostilely. **Those persecuted for righteousness' sake** (5:10a) are disciples who are suffering not because they have done wrong but because they have done right. In Wis. 2:12 the wicked say, "Let us lie in wait for the righteous." In 1 Pet. 3:14 the author encourages his audience: "But even if you do suffer for righteousness' sake, you will be blessed" (RSV). What is their blessing? **The kingdom of heaven is theirs** (5:10b).

Matthew 5:11–12 continues the theme of persecution of disciples that was heard in 5:10. Here the persecution is not because of righteousness but **on my account** (5:11b). There is also a shift from third person (blessed are they) to second person (blessed are you). The reward **will be great in the heavens because so they persecuted the prophets before you** (5:12). The suffering disciples are in good company.

In the beatitudes, Jesus has provided his auditors with a portrait of disciples in both their relation to God and their relations with other humans, on the one hand, and a promise of blessings on such people, on the other. In the Matthean plot, Jesus has been depicted as one who knows about the kingdom of heaven (4:17, i.e., its imminence and its demand for repentance). Matthew 5:3–12 assumes that Jesus not only has a knowledge of the character of the kingdom and the criteria of the last judgment but also has the authority to pronounce that judgment (cf. 7:21–23 for similar assumptions). Consequently, Jesus can issue congratulations to those who will benefit from the kingdom's coming. The poem (5:3–12) is in effect *eschatological judgment proleptically given, on the basis of Jesus's assumed knowledge of the end times and authority at the last judgment*. It also assumes that Jesus's disciples are attached to him (5:11) and that they resemble the portrait of 5:3–12 (this is implied in 5:13–16: "you are salt" and "you are light").

5:13–16. The second subunit, 5:13–16, consists of two metaphors, one with a warning and the other with an exhortation, providing a portrait of disciples and their mission in the world (see table 6). The first description is **You are the salt of the earth** (5:13); the second, **You are the light of the world** (5:14). The sayings associated with each metaphor are essentially a call for disciples to "be who you are" in your relations in the world.

Table 6
Two Metaphors (Matt. 5:13–16)

Portrait	Mission
You are the salt of the earth	*Warning:* Be what you are or be discarded.
You are the light of the world	*Admonition:* Be what you are for God's glory.

How does this portrait of disciples and promises to them function for Matthew's auditors? The portrait serves two purposes. First, it sketches the outlines of a good person, a person of piety toward God and right behavior toward other humans. Plutarch (*Virt. prof.* 84d) tells how such a portrait would affect the auditors. He says that one's being in the presence of a good person has the effect: "Great is his craving all but to merge his own identity in that of the good man." Elsewhere, Plutarch expounds,

> Our intellectual vision must be applied to such objects as, by their very charm, invite it onward to its own proper good. Such objects are to be found in virtuous deeds; *these implant in those who search them out a great and zealous eagerness which leads to imitation.* . . . Virtuous action straightway so disposes a man that he no sooner admires the works of virtue than he strives to emulate those who wrought them. . . . The Good *creates a stir of activity towards itself, and implants at once in the spectator an active impulse; it does not form his character by ideal representation alone; but through the investigation of its work it furnishes him with a dominant purpose.* (*Per.* 1–2, trans. Perrin 1914–26, 2–7, emphasis mine; cf. also Plutarch, *Aem.* 1.1–5)

The vision of the good is transformative. Second, the ninth beatitude shifts to second person, thereby drawing the auditors into an identification with the portrait given. A new way of seeing themselves occurs. This is who we are. Participation in the dispositions and intentions reflected in the portrait is effected. This is *really* who we are. Jesus sees us this way! The poem, then, in its portrait of disciples, functions to form the character of the auditors in their vertical and horizontal relations.

What about the promises? They constitute eschatological judgment proleptically given on the basis of Jesus's assumed knowledge of the end times and authority at the last judgment. They promise fullness of eschatological blessing to those who participate in the portrait sketched. Promises are performative language (Austin 1962). Something occurs in the utterance itself. To issue a promise does not just provide information; it also performs an action. It obliges the one who utters it; it puts on record one's assumption of a spiritual shackle. So the promises of the beatitudes oblige their speaker. They put him on record as assuming responsibility for the disciples' ultimate destiny. The disciples now *see* their destiny differently. This is the way Jesus sees us. There is one who by his promises has now undertaken responsibility to enable the fulfillment of the beatitudes. The disposition that flows from this insight is to trust him. Character is being formed.

Six Antitheses: Deficient and Surpassing Righteousness (5:17–48)

The next large thought unit in the sermon is 5:17–48. There is an introduction in 5:17–20, followed by the so-called six antitheses (5:21–48). This unit contrasts two types of covenant faithfulness. There is a *deficient* righteousness, that of the scribes and Pharisees, and a *surpassing* righteousness, that of those who will enter the kingdom of heaven.

What is this surpassing righteousness? There are four large thought units in the heart of the Sermon: 5:17–48; 6:1–18; 6:19–34; and 7:1–12. Each of the four thought units contrasts the higher righteousness with that of the scribes and Pharisees. With 5:21–48, one should compare 15:1–9 (you break the command of God for the sake of your tradition); with 6:1–18, compare 23:5 (they do all their deeds to be seen by others); with 6:19–34, compare 15:1–12 and 23:25 (you cleanse the outside of the cup and plate but inside you are full of greed); and with 7:1–12, compare 9:11; 12:2; 15:2; and 23:2–4 (they judge but do not practice what they preach). The surpassing righteousness in the sermon is illustrated in these four thought units. Matthew 5:21–48 asks, What is the purpose of your Bible reading? It advocates a radical, as opposed to a formal, obedience to Scripture. The surpassing righteousness does not seek to evade the intent of the law. Matthew 6:1–18 asks, Whose attention are you trying to get? It advocates a piety that avoids ostentatious displays because they are directed to the wrong audience. The surpassing righteousness does not seek human approval. Matthew 6:19–34 asks, How do possessions function in your life and why? It advocates a piety that is neither greedy nor anxious because it trusts God's providential goodness. The surpassing righteousness does not act out of either greed or anxiety

---

An Outline of Matthew 5:17–48

Six antitheses: Deficient and surpassing righteousness (5:17–48)

   The law's continuing validity (5:17–20)

   Antithesis 1: Murder and anger (5:21–26)

   Antithesis 2: Adultery (5:27–30)

   Antithesis 3: Divorce (5:31–32)

   Antithesis 4: Oaths (5:33–37)

   Antithesis 5: Revenge or nonretaliation (5:38–42)

   Antithesis 6: Love neighbors or enemies (5:43–48)

---

with reference to possessions. Matthew 7:1–12 asks, When you exercise your critical function, where do you direct it first? It advocates a lifestyle in which one walks the talk, directing one's critical function first toward oneself. The surpassing righteousness practices what it verbally advocates.

In 5:21–48 the Matthean Jesus shows he is not abolishing the Scriptures but rather properly interpreting them (Snodgrass 1996) and indicating what the greater righteousness looks like with reference to one's use of the Bible. Six examples follow, in two groups of three each, contrasting how Jesus reads Scripture over against how others have traditionally read it.

5:17–20. The introductory subunit, 5:17–20, is composed of four sayings (5:17, 18, 19, and 20). It functions as a control on the way 5:21–48 is to be read. It aims to protect against any interpretation of what follows that would depict Jesus as doing away with the observance of the law or the prophets. In outline form, the unit looks like this:

1. Jesus's intent is *not* to cause observance of the Scriptures to cease *but* to realize the intent of God's will in the Scriptures (5:17; cf. Rom. 8:4).
2. The ground of Jesus's intent is that the Scriptures endure to the eschaton (5:18; cf. Bar. 4:1; 2 Esd. [*4 Ezra*] 9:37; *Jub.* 3.14).
3. Two consequences of Jesus's intent and its basis, one for teachers and one for all auditors:
   a. *For teachers.* Implications for a teacher's status in the kingdom of heaven (5:19; cf. 28:18: "All authority in heaven and on earth has been given to me"; i.e., Jesus's status indicates he has not relaxed even the least of the commandments).
   b. *For all auditors.* Implications for a person's entry into the kingdom of heaven (the righteousness demanded of humans; 5:20).

Verse 17 contradicts a false saying with a correct one. The false saying attributed to Jesus ran thus: "I have come to abolish the law and the prophets." The evangelist corrects it with a true saying: "**I have come not to abolish** (to rescind the whole web of traditional observance; cf. 2 Macc. 2:22; 4:11) **but to fulfill** (to expound the true meaning and intent of the law as opposed to the wrong or shallow understandings of it)."

Verse 18 falls into an ABA′ pattern to aid interpretation.

A **Until heaven and earth pass away;**
　B **not an iota nor a dot will pass from the law**
A′ **until all is accomplished.**

Iota is the Greek equivalent of the Semitic *yod*, the smallest letter in the alphabet. A **dot** is literally a "horn" (i.e., a projection or hook of a letter). The central point is the enduring character of even the smallest part of the law

The Historical Pharisees

Scholars disagree on what the historical Pharisees were like. Ellis Rivkin (1978) regards the Pharisees as a scholarly class of teachers of the twofold law. Jacob Neusner (1973) sees them as a group concerned with ritual purity that tried to extend it to the whole population. Modern scholars generally regard them as the best of the Judaism of their time. The rabbis, however, sometimes criticized certain Pharisees in ways similar to Matthew's depiction of them (*y. Ber.* 14b; *b. Sotah* 22b; *Avot R. Nat.* [A] 37; [B] 45: e.g., the ostentatious Pharisee who wears his good actions on his shoulder; cf. Matt. 6:1–18). The First Evangelist's intensity in evaluating the Pharisees negatively likely derives from the historical context after AD 70, in which competition between Matthew's community and the Pharisee-led Jamnia movement was fierce.

(Bar. 4:1; 2 Esd. [*4 Ezra*] 9:37; *Jub.* 3.14). The question is, when will the law pass away? That **until heaven and earth pass away** (Mark 13:31; Rev. 21:1; cf. 1 Cor. 7:31) and **until all is accomplished** (Mark 13:30; Rev. 1:1, 19; 4:1) are synonymous expressions in Matt. 24:34–35 favors the answer "not until the end of the age" (also the position of Philo, *Mos.* 2.14).

Matthew 5:19 is addressed to teachers. The danger faced is a teacher's tendency to evade the clear intent of the Scriptures (cf. 15:9 for an example; also *y. Sotah* 19a: scholarly Pharisees who give counsel by which the law may be circumvented). Verse 20 presents a conditional judgment. *Unless* **your righteousness exceeds that of the scribes and Pharisees, you will not enter into the kingdom of the heavens.** By "righteousness" the First Gospel means "covenant faithfulness." In 5:20 the covenant faithfulness referred to is that which God expects of humans. This surpassing righteousness is contrasted with the deficient righteousness of the Pharisees.

5:21–26. The first of the six examples showing what the "surpassing righteousness" is like comes in 5:21–26. Like the other five examples, it begins with a contrast: **You** (disciples) **have heard** (in the synagogue) **that it was said to the ancestors . . . , but I say to you** (5:21–22). What was said to the ancient Israelites? **You shall not murder** (Exod. 20:13//Deut. 5:17). What are the consequences of such behavior? **Whoever murders will be liable to judgment** (5:21; cf. Exod. 21:12; Lev. 24:17; Num. 35:12). This traditional interpretation of Scripture limited the intent of Exod. 20:13 to physically taking the life of another human and restricted the punishment to being brought before the court. To this reading the Matthean Jesus responds with his own. There are three parts, each describing the *behavior* and then the *consequences*. (1) **Everyone who continues to be angry with his brother will be liable to the** (local) **court** (cf. Eph. 4:26–27). (2) **Whoever says "Raka"** (Empty Head) **to his brother will be liable to the Sanhedrin** (the Jewish supreme court). (3) **Whoever says "Fool" will be liable to the Gehenna of fire** (hell; 5:22). (In *m. Avot* 3.12, R. Eleazar of Modiim says, "If a man . . . puts his fellow to shame publicly . . . even though a knowledge of the Law and good works are his, he has no share in the world to come" [trans. Danby 1933, 451].) Jesus's interpretation of **You shall not murder** indicates that God's intent in giving the command is to prohibit more than just eliminating another by killing the body. The divine intent is that one not eliminate another from a relationship by holding a grudge or by shaming. The judgment for such relational elimination of the other is much more severe than traditional interpretation of the Decalogue supposes. Two illustrations follow that speak about taking the initiative to restore broken relationships. **If you are offering your gift upon the altar and you remember that your brother has something against you, leave your gift there upon the altar and go, first be reconciled with your brother, and then come offer your gift** (5:23–24). This is hyperbole. The imaginary situation is impossible to fulfill. Nevertheless, it makes its point. **Settle with your adversary quickly while you are on the way with him** (Prov. 6:1–5) **lest your adversary deliver you to the judge, and the judge to the guard, and he cast you into prison. Truly I say to you, you will not come out until you pay the last amount owed** (5:25–26). If 5:22's concern is with not causing broken relationships, 5:23–26's point is about taking the initiative to restore broken relationships. The divine intent, says Jesus, is that disciples be persons who neither break relationships nor fail to restore broken ones. A different perception is a catalyst to change character.

5:27–30. The second contrast between traditional interpretation and that of Jesus comes in 5:27–30. **You have heard that it was said, "You shall not commit adultery"** (5:27; Exod. 20:14//Deut. 5:18). No explicit interpretation is given of the biblical command. To make sense of what follows (5:28), we must assume the accepted interpretation that the physical act of sex with another man's wife is what is prohibited. **But I say to you, everyone who goes on looking at another man's wife for the purpose of coveting her has already committed adultery with her in his heart** (cf. 15:19: "out of the heart come forth evil thoughts . . . adultery"). The reference is to the deliberate harboring of desire for an illicit relationship. Although ancient courts did not assess liability for intention, Jewish and pagan moralists sometimes did. In *T. Iss.* 7.2 we read, "I have not had intercourse with any woman other than my wife, nor was I promiscuous by lustful look" (*OTP* 1:804). Xenocrates, the companion of Plato, said that it made no difference whether one set one's eyes in a strange house or placed one's feet there, for the one who looks on forbidden places is guilty of the same sin as the one who goes there (Aelian, *Var. hist.* 14.42).

In matters of intention, however, God or the gods would be the judge, not human courts. Two illustrations follow. The first: **If your right eye causes you to stumble, tear it out and cast it from you. It is better for you to lose one of your members and not have your whole body cast into Gehenna.** The second: **If your right hand causes you to stumble, cut it off and cast it from you. It is better for you to lose one of your members and not to have your whole body go to Gehenna** (5:29–30). These two illustrations are hyperbole; they are not to be taken literally. Together they call for a radical integration of the self. Whatever does not fit into the self's integration around God's will, be it intent (eye) or action (hand), is to be jettisoned. The point of 5:27–30 is that the divine intent behind "Do not commit adultery" is that one not violate another's spouse. Such violation may be due to covetousness as well as the physical act. Be a person who is whole in avoidance of adultery. To *see* God's intent in this new way alters not only one's perception but also one's disposition, intention, and motivation. Character is being formed.

5:31–32. The third pericope in this study of contrasting interpretations of Scripture is 5:31–32. **It has been said, "Whoever divorces his wife, let him give her a bill of divorce"** (5:31). This is a reference to Deut. 24:1 as understood in Jesus's time. Divorce was assumed to be permissible in a Jewish context. The issue was, on what grounds is divorce possible? (cf. 19:3). The interpretation of Deut. 24:1–2 assumed by Matt. 5:31 holds that divorce is permissible on any grounds so long as a bill of divorce is given to the woman. The essential formula in the bill of divorce was "Lo, you are free to marry any man" (*m. Git.* 9.3; cf. Danby 1933, 319). It was a writ of emancipation. The purpose of the writ was to protect the woman and any man who might marry her from the charge of adultery. The assumption was that the writ sundered the marital relation with the divorcing husband. **But I say to you, everyone who divorces his wife except on the basis of unfaithfulness makes her commit adultery, and whoever marries her commits adultery** (5:32).

From the Matthean Jesus's perspective, the writ of divorce does not protect either the divorced wife or the second husband from the charge of adultery. Jesus's assumption must be that the woman is still the first husband's wife (cf. 19:4–6). The Matthean Jesus is saying that the divine intent behind Deut. 24:1–4 was to limit divorce. Protection from charges of adultery is not given by issuing a writ of divorce but by forgoing divorce altogether. The only exception is **on the basis of unfaithfulness.** Jewish (e.g., 2 Sam. 20:3; *T. Reu.* 3.10–15; cf. Matt. 1:18b–19) and Roman (e.g., *Lex Julia de adulteriis* of 18 BC) law mandated divorce in the case of adultery. Unfaithfulness was not only sufficient grounds for divorce; it was also something that necessitated it. Divorce, then, was allowed because the marriage had already been dissolved by the unfaithful partner. This pericope calls for a disciple to be a person who does not violate the indissoluble marriage bond. *Seeing* the divine intent behind Deut. 24:1–2 is a catalyst for the formation of character. At this point the first subunit of three contrasts is complete.

5:33–37. The second subunit of three begins at 5:33, signaled by the term *palin* (again) and the repetition of the full formula of contrast. The first of the second set of three pericopes is 5:33–37, concerning oaths. **You have heard that it was said to the ancestors, "You shall not swear falsely** (using God's name, *epiorkēseis*; Lev. 19:12), **but you shall give to the Lord what you have sworn to do"** (5:33; Deut. 23:21, 23; Num. 30:2; Ps. 50:14b). The traditional interpretation the disciples have heard is that using God's name when swearing means one must then tell the truth and do what one has promised. Implied is the assumption that if God's name is not used, then one may play fast and loose with the truth. **But I say to you, Do not swear at all** (5:34a). (Philo, *Decal.* 92, says, "From much swearing springs false swearing.") What follows is a list of four examples of oaths that were considered not binding by some (5:34b–36; cf. 23:16–22): (1) **not by heaven, because it is the throne of God,** (2) **nor by the earth, because it is the footstool for his feet,** (3) **nor by Jerusalem, because it is the city of the great king,** (4) **nor should you swear by your head, because you are not able to make a single hair white or dark.** The Mishnah lists oaths that are not binding:

> If a man said, "I adjure you," or "I command you," or "I bind you," they are liable. But if he said "By heaven and by earth," they are exempt. (*m. Shevu.* 4.13, trans. Danby 1933, 415; cf. Matt. 23:22)

> If he said, "May it be Jerusalem," he has said naught. (*m. Ned.* 1.3, trans. Danby 1933, 264)

> If a man take an oath before his fellow, and his fellow said to him, "Vow to me by the life of your head," R. Meir says he may retract. (*m. Sanh.* 3.2; cf. Danby 1933, 385)

Let your word be "Yes, yes; no, no"; that which is more than this is from the evil one (5:37). (Josephus, *J.W.* 2.135, says about the Essenes that any word of theirs has more force than an oath; they avoid swearing, regarding it as worse than perjury.) When the Matthean Jesus says that one should not swear at all, is the prohibition specifically against oaths that function as loopholes for escape from truthfulness? Or is it against oaths in general because they allow people to try to evade the truth? Either way, the higher righteousness does not look for loopholes. This pericope causes its auditors to *see* speech entirely differently. God's intent is that we be truthful. This alters the audience's dispositions and intentions. Character is being formed.

5:38–42. The second contrast of the second triad comes in Matt. 5:38–42. **You have heard that it has been said, "An eye for an eye and a tooth for a tooth"** (5:38; Exod. 21:23–24; Lev. 24:17, 19–20, 21b; Deut. 19:21 LXX). This OT command was intended as an official regulation (as opposed to taking the law into one's own hands) to prevent vengefulness blinded by rage. In its time it was a social advance. It ended vendettas, blood feuds that permitted unlimited retaliation. The *lex talionis* continued into the NT period in some circles (cf. 11QT[a] 61.10–12; *Jub.* 4.31–32; Philo, *Spec.* 3.182; Josephus, *Ant.* 4.280). In other circles contemporary Jewish law provided monetary restitution as an alternative to maiming the offender (Josephus, *Ant.* 4.280). Apparently some who continued its strict usage took it as justification for personal acts of vengeance by the one wronged. Such an assumed interpretation seems necessary to make sense of the response by the Matthean Jesus: **But I say to you, Do not retaliate against the evil person** (5:39a). If Jesus is following the same practice as before, this statement must be understood as his interpretation of the divine intent behind the *lex talionis*. The true intent of the principle, he says, is to limit revenge. So if God's intent is to limit revenge, then that intent is better realized through nonretaliation than literal application of the principle of an eye for an eye. The issue is how to understand the *lex talionis* properly.

There follow four illustrations of the renunciation of retaliation. (1) **Whoever strikes you on the right cheek, turn to him also the other** (5:39b). This backhanded slap was a way of humiliating a person (Job 16:10; Lam. 3:30; 1 Esd. 4:30 LXX). Do not retaliate. (2) **To the one wanting to sue you and to take your inner garment, give him also your outer garment** (5:40). Whereas in Luke 6:29 the situation assumed is robbery (so one takes possession of the outer garment first), here the context is the courtroom. Exodus 22:25–27 and Deut. 24:10–13 do not allow the one suing to demand the outer garment, which was used as a blanket at night. Hence the one suing in Matthew is demanding the inner garment. Let there be no retaliation; give the outer garment as well. (3) **And whoever conscripts you for one mile, go with him two** (5:41). Roman soldiers could commandeer citizens to carry their burdens for one mile (Matt. 27:32; Epictetus, *Diatr.* 4.1.79: "If a soldier commandeers your donkey, let it go. Do not resist or grumble. If you do, you will get a beating and lose your little donkey just the same" [trans. W. Oldfather 1925–28]). Do not retaliate. (4) **To the one asking you, give, and do not refuse the one wanting to borrow from you** (5:42). How does this logion fit with the theme of nonretaliation? In *b. Yoma* 23a, one reads: "But is it not written: Thou shalt not take vengeance nor bear any grudge (Lev. 19:18). That refers to monetary affairs, for it has been taught: What is revenge and what is bearing a grudge? If one says to his fellow: Lend me your sickle, and he replied No, and tomorrow the second comes to the first and says: Lend me your axe! And he replies: I will not lend it to you, just as you would not lend me your sickle, that is revenge" (trans. Epstein 1948). If some such tradition circulated in Matthew's time, then verse 42 makes sense within the pattern of the previous three illustrations.

All four illustrations focus on nonretaliation. Note that the four are very specific. How often is one backhanded on the right cheek, sued for one's underwear, or forced by a soldier to carry his gear for a mile? They are also extreme. If one did as verse 40 advocates, one would stand naked in court, a practice eschewed by Jewish tradition. They are part of a series whose effect is to establish a pattern that can be extended to other instances. It is open-ended. The meaning of the text, therefore, cannot be restricted to what it says literally. It does not consist of legal rules. The language of this pericope gives a shock that arouses the moral imagination, enabling the auditors to *see* their situations in a new way and to contemplate new possibilities of action. This shapes moral character.

5:43–48. The last of the six contrasts is 5:43–48. **You have heard that it was said, "You shall love your neighbor** (Lev. 19:18 LXX) **and hate your enemy"** (5:43; Pss. 26:5; 139:21–22; 1QS 1.10–11; 9.21–23; Josephus, *J.W.* 2.139). The second part, which is not a quotation from Scripture, functions as the interpretation of the first. Loving the neighbor implies hating the enemy. Such sentiments are heard at Qumran (1QS 1.3–4, 9–10). They can also be found in Greco-Roman circles (Anaximenes of Lampsacus, *Rhet. Alex.* 1.38–40: Do good to one's friends, . . . do harm to one's enemies). The interpretation, then, reflects popular sentiment of the time. **But I say to you, love your enemies, and pray for those who persecute you so that you may become children of your Father in the heavens** (5:44–45a). Children act like their parents (Philo, *Virt.* 195, says: "Kinship is not measured only by blood, but by similarity of conduct"). How does God act? **He makes his sun rise upon the evil and good and sends rain upon the righteous and unrighteous** (5:45b). The inference is drawn. **Be inclusive** (*teleioi*) **in your love as your heavenly Father is inclusive** (*teleios*; 5:48). To do otherwise is to fall short of the surpassing righteousness. God's intent in the love command is that disciples be persons who do not exclude their enemies from the love shown to their friends. A new way of *seeing* leads to the formation of character. With this, the major thought unit of 5:17–48 is at an end. The next major unit is 6:1–18.

Outward and Inward Piety (6:1–18)

In 5:20 the Matthean Jesus spoke of a righteousness that exceeds that of the scribes and Pharisees. In 5:21–48, in a set of six contrasts, he showed what such a righteousness looks like in one's relationships with others as discerned through interpreting Scripture. Now in 6:1–18 Jesus continues to elaborate on the higher righteousness by focusing on three acts of piety done before God. The spotlight is on the necessary inwardness in the practice of these three external acts. This thought unit, 6:1–18, consists of a statement of principle (6:1) followed by four paragraphs following the same basic arrangement (6:2–4, almsgiving; 6:5–6, prayer; 6:7–15, prayer; 6:16–18, fasting). Paragraphs 1, 2, and 4 make one point: appropriate piety is done *for* God; paragraph 3 makes another point: appropriate piety is done in line with God's character.

6:1. The statement of principle runs, **Be on your guard that you do not do your righteousness** (acts that reflect your

---

An Outline of Matthew 6:1–18

Outward and inward piety (6:1–18)

The principle of piety (6:1)

Almsgiving (6:2–4)

Private prayer (6:5–6)

How to pray (6:7–15)

Fasting (6:16–18)

faithfulness to God) **in the presence of others with the aim of being seen by them** (cf. 23:5; *y. Ber.* 14b: the "shoulder Pharisee," who packs his good works on his shoulder to be seen by others; Rom. 2:28–29). This makes your righteousness "theater, not worship" (H. Betz 1995, 353). **If you should do so, you do not have a reward from your Father in the heavens.**

6:2–4. The first of the four examples focuses on almsgiving (cf. Tob. 4:7–11; 12:8). The structure includes a prohibition plus a basis, followed by a prescription plus a basis.

> Prohibition: **When you do deeds of mercy, do not blow a trumpet before you as the hypocrites do in the synagogues and in the streets so that they may be honored by the observers** (6:2a; Mark 12:41–44 indicates it was possible to observe people's giving; Sir. 31:11b says the assembly proclaimed one's acts of charity).
> Basis: **Truly I say to you, they have been fully compensated** (6:2b).
> Prescription: **When you do your deeds of mercy, do not let your left hand know what your right hand is doing so your almsgiving may be in secret** (6:3–4a).
> Basis: **Your Father who sees in secret will reward you** (6:4b).

Hyperbole is used throughout to ensure awareness.

6:5–6. The second example concerns prayer (6:5–6). The structure is the same as in the previous example.

> Prohibition: **When you pray, do not be as the hypocrites because they love to pray in the synagogues and standing on the corners of the streets so they may be observed by others** (6:5a).
> Basis: **Truly I say to you, they have been fully compensated** (6:5b).
> Prescription: **When you pray, enter into your room, and when you have closed the door, pray to your Father in secret** (6:6a; Dan. 6:11; Philo, *Contempl.* 3.25: the Therapeutae hid themselves away in private rooms).
> Basis: **Your Father who sees in secret will reward you** (6:6b).

Hyperbole is again used to accent the problem.

6:7–15. The third subunit, a second one devoted to prayer, detours from the theme of inward motivation to advocate prayer in line with God's character. The structure is the same as the other three subunits, however.

> Prohibition: **When you are praying, do not babble as the gentiles do, for they think they will be heard because of their many words** (cf. 1 Kings 18:26–29: the prophets of Baal prayed all day). **Do not be like them** (6:7–8a).

> Basis: **Your Father knows what you have need of before you ask him** (6:8b; Ps. 139:3–4; Isa. 65:24).
> Prescription: **You pray like this** (Luke 11:2–4; *Did.* 8.2). **Our Father in the heavens: May your name be reverenced; may your kingdom come; may your will be done, as in heaven so on earth** (6:9–10).

The three "Thou-petitions" (may your . . .) of the prescription are virtual synonyms. They are a prayer for the speedy coming of the eschatological kingdom. Three "us-petitions" follow. **Give to us today our *epiousion*** (either "necessary for life" or "future") **bread** (6:11). Luke 11:3 ("Give us *each day* our daily bread") makes clear that some early Christians understood this to be a petition for God's provision of one's daily nourishment. In Matt. 8:11–12 the eschatological future is imaged as a great banquet. If so, then in the First Gospel the reference could be to the future bread (when the heavenly manna would return). **Forgive us our debts as we have forgiven our debtors** (6:12). Sirach 28:2 ("Forgive your neighbor the wrong he has done, and then your sins will be pardoned when you pray") points to the daily life of disciples in this world. Matthew 18:23–35 seems to speak of an eschatological forgiveness and its link to disciples' forgiveness within history. There may well be both a present and a future reference here (as in the previous petition). **Do not bring us into the time of trial, but deliver us from the evil one** (6:13). Again, this could refer to testing in the present time (26:41) or to the great testing at the end of history (24:4–26). All three of the "us-petitions" seem to contain both an eschatological and a present, existential meaning.

The doxology in 6:13b is missing in early textual witnesses (Sinaiticus, Vaticanus, Bezae, etc.) and is not an original part of the prayer. It was likely added because Jews tend to end their prayers with a doxology (e.g., Pss. 41:13; 72:18; 89:52; 106:48; 150:6; 1 Chron. 16:36; cf. 1 Chron. 29:11). This lengthy prescription (6:9–13) is followed by the typical basis (6:14–15).

> Basis: **For if you forgive others their trespasses, your Father in the heavens will also forgive you. If you do not forgive others, neither will your Father forgive your trespasses** (6:14–15; cf. 18:35).

The Lord's Prayer causes the auditors to *see* what their needs really are, what their petitions should really be—that is, to see prayer differently. As such, in changing their perceptions, it alters their dispositions and intentions. Character is being purified in light of a higher righteousness.

6:16–18. The fourth subunit, on fasting (a common Jewish practice: Dan. 9:3; Mark 2:18; Luke 18:12), returns to the point of the first and second units regarding inward piety. The structure is again the same.

Prohibition: **When you fast, do not be dismal like the hypocrites, for they disfigure their faces so they may show others that they are fasting** (6:16a).

Basis: **Truly I say to you, they have been fully compensated** (6:16b).

Prescription: **When you fast, put oil on your head and wash your face so your fasting may be manifest not to others but to your Father in secret** (6:17–18a).

Basis: **Your Father who sees in secret will reward you** (6:18b).

Again hyperbole plays its role. The point of the first (6:2–4), second (6:5–6), and fourth (6:16–18) subunits of Matt. 6:1–18 is that piety before God is done for God alone and not for oneself, to enhance one's standing before other humans. The language has been very specific and extreme, and it belongs to a pattern. This makes the auditor aware of a tendency that is often concealed but that can be recognized in an extreme form. The auditors are enabled to *see* differently and have their character shaped as a result.

Possessions: Priorities and Trust (6:19–34)

If 5:17–48 and 6:1–18 are clearly defined units of thought in the Sermon, each introduced by a heading (5:17–20 and 6:1), the same is not true for 6:19–34. Yet this subsequent material has its own defining arrangement. Matthew 6:19–34 is composed of two subunits, each introduced by a prohibition: **Do not store up for yourselves treasures on earth** (6:19) and **Do not be anxious** (6:25). Each subunit has three parts. Matthew 6:19–24 breaks into verses 19–21, 22–23, and 24. Matthew 6:25–34 falls into verses 25–30, 31–33, and 34. The first subunit (6:19–24) deals with getting one's priorities straight about possessions. The second (6:25–34) focuses on trusting God to provide for one's needs. Matthew 7:1–12 also falls into two subunits, each introduced by a prohibition: **Do not judge** (7:1) and **Do not give what is holy to dogs** (7:6). Each subunit consists of three parts. Matthew 7:1–5 consists of verses 1, 2, and 3–5. Matthew 7:6–12 consists of verses 6, 7–11, and 12. The former (7:1–5) concentrates on judging as condemnation; the latter (7:6–12) on judging with discernment. Matthew 6:19–7:12, then, consists of two large thought units (6:19–34 and 7:1–12), each organized the same way.

An Outline of Matthew 6:19–34

Possessions: Priorities and trust (6:19–34)

Priorities (6:19–24)

1. Two treasures (6:19–21)
2. Two eyes (6:22–23)
3. Two masters (6:24)

Trusting God (6:25–34)

1. Four reasons not to be anxious (6:25–30)
2. Two reasons, a command, and a promise (6:31–33)
3. Two more reasons not to be anxious (6:34)

6:19–24. This first subunit in the large thought unit 6:19–34 is composed of three logia: (1) the two treasures (6:19–21), (2) the two eyes (6:22–23), and (3) the two masters (6:24).

1. Verse 19 provides the controlling prohibition. **Do not make a habit of storing up as treasure for yourselves treasures on earth. . . . Habitually store up as treasure for yourselves treasures in heaven** (sharing of one's possessions with the needy; 6:19–20a; cf. Tob. 4:8–9; Sir. 29:10–12; *t. Pe'ah* 4.18d: "My ancestors stored up treasures for this lower world, but I, through giving charity, have stored up treasures for the heavenly world above" [trans. Neusner 1981]). Why? **Where your treasure is, there your heart will be also** (6:21). The implied exhortation is to choose properly between the two treasures.

2. The logion of the two eyes comes in 6:22–23. **The eye is the lamp of the body** (6:22a). Here "eye" is used metaphorically for one's disposition toward others (e.g., Deut. 15:9 RSV: "lest . . . your eye be hostile to your poor brother and you give him nothing"; Tob. 4:7; Sir. 14:9–10). **If your eye is sound** (*haplous*), **your whole body will be full of light** (6:22b). In ancient Judaism a sound eye is a generous eye (a generous intent or disposition; e.g., *T. Benj.* 4.2). **If your eye is unsound** (*ponēros*, evil), **your whole body will be full of darkness** (6:23a). In this context, an unsound, evil eye is a stingy spirit (e.g., Deut. 15:9 LXX; Sir. 14:8; Matt. 20:15). If one's eye (ethical perception) becomes clouded by greed, the result is darkness (selfishness) in the whole self (cf. *T. Jud.* 18.2–3, 6). Character is shaped by intent or disposition.

3. Verse 24 contains the logion **No one can serve two masters.** In antiquity, this was recognized as true at the spiritual level (Rom. 6:16; Philo, *Frag.* 2.649 [= 370B]: "It is impossible for love of the world to coexist with the love of God" [trans. Colson 1929–62]). Why? **For the slave will either hate the one and love the other, or be devoted to the one and despise the other. You cannot serve God and mammon** (materialism as a pseudo-god). All three of these sayings concern appropriate relation to one's possessions. They are three ways of saying basically the same thing. "We are asked . . . to turn our backs on the goals and goods of this world, to be the *real* atheists of our culture—denying the gods to whom most give unquestioning fealty" (Bruner 2004, 1:327). *Seeing* the divine will about such matters results in the auditor's character formation as a nongreedy person. Be a person whose priorities are straight about possessions.

6:25–34. This second subsection on possessions deals with trusting God to provide for one's needs. Here food, drink, and clothing are regarded as the necessities for human life. The unit functions not to offer concrete counsels on what to do with wealth but to reassure believers about God's trustworthiness. Rather than being an ethical text with a horizontal focus, 6:25–34 is concerned with the vertical dimension. It consists of three paragraphs, each beginning with "Do not be debilitatingly anxious": (1) four reasons not to be anxious (6:25–30); (2) two reasons, a command, and a promise (6:31–33); and (3) two more reasons not to be anxious (6:34).

1. The first paragraph, 6:25–30, consists of a prohibition and four reasons. *Prohibition* (6:25a): **Do not be debilitatingly anxious** (1 Macc. 6:10; Sir. 42:9) **about your life, what you may eat or what you may drink, or about your body, what you shall wear.** *Four reasons* (6:25b–30): (1) **Is not life more than food and the body than clothing?** (6:25; cf. 4:4). (2) **Observe the birds of the heaven that they neither sow nor reap nor gather into barns, and your heavenly Father takes care of them** (Ps. 147:9). **Are you not more valuable than they are?** (6:26). (3) **Which of you by being anxious is able to add one hour to his lifespan?** (6:27). Anxiety is futile. (4) **Learn from the flowers of the field, how they grow. They do not toil or spin. But I tell you that Solomon in all his glory was not dressed as one of these. Now if God so clothes the grass of the field that is today and tomorrow is cast into an oven, will he not much more clothe you little-faith ones?** (6:28b–30).

2. The second paragraph, 6:31–33, consists of a prohibition and two reasons plus a command and a promise. *Prohibition* (6:31): **Do not be debilitatingly anxious, saying, "What shall we eat, or what shall we drink, or what shall we wear?"** *Reasons* (6:32): (1) **All these things the gentiles are seeking.** (2) **Your heavenly father knows that you have need of all these things** (cf. 6:8). *Command* (6:33a): **Seek first the kingdom and his righteousness.** *Promise* (6:33b): **and all these things will be given to you.** When the ultimate good is acknowledged (God's lordship), then the relative goods (Gen. 1:29) can be received.

3. The third paragraph is very brief (6:34), consisting of a prohibition and two reasons. *Prohibition* (6:34a): **Do not be debilitatingly anxious about tomorrow.** *Reasons* (6:34b–c): (1) **Tomorrow will be anxious for itself.** (2) **Today's trouble is enough for today.** (*Mekilta* on Exod. 16:4: "He who has what he will eat today and says, 'What shall I eat tomorrow?' Behold, this man has little faith" [trans. Lauterbach 1961]).

Matthew 6:25–34 does not simply command. One does not stop worrying or avoid debilitating anxiety by obeying a command to do so. "Our involvement in these structures of care is too deep to be uprooted by a simple command. . . . A change could only take place if we were to *see* the world in a fundamentally new way" (Tannehill 1975, 67). The passage functions as performative language. It sets two structures opposite one another: debilitating anxiety is on one side, and on the other is the world of birds and flowers, in which anxiety is absent yet life goes on. The auditor is challenged to say which is the real world. If the auditor *sees* the deeper reality (God's providential care for created beings), this opens a new possibility of life, and character can be shaped around trust in God's providential goodness. This is the higher righteousness as regards possessions.

Judging: Condemnation and Discernment (7:1–12)

This next major thought unit sets the Matthean Jesus's teaching about the higher righteousness in opposition to Pharisees who are judgmental (e.g., 9:11;

12:2; 15:1–2) while not practicing what they preach (23:2–4). This pericope is composed of two subunits (7:1–5 and 7:6–11), each controlled by an opening prohibition (**Do not judge** [7:1] and **Do not give** [7:6]) and composed of the same three components: what we are not to do (7:1, 6); what God will do (7:2, 7–11), and what we are to do (7:3–5, 12).

7:1–5. This first subunit deals with judging as condemnation of another by one who has not judged himself or herself (so contra severity). *What we are not to do* (7:1): **Do not judge in order that you may not be judged.** *What God will do* (7:2): **With the judgment you judge, you will be judged; and with the measure you measure, it will be measured to you.** *What we are to do* (7:3–5): **Why do you notice the splinter in the eye of your brother but do not recog-**

> ### An Outline of Matthew 7:1–12
>
> **Judging: Condemnation and discernment (7:1–12)**
>
> Against condemnation (7:1–5)
>
> The case for discernment (7:6–12)

nize the log in your eye? How can you say to your brother, "Let me remove the splinter from your eye," when the log is in your eye? Hypocrite, remove first the log from your eye, and then you will see clearly to remove the splinter from the eye of your brother. Reprove yourself first; then you will be able to reprove others (cf. Sir. 18:20; Cicero, *Tusc.* 3.73: "It is a peculiarity of folly to discern the faults of others and to be forgetful of one's own" [trans. King 1945]).

7:6–12. Subunit two deals with judging as discernment necessary for appropriate action (so contra moral laxity). It also consists of three parts. *What we are not to do* (7:6): **Do not give holy things to dogs, and do not cast your pearls before pigs lest they trample them with their feet and turn and attack you.** Do not fail to discern the difference between holy and unclean things, and do not fail to act appropriately (cf. *m. Tem.* 6.5: "Do not give to dogs what is holy," meaning in context that one should use discernment and should not act inappropriately). Verse 6, then, qualifies the prohibition against judging in 7:1–5.

What God will do (7:7–11): God will supply wisdom to enable this discernment. So **ask, seek, knock**—typical language about prayer (cf. Jer. 29:12–14; Isa. 65:1). In context, this is not an affirmation of the efficacy of unrestricted prayer. The language is typical of prayers for wisdom (e.g., Prov. 8:17; Wis. 6:12; James 1:5). Those who ask for wisdom to discern correctly will be heard and given this treasure. After all, God is good and willing to answer prayer.

What we are to do (7:12): **In everything, whatever you want others to do to you, you also do to them. For this is the law and the prophets.** When judging and evaluating, do it in the spirit of the golden rule. (In *Let. Aris.* 207, the king asks, "What is the teaching of wisdom?" The sage answers that it is the golden rule.) In 7:1–12 a grotesque contrast (splinter . . . log) provides a metaphoric shock to the auditor. The extreme picture helps illumine a whole range of situations that we would otherwise miss. The auditor who is enabled to *see* differently

The Golden Rule

This ethical guideline was widespread in antiquity in both positive and negative terms (e.g., Tob. 4:15; *Let. Aris.* 207; Sir. 31:15 LXX; *T. Naph.* 1.6 Heb.; *Ahiqar* 53 Aramaic B; Philo, *Hypoth.* in Eusebius, *Praep. ev.* 8.7.6; *Syr. Men.* 39; *2 En.* 61.1–2; *Avot R. Nat.* 15; Dio Cassius, *Rom. Hist.* 51.34.39; Isocrates, *Nic.* 49, 61; Herodotus, *Hist.* 3.142; Homer, *Od.* 5.188–89; Acts 15:20, 28 in Codex Bezae; *Did.* 1.2). Positive and negative forms of the golden rule are moral equivalents. One is not superior to the other.

can then be a different person. Character formation is in view. Matthew 7:12 echoes 5:17 (law and prophets), providing an inclusio to hold together 5:20–7:12 and its four examples of the higher righteousness (5:21–48; 6:1–18; 6:19–34; 7:1–12).

Warnings of Catastrophe (7:13–27)

Matthew 7:13–8:1 is comprised of two parts: 7:13–27 and 7:28–8:1. The former falls into an ABB′A′ pattern. A and A′ focus on everyone; B and B′ concentrate on false prophets. All of the material is related to the expectation of the end and the prospect of judgment. The warning of catastrophe predominates.

(A) **7:13–14.** In section A, the auditor is confronted by the two gates, the two roads, and the two destinations. A preferred choice is encouraged. **Enter in through the narrow gate. . . . Narrow is the gate and hard is the road that leads to life. Few there are who find it** (Sir. 21:10; Philo, *Spec.* 4.112). In the First Gospel, this way has already been spelled out: "Follow me" (4:18–22).

An Outline of Matthew 7:13–27

Warnings of catastrophe (7:13–27)

(A) Exhortation: The narrow gate (7:13–14)

(B) False prophets: Wolves and bad trees (7:15–20)

(B′) False prophets: "Lord, Lord" (7:21–23)

(A′) Exhortation: House on a rock (7:24–27)

(B) **7:15–20.** Section B lays out the criterion for recognizing a false prophet. **From their fruits you will recognize them** (7:16a); **from their fruits you will recognize them** (7:20). This inclusio makes the criterion clear. The nature and destiny of a tree are revealed by its fruit.

(B′) **7:21–23.** Section B′ focuses on a false prophet's destiny. The scene is the last judgment, with Jesus as judge. The criterion is specified. **Not everyone who says to me, "Lord, Lord," will enter into the kingdom of the heavens, but the one who does the will of my Father in the heavens** (cf. 12:50). **Many will say to me on that day, "Lord, Lord, did we not prophesy in your name, and in your name we cast out demons, and in your name we did many miracles?" And then I will confess to them, "I never knew you. Depart from me, workers of lawlessness."** Again the same note is sounded. One's ultimate destiny is tied to hearing and doing Jesus's words (cf. 28:19–20).

True and False Prophets

Early Christians employed a variety of tests to distinguish between true and false prophets. In 1 Cor. 12:3, false prophets do not confess Jesus as Lord. In 1 John 4:2, false prophets do not confess that Jesus came and remained in the flesh. In Matt. 24:24–27, false prophets do not view the parousia as a cosmic event. In 2 Pet. 2, false prophets have false doctrine and libertine ethics. *Didache* 11.10 says false prophets do not do the truth they teach, and in 11.5 they ask for money. According to Herm. *Mand.* 11.12–13, false prophets do not go to church, and they take money. In Ps.-Clem., *Homilies* 2.10, only those whose prophecies come to pass are said to be true prophets. There were behavioral and doctrinal tests. Matthew 7:16, 20 falls into the camp of those who test behavior by its ethical fruit.

(A') **7:24–27.** Section A' consists of a parable about the two houses that includes a promise (7:24–25) and a warning (7:26–27). The stress is on the fate of the two houses. Will they be standing when the storm is over? *Promise* (7:24–25): **Everyone who hears these words and does them will be like a wise man who built his house on the rock. The rain descended and the floods came and the winds blew and beat on that house, and it did not fall, for it had been founded on the rock.** The Palestinian house had no foundations as such. Its stability depended on the soil on which it was built. Hearing and doing Jesus's teaching is the proper foundation for those who stand before God at the judgment. *Warning* (7:26–27): **Everyone who hears these words and does not do them will be like a foolish man who built his house on the sand. The rain descended and the floods came and the winds blew and beat on that house, and it fell—and the collapse was great.** The sermon has provided guidance about the higher righteousness that enables entrance into the kingdom of heaven (5:20). To fail to hear and do leads to disaster at the last judgment. The sermon ends with its auditors being confronted by these two possibilities.

Conclusion: Effects of Jesus's Teaching (7:28–8:1)

This final segment of the Sermon on the Mount forms an inclusio with 4:32–5:2. This conclusion indicates that the evangelist understood the sermon as teaching (7:28) and that the crowds perceived Jesus's teaching as different in style from that of the scribes (7:29—**He was teaching them as having authority, and not as their scribes**). In the scribal culture, authority resided in the past, in one's teacher and his teacher and his teacher. One appealed to those who had come before. A rabbinic text illustrates the issue. In *b. B. Metzi'a* 58b–59a, set during the second generation of Tannaim (AD 90–130), a debate between R. Eliezer and R. Joshua was resolved against Eliezer. This was done in spite of miracles supporting R. Eliezer's position (the uprooting of a carob tree and its relocation; water flowing uphill; and a *bath qol* [heavenly voice]) because the Torah had already been given on Sinai. That is, authority did not reside in spiritual power in the present but in the established tradition from the past. In *y. Pesah.* 6.1.33a, a similar tradition is found. The great teacher Hillel had discoursed on a matter all day, but the other rabbis did not receive his teaching until he said: "Thus I heard it from Shemaiah and Abtalion." Again, it is the succession of tradition from the past that settles an issue. By contrast the Matthean Jesus is said to have taught with authority (out of himself), with no appeal to a chain of tradition (e.g., you have heard that it was said to the ancestors, but I say). The difference in style was striking to the auditors and functioned as a catalyst for the character formation of the disciples who heard Jesus.

Table 7
Parallels between Matthew 4:23–5:2 and 7:28–8:1

4:23–5:2	7:28–8:1
great crowds followed (4:25)	great crowds followed him (8:1)
the crowds are present (5:1)	the crowds are present (7:28)
the mountain (5:1)	the mountain (8:1)
Jesus goes up (5:1)	Jesus comes down (8:1)
Jesus teaches (5:2)	Jesus's teaching (7:29)
opening his mouth (5:2)	when Jesus finished speaking (7:28)

Functions of the Unit as a Whole

In listing the elements of confirmation in an oration, Cicero includes several attributes of a person that might be used to persuade an audience. One of those was "speeches made" (*Inv.* 1.24.34). Powerful speakers were highly regarded in all of Mediterranean culture. By presenting Jesus as such a speaker in Matt. 5–7 (and elsewhere throughout the Gospel), the evangelist is praising him and using Jesus's rhetorical power to persuade the auditors. Quintilian (*Inst.* 3.7.15) says that in collecting material to praise a person, one component would be that person's words. Being a forceful speaker who addresses right behavior in society falls under deeds of prudence and wisdom. This fits Aelius Theon's category of "mind and character" as one of the three categories used to construct an encomium (*Progym.* 8.109–12). The encomiastic character of Matthew's depiction of Jesus continues (Neyrey 1998).

Theological Issues

Is it with ethics that the Sermon on the Mount is concerned? (see Talbert 2004a for what follows). To ask this question is to evoke a nearly unanimous response: Yes, of course. Consider a recent claim by a leading NT scholar.

The Sermon on the Mount is a "call to Christian ethics." Its aim is the morality of the individual (Hagner 1997, 45, 53). This assertion is no innovation. It is representative. Virtually all secondary literature on the Sermon on the Mount assumes that Matt. 5–7 is an ethical text, aiming to provide guidance for decision making. Is this assumption appropriate? Is the sermon's primary aim to provide guidance for ethical decision making? This is an incorrect assessment for two reasons.

First, note that "there is not just ethical instruction in the Sermon but instruction in worship and prayer" as well (Riches 1996, 68). Matthew 5–7 is concerned with the vertical (Matt. 5:3, 4, 5, 6; 5:33; 6:1–18; 6:24; 6:33; 7:7–11) as well as the horizontal (e.g., Matt. 5:21–26; 5:27–30; 5:38–42; etc.) relations of life. In this the Sermon on the Mount is like biblical law (vertical: Exod. 20:3, 4–6, 7; horizontal: Exod. 20:13–17), prophecy (vertical: Jer. 4:1–2; Hosea 14:1–8; horizontal: Hosea 4:1–3; Amos 6:4–7), and wisdom (vertical: Prov. 3:11–12; 3:9–10; horizontal: Prov. 15:1; 16:32) that also address both vertical and horizontal dimensions of life. The teaching of the sermon—like that of biblical law, prophecy, and wisdom—cannot be reduced to ethics (the horizontal). In all these streams of biblical material, the ethical is but one dimension of the larger concern for "covenant faithfulness," which includes the vertical. The Sermon on the Mount contains material focused on piety as well as that concerned with ethical behavior. Is it with ethics that the Sermon on the Mount is concerned? Yes and no. Yes, the sermon is concerned with ethics. No, that is not all with which it is concerned.

Second, as already suggested above, the Sermon on the Mount functions primarily as a *catalyst* for the formation of identity or character. Only in a secondary way can it serve as a *contributor* to the task of decision making. The ethical material contained in the Sermon is directed not in the first instance to decision making but rather to the formation of moral character, just as the material focused on the vertical dimension is aimed at the formation of character in one's relation with God. There is a need to clarify these categories before proceeding further.

What exactly is meant by decision making? Suppose a person is confronted with a problem and must make a decision about the right thing to do under the circumstances. The question arises: is there a norm, a principle, a rule, a law that will inform the decision? If the Sermon on the Mount is designed to assist in decision making, it will provide norms, rules, laws to guide a person's decision about the right thing to do in this or that circumstance. Dilemma-based ethics, then, are reactive.

What exactly is meant by character formation? Character and identity may be regarded as interchangeable terms. The chief elements in character or identity are perceptions (how one sees things), dispositions (persisting attitudes that flow from the overarching orientation or vision), and intentions (deliberately chosen or self-conscious activity, motivation). If the Sermon on the Mount is designed for character formation, it will facilitate a new way of seeing life (seeing the world with eyes that are Christlike), issuing in new dispositions and intentions/motivations toward life. Character ethics, then, are proactive.

There are, therefore, two questions to distinguish. First, what is a disciple of Jesus to *be* (virtue ethics)? Second, what is a disciple of Jesus to *do* (dilemma-based ethics)? The first is a question of character or identity; the second is a question of decision making to enable proper action. The First Evangelist reflects this distinction between being and doing. Matthew distinguishes between tree and fruit (7:16–18; 12:33), heart and mouth (12:34; 15:18–19), being and speaking (12:34), and person and things (12:35). These distinctions are what we would refer to as character or identity on the one side and behavior or actions on the other. In Matt. 5:14–16 the distinction is expressed as "You are the light of the world" (character/identity) and "Let your light shine" (behavior/actions)—that is, act in accordance with your nature; let your actions reflect your character. In light of this distinction between *being* and *doing*, let me repeat my contention. The Sermon on the Mount functions primarily as a *catalyst* to enable an auditor to become a person whose identity or character is appropriate to one who follows Jesus. Only secondarily does the Sermon function as a *contributor* to the task of decision making that is appropriate to a disciple of Jesus.

The Sermon on the Mount as a Catalyst for Character Formation

The contention of this commentary, as seen in the previous section, is that the Sermon on the Mount is aimed at character formation rather than decision making. Its primary concern is with the kind of person the decision maker is.

An objection must be faced from the first. Does not the very *form* of much of the material in the Sermon on the Mount raise questions about the contention that the sermon's *content* is focused on character formation? True, the beatitudes seem directed, in some respects, to character: for example, poor in spirit, merciful, pure in heart. But in most places in the Sermon on the Mount, attention is directed, on first glance at least, not to being but to doing: for example, insulting a brother, looking lustfully, divorcing a wife, swearing, retaliating, hating enemies, judging others before having judged oneself. Does not the focus on doing mean that the Sermon aims to provide guidance for ethical decision making? Both Robert C. Tannehill (1975, 67–77) and John Dominic Crossan (1975) have addressed this issue. Both contend that the material is not to be taken as casuistic law. Tannehill's alternative category is "focal instance"; Crossan's is "case law parody." Both rightly sense that in spite of the Sermon on the Mount's apparent focus on actions, the language functions very differently. Furthermore, a consideration of Mediterranean ways of thinking about acting and being deflects the claim that the Sermon's focus is on decision making.

By recognizing that the Sermon on the Mount comes from a culture that thinks in terms of actions and assumes that one's character is produced by and is a reflection of what one repeatedly does, one may properly appreciate the texts in the sermon that seem to be focused on actions. For example, 1 John 3:7–8a says: "The one who habitually does right is righteous. . . . The one who habitually does sin is of the devil" (author's trans.). If so, then the language of doing does not, of necessity, exclude a focus on character. This mind-set is reflected in Matt. 6:19–21. In this logion an action is prohibited (do not continually act greedily, 6:19); an action is commanded (continually act generously, 6:20); the command and prohibition are issued because how one acts will determine one's character (6:21). One's character is determined by and reflects what one habitually does. The Sermon on the Mount shares the general cultural assumptions about the relations between actions and character. A focus on actions, then, does not detract from the sermon's emphasis on character. Ultimately, examination of specific texts shows that the focus on actions leads to a concern for character formation at both the horizontal and vertical levels.

The horizontal: Ethics as character formation. Two examples show how the Sermon on the Mount's ethical material is oriented to character formation.

The first, Matt. 5:38–42, offers a series of four examples that advocate nonretaliation. (1) "If anyone strikes you on the right cheek, turn the other also." (2) "If anyone wants to sue you and take your inner garment, give your outer garment as well." (3) "If anyone forces you to go one mile, go also the second mile." (4) "Do not refuse anyone who wants to borrow from you" (even if that one has refused you earlier). The examples are specific and extreme. How often is one struck on the right cheek? If the advice of the second one is followed, the disciple will be left standing in court naked. They reverse our natural tendency; they are the opposite of what we normally do. They appear in a series, which establishes a pattern that can be extended to other instances. It is open-ended. Much more is at stake, therefore, than behavior in the situations explicitly mentioned. The series suggests an alternative to what we normally do. Verse 39 offers it: "Do not retaliate against an evildoer." The pericope causes the auditor to *see* life in a new way: nonretaliation. The effect, then, is to enable the auditor to see nonretaliation as the pattern for relating, to be disposed toward nonretaliation, and to intend nonretaliation. If so, then this text would be aiming at the formation of character.

Is not this statement, "Do not retaliate against an evildoer," rather a norm or rule or law to cover a general area of human behavior? Is not this the obvious reading? No. To take it as a norm/rule/law providing guidance for decision making would contradict the Matthean Jesus's priorities. How? Jesus in Matthew sets love (22:37–40) and mercy (12:7) and the golden rule (7:12) at the center of God's intention for human behavior. All of Scripture must be read in this light (22:40; 7:12); all of Jesus's teachings must be heard in these terms. If "do not retaliate" is taken as a general rule, however, when the neighbor is violated by another, the disciple will be obligated to abstain from defending, protecting, or vindicating the neighbor because of obedience to the rule. In so acting, the disciple will sacrifice the love of the neighbor to the rule "do not retaliate against evil." This contradicts the Matthean Jesus's stated priorities. Assuming that the Matthean Jesus's teaching represents a rationally coherent stance, "do not retaliate against evil" cannot be taken as a general rule for an area of life. If, however, it is a provocation that arouses the hearers' moral imagination so that they are enabled to *see* their situation in a new way with a resultant change of disposition and intention, it is a catalyst to create a nonretaliatory character. If so, then the hierarchy of values making up the selfhood of the disciple incorporates both love of neighbor and nonretaliation against evildoers, with the former being more basic. If so, then when confronted by an evildoer, the disciple with such a character will likely retaliate if necessary to defend, protect, and vindicate the neighbor.

Variations on the Good Samaritan story illustrate the two options. Suppose on the one hand the Good Samaritan had come upon robbers attacking a fellow traveler on the road to Jericho, and he had earlier heard Jesus's words, "Do not retaliate against an evildoer," and had taken them as a norm/rule/law. Then he would likely have waited until the attack was over, the robbers were gone, and made his way to the victim, binding up his wounds with oil and wine, setting him on his animal, and taking him to the inn to provide care for him. The Samaritan would have thereby satisfied the two commands: do not retaliate, and love the neighbor, in that order. Judged by the Matthean Jesus's value system, however, he would have acted improperly because love of the neighbor was not central to his behavior. If on the other hand the Good Samaritan, with a character shaped by the Matthean Jesus's priorities, had come along when robbers were attacking someone on the road to Jericho, he likely would have taken his staff, cuffed the robbers about their ears, and driven them off, and then gone to the man with oil and wine, binding up his wounds before setting him on his donkey to go to the inn to take care of him. In so doing, he would have made his ethical decision out of a character that gave priority to mercy and love for the neighbor. He remained a nonretaliatory person, but he was a loving person above all.

The second example, Matt. 5:33–37, is spoken in a culture in which oaths were widely used, ostensibly to guarantee the truthfulness of what was said. Distinctions came to be made, however, between oaths that were binding and those that were not. For example, if people swore "by heaven and earth," they were not bound (*m. Shevu.* 4.13); if they swore "by Jerusalem," it was not binding (*m. Ned.* 1.3); if they swore "by one's head," they were not bound (*m. Sanh.* 3.2). In this context, oaths were used to conceal dishonesty. As Philo put it, "From much swearing springs false swearing" (*Decal*. 92). The Matthean Jesus says the intent of Scripture (do not swear falsely: Lev. 19:12; cf. Deut. 6:13; perform what you have sworn: Ps. 50:14b; Deut. 23:21, 23; Num. 30:2) is truthfulness in relations among humans and with God. Sweeping aside the non-binding oaths, he says simply: "Do not swear at all" (5:34). Instead of looking for loopholes in the demand for truthfulness, act in line with God's intention. "Let what you say be simply 'Yes' or 'No'" (5:37). Be truthful! The pericope functions as a lens to enable a new way of *seeing* human communications: in terms of honesty. From this perception flow a disposition to tell the truth and the intent to be truthful, not deceptive. Character is being formed.

Should not this teaching rather be understood as a general rule: always tell the truth? Does not this seem the obvious way to read it? No. To do so would once again contradict the primacy of love and mercy in the Matthean Jesus's teaching. This is best grasped from an illustration. The example comes from a story told to me in my youth that may have had its origins in Hilary of Poitiers (*Hom. Ps.* 10). Suppose you were in your house and heard a frantic knocking on your door. You opened it to find a young woman, blood-smeared, eyes wild with fright, who said: "Let me in, hide me; I am being chased by a maniac who wants to kill me." You hurriedly let her in and motion her to the back room where she can hide. Then there is more pounding on your door. You open it and see a wild-eyed man, breathing heavily, with a huge knife in his hand. He asks, "Did you see a young woman run this way?" Now the question is, Is Jesus's disciple obligated to tell the truth regardless of the circumstances? If the pericope is understood as setting forth a rule or law to govern human decision making, then the answer is yes. If, however, the text aims at character formation and if the disciple acts out of a hierarchy of values in which what is central to Jesus's teaching (love and mercy) is primary, then no. The disciple replies, "Why, no, I have not seen any such person," then closes and locks the door. One cannot take 5:33–37 as a general rule without violating the coherence of the Matthean Jesus's teaching. If, however, the pericope is understood to provide a new way of seeing human communication, it functions as a catalyst enabling one to be a truthful person. Then the problem is solved. A truthful person does not always tell the truth no matter what the circumstances. Sometimes love and mercy trump truthfulness. The unit, then, is designed to form the character of the disciple to be a truthful person.

These two examples show clearly how the ethical material in the Sermon on the Mount does not function adequately as norms, rules, laws to be used in decision making. Rather, the contents that address the horizontal level function to provoke the auditor into a new way of seeing life, a way of perceiving that will change dispositions and intentions.

The vertical: Piety as character formation. Two further examples show how the material in the Sermon on the Mount that is focused on the vertical relation is also directed to the formation of character.

The first, Matt. 6:2–4, 5–6, 16–18, offers three specific examples of how to relate to God properly in the areas of almsgiving, prayer, and fasting. The specific cases are extreme (sounding a trumpet as one contributes, praying on street corners, disfiguring one's face when fasting). They are part of a series that establishes a pattern causing the auditor to see beyond these three specific instances. The series is open-ended. In each case the emphasis is on the worshiper's motivation in performing these acts of piety. A different kind of person is called for. That the evangelist intended the admonitions about these three acts to be something more than case law may also be seen from the introduction to the series (6:1): "Beware of practicing your righteousness [covenant faithfulness] before others in order to be seen by them; for then you have no reward from your Father in heaven" (cf. 23:5–7, 28). A consequential-ist argument is used to enable the reader to *see* an orientation toward God in which a person relates to God for God's sake and not merely to enhance one's status among other humans. The unit introduces the auditor into an alternative world of relating to God.

Should not the injunction in 6:1 be taken rather as a rule that one's piety be kept private? No. To take it this way would violate other teachings of the Matthean Jesus. In 5:16 Jesus exhorts his disciples: "Let your light so shine before others that they may see your good works and glorify your Father who is in heaven." Matthew 10:32–33 has Jesus say that one's ultimate destiny depends upon acknowledging him publicly. It is clear that the Matthean Jesus does not advocate a "private piety" in texts such as these. Again, assuming a rational coherence for the teaching of the Matthean Jesus, 6:1–18 cannot be understood as a rule that one's piety be kept private. If understood as the formation of character in a way that relates to God for himself, not for the status it gives one among other humans, however, 6:1–18 makes sense.

The second example that focuses on the vertical dimension requires some justification for its being so classified. Matthew 6:25–34 has sometimes been read as an ethical text. Live like the birds and flowers! Make no provision for the future. To do so, however, would lead to the divestment of one's savings, retirement plans, and insurance policies. This is a misreading. "The image [of the birds] is meant to evoke an awareness of God's pervasive care and provision, not to give encouragement to be as careless as the ravens" (Nolland 1993, 692). Rather than being an ethical text with a horizontal focus, 6:25–34's focus is on the vertical dimension. The threefold "do not be debilitatingly anxious" (6:25, 31, 34) involves one in an alternative world of birds and flowers, where anxiety is absent, and it activates one's imagination so that one can begin to *see* self and world from a new perspective. It does not simply command but also seeks to make possible what it commands, shaping the character of the auditor. It functions to facilitate being a person who trusts God's providential care.

Should not this material rather be read as a rule prohibiting anxiety or worry? Note the threefold repetition of "Do not be anxious." If it is so understood, its message is futile. One does not stop worrying or being anxious by obeying a command. Indeed, such a command would further complicate the situation. From my youth I remember a ditty that makes the point.

> I've joined the new "don't worry club,"
> In fear I hold my breath,
> I'm so afraid I'll worry,
> I'm worried half to death.

It takes more than a rule or law to deal with human anxiety. Only divine enablement makes trust in God possible. That is how Matt. 6:25–34 functions: as a catalyst enabling trust in God's providence.

The argument so far shows, first, that the Sermon on the Mount is not to be reduced to ethics (horizontal relationships) and, second, that the ethical material in the Sermon is not to be restricted to a decision-making function. Rather, the material with a horizontal focus, just as the texts with a vertical orientation, is aimed at the formation of character, a character of covenant faithfulness. This is what is properly called spiritual formation. Such a conclusion, however, inevitably raises a further question: can the Sermon on the Mount be used at all in decision making?

The Sermon on the Mount's Contribution to Decision Making

The Sermon on the Mount can also contribute to decision making, but in order for it to do so, the interpreter must take a further step. One must read in context. To read in context means (1) in the context of the whole Gospel of Matthew, (2) in the context of the whole of the NT, and sometimes (3) in the context of the entire biblical plot. Examples are in order both for texts that deal with the horizontal relationships and for those that focus on the vertical dimension. Because of the previous analysis, some repetition may be expected.

The horizontal: Ethics and decision making. We begin with Matt. 5:38–42, a text aiming to shape a disciple's character in the direction of nonretaliation. The question for decision making raised by this text is, If one is a nonretaliatory person, does this mean one never resists evil people? Let us read in context. (1) In the context of Matthew as a whole, Matt. 22:36–40 gives the commandments to love God and to love the neighbor the highest priority, alongside the golden rule (7:12) and mercy (12:7). Matthew 5:39 must be read in connection with these texts. Love of the neighbor may demand retaliation against an evildoer. (2) In the context of the NT as a whole, Rom. 12:17, 19; 1 Thess. 5:15; and 1 Pet. 3:9 speak on behalf of nonretaliation. Romans 13:1–7, however, relegates vengeance against and retaliation for evildoing to the state in this present evil age. Matthew 5:39 must be read in connection with Rom. 13:1–7. (3) In the context of the Bible as a whole, Lev. 19:18 and

Prov. 20:22 speak against vengeance and for leaving it to God. Psalm 72:1–2 is representative when it assumes that the king judges evildoers and vindicates the vulnerable. In light of these three contexts, one may say (a) that there may be occasions when the love of the neighbor trumps one's commitment to nonretaliation, and (b) that a Christian who works for the state may find it necessary to retaliate/resist in his or her role. Being a nonretaliatory person does not relieve one of the responsibility to defend the neighbor and does not negate the state's role as bearer of the sword. At this point, Matt. 5:38–42 is ready to make a contribution to ethical decision making.

Next we turn to Matt. 5:33–37, a call for Jesus's disciple to be a truthful person, given in the form of a prohibition of oaths. The question raised by this text for ethical decision making is, Does being a truthful person mean that one always tells the truth no matter what the circumstances? Let us read in context. (1) In the context of Matthew as a whole, in 7:12; 12:7; 22:36–40 the Matthean Jesus sets up the golden rule, mercy, and love as primary values. In the First Gospel, Jesus follows "a generally accepted juridical axiom: that fundamental law takes precedence over all other law; that each individual statute and paragraph must give expression to the demand and spirit of that fundamental law" (Gerhardsson 1981, 41). According to Matthew, Jesus has adopted this principle and carried it out in a radical way. Everything is seen in light of the golden rule, mercy, and love. If so, then the call to be a truthful person is conditioned by mercy and love of the neighbor. This perspective comes from reading 5:33–37 in the context of the entire First Gospel. (2) In the context of the NT as a whole, God does not lie (Titus 1:2; Heb. 6:18), though the devil does (John 8:44); Christians are exhorted to speak the truth to their neighbors (Eph. 4:25); Christians are not to lie to God (Acts 5:4). In the NT, however, Matt. 26:64a//Luke 22:70b; Luke 23:3; and John 18:37a show Jesus, while on trial, being evasive in his answers to questions from the authorities. This was a mainline Jewish value. When facing possible death at the hands of the authorities, one is not obligated to speak the absolute truth; one may be evasive (Daube 1972, 112–14). To do otherwise is to manifest a lust for martyrdom. Such a lust for death was frowned upon by pagans (Seneca the Younger, *Ep.* 24.25), the rabbis (*Gen. Rab.* 82), and early Christians (*Mart. Pol.* 4) alike. From the NT at large, the example of Jesus conditions the call for truthfulness in a certain context. A reading of Matt. 5:33–37 in the context of the First Gospel and in the context of the NT leads to the conclusion that truthfulness in every situation is not an ethical imperative for Jesus's disciples. Other priorities may sometimes overrule the demand for honesty. (3) In the context of the Bible as a whole, specifically the OT, God's people are exhorted not to lie in court (Prov. 6:19; Isa. 59:3–4), to a neighbor/one another (Lev. 6:2–3), or to God (Ps. 78:36). Nevertheless, the obligation to speak the truth may be qualified by the need to protect someone's life (Exod. 1:19; Josh. 2:4–6;

1 Sam. 16:2–3; 2 Sam. 17:14, 20; Jer. 38:27). Again, truthfulness is sometimes subordinated to other values.

From this reading of Matt. 5:33–37 in context, one concludes: (1) truthfulness is a value because it is fundamental to the establishment and continuance of relationships; lying is a vice because it undermines relationships, but (2) truthfulness is not an absolute/fundamental value; love and mercy are more basic because they are more basic to maintaining relationships. At this point one is ready to use Matt. 5:33–37 properly in decision making.

The vertical: Piety and decision making. Turning now to two texts with a focus on the vertical relationship, we look first at Matt. 6:2–4, 5–6, 16–18; the aim of these verses is to shape persons whose piety before God is done for God alone and not for themselves, to enhance their standing before other humans. The question this text raises for decision making is, Must Christian piety be totally private and never public? Let us read in terms of three contexts. (1) In the context of Matthew as a whole, Matt. 5:16 encourages Jesus's disciples to let their light shine before others so that the others may see the disciples' good works. Matthew 10:32–33 calls for disciples' public acknowledgment of Jesus. Matthew 11:25–27 shows Jesus praying before his disciples. (2) In the context of the NT as a whole, Luke 11:1 has Jesus pray before his disciples. First Thessalonians 1:8 says the recipients' faith is spread abroad. In 2 Cor. 9:2, the recipients' zeal has stirred up many others. Colossians 4:5–6 calls the readers to conduct themselves wisely before outsiders, making the most of the time. First Peter 2:12 likewise calls the readers to conduct themselves honorably among the gentiles, so that, though they malign you as evildoers, they may see your honorable deeds and glorify God. (3) In the context of the Bible as a whole, in Gen. 41 Joseph's actions are witnessed by Pharaoh; in Dan. 6:11, Daniel is seen at his prayers by his enemies. The conclusion reached is inevitable. The aim of Matt. 6:2–4, 5–6, 16–18 is not the privatization of piety but the purification of motive in relating to God. Piety may be public, but when it is, it should be for God's sake.

We turn now to Matt. 6:25–34. Does this passage encourage idleness? Is there a difference between not being anxious and being irresponsible? Reading 6:25–34 in three contexts enables one to understand how it should be used in a disciple's decision making. (1) In the context of Matthew as a whole, Matt. 25:14–30, the parable of the talents, encourages both work and forethought. (2) In the context of the NT as a whole, on the one hand, the NT encourages work: in Acts 20:34–35, Paul works with his own hands; Eph. 4:28 admonishes Christians to work honestly with their own hands; 1 Thess. 5:14 says to warn the idlers; 2 Thess. 3:6–13 commands the believers to keep away from other believers who are living in idleness. On the other hand, the NT encourages forethought: Luke 14:28–32 says one should count the cost of an action; 2 Cor. 12:14 says parents ought to lay up for their children; 1 Tim. 5:8, 16 says whoever does not provide for family members is worse than an unbeliever.

(3) In the context of the biblical plot as a whole, on the one hand, passages like Prov. 6:6 ("Go to the ant, you lazybones; consider its ways, and be wise") encourage work. On the other hand, passages like Gen. 50:20–21 ("I myself will provide for you and your little ones," v. 21a) speak of forethought and its advantages. Reading Matt. 6:25–34 in these three contexts leads to a dual conclusion. First, there is a difference between being anxious and being idle. To trust God's goodness does not relieve one of the responsibility to work. Second, there is a difference between being anxious and being irresponsible. To trust God's goodness does not relieve one of the responsibility to provide for others in one's care (parents, children, family). At this point, one is ready to use 6:25–34 in decision making.

Conclusion

This discussion began with the thesis that the Sermon on the Mount functions first of all as a catalyst for the formation of character/identity but that it can contribute to a disciple's decision making if read in context. By this point, hopefully enough evidence has been provided to enable the reader's assent to the legitimacy of this thesis. Is it with ethics that the Sermon on the Mount is concerned? Yes and no. Yes, the Sermon contains material that must be considered ethical. No, the Sermon cannot be reduced to ethics. It is concerned with piety as well. Furthermore, both the material with an ethical focus and that devoted to piety aim first of all at the shaping of character. Only after being read in the contexts of Matthew, the NT, and the Bible can either type of material be used in Christian decision making.

PART 2

Matthew 8:2–11:1

Jesus's Authority Is Revealed

After the first major cycle (3:1–8:1), the next major grouping of material in Matthew is found in 8:2–11:1. It also consists of a narrative (8:2–9:34) and a discourse (9:35–11:1). The two parts are held together by the thematic link of Jesus's authority. In the narrative, it is demonstrated by his deeds, and at the beginning of the discourse it is imparted to his disciples.

Matthew 8:2–11:1 in Context

Birth narratives (1:1–2:23)

Jesus's ministry begins (3:1–8:1)

▶ **Jesus's authority is revealed (8:2–11:1)**

Narrative: Jesus's authority is manifest in his mission (8:2–9:34)

Discourse: Jesus's authority enables disciples' mission (9:35–11:1)

Jesus's ministry creates division (11:2–13:53)

Jesus focuses on his disciples (13:54–19:2)

Jesus and judgment (19:3–26:1a)

Passion and resurrection narrative (26:1b–28:20)

Matthew 8:2–9:34

Narrative 2:
Jesus's Authority Is Manifest in His Mission

Introductory Matters

The narrative (8:2–9:34) contains a core of miracle stories, ten in number. They are supplemented by a summary of miracle activity (8:16–17), material about following Jesus (8:19–20, 21–22; 9:9), reactions to Jesus's healings (wonder: 8:27; 9:26, 33b; hostility: 8:34; 9:34), and a series of connecting links (8:1, 5, 14a, 23, 28; 9:9a, 10a, 14a, 18a, 27a, 32a).

The Relation of Matthew 8–9 to 5–7

Several introductory matters need attention. First, what is the relation of chapters 8–9 to chapters 5–7? W. Grundmann (1971, 110), followed by many others, argues that Matt. 5–7 and Matt. 8–9 are linked. This is shown by the compositional frame created by the summaries in 4:23 ("And he went around in all of Galilee teaching in their synagogues and preaching the gospel of the kingdom and healing every illness and every malady among the people") and 9:35 ("And Jesus went around all the cities and villages, teaching in their synagogues and preaching the gospel of the kingdom and healing every illness and every malady"). Matthew 4:23 acts as an introduction, and 9:35 rounds up the whole unit. The Sermon on the Mount he labels "The works of Jesus through his word" and the miracle cycle "The works of Jesus through his deeds." If, as has been contended, the First Gospel is built around five big discourses, each of which ends with a common refrain ("and when Jesus had finished") and each of which is preceded by a narrative section linked with the discourse thematically, then 4:23 and 9:35 are signals of the ends of the narrative sections and the beginnings of the discourse sections and not an inclusio holding 5–7 and 8–9 together. In this commentary they will be so understood.

The Significance of Ten Miracles in Matthew 8–9

A second question has to do with the number of mighty deeds found in Matt. 8–9. Why are there ten? Eric Klostermann (1927, 72) contends that in Matt. 8–9 Jesus's ten miracles alludes to the ten wonders Moses worked in connection with the exodus (Exod. 7–12). It was a Jewish conviction that "ten wonders were done for our forefathers in Egypt" (*m. Avot* 5.5). As Micah looked forward to a new exodus after the exile, he could say, "As in the days when you came out of the land of Egypt I will show them marvelous things" (7:15 RSV). Some early Christians applied such a hope to Jesus's ministry. The Pseudo-Clementine *Recognitions* 1.57 says, "As Moses did signs and miracles, so also did Jesus. And there is no doubt but that the likeness of the signs proves him [Jesus] to be that prophet of whom he [Moses] said that he should come 'like myself'" (cf. *ANF* 8:92). Given this context and given the Mosaic typology that pervades the First Gospel, it is surprising that there have been reservations about this matter. One critique is that Matt. 8–9 consists of three triads, not ten separate miracle stories. There are indeed ten miracle stories; structurally, however, one is sandwiched within another. Moreover, Philo (*Mos.* 1.97–139) discusses the plagues in Exod. 7–12 in terms of three triads. Of course, the nature of these miracles is different, but that is due to the context that controls the parts. This commentary, therefore, sees Matt. 8–9 as a fulfillment of hopes expressed in the prophecy of Mic. 7:15 that as in the days of the exodus, they would see marvelous things.

The Arrangement of Matthew 8–9

A third introductory matter concerns the arrangement of the two chapters. The structural suggestions are legion. For example, are chapters 8–9 arranged into two groups of five miracles each (Fenton 1978, 119–20), or by the things expected in the messianic times according to Isa. 35 (Albright and Mann 1971), or around OT liturgical readings (Goulder 1974, 325–26), or parallel to the order of the Sermon on the Mount (Moiser 1985), or in terms of four segments with each having a distinctive theme (W. Thompson 1971; Burger 1973), or as a chiasm: A (8:1–17), B (8:18–9:17), A' (9:18–34; Garland 2001, 92–93), or in terms of triads (Davies and Allison 1991, 2:3–4)? The last suggestion seems to have the largest following. Within this camp, however, there are variations depending on what is done with 8:18–22 and 9:9, 10–13, 14–17 (e.g., Wainwright 2001, 82; Vledder 1997, 172–73). The suggestion offered here is that there are three subunits: 8:2–17; 8:18–9:17; and 9:18–34 (Garland

2001, 92). The contribution that this attempt makes may be seen in its treatment of 8:18–22 and 9:9–17.

Tracing the Narrative Flow

The first triad shown in the accompanying outline—three miracles plus a summary—begins with the healing of a leper outside Capernaum, continues with the healing of a paralytic after Jesus enters Capernaum, then the healing of Peter's mother-in-law's fever, plus many other healings. In 8:17 the quotation from Isa. 53:4 interprets what has come before.

The second triad consists of three miracles, preceded by two episodes about disciples and followed by a call story and two conflict stories. Matthew 8:18–22 and 9:9–17 constitute an inclusio around the three miracles. The opening frame, 8:18–22, gives two episodes about discipleship ("follow" in 8:19, 22). The first episode poses the question, Have you counted the cost? The second episode issues the challenge, Get your priorities straight! The miracle of the stilling of the storm occurs in a boat on the way from Capernaum; the two demoniacs are healed on the other side; then Jesus goes back to Capernaum for the healing of the paralytic. The closing frame (9:9–17) gives the call of Matthew and two controversy stories. The call story is about getting one's priorities straight (followed, 9:9b); the two controversies pose the question, Have you counted the cost of discipleship (criticism and change)?

The third triad actually includes four miracles, but the second (the healing of the woman with the hemorrhage) is sandwiched inside the first (the dead girl raised at Capernaum). The other two (two blind men and a dumb demoniac) take place inside the house in Capernaum.

Matthew 8:2–9:34 in the Narrative Flow

Birth narratives (1:1–2:23)

Jesus's ministry begins (3:1–8:1)

Jesus's authority is revealed (8:2–11:1)

▶ *Narrative*: Jesus's authority is manifest in his mission (8:2–9:34)

First triad of miracles (8:2–17)

Healing a leper (8:2–4)

Healing a paralytic (8:5–13)

A fever and other healings (8:14–16)

An Isaianic interpretation (8:17)

Second triad of miracles (8:18–9:17)

Framing: The cost of discipleship (8:18–22)

First miracle: Stilling a storm (8:23–27)

Second miracle: Exorcising two demoniacs (8:28–9:1)

Third miracle: Healing a paralytic (9:2–8)

Framing: The cost of discipleship (9:9–17)

1. The call of Matthew (9:9)

2. Controversy: Dining with sinners (9:10–13)

3. Controversy: Fasting (9:14–17)

Third triad of miracles, with a fourth embedded (9:18–34)

Raising a dead girl and healing a hemorrhage (9:18–26)

Healing two blind men (9:27–31)

Healing a dumb demoniac (9:32–34)

Jim Yancey

Figure 6. The remains of this synagogue in Capernaum are probably from the fourth century. It rests on the foundations of the first-century synagogue.

First Triad of Miracles (8:2–17)

The first of the triads in Matt. 8–9 comes in 8:1–17. Each of the three episodes begins with Jesus's movement (8:1: "coming down from the mountain"; 8:5: "entering into Capernaum"; 8:14: "coming into the house of Peter"), and if 8:16 is taken together with 8:14–15, in each case someone comes to Jesus (8:2: "and behold a leper coming paid homage to him"; 8:5: "a centurion came to him beseeching him"; 8:16: "and when evening came they brought to him many demon possessed"). The three components are structurally linked.

8:2–4. Matthew 8:2–4 (cf. Mark 1:40–45) is a healing of a leper with a touch and a word. (Both Jewish and pagan traditions relate healings of lepers. In 2 Kings 5, Naaman is healed of leprosy through the agency of Elisha. Galen, *Subfiguratio Empirica* X, tells of Asclepius healing a man with leprosy.) In a Jewish context, lepers were considered unclean (Josephus, *Ant.* 3.261 put them in the same category with those who had touched a corpse) and were social outcasts (Lev. 13:45–46; Josephus, *Ag. Ap.* 1.281; 11QT^a 45.17–18; 46.16–18; 49.4). This leper said to Jesus, **If you want to, you are able to cleanse me. And stretching out his hand, he touched him, saying, "I want to; be cleansed"** (8:2b–3a). Touching a leper was believed to make the one who touched him unclean (Lev. 5:3). The Matthean Jesus seems unconcerned about such matters. The result: **And immediately his leprosy was cleansed** (8:3b). Then Jesus told him to do two things. First, **Tell no one**; second, **Go show yourself to the priest and offer the gift that Moses commanded** (Lev. 14), **as a witness to them** (8:4). This little story not only is a testimony that the messianic times have arrived (*2 Bar.* 73.1–2 says health and absence of illness are to be part of the new age) but also shows Jesus concerned to be a law-abiding Jew (cf. 5:17).

At the same time, Jesus is one who is concerned to actualize the intent of the law (cf. 5:21–48): the healing of the leper (Gundry 1982, 138, 140).

8:5–13. Matthew 8:5–13 (cf. Luke 7:1–10 and 13:28–30) is a healing of a paralytic from a distance. (Both Jewish and pagan traditions recount healing from a distance. In *b. Ber.* 34b, Rabbi Hanina ben Dosa prays and heals from a distance on two occasions. Cf. also *y. Ber.* 5.5.2a–c. Philostratus, *Vit. Apoll.* 3.38, tells of the philosopher healing from a distance. Marinos, *Vit. Proc.* 29, tells of Proclus assisting in healing from a distance. An Epidaurian inscription, stele 2.21, says that Asclepius healed from a distance.) The centurion comes to Jesus, saying, **Lord, my slave/child** (*pais*) **is lying in the house paralyzed, suffering terribly** (8:6). Jesus replies with a question (Boring 1995, 8:226), **Shall I, by coming, heal him?** (8:7). This takes place in Capernaum, Jewish territory where Jews were not supposed to enter a gentile's dwellings because they were unclean. Herod Antipas, like his father, primarily used non-Jewish soldiers (Josephus, *Ant.* 17.198; 18.113–14). Jews considered contact with gentiles contaminating (Acts 10:28; Josephus, *J.W.* 2.150; *m. Ohol.* 18.7). Sensitive to this, the centurion replied, **Lord, I am not worthy that you should enter, . . . but only say a word and my servant/child will be healed** (8:8). The reason: the centurion believes that Jesus has authority to command it to be done and it will be done (8:9). **Jesus marveled and said to those following, "Truly I say to you, from no one in Israel have I found such faith** (8:10).

Jesus's response to the centurion's faith is twofold. First, to those following him Jesus says, **Many will come from east and west and share the table with Abraham, Isaac, and Jacob in the kingdom of heaven, and the children of the kingdom will be cast out into eternal darkness** (8:11–12). To Abraham, God's promise had been given that through Abraham's offspring the nations would

---

Example of a Jewish Miracle Story

In *b. Ber.* 34b is an account of a miracle associated with a mid-first-century Palestinian, Hanina ben Dosa:

> *"Our rabbis say, once upon a time Rabban Gamaliel's son got sick. He sent two men of learning to Rabbi Chanina ben Dosa to beg him mercy from God concerning him. He saw them coming and went to a room upstairs and asked mercy from God concerning him. When he had come back down he said to them, 'Go, the fever has left him.' . . . They sat down and wrote and determined exactly the moment he said this, and when they came back to Rabban Gamaliel he said to them, 'By the temple service! You are neither too early nor too late but this is what happened: in that moment the fever left him and he asked for water!'"* (Cartlidge and Dungan 1980, 158)

Example of a Greco-Roman Miracle Story

Lucian, a second-century satirist, relates this story of an exorcism through the words of one Ion (*Philops.* 16):

> *"Everyone has heard of the Syrian from Palestine, so skilled was he in these things. Whomever he received, those who were moonstruck and rolled their eyes and filled their mouths with foam, they arose, when they were free of the terror, and he sent them away healthy, for a large fee. When he stands by them as they lie there, he asks [the demons] from whence they came into the body. The sick man is silent, but the demon answers in Greek or some barbarian tongue, or in the language of the country from which he comes, how and from whence he came into the man. The Syrian then levels oaths at him [to drive him out], but if the demon is not persuaded, he threatens [even worse punishments] and expels the demon. I actually saw one coming out, black and smoky in color."* (Cartlidge and Dungan 1980, 157)

---

be blessed (Gen. 12:2–3). The prophets looked forward to the day when the gentiles would come to the Lord (e.g., Isa. 2:2–4; Jer. 3:17; Mic. 4:1–2; Zech. 8:20–22; Tob. 14:5–7). John the Baptist had said that Abraham's descendents were not such by genetics but by a proper response to God (Matt. 3:9). There will be no ritual purity issues in the kingdom. Jews and gentiles will sit at table together. So also, Jesus sees in this gentile's faith a foreshadowing of the ingathering of the gentiles in the end time. Second, to the centurion he says, **Go; as you have believed may it be done for you** (8:13a). **And the servant/child was healed in that hour** (8:13b).

8:14–16. Matthew 8:14–15 and 16 (cf. Mark 1:29–31 + 32–34) is a combination of the healing of Peter's mother-in-law of a fever by a touch (Plutarch, *Pyrrh*. 3.4–5: the king is able to heal by his touch) and a summary of an evening of exorcisms and healings with a word. (In *b. Ber.* 34b, Rabbi Hanina ben Dosa prays for the son of Rabbi Gamaliel, and the child is healed of a fever. Oxyrhynchus Papyrus 11.1381 tells of Asclepius healing a fever. Also, 1Qap-Gen ar 19.10–20.32 speaks of Abraham's exorcism of Pharaoh's evil spirit. And 11Q11 2.2–3; 3.2–9; 5.4–10 is a Davidic hymn describing Solomon as an exorcist. Josephus, *Ant.* 8.45–49, relates one Eleazar's exorcism of a demon by knowledge revealed to Solomon. In Philostratus, *Vit. Apoll.* 4.20, the philosopher casts a demon out of a young boy.) Again, Jesus's activity on behalf of physical well-being is thought to characterize the messianic age (Isa. 29:18; 32:3–4; 35:5–6). Again, it fits with the activity of a son of Abraham and a son of David. This pericope may serve with 8:1–4 as an inclusio holding the first triad together (8:3, touch plus word; 8:15–16, touch plus word).

8:17. The entire first triad is closed with a quotation from Isa. 53:4 MT. **So the word through Isaiah the prophet was fulfilled, saying, "He took our illnesses and bore our sicknesses."** This does not mean that Jesus became vicariously sick. Rather, he took the diseases away (Gundry 1982, 150). Here as elsewhere in Matthew, references to the servant of Deutero-Isaiah do not mean that the evangelist has adopted an existing Suffering Servant concept and applied it to Jesus. No such servant figure was present in Matthew's encyclopedia either for Matthew to appropriate or for his hearers to appreciate. The Isaianic servant material in Matthew has other functions besides presenting Jesus as *the* Servant. Context controls the meaning (Huizenga 2005).

Second Triad of Miracles (8:18–9:17)

The second triad is composed of three miracle stories (8:23–27; 8:28–9:1; 9:2–8) and is held together by an inclusio: 8:18–22 and 9:9–17.

8:18–22. This unit consists of a setting (8:18) plus two scenes (8:19–20; 8:21–22). In the first scene, an enthusiastic scribe, presumably a disciple to whom the command has been given to go to the other side of the lake (Gundry 1982, 151), says to Jesus, **Teacher, I will follow you wherever you may go** (8:19). Jesus responds, **The foxes have holes, and the birds of the heaven have nests, but the son of man does not have anywhere he may rest his head** (8:20). Is the scribe not yet a disciple and is rejected because he wants to enable himself to become Jesus's disciple (Kingsbury 1988, 49)? Hardly. As we saw in 4:23–25, disciples are made in two ways: some are drawn to Jesus as to a magnet, some are summoned. There is no presumption here, just enthusiasm. Countering this excitement, Jesus asks whether he has counted the cost of following (cf. 13:20–21).

In the second scene, a concerned individual who wants to satisfy a major religious and familial obligation before following asks Jesus, **Lord, allow me first to go away and to bury my father** (8:21). In his Jewish culture this was a reasonable request. In *m. Ber.* 3.1 the rabbis teach that one who is confronted by a dead relative is freed from reciting the Shema, from the Eighteen Benedictions, and from all the commandments stated in the Torah in order to bury the dead one (cf. 1 Kings 19:20; Tob. 4:3–4). Greco-Roman culture shared the same values. Philostratus (*Vit. Apoll.* 1.13) tells how when Apollonius heard of his father's death, he hurried to Tyana to bury him with his own hands beside his mother's grave. Jesus responds,

---

The Cost of a Committed Life

Epictetus (*Diatr.* 3.22.45–49) says of himself, as a committed philosopher, that he is "without house, without home, without property, without slaves! I sleep on the ground, I have no wife, children, no palace from which to rule but only the earth and sky and one rough coat. . . . My concern is not with my father (cf. 8:21–22) but with the good" (trans. W. Oldfather 1925–28).

Follow me, and leave the dead to bury their own dead (8:22). There are analogies. In Ezek. 24:15–24 Yahweh forbids the prophet to lament the dead and to carry out the mourning ritual on the occasion of his wife's decease. In Jer. 16:5–7 Yahweh forbids Jeremiah to visit a house of mourning and to take part in lamentations for the dead. Why? There were other more-pressing matters before these two prophets. As Epictetus puts it: The good has priority over any relationship. Therefore, one's concern is not with one's father but with the good (*Diatr.* 3.3.5). So the Matthean Jesus says to the disciple that whatever other commitments he may have, they can have no prior claim to his devotion. Get your priorities straight! (Hengel 1981, 29–33).

8:23–27. In the three miracle stories that follow, Jesus is going somewhere (8:23; 8:28; 9:1). In all three someone comes to Jesus (8:25; 8:28; 9:2). The pattern is the same as in the first triad.

The first miracle in the second triad comes in 8:23–27 (cf. Mark 4:35–41). As 8:18 stated, Jesus gave orders to go to the other side of the lake. The other side from Capernaum was gentile territory (Gadarenes). Gadara was a Hellenistic city about six miles from the lake. Josephus (*Life* 42) tells us, however, that Gadara had territory that extended to the lake. While the disciples are following Jesus into gentile territory, they encounter a storm on the way. And behold, a great storm happened in the sea so that the boat was being filled by the waves. Now Jesus was asleep. And coming to him, they awakened him, saying, "Lord, save! We are perishing!" And he said to them, "Why are you fearful, little-faith ones?" (8:24–26). Then Jesus rebukes the winds and the sea. There is then a great calm (cf. Ps. 107:23–29). Those with him marvel and say, What kind of man is this that even the winds and the sea obey him? (8:27). In addition to testifying to Jesus's authority and power over the natural world (a divine attribute, Ps. 89:8–9), this miracle prefigures Jesus's leading his disciples into gentile territory in spite of a storm that threatens their existence.

8:28–9:1. The second miracle in the second triad comes in 8:28–9:1, a unit held together by 8:28 and 9:1 (Jesus's coming to the other side and his coming to his own town; cf. Mark 5:1–20). This story reflects the Matthean technique of doubling. Here are two demoniacs, not Mark's one (cf. also 9:27 [two blind men];

Stilling Storms at Sea

Both Jewish and pagan traditions tell of individuals stilling storms at sea. In *y. Ber.* 9.1.10.e–k, a Jewish boy prays and a storm stops. In *b. B. Metziʾa* 59b, Rabbi Gamaliel is instrumental in God's stilling a storm. In *T. Naph.* 6.1–10 God stills a storm at sea in answer to prayer. In Athenaeus, *Deipn.* 15.676a–b, Aphrodite calms a storm. Apollonius of Tyana is said to be master of tempests (Philostratus, *Vit. Apoll.* 4.13). Pythagoras, it is said, calmed waves (Iamblichus, *Vit. Pyth.* 28). Ovid says Medea was able to soothe stormy seas and dismiss the winds by the power of Hecate (*Metam.* 7.200–205).

Miracle by Command and Miracle by Prayer

One should not exaggerate the difference between a miracle accomplished through the form of a command and a miracle effected by prayer. In Josh. 10:12–14 Joshua's command to the sun and moon to stand still is clearly interpreted as a prayer heeded by God. In Acts 9:40 Peter prays and commands, indicating their virtual identity. John 11:41–44 has the same combination of praying and commanding. In *b. Ta'an.* 23a, the effectiveness of Honi the Circle Drawer's command that it rain is interpreted as God's answer to his prayer (Blackburn 1991, 131).

20:30 [two blind men]; 26:60 [two false witnesses]; 21:7 [two animals being ridden]). These demoniacs are in gentile territory, as the commercial keeping of pigs indicates (Lev. 11:7–8; Deut. 14:8; *m. B. Qam.* 7.7: No Israelite may raise swine anywhere). When the fierce demoniacs meet Jesus, they recognize him. They cry out, **What do we have in common, son of God? Have you come here before the time in order to torment us?** (8:29). Demons were believed to be free to torment humans prior to the last judgment. At that time, the demons would be tormented (*1 En.* 10.4–6, 11–14; *Jub.* 10.5–9; *T. Levi* 18.12). So, they ask, why is the one who would be their judge then here now? The answer will be made explicit in 12:28 ("But if it is by the Spirit of God that I cast out demons, then the kingdom of God has come to you," NRSV). When the demons ask for permission to enter the swine (the unclean going into the unclean), Jesus gives his permission. The herd rushes down the steep bank and perishes in the water. Even in the sea, however, the evil powers cannot escape Jesus's power. He has just proved that he commands the sea (8:26)! Because of their financial loss, the locals ask Jesus to leave. This he does. Gentiles put economics above deliverance (cf. Acts 16:16–24). So Jesus comes back to his own town, Capernaum (9:1).

9:2–8. The third miracle story in the second triad comes in 9:2–8 (cf. Mark 2:1–12). It is once again a healing of a paralytic (cf. 8:6). (Asclepius apparently was an effective healer of paralytics. Cf. Epidaurian inscriptions, stele 1.3 [healing of paralyzed fingers], stele 1.15 [healing of paralyzed Hermodicos], stele 1.16 [healing of lame Nicanor], stele 2.37–38 [paralytics healed; hope required]). When Jesus is back in Capernaum, **behold, they are bearing to him a paralytic lying on a pallet** (9:2a).

And seeing their faith, Jesus said to the paralytic, "Cheer up, son, your sins are being forgiven" (9:2b; note the present indicative passive form of the verb). Certain scribes agreed among themselves that Jesus was blaspheming (9:3). Jesus responds, saying, **"Which is easier, to say, 'Your sins are being forgiven,' or to say, 'Get up and walk?'"** (9:5). Jesus continues, **"In order that you may know that the son of man has authority upon the earth to forgive sins"**—then he says to the paralytic, "Get up, take your pallet and go to your house" (9:6). The man got up and went home (9:7). This produced a reaction among the crowd. **They glorified the God who had given such authority to humans** (9:8).

Two matters of background assist in understanding this story. First, in ancient Judaism it was believed there was a close connection between sin and sickness (e.g., Lev. 26:14–16, 21; Deut. 28:15, 22, 27–28, 35; 2 Chron. 21:12–15, 18–19; John 5:14; 9:2). This story assumes such a link. The paralytic's physical condition is due to his spiritual condition. The latter has to be taken care of before the former can be remedied. Second, when Jesus says the man's sins "are being forgiven," the passive implies that God is forgiving the man's sins (Witherington 2006, 195). Jesus's role is to pronounce God's decision. In 2 Sam. 12:13, when the prophet Nathan says to David, "The LORD has put away your sin," he is pronouncing God's forgiveness. In 4QPrNab ar, we hear how a Jewish exorcist remitted king Nabonidus's sins, restoring him to health (García Martínez 1996, 289). Here, as in the case of Nathan the prophet, when the Jew remitted the king's sins, he was pronouncing God's decision in the matter (cf. Luke 7:36–50). In this story, Jesus's self-designation as son of man should be understood from his acting in a prophetic role, like Nathan. The scribes' label of blasphemer is, then, to be taken as a reflection of their own spiritual darkness.

9:9–17. At the end of the second triad of miracles is 9:9–17, the other half of the inclusio that frames this triad. The subunits are (1) a call story (9:9), (2) a controversy regarding Jesus's meal fellowship with sinners (9:10–13), and (3) a controversy over fasting (9:14–17).

1. Matthew 9:9 (cf. Mark 2:14, where the name of the person is Levi, not Matthew) is a brief call story similar to the two in 4:18–22 (cf. 1 Kings 19:19–21). Jesus passes by; he sees someone; he summons that one to follow him; the person follows, leaving everything behind. Such a story speaks about getting one's priorities in order. Following Jesus takes precedence over all else.

2. The first controversy story is 9:10–13 (cf. Mark 2:15–17). Jesus and his disciples (Matthew included?) are eating with **many tax collectors and sinners** (9:10). This prompts a Pharisaic question addressed to the disciples: **Why is your teacher eating with the tax collectors and sinners?** (9:11). Jesus answers with a proverb: **The strong have no need of a physician, but those who are sick** (9:12; cf. Plutarch, *Apoph. lac.* 230f: physicians are not among the healthy but spend their time among the sick); a challenge: **Go and learn what it means, "I desire mercy and not sacrifice"** (Hosea 6:6); and a statement of the aim of his ministry: **I did not come to call righteous but sinners** (cf. Luke 5:32; 1 Tim. 1:15; *Barn.* 5.9; *2 Clem.* 2; Justin Martyr, *1 Apol.* 15.8). Taken in context, this pericope says that discipleship entails suffering criticism. Have you counted the cost?

3. The second controversy story comes in 9:14–17 (cf. Mark 2:18–22). In it Jesus is apparently still in the house (9:10), eating in the company of tax

Another Jewish Use of Hosea 6:6

In *Avot R. Nat.* 4, a story explains the third part of the saying of Simeon the Righteous: On three things the world stands—on the Torah, on the temple service, and on acts of loving-kindness. The section "on acts of loving-kindness" begins with a question. How so? "Lo, it says, *For I desire mercy and not sacrifice*" (Hosea 6:6). The haggadic (story) explanation follows. Once as Rabban Johanan ben Zakkai was coming forth from Jerusalem, Rabbi Joshua followed after him and beheld the Jewish temple in ruins. "Woe unto us!" Rabbi Joshua cried, "that this place where the iniquities of Israel were atoned for, is laid waste!" "My son," Rabban Johanan said to him, "be not grieved; we have another atonement as effective as this. And what is it? It is acts of loving-kindness, as it is said, *For I desire mercy and not sacrifice*" (Hosea 6:6; Goldin 1955, 34). This tradition seems to indicate that the Matthean Jesus was challenging the Pharisees on the basis of their own accepted values.

collectors and sinners (9:11). Disciples of John the Baptist come asking, **Why do we and the Pharisees fast but your disciples do not fast?** (9:14; cf. 11:19). Jesus answers with a rhetorical question. **The sons of the bridegroom are not able to mourn for as long as the bridegroom is with them, are they?** (9:15; cf. 1 Macc. 9:37). By analogy, Jesus's disciples cannot fast, because they are in a time of celebration (cf. 25:1–12). Fasting and celebrating are an impossible combination. A double parable with two more impossible combinations follows (9:16, 17). The first reads: **No one sews an unshrunk patch on an old cloak, for** (when washed and the patch shrinks) **the patch tears the overlapping section from the cloak, and a greater tear occurs** (Davies and Allison 1991, 2:113). The second is similar: **They do not pour new wine into old wineskins, and if they did, the skins would burst and the wine pour out and the skins be ruined. Rather, they pour new wine into new skins, and both survive.** The point: my disciples reflect the forms of piety that are appropriate to the new reality they are experiencing. The new disciplines of piety cannot be constrained by the old forms. To be my disciple, Jesus says, will involve change. Have you counted the cost?

Third Triad of Miracles, with a Fourth Embedded (9:18–34)

The third triad actually contains four miracle stories, the first two being one within another, sandwich style (9:18–34). In the first three stories, Jesus is going somewhere (9:19, 23, 27). In all four, people come to Jesus (9:18, 20, 27, 32). The same pattern continues.

9:18–26. The first unit, containing two healings, comes in 9:18–26 (cf. Mark 5:21–43). Apparently while Jesus is still at a meal in the house (9:10), a synagogue official comes, kneels before him, and says, **My daughter has just now**

Raising the Dead

Although the Jewish tradition said that only God has the keys to raising the dead (*b. Ta'an.* 2a) and the Greek Aeschylus could say there is no return to life after death (*Eum.* 647–48), there were claims that some did in fact resuscitate the dead. In 1 Kings 17:17–24 and 2 Kings 4:18–37, Elijah and Elisha perform such miracles. Asclepius allegedly raised several back to life (Apollodorus, *Bibl.* 3.10.3–4). Apollonius of Tyana resuscitated a young bride (Philostratus, *Vit. Apoll.* 4.45). This was deemed so incredible by the Greco-Roman world that Lucian constructed cynical accounts of such raisings (*Philops.* 26; *Alex.* 24). That Lucian would satirize such stories, however, indicates that they circulated and were known in his culture. In addition to this story in the triple tradition (i.e., appearing in three of the four Gospels), the Gospels relate other such events found only in Luke 7:11–17 and John 11.

---

died. **Come and lay your hand upon her, and she will live** (9:18). Jesus and his disciples get up and follow the man.

On the way a woman who has suffered twelve years from hemorrhages comes up behind Jesus and touches the fringe (Num. 15:38–39; Deut. 22:12) of his cloak, believing this will effect her cure (Matt. 9:20–21). Such a touch was believed to render the one touched unclean (Josephus, *Ant.* 3.261; *m. Zavim* 5.1, 6, 11; *m. Kelim* 1.4). Unconcerned with such, Jesus turned and said to her, **Take courage, daughter, your faith has saved you** (9:22a). **And the woman was saved from that hour** (9:22b).

Upon arrival at the official's house, Jesus dismisses the flute players and the mourning crowd (cf. John 11:31), saying, **The girl is not dead but is sleeping** (9:24a). **Now when the crowd was put out, entering he took her hand, and the girl was raised** (9:25). The report of this event spread throughout the region. Matthew's abbreviated form of the longer Markan narrative leaves Jesus center stage throughout and his power unsurpassed. He can even resuscitate the dead!

9:27–31. The second segment of the third triad comes in 9:27–31 (no true parallel in Mark or Luke). When Jesus leaves, two blind men cry out, **Have mercy on us, son of David** (9:27; cf. 12:23; 15:22; 21:9, 15).

When Jesus enters the house, the two blind men come to him. Jesus says to them, **Do you believe that I am able to do this?** (9:28). When they say yes, Jesus **touched their eyes, saying, "According to your faith may it be done for you"** (9:29). Then they can see (9:30). This kind of event was believed to belong to the messianic time of fulfillment (cf. 11:5). Jesus then unsuccessfully orders them not to make it known; they spread the news throughout the district (9:30–31).

9:32–34. The final miracle in the third triad is a brief story about Jesus's healing of a demoniac who was mute (9:32–34, without parallel in the other

The Son of David and Healing

Why is the son of David associated with healing in Matthew? A number of answers have been proposed. One option is that Solomon, a son of David, was an exorcist and so a healer (Duling 1978; Charlesworth 1996). Another is that the connection between a Davidic healer and Jesus is grounded in a midrashic understanding of Scripture, particularly of Isaiah. For example, by its reference to the servant of Yahweh, Matt. 8:16–17 (citing Isa. 53:4a) refers to physical illness. Because the messiah is described as God's servant in Ps. 89:39 and Ezek. 34:23, the reference to "my servant" in Isa. 52:13 must also signify the Messiah. Also, Matt. 12:15–21 cites Isa. 42:1–4, where "my servant" and "my beloved" are linked. "My beloved" is also linked with Matt. 3:17, where "my beloved" is identical with "my son." In this way son of David is linked with healing (Novakovic 2003). Yet another attempt to explain the link between son of David and healing is the appeal to the Davidic shepherd tradition found in places such as Ezek. 34 and 37. There the false shepherds have not healed the sick or bound up the injured (34:4). God, therefore, will set up over his people one shepherd, David, who will do what the false shepherds have not done (34:23–24; Chae 2006). Given the Matthean emphasis elsewhere on Jesus as the Davidic eschatological shepherd with strong roots in Ezek. 34 and 37, this last explanation seems probable. It would not, however, rule out the links to Isaiah's servant. It is rather a case of both-and, not either-or (Baxter 2006).

Gospels). Actually the term *kōphos* can mean either deaf or mute or both (11:5 mentions the deaf). Such people were ostracized in Jewish society (*m. Menaḥ.* 9.8; *m. Ḥul.* 1.1; *m. Rosh HaSh.* 3.8). (Stories of such healings are known from elsewhere in antiquity. In *b. Ḥag.* 3a, a rabbi prays for two mute men, and they are healed. Among the Epidaurian inscriptions, stele 1.5 tells of Asclepius's healing of a mute boy.) In this brief healing story, the focus is on the two contrasting reactions to the man's speaking (Nolland 2005, 402). First, **the crowds marveled, saying, "Never has such been seen in Israel"** (9:33b). Second, **the Pharisees were saying, "By the ruler of the demons he is casting out demons"** (9:34; cf. 10:25 and 12:24 that mention Beelzebul, prince of the demons; on Beelzebul, cf. *T. Sol.* 3.1–6). The Pharisees do not deny Jesus's expulsion of the demon. They question the source of his power. This ending to Matt. 8–9 leaves the impression that the miracle collection begins with faith and ends with unbelief. Miracles are not a sure guarantee of faith!

Functions of the Unit as a Whole

"Meaning resides not just in the parts but in the whole" (Davies and Allison 1991, 2:141). How then do chapters 8–9 function within the overall Matthean plot? The miracle collection has multiple functions.

Healing the Blind

Stories about healing blind persons are known from antiquity. Jewish stories (e.g., Tob. 2:10; 3:16–17; 11:7–15) do not involve a blind person being directly healed by another individual. Greco-Roman accounts, however, do. The Epidaurian inscriptions (steles 1.18; 2.22; 2.32) speak of Asclepius's healing of three named individuals. Pausanias (*Descr.* 10.38.13) tells of Asclepius's healing of blind Phalysios. Tacitus (*Hist.* 4.81), Suetonius (*Vesp.* 7.7.2–3), and Dio Cassius (*Rom. Hist.* 65.8) tell of Vespasian's healing of a blind man in Alexandria with a touch. John 9 is a non-Matthean Gospel account of such a healing.

1. First and foremost, the ten miracles show the authority of Jesus. This is crucial for the discourse that follows. There Jesus gives authority to his twelve disciples to cast out demons, to heal the sick, to cleanse lepers, and to raise the dead (10:1, 8). Jesus, however, can only give to his disciples what he himself possesses. It is therefore necessary first to show Jesus's power before saying that this power is given to the twelve disciples.

2. This section shows the identity of Jesus as "the one who is to come." The Baptist in prison sends his disciples to ask Jesus, "Are you the coming one, or should we expect another?" (11:3). Jesus's response is to have the Baptist's disciples tell John what they have heard and seen (11:4). This list (11:5) includes the blind seeing, the lame walking, lepers being cleansed, the deaf (*kōphoi*; cf. 9:32) hearing, and the dead being raised—an overlap with the miracles in Matt. 8–9. These are the things the coming one is expected to do (Isa. 29:18; 35:5–6). This coming one is son of God (8:29), son of man (9:6), son of David (9:27), and a second Moses with his ten wonders on behalf of Israel. The coming one has many names!

3. Matthew 8–9 functions to show a wide range of responses to Jesus (cf. 13:18–23). The responses range from positive (8:2, 10, 16, 23; 9:2, 7–8, 9, 18, 21–22, 29–30a) to incomplete or inadequate (8:19–20, 21–22, 27; 9:33a) to negative (gentiles: 8:28–29, 34; scribes: 9:3; Pharisees: 9:11, 34; John's disciples: 9:14; the crowd: 9:24). The final miracle and the Pharisaic response to it (9:34) leaves one with the impression of a growing negative response to Jesus's miracle-working activity.

4. Also in Matt. 8–9 are foreshadowings of Jesus's concern for the gentiles, something appropriate for a son of Abraham (8:5–13, a gentile's faith foreshadows the inclusion of the gentiles in the end times; 8:23–9:1, Jesus's crossing into gentile territory to aid two demoniacs, in spite of a storm that seeks to impede the progress of Jesus and his disciples, foreshadows a mission to gentiles). Jesus's concern for gentiles is sometimes met with faith (8:5–13), sometimes with rejection (8:28–34).

5. These miracle stories "function for Matthew and his church as 'parenetic paradigms,' i.e., these stories invite the Christians of this community, as

people who have been baptized (28:19) and therefore are themselves persons of faith, to approach the exalted Son of God, under whose aegis they live, with their own petitions for help in the firm assurance that he will hear them and mercifully employ his divine power to sustain them in time of distress and affliction" (Kingsbury 1978, 572).

6. The focus on the praise of Jesus (encomium) continues. Quintilian (*Inst.* 3.7.15) urges praising the whole course of a hero's life, "including words as well as deeds." In Matt. 5–7 the focus was on Jesus's words; in Matt. 8–9 it is on his deeds. What kind of deeds? Among the various categories of deeds, the miracles of Matt. 8–9 appear to fall in the category of deeds of magnanimity, deeds done for others. While all of Jesus's deeds in the First Gospel are for others, those of Matt. 8–9 focus on the magnanimous nature of Jesus's miracles.

Theological Issues

Collections of Miracle Stories

In a papyrus of the second century AD by an unnamed author, we hear about the translation into Greek of a book about the god Imouthes, an Egyptian deity commonly identified with Asclepius, who was part of a circle of deities around Serapis at Memphis. It was a book of his mighty deeds and marvelous epiphanies. The book was said to have been a factor in causing the god to be greatly revered. At the end of the work, the author tells of his editorial procedure: "Through the whole writing I have supplied what was lacking and removed what was superfluous, and I have told shortly a tale sometimes long, simply a story which is complicated" (Nock 1998, 88). It is significant that these miracles were written down in book form. The literary propaganda that made known the miracles of the gods was one way of winning adherents (Nock 1998, 83, 89).

In the early Christian movement, Jesus material circulated in a variety of forms: collections of Jesus's sayings (e.g., Q; Coptic *Gospel of Thomas*), collections of Jesus's miracles (e.g., Semeia source behind the Fourth Gospel; *Childhood Gospel of Thomas*), revelation collections in which the risen Christ disclosed either the ultimate origins of the universe or its ultimate destiny (e.g., Revelation to John; *Apocryphon of John*), and composite collections (containing sayings, miracles, and prophesies of the ultimate end of things) plus a narrative of Jesus's passion and resurrection (the four canonical Gospels). The First Gospel is a composite plus a narrative of Jesus's death and resurrection. Chapters 8–9 represent a collection of miracles, set within a whole that controls the way they are to be read. This yields the result: Power is a part of who Jesus is but it is not the whole. That whole includes virtue, knowledge of heavenly secrets, and divine forgiveness above all (Talbert 1988).

Making Sense of the Miracle Stories

In the history of the interpretation of the Gospel miracle stories, there have been several distinct periods, each with its own way of reading.

The first is the period in which the *evidential value* of miracles was primary. Assuming that the miracle stories were true narratives of historical facts, this approach contended that the miracles were not part of Jesus's message but were proofs of its truth and evidence of Jesus's supernatural nature. Although its roots are in Christian antiquity, in modern times this approach was popularized by William Paley's *Evidences of Christianity* (1794). This interpretation of the Gospel miracles was only possible for as long as the historicity of the miracles could be assumed. When their historicity was questioned, the miracles ceased to function as proofs and instead became the problem. B. F. Westcott (1859, 4) states it plainly: "In nothing has the change of feeling during the last century been more violent than in the popular estimation of miracles. At the beginning they were singled out as the master-proof of the Christian faith: now they are kept back as difficulties in the way of reception." As a result, the Gospel miracles were discussed primarily in terms of whether or not they actually happened.

In the second phase of interpretation of the Gospel miracles, the *historicity* of the miracles was the primary focus. A variety of approaches evolved. One was supernaturalistic explanation: if God is who we believe God to be, then of course the miracle stories in the Gospels refer to historical occurrences. This reading may be found as late as A. M. Hunter (1950, 59) who says, "If Jesus was, and is, what Christians have always believed Him to be, the Son of God in a unique . . . sense; if in Him the Spirit of the living God was uniquely incarnated; . . . then there is nothing inherently absurd or incredible in the supposition that such a one must have had control over the great frame of nature itself."

Another was the rationalistic approach, which tried to make all events intelligible as natural occurrences whose secondary causes could be discerned. Its classic representative was H. E. G. Paulus (1828), whose life of Jesus focuses on the explanations of the miracles. In the so-called miracles of healing, Jesus worked through his spiritual power upon the nervous system of the sufferer or used medicines known to him alone. Diet and aftertreatment played their part as well. The nature miracles, like stilling the storm at sea, were illusions. When awakened, Jesus spoke about the wind and waves just as the boat gained shelter of a hill that protected them from the wind that swept down the valley. The disciples interpreted it as a miraculous event. (See an extensive survey of Paulus's explanations in Schweitzer 1910, 48–57.)

Mythical interpretation was a third approach to the historicity question. D. F. Strauss (1972) represents this reading of the Gospel miracles. (See an extensive discussion of Strauss in Schweitzer 1910, 78–95.) The miracle stories are not accounts of historical events but were created by the early Christians out of

OT prophecies (e.g., Isa. 35:5–6 says the messianic age will be characterized by the blind seeing, the deaf hearing, the lame leaping, and the dumb singing), sayings of Jesus (e.g., Luke 13:6–9, a parable about a fig tree that does not bear fruit), and theological tendencies of the later church (e.g., Col. 2:15, where it is said that Christ defeats the evil spiritual powers).

A fourth approach in this era of interpretation is agnostic. Here one refuses to assert either the possibility or impossibility of the miracles. R. H. Fuller (1963, 38) asks, "Why not put them into a *historical* suspense account? At all events, we must avoid *a priori* judgments either for or against them."

A reaction inevitably set in against the overabsorption with the question of the historicity of the Gospel miracles. This led to another way of reading. In this third period, the focus was on *the meaning of the miracles for the evangelists.* The dominant reading has been and continues to be eschatological. Within the context of an inaugurated eschatology, Jesus's miracles came to be seen as having the same message as Jesus's words. If the words of Jesus concentrated on the coming kingdom of heaven (verbal announcements), the mighty works showed what the kingdom would be like (physical anticipations; cf. Matt. 12:28; e.g., Kallas 1968, 161). At the same time, others have tried to broaden the scope of their significance. For example, Ernst Bloch (1986, 1303–11), a Marxist, points out that daydreams, visions, myths, and miracles all provide material for a critique of the present situation and the impetus for revolution. Miracle is characterized both by an interruption of the status quo and by the realization of part of a better situation. Miracles offer a vision of a better world and unmask the insufficiency of the contemporary world. They thereby provide a vision of the unrealized opportunities of human existence. This, of course, is a secularized, generic form of the more contextual eschatological reading of the Gospels.

Another example, Eugen Drewermann (1992, 2:43–309), using Jungian depth psychology, analyzes the human situation in terms of psychological rather than physical reasons as a cause for illness. Jesus is seen as a shaman in a primitive society whose miraculous healings caused harmony of body and soul, effecting a reintegration of humans into the unity of the universe. So the miracle stories are read as answers to the timeless experience of anxiety and desperation. In them are archetypical patterns of behavior that provide healing. Yet another example is that of feminist theology, whose goal is to break the patriarchal shell of Scripture and to unwrap a kernel of traditions that show the equality of the sexes. In the miracle stories as interpreted, males are shown to be passive and females active, females teaching and males learning (Korte, 2001). (For an up-to-date survey of the history of the interpretation of miracle stories in the Gospels, see Kollmann 2006, 244–64.)

But the historicity of the Gospel miracles is still a matter of debate, with healings and exorcisms often given more credibility and nature miracles often put in a historical suspense account. The meaning of the Gospel wonders for the evangelists has not gone beyond the eschatological reading of an inaugurated eschatology. Certainly in the First Gospel, this is how the stories are understood (Matt. 12:28).

The miracle stories in the collection of Matt. 8–9, as has been pointed out, have parallels in both Jewish and Greco-Roman cultures. The Matthean Jesus is a miracle-working figure in a Mediterranean context where other miracle workers (some demigods like Asclepius or Isis [Diodorus Siculus, *Bib. hist.* 1.25.2–7: Isis delights in healing many diseases]; some philosophers like Apollonius and Pythagoras; some rulers like Vespasian; some rabbis or prophets) were active. Indeed, in Matt. 12:27 the Matthean Jesus defends himself by an appeal to similar activity by others ("If I by Beelzebul am casting out the demons, by whom are your sons casting [them] out?"). How is one to evaluate this evidence?

The First Gospel does not claim that Jesus's actions are unique (cf. 12:27). Parallels, moreover, prove that his mighty deeds were similar to those of other healers, Jewish and Greco-Roman. Wherein, then, does his uniqueness lie? The issue of the miracles' uniqueness is analogous to the uniqueness of Jesus's teaching. For the Sermon on the Mount, there is a Jewish and/or Greco-Roman parallel to almost everything said by Jesus. His uniqueness lies in what he selected from his religious milieu, what he left out, and how what was accepted fit into a coherent hierarchy of values. With regard to the mighty deeds, the uniqueness of Jesus's actions does not consist in his doing things others did not do. His distinctiveness lies in the context of meaning within which his activity took place. These deeds are signs of the coming of God to reclaim the creation corrupted by evil powers; they are, moreover, signs of what God's kingdom will be like when fully actualized. This context is provided by the Scriptures and later hopes of the Jewish people. In performing his mighty deeds, the Matthean Jesus is saying that in him the hopes of Israel are being actualized.

A Didactic Function of Miracle Stories

In Matthew, miracles are important not for their own sakes but because of the message they convey. (See Held 1963, 210; Blomberg 1986, 330, says the miracles "correspond to and cohere with the fundamental message of his [Jesus's] teaching.") Each of the nineteen miracle stories in Matthew functions to instruct about some aspect of the Christian life. Emily Cheney (1986) argues that there are four aspects of the lives of Jesus's followers that are addressed: (1) instruction about the law (8:1–4; 9:1–8; 12:9–14; 17:24–27), (2) instruction about the difficulties of discipleship (8:14–15, 23–27, 28–34; 9:32–34; 14:13–21, 22–33; 20:29–34), (3) instruction about acceptance of gentiles into the Jesus movement (8:5–13; 15:21–28, 32–39), and (4) instruction about miracle-working faith (9:18–19 with 23–26, 20–22, 27–31; 17:14–21; 21:18–22). In this practice, the First Evangelist followed cultural norms. A good example from the Greco-Roman world is found in the Pythagorean tradition. Blocks of miracle stories are found in the biographies of Pythagoras by Diogenes Laertius, Porphyry, and Iamblichus. Careful attention to these miracles shows that they serve as illustrations of Pythagorean doctrines (e.g., the immortality of the soul, reincarnation, metempsychosis and the possibility of communicating with the souls within animals, and dietary taboos like abstinence from meat, beans, and fish; Williams 1988). From the Jewish world, examples may be found in Wisdom of Solomon and Philo's *De vita Mosis*. In Wis. 16:26 the sending of manna occurred to teach the Israelites in the wilderness that God preserves those who trust him. In *Mos.* 1.207, Philo explains that the sending of a double portion of manna on Friday gave the people proof of the proper time of the Sabbath. Recitation of miracles in antiquity functioned not only evangelistically to make converts but also didactically to shape converts according to the group's beliefs and values.

Matthew 9:35–11:1

Discourse 2:
Jesus's Authority Enables Disciples' Mission

Introductory Matters

The Relation of Matthew 10 to 8–9

Matthew 9:35–11:1 is a composite unit arranged by the First Evangelist out of diverse materials (Gnilka 1986, 1:358–59, 361). The first introductory question that needs to be addressed is, how is 9:35–11:1 related to Matt. 8–9? In Matt. 8–9 Jesus is shown performing ten miracles of the types expected to occur in the messianic age. His authority or power is the focus throughout. Now in Matt. 10, Jesus gives his power or authority to the twelve disciples to enable them to participate in his mission. They will say the same things and do the same things that Jesus said and did in Matt. 8–9. It is this link above all else that ties the narrative of Matt. 8–9 together with the discourse of Matt. 10.

The Relation of Discourse and Framework

A second question concerns how the discourse is related to its narrative framework. The problem may be stated like this. The framework (9:35–10:5a; 11:1) assumes a missionary enterprise undertaken by the twelve disciples and directed to Israel. Matthew 10:5b–15 is congruent with this setting. It may be understood solely in relation to this particular mission of the Twelve. In Matt. 10:16–23, most parts are congruent with the narrative framework, but some parts may not be (e.g., 10:18). In Matt. 10:24–42, no elements specifically link up with the particular mission of the Twelve mentioned in the framework. These sayings are so general in nature that they may point to a wider mission and a post-Easter one (D. Weaver 1990, 74). Once noted, this fact should not signal discontinuity with the evangelist's normal way of working. All of the other discourses in Matthew are not solely part of the narrative plot of Jesus's career but rather transcend it at points and address the post-Easter auditors of the Gospel (Luz 1994, 39).

The Organization of Matthew 10

The third introductory question to be asked is, how is this unit organized by the evangelist? There is as yet no agreement about the structure of Matt. 10 (Witherington 2006, 228n6). The proposals are legion. Some scholars find a chiastic pattern controlling the material (see table 8). Robert Morosco (1984, 539–56) argues unsuccessfully that 9:35–11:1 is a commissioning story patterned after the literary convention used in the OT, like Exod. 3:1–4:17. Most scholars, however, try to break up the discourse segment into subunits (see table 9). The proposal espoused here sees the discourse breaking into two parts: the mission of the Twelve to Israel (10:5b–23) and the ongoing mission of disciples generally (10:24–42). Within the first part are two subunits (10:5b–15 and 10:16–23). Within the second part there are four subunits (10:24–25, 26–31, 32–39, 40–42). The accompanying outline shows how this commentary tracks the structure of this discourse.

> **Matthew 9:35–11:1 in the Narrative Flow**
>
> **Birth narratives (1:1–2:23)**
>
> **Jesus's ministry begins (3:1–8:1)**
>
> **Jesus's authority is revealed (8:2–11:1)**
>
> *Narrative*: Jesus's authority is manifest in his mission (8:2–9:34)
>
> ▶ *Discourse*: Jesus's authority enables disciples' mission (9:35–11:1)
>
> Opening narrative frame (9:35–10:5a)
>
> The mission of the Twelve to Israel (10:5b–23)
>
> The ongoing mission of disciples generally (10:24–42)
>
> Closing narrative frame (11:1)

Table 8
Proposed Chiastic Analyses of Matthew 10

Davies and Allison 1988, 1:162; Gaechter 1965, 41	Combrink 1980	Boring 1995, 255	Arens 1976, 63
A 10:5–15 (or 11–15)	A 9:35–10:5a	A 10:5b–15	A 10:5–15
B 10:16–23	B 10:5b–15	B 10:16–23	B 10:16–31
C 10:24–25	C 10:16–23	C 10:24–33	B′ 10:32–39
D 10:26–31	D 10:24–25	B′ 10:34–39	A′ 10:40–42

Davies and Allison 1988, 1:162; Gaechter 1965, 41	Combrink 1980	Boring 1995, 255	Arens 1976, 63
C' 10:32–33	C' 10:26–31	A' 10:40–42	
B' 10:34–39	B' 10:32–42		
A' 10:40–42	A' 11:1		

Table 9
Proposed Analyses of Matthew 10 into Sections

D. Weaver 1990, 123–24; Carter 2000, 232	Patte 1987	Harrington 1991	Park 1995, 41
10:5b–15	10:5b–15	10:5–15	10:5b–15
10:16–23	10:16–31	10:16–25	10:16–33
10:24–42	10:32–42	10:26–42	10:34–39
			10:40–42

Tracing the Narrative Flow

Matthew 9:35–11:1 is a discourse enclosed in a narrative framework: 9:35–10:5a is a third-person narration that gives the setting for the discourse; 10:5b–42, using the second person, is the discourse proper; and 11:1 is a third-person summary (the conclusion for the discourse). The discourse proper contains two main parts: the mission of the twelve disciples to Israel (10:5b–23) and the ongoing mission of the post-Easter disciples (10:24–42).

Opening Narrative Frame (9:35–10:5a)

Matthew 9:35–10:5a (third-person narration) is the opening part of the frame within which the discourse of 10:5b–42 is set. Matthew 9:35 (cf. Mark 6:6) echoes 4:23, signaling for the reader that this is the end of the narrative of Matt. 8–9 and the beginning of the discourse in Matt. 10. The focus is on Jesus's activity: itinerant teaching, preaching, and healing. Matthew 9:36 (cf. Mark 6:34) speaks about Jesus's motivation. **And seeing the crowds, he had compassion on them because they were troubled and vulnerable, like sheep who have no shepherd** (Num. 27:17). His words to the disciples (9:37–38; cf. Luke 10:2) speak of the need for help in his task. **The harvest is great but the workers are few. Pray therefore to the lord of the harvest that he would send forth workers into his harvest.** Unlike 13:30, where the harvest refers to the last judgment, here the harvest is a present evangelistic task. And as if in answer to such a prayer, **calling his twelve disciples he gave them authority to cast out unclean spirits and to heal every disease and illness** (10:1; cf. Mark 6:7). Who were these twelve apostles (10:2–4; cf. Mark 3:16–19; Luke 6:14–16; Acts

1:13)? Matthew's list consists of six pairs of names. The first four come in the order found in their call in 4:18–22. In the fourth pair, Thomas and Matthew, the evangelist adds, **the tax collector**, echoing 9:9. **These twelve Jesus sent out** (10:5a). The setting for Matt. 10's discourse is a mission of the twelve disciples during Jesus's pre-Easter career.

The Mission of the Twelve to Israel (10:5b–23)

The first half of the discourse is congruent with the setting in the time of Jesus's pre-Easter ministry (with the possible exception of 10:18). It is held together by an inclusio (Israel, 10:6; Israel, 10:23). It has two parts, each opening signaled by the same language (Jesus sent out, 10:5; "I send you out," 10:16) and each closing signaled by the same language ("Truly, I say to you," 10:15 and 23). These two parts respectively focus on the sending of the Twelve (10:5b–15) and indicate that his own help will be required before they can complete their mission (10:16–23). The latter section takes chiastic form.

10:5b–15. The discourse begins in 10:5b. The first subunit is 10:5b–15, a segment entirely congruent with the opening frame. Jesus tells them to whom they are to go (10:5b–6). **Into a way of the gentiles do not go, and into a city of Samaritans do not enter. Go rather to the lost sheep of the house of Israel.** For what purpose the Twelve are on mission is specified in 10:7–8a (cf. Luke 9:2). **As you go, preach, saying that the kingdom of the heavens has come near. Heal the sick, raise the dead, cleanse lepers, cast out demons.** How the Twelve are to behave on their journey is clarified in 10:8b–14. **You have received a gift, give a gift** (10:8b). **Do not take gold or silver or copper in your belts** (a long cloth wrapped around the waist several times, in which one would fold money, *m. Shabb.* 10.3; *m. Ber.* 9.5), **no bag for the way, nor two tunics,**

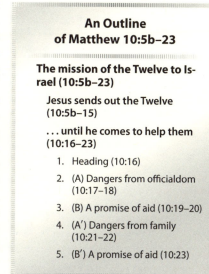

An Outline of Matthew 10:5b–23

The mission of the Twelve to Israel (10:5b–23)

Jesus sends out the Twelve (10:5b–15)

. . . until he comes to help them (10:16–23)

1. Heading (10:16)
2. (A) Dangers from officialdom (10:17–18)
3. (B) A promise of aid (10:19–20)
4. (A′) Dangers from family (10:21–22)
5. (B′) A promise of aid (10:23)

nor sandals, nor a staff (10:9–10a; cf. Mark 6:8–9). In Mediterranean culture, Cynics were characterized by a double cloak, a purse, and a staff (Diogenes Laertius, *Vit. phil.* 6.22–23; *Cynic Epistles*, Diogenes 7, trans. Malherbe 1977). Essenes carried nothing with them except their weapons. They did not allow a change of garments or shoes (Josephus, *J.W.* 2.125–26). The Twelve in Matt. 10 are depicted as more restricted in what they carry than either Essenes or Cynics. The Twelve can travel light because **the workman is worthy of his food** (10:10b; cf. Luke 10:7b; 1 Cor. 9:14; 1 Tim. 5:18; *Did.* 13.1–2). Verses 11–13 (cf.

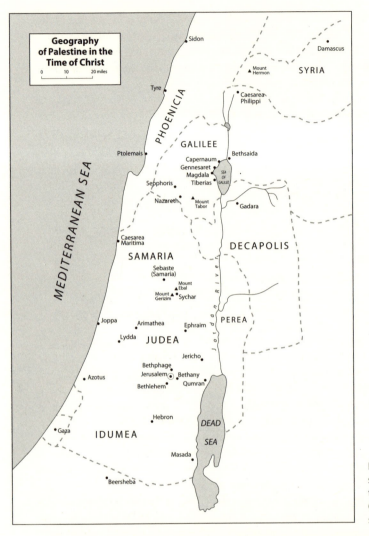

Geography of Palestine in the Time of Christ

0   10   20 miles

Sidon

Damascus

Mount Hermon ▲

SYRIA

Tyre

Caesarea Philippi

PHOENICIA

GALILEE

Ptolemais

Bethsaida

Capernaum

Gennesaret

Magdala

Tiberias

SEA OF GALILEE

Sepphoris

Nazareth

Mount Tabor ▲

Gadara

MEDITERRANEAN SEA

Caesarea Maritima

DECAPOLIS

SAMARIA

Sebaste (Samaria)

Mount Ebal ▲

Mount Gerizim ▲

Sychar

Jordan River

Joppa

Arimathea

Ephraim

PEREA

Lydda

JUDEA

Jericho

Bethphage

Jerusalem

Bethany

Azotus

Bethlehem

Qumran

Hebron

DEAD

Gaza

IDUMEA

SEA

Masada

Beersheba

Figure 7. Map of Palestine showing gentile regions to the north and east of Galilee, and Samaria to the south.

Mark 6:10; Luke 10:5–7) say that when a missionary enters a village, he should stay where the proclamation has already found a favorable reception (Gundry 1982, 188). If the proclamation is rejected, leave (10:14; cf. Mark 6:11; Luke 10:10–11). In support of the efforts of the Twelve, there is Jesus's proleptic pronouncement of judgment (10:15; cf. Luke 10:12): **If anyone will not receive you and does not listen to your words, . . . truly I say to you, it will be better for the land of Sodom and Gomorrah** (Gen. 19:24–28; Isa. 1:9–10) **on the day of judgment than for that city.** How one treats the emissaries is how one treats Jesus (Matt. 10:40; *Mek.* 18.12: "Whoever receives the Sages is as if he received the Shekinah"). The missionaries have not only Jesus's authority in the present but also his promise of ultimate support. With this promise of support, the first segment of the harvest mission to Israel comes to an end.

10:16–23. This is the second subunit that has a link with the frame of the discourse (Jesus's disciples on a pre-Easter mission to Israel). Only at 10:18 is there material that evokes a possible post-Easter setting. This subunit begins with (1) a heading. The material that follows (10:17–23; cf. Mark 13:9–13) falls into an ABA′B′ pattern: (2) A, dangers from officialdom (10:17–18), (3) B, a promise of aid (10:19–20), (4) A′, dangers from family (10:21–22), and (5) B′, another promise of aid (10:23).

1. Matthew 10:16 (cf. Luke 10:3) functions as the heading for the unit (10:16–23). **Behold, I send you out as sheep in the midst of wolves. Therefore, be as wise as serpents and as harmless as doves.**

2. Section A, 10:17–18, speaks about dangers from officialdom, Jewish and gentile. **Beware of humans. They will deliver you to councils** (local Jewish courts; cf. *m. Sanh.* 1.1–6), **and in their synagogues they will flog you. And before governors and kings they will bring you on account of me, for a witness to them and to the gentiles.** The question is, Were Jesus's followers brought before kings and governors during the pre-Easter period? One might say that, because of King Herod's threat (2:3, 16) to the baby Jesus and because of the Baptist's arrest (4:12) and martyrdom (14:10; 11:12), it would not be a stretch for the Matthean Jesus to anticipate in general terms such a danger during his ministry.

3. Section B, 10:19–20, offers a promise of aid. **When they deliver you up, do not be anxious about how or what you will say. For it will be given to you in that hour what you will say. For it is not you who speak but the Spirit of your Father that speaks through you.**

4. Section A′, 10:21–22, returns to a warning, this time of dangers from family. **Brother will deliver up brother to death and a father his child, and children will arise against parents and they will kill them** (cf. Mic. 7:6; *m. Sotah* 9.1; *b. Sanh.* 97a). **And you will be hated by all because of my name. And the one who remains faithful to the end, this one will be saved.**

5. Section B′, 10:23, returns to a promise of aid. **When they persecute you in this city, flee to the other. For truly I say to you, you may not finish going to all the cities of Israel until** (*heōs*) **the son of man comes.** Exactly how 10:23 should be read is a matter of debate (Sabourin 1977).

The dominant reading is that Matt. 10:23 is a reference to the parousia (as in 13:41–42; 16:27; 25:31). If the logion is taken this way, then it predicts the son of man's parousia within the time span of the mission of the Twelve to Israel. It is a prediction of an imminent parousia. This is precisely how A. Schweitzer (1957, 165–66) took the saying. The appearing of the son of man would overtake them before they had gone through the cities of Israel. In spite of its popularity, this reading faces real difficulties. First, the Matthean Jesus is then made to contradict himself about his knowledge of the time of the end (24:36: "Now concerning that day and hour, no one knows, neither the angels of the heavens nor the Son, but only the Father"). Second, the Matthean Jesus is made to contradict himself regarding the gentile mission (24:14: "This gospel of the kingdom will be preached in the whole world for a witness to all the nations, and then the end will come"; 28:19–20: "As you go, make disciples of all the nations, . . . and behold, I am with you all the days until the end of the age"). Third, the Matthean Jesus then contradicts himself about a delay in the time of the parousia (24:48: "my master is delayed"; 25:5: "when the bridegroom was delayed"; 25:19: "after a long time the master comes"). Matthew does not expect an imminent end (McDermott 1984). Fourth, when Matthew speaks about the son of man in connection with the parousia, he usually makes reference to a coming on the clouds or a coming with angels. Matthew 10:23 has neither connection. Further, sayings about the son of man's coming fall into two camps: those that refer to Jesus's coming in the present (5:17; 9:13; 10:34–35; 18:11) and those that refer to his coming at the parousia (16:27; 25:31). The usage that occurs nearest to 10:23 is a historical coming (9:13; 10:34–35).

The difficulties an interpreter faces when 10:23 is taken as a logion about the parousia has led others to read it as a reference to a different event, such as the resurrection of Jesus (Cullmann 1948, 8; Morris 1992, 258), Pentecost (a view known to Calvin 1972, 302), the destruction of Jerusalem in AD 70 (Feuillet 1961; Hagner 1993, 1:278–80), or a series of events preceding the parousia of which the parousia is the type (Giblin 1968). The fact that none of these offered solutions fits the Matthean context renders them useless for reading Matthew's plot.

Is there another explanation for 10:23 that fits better in its Matthean context? First, consider the language. To whom is 10:23 addressed? The "you" (pl.) is the same "you" as in 10:16, that is, the Twelve. How should *heōs* be translated? The English translations vary between "before" (RSV, NJB, NAB, NIV, TEV, REB) and "until" (KJV, NASB). *Heōs* with an aorist subjunctive denotes that the commencement of an event is dependent on circumstances (e.g., Matt. 2:13: Joseph is told by the angel to remain in Egypt "until I tell you"). So in 10:23, the disciples may not finish their mission to the cities of Israel **until the son of man comes.** The meaning, then, is that the disciples will not complete their mission to Israel until Jesus comes to help. Finishing depends on that circumstance (BDAG 422–23.1β). This statement, then, is not a consolation of the Twelve in the midst of their suffering but rather a promise of aid in the completion of their mission.

Second, consider the context. On the one hand, 10:23 is in the mission discourse rather than in the eschatological speech of Matt. 24–25. This places the burden of proof on those who want to read 10:23 in apocalyptic terms. On the other hand, the organization of Matt. 10 places verse 23 within the context of the sending out of the Twelve (Luz 1994, 42). This puts the burden of proof on those who want to read 10:23 in terms of a later time.

Third, consider the usage of "son of man" within Matthew's narrative development. The only son-of-man sayings in Matthew so far have been 8:20 and 9:6. In the former, son of man could be a circumlocution for "I" or it could be a reference to a prophetic figure like Ezekiel. In the latter case, son of man almost certainly is used as a referent for a prophetic figure like Nathan. Neither has any eschatological connotations. In 11:19, son of man is either a circumlocution for "I" or a reference to a prophetic figure. In 13:37, the son of man is the sower, a prophetic figure active in the present. Not until 13:41 does the auditor hear a reference to son of man that has any eschatological overtones. The development of the narrative would therefore not demand an apocalyptic reading of son of man. Indeed, it would incline the auditor to take son of man either as a circumlocution for "Jesus" or as a reference to a prophetic figure who proclaims the word.

Fourth, consider the depiction of Jesus in the thought unit 9:35–11:1. The unit begins in 9:35 with the statement "Jesus went around all the cities and villages, teaching in their synagogues and preaching the gospel of the kingdom and healing every disease and illness." The unit continues with Jesus giving the twelve disciples authority to do what he has been doing (10:1). The discourse ends in 11:1 with the statement that Jesus "went on from there to teach and to preach in their cities."

These various observations about the Matthean setting for the logion lead one to read 10:23 as Jesus's saying that it may take the son of man's presence and help to complete the Twelve's mission. This meshes nicely with the need expressed in 9:37 for more workers to help with the plentiful harvest. To meet the great need, Jesus sends out the Twelve. The harvest is so great that they may not be able to finish their assignment until Jesus comes to help. In Matthew, the Twelve do not return to report. Instead, they go and Jesus also goes and eventually joins them to help complete the task. (Examples of scholars who see 10:23 as a reference to Jesus coming to join the disciples at some point in his ministry include John Chrysostom, *Hom. Matt.* 34 [*NPNF* 10:226]; Dupont 1958; D. Wenham 1984, 219–52; Witherington 2006, 223.)

Once one has read Matt. 10:23 in light of its Matthean context, one should then look at Luke 9:52, where Jesus sends messengers ahead of him, and 10:1, where Jesus sends disciples ahead of him to every town and place where he intends to go. There was, then, a tradition about disciples being sent out on mission and about Jesus joining them later. This is not precisely the Matthean point, but it is close. To sum up: 10:23 refers to the unrepeatable mission of the Twelve to the lost sheep of Israel, a mission that will not be completed until Jesus comes to help.

The Ongoing Mission of Disciples Generally (10:24–42)

After completing his discussion of the mission of the Twelve to Israel (10:5b–23), the evangelist turns to the ongoing mission of disciples generally

(10:24–42). This section has no specific ties with the sending out of the Twelve during Jesus's pre-Easter ministry. It gives timeless teaching relevant for later disciples on mission. There are four subunits: 10:24–25 (negative responses are to be expected; unique to Matthew), 10:26–31 (negative responses are not to be feared; cf. Luke 12:2–7), 10:32–39 (the important thing is faithful discipleship; cf. Luke 12:8–9, 51–53; 14:26–27; 17:33), 10:40–42 (a promise of Jesus's solidarity with disciples; unique to Matthew). The section is held together by an inclusio, beginning with 10:24–25 (a disciple's identification with the master) and ending with 10:40–42 (Jesus's identification with the disciples).

> ### An Outline of Matthew 10:24–42
>
> **The ongoing mission of disciples generally (10:24–42)**
>
> Negative responses to be expected (10:24–25)
>
> ... but not feared (10:26–31)
>
> Faithful discipleship (10:32–39)
>
> Jesus's solidarity (10:40–42)

10:24–25. The first subunit comes in 10:24–25. It consists of a principle and an application. The principle is found in 10:24–25a. **A disciple is not above the teacher nor a slave above his lord. It is sufficient for the disciple to become as his teacher and the slave as his lord.** The principle was common. *Sifra* on Lev. 25:23 has God speaking to Israel: "You are servants." *Sifra* comments: "It is enough for the servant that he be as his master." The application is found in 10:25b: **If they have called the master of the household Beelzebul, how much more the members of his household** (cf. 9:34; 12:24, 27). Negative responses are to be expected.

10:26–31. The second subunit consists of three admonitions built around **do not fear** (10:26a, 28, 31a) and their reasons (10:26b–27, 29–30, 31b). The reasons offered are that there will be an ultimate, public vindication (10:26b–27), and the disciples are precious to their heavenly Father (10:29–30, 31b). Negative responses are not to be feared.

10:32–39. The third subunit has two parts: 10:32–33, making a public confession of Jesus, and 10:34–39, placing Jesus ahead of one's family. Why is Jesus responsible for division within families? It is because he demands an ultimate loyalty to himself. "The ties that bind are relativized in favour of a newly found, more fundamental tie" (Nolland 2005, 441). The important thing is faithful discipleship (cf. 8:21–22; 19:16–22).

10:40–42. In the fourth subunit Jesus expresses his identification with his disciples in a fourfold refrain. (1) **The one receiving you receives me, and the one receiving me receives the one who sent me.** (2) **The one receiving a prophet because he is a prophet will receive a prophet's reward.** (3) **The one receiving a righteous person because he is a righteous one will receive a righteous one's reward.** (4) **Whoever gives only a cup of cold water to one of these little ones because that one is a disciple, truly I say to you, he will not lose his reward.** In this context, "the little ones" are explicitly disciples of Jesus (cf. Zech. 13:7 and

2 Bar. 48.19, where "little ones" are the people of God; cf. Matt. 18:6, 10, where "little ones" are disciples of Jesus). How the disciples are received is regarded as how Jesus is received. This is the Matthean Jesus's promise of solidarity with his disciples, who are on mission at any time and in any place.

Closing Narrative Frame (11:1)

Having covered two sections of the discourse proper, the evangelist returns to the narrative framework (third-person narration) and brings this section to its close. **And it came to pass when Jesus had finished instructing his twelve disciples, he went away from there to teach and to preach in their cities** (11:1; cf. 8:1; also 13:53; 19:1; 26:1).

Functions of the Unit as a Whole

Looked at in terms of the forest instead of the trees, the focus of Matt. 9:35–11:1 is on mission. The unit begins and ends with statements about Jesus's mission (9:35; 11:1) arising out of his compassion for the crowds (9:36). Because the task is so great (9:37a), and sensing the need for more workers (9:37b–38), Jesus gives his twelve disciples authority to participate in his mission (10:1, 7–8a). The discourse proper gives instructions to the Twelve (10:5b–23) and then to others beyond that time (10:24–42) about the conduct of mission. This simple plot development raises two questions regarding how these words about mission function in the overall Matthean context.

First, does the focus on mission in 9:35–11:1 function to define Matthew's understanding of the nature of the church? Ulrich Luz (1994, 39–55) contends that Matt. 10 provides a basic direction for a new ecclesiology. On the one hand, Protestant ecclesiology, he says, interprets the visible church as the assembly where the gospel is taught purely and the sacraments are administered rightly. The proclaimed gospel and the two sacraments are the only visible marks of the church in the world. If so, then what the church actually looks like (whether it is rich or poor, democratic or hierarchical, a lay church or a theologian's church) and what it does (whether it is politically engaged or not, whether it supports apartheid or socialism or capitalism) is irrelevant as long as the word is preached and the sacraments observed. On the other hand, for Roman Catholics the church is visible not only in word and sacrament but also in its institutional forms—in the visible office of the bishop, the visible priesthood, the visible sacramental ministry, and in the whole visible body of the church. The line between the visible and invisible church is virtually obscured.

Matthew's concept of the church, Luz argues, is very different. In Matt. 10, the church consists of the disciples who follow Jesus. It is neither the church's teaching and sacraments nor the church's institutional hierarchy that are the visible marks of the church. For Matthew, the visible marks of the church of Jesus's disciples are its life of poverty (10:9–10), its defenselessness (10:17–23a), its persecution (10:24–25, 26–31), its deeds of justice (10:8). The visible marks of the church in Matthew are the disciples' life of obedient mission, practicing what is commanded by Jesus. The Matthean view of the church is that of a dynamic community of obedient disciples on mission. Matthew's church is a community on the way. This concept, however, has been marginalized in the history of the mainline churches.

What shall one say to this presentation? Yes . . . but. Yes, this is part of Matthew's view of the church, but it is only a part of it. Matthew 9:35–11:1 is only one of the five designated discourses in the First Gospel. Matthew 5–7 has its contribution to make, as do Matt. 13; 18; and 24–25. Mission is at the heart of the Matthean view of the church, but so are the surpassing righteousness, received revelation, congregational relations, and eschatological perspective. As a corrective, Matt. 10 is an effective agent, but as a balanced perspective, it is defective and in need of supplementation from the other four discourses. The first function of 9:35–11:1, therefore, is as a corrective for deficient ecclesiologies that ignore the comprehensive nature of Matthew's view of the church. It functions to make mission central to the life of disciples.

Second, Matt. 9:35–11:1 also functions to make clear that the granting of authority by Jesus must precede the disciples' mission. Enablement *precedes* commissioning. So Jesus "gave them authority" (10:1) *before* "these twelve he sent out" (10:5a) and *before* he gave instructions about how to proceed (10:5b–14). Gift precedes demand not only when one begins the life of discipleship (cf. 4:18–5:2) but also throughout the disciples' following Jesus on mission (cf. Luke 24:49; Acts 1:8).

Matthew 9:35–11:1 also continues the First Gospel's concern to be heard as an encomium (praise) to Jesus. This segment of Matthew first of all praises Jesus's deeds of magnanimity. In 9:36 "when [Jesus] saw the crowds, he had compassion on them because they were . . . like sheep having no shepherd." Everything that follows in this discourse section arises out of and is an expression of Jesus's compassion (cf. 14:14; 15:32; 20:34). This segment also praises Jesus for his wisdom. According to Quintilian's categories (*Inst.* 3.7.15), this large discourse that gives guidance to his disciples would have been regarded as reflecting his wisdom. Both of these matters would have been heard in Mediterranean antiquity as praiseworthy (Neyrey 1998).

Theological Issues

To the Lost Sheep of Israel versus To All the Nations

One of the more perplexing issues raised by Matt. 10 is the contrast between 10:5b–6 ("Into the way of the gentiles/nations do not go, and into a city of the Samaritans do not enter. Go rather to the lost sheep of the house of Israel"), on the one hand, and 28:19 ("As you go, make disciples of all nations"; cf. 24:14:

"This gospel of the kingdom will be preached in all the world as a witness to the nations"), on the other. How is this difference to be explained?

Any explanation must begin with the recognition that Matthew sees a number of periods in the history of salvation's final phase (Davies and Allison 1988, 1:167). John the Baptist represents one such period. It is a time of preparation for the coming one, Jesus (3:11, 14; 11:9–11; 17:10–13). In Jesus's career, the evangelist draws a distinction between pre- and post-Easter periods (9:14–15; 13:37–43; 17:9). Within the pre-Easter period are two observable phases: a time when Jesus's ministry is directed to Israel as a whole (4:12–16:12) and a time when he focuses primarily on his disciples (16:13–20:28). The key distinction here is between pre- and post-Easter phases of Jesus's career. Simply put, the Matthean Jesus reflects a certain Jewish missionary theology that allows for both 10:5–6 and 28:18–20.

In Mic. 4:1–14 (MT); Isa. 2:2–4; and Tob. 14:5–7 is a similar oracle that speaks about God's ultimate redemption of the people of Israel. This is done in terms of Mount Zion being exalted, the temple in Jerusalem being elevated, so that all nations see that God is with Israel. As a result of seeing God's restoration of Israel, the nations flow toward Jerusalem and worship the true God. As Tob. 14:6–7 puts it, "Then the nations in the whole world will all be converted and worship God in truth. They will all abandon their idols, . . . and in righteousness they will praise the eternal God." The same viewpoint is reflected in yet other oracles found in Zech. 8:20–23; *1 En.* 10.21; and *Sib. Or.* 3.710–20.

In Isa. 25:6–8 the ingathering is portrayed in terms of a great feast at which all people are assembled, the messianic banquet. In all such oracles the perspective is the same. First is the restoration of Israel. Then, as the result of this display of God's might, the nations come to worship the true God. There are two stages in this Jewish eschatological soteriology: first the restoration of Israel, then the inclusion of the gentiles.

The Matthean Jesus subscribes to this theological position. In 8:11–12, he says, "Many from the east and the west will come and will recline at table with Abraham, Isaac, and Jacob in the kingdom of heaven, and the children of the kingdom will be cast out into the outer darkness." In this context, the people from east and west are gentiles, and the children of the kingdom are Jews who have rejected the presence of God in Jesus. That is, the Matthean Jesus stands within the Jewish theology that expected the gentiles to be gathered in at the messianic banquet. He, however, works for the restoration of the lost sheep of the house of Israel in the here and now (cf. 15:24). Since the twelve disciples are to participate in his mission in 9:35–11:1, Jesus sends them also only to the lost sheep of the house of Israel (10:6). When the risen Christ, however, commissions his disciples to make disciples of all nations (28:19), it is because after the resurrection the gentiles are to be gathered in. The two perspectives about a mission to Jews only and about a mission to all nations represent two stages in a Jewish mission theology subscribed to by the Matthean Jesus (Jeremias 1958, 55–73, who tries to relate it to the historical Jesus).

How Long Does the Mission to Israel Last?

A second question raised by the Matthean section on mission (9:35–11:1) has to do with the time frame of the mission to Israel. Does it belong strictly to the pre-Easter period so that after Easter there is only a mission to gentiles? Or does the mission to Israel continue after Easter? On the one hand, D. R. A. Hare (1967, 147–57) is a representative of the former view. He contends that the First Gospel assumes the abandonment of the mission to Israel after Easter. "Matthew sees both Jesus's mission and the mission of his messengers as having the purpose of exhibiting and bringing to completion the already existing guilt of Israel" (Hare 1967, 151). The purpose of Jesus's mission is to accomplish the transfer of the kingdom from Israel to the church. After Easter, there is no mission to Israel (cf. also Meier 1979, 30–31). On the other hand, Ulrich Luz (1989, 1:84–86) thinks that the Matthean community is still engaged in the mission to Jews but has not yet fully accepted the gentile mission, while Ferdinand Hahn (1965, 127) argues that the Matthean community has fully accepted the gentile mission but also continues the mission to the Jews. Luz and Hahn agree that the Jewish mission continues after Easter (cf. also Trilling 1959, 47, 68, 75, 76). Axel von Dobbeler (2000) contends that the two missions are complementary expressions of the one mission of Jesus. A final decision on this matter must be postponed until the discussion of Matt. 28:18–20.

PART 3

Matthew 11:2–13:53

Jesus's Ministry Creates Division

This third major section of Matthew consists once again of a narrative (11:2–12:50) and a discourse (13:1–53). The distinction between the disciples, who see and understand, and most others, who do not, becomes apparent in the narrative and is reflected upon in the discourse.

Matthew 11:2–13:53 in Context

Birth narratives (1:1–2:23)

Jesus's ministry begins (3:1–8:1)

Jesus's authority is revealed (8:2–11:1)

▶ **Jesus's ministry creates division (11:2–13:53)**

  Narrative: Jesus encounters a divided response (11:2–12:50)

  Discourse: Jesus reflects on the divided response (13:1–53)

Jesus focuses on his disciples (13:54–19:2)

Jesus and judgment (19:3–26:1a)

Passion and resurrection narrative (26:1b–28:20)

Matthew 11:2–12:50

Narrative 3:
Jesus Encounters a Divided Response

Introductory Matters

The Relation of Matthew 11–12 to What Precedes and Follows

On the one hand, Matt. 10 is linked not only with chapters 8–9 but also with chapters 11–12. Matthew 10 prepares for the rejection of Jesus by Israel in chapters 11–12. In particular, 11:20–24 echoes 10:14–15 and 12:24 echoes 10:25 (Bauer 1988, 130). Also, 11:5 reprises the miracles of chapters 8–9, and 12:23 echoes 9:27 (Garland 2001, 125). On the other hand, Matt. 11–12 is the narrative section tied closely to the third discourse that follows (13:1–53). As is customary in the First Gospel's arrangement, the link between the two is thematic. So in 11:2–13:53 are three themes that occur in both narrative and discourse: divine revelation (11:25–27; 13:11–17); diverse responses, positive and negative (11:3, 16–19, 20; 12:2, 14, 23, 42, 45, 50; and 13:3–9, 18–23); and coming judgment on wrong responses (11:24; 12:30–32, 33–37, 41–42, 43–45; and 13:24–30, 36–43, 47–50).

The Structure of Matthew 11–12

A variety of proposals have been offered regarding the structure of chapters 11–12. Most commentators find little coherence in these two chapters and deal with the material mostly pericope by pericope. A few, however,

Matthew 11:2–12:50 in the Narrative Flow

Birth narratives (1:1–2:23)

Jesus's ministry begins (3:1–8:1)

Jesus's authority is revealed (8:2–11:1)

Jesus's ministry creates division (11:2–13:53)

▶ *Narrative*: Jesus encounters a divided response (11:2–12:50)

  Jesus the Christ: Rejection brings judgment (11:2–24)

    Who is Jesus? (11:2–6)

    Who was John? (11:7–15)

    Rejection of Jesus and John (11:16–19)

    Pronouncement of woe (11:20–24)

  Jesus the Son: Conflict and withdrawal (11:25–12:21)

    Son, revealer, and giver of rest (11:25–30)

    Rejection: Picking grain on the Sabbath (12:1–8)

    Rejection: Healing on the Sabbath (12:9–14)

    Jesus withdraws (12:15–21)

  Jesus, the Spirit-anointed servant (12:22–50)

    Rejection: Casting out Beelzebul (12:22–37)

    Rejection: The demand for a sign (12:38–45)

    Warnings and a pronouncement (12:46–50)

try to find an overall pattern. Daniel Boerman (2005) suggests a chiastic arrangement:

> A 11:1–19
>   B 11:20–24
>   C 11:25–30
>   D 12:1–14
>   C′ 12:15–21
>   B′ 12:22–45
> A′ 12:46–50

W. D. Davies and Dale Allison (1991, 2:233–34) argue for three triads (11:2–30; 12:1–21; 12:22–50), each of which follows the pattern unbelief/rejection, unbelief/rejection, and invitation/acceptance. David Verseput (1986) also sees three major divisions in chapters 11–12, each with a similar arrangement. He contends, however, that there are three cycles of material portraying Jesus as the Christ, the Son, and the Servant. They are followed by a general rejection. In cycles one and three, the cycles end with warnings of judgment. This proposal, as adapted in the accompanying outline, seems best to reflect the flow of the narrative.

In Matt. 11:2–24, Jesus is the Christ (11:2–6), and John is Elijah (11:7–15). Both meet rejection (11:16–19). Those who have rejected them will face judgment (11:20–24). (Cf. also Gundry 1982, 204, who recognizes the unity of 11:2–24.)

In 11:25–12:16, Jesus is the Son, the revealer, and the giver of rest (11:25–30). He meets rejection in two conflict stories (12:1–8, 9–14). In response to a plot against him, Jesus withdraws (12:15–16). The transitional quotation from Isa. 42:1–4 in Matt. 12:17–21 links what has come before with what is to follow. The quotation explains Jesus's withdrawal, which precedes, and his link with the Spirit, which follows.

In 12:22–50, Jesus is the Spirit-anointed servant/child whose exorcisms show that the kingdom is active in Jesus's ministry. He meets with rejection in two controversy stories (12:22–37; 12:38–45), rejection that results in warnings of judgment, and in a pronouncement story about true family (12:46–50).

By the end of the narrative section (11:2–12:50), the reader is aware that Jesus's ministry has met with widespread rejection. The reader is also aware that the disciples who have responded positively make up Jesus's true family.

Tracing the Narrative Flow

Jesus the Christ: Rejection Brings Judgment (11:2–24)

The first of the three triads comes in 11:2–24. The pattern is (1) Jesus is the one who is to come, (2) he meets rejection, and (3) this results in warnings of judgment.

Its pieces are held together by four sets of questions:

John asks, "Are you the coming one?" (11:3)

Jesus asks, "What did you go out into the wilderness to see?" "What did you go out to see?" "Why did you go out?" (11:7, 8, 9)

"To what shall I liken this generation?" (11:16)

"And you, Capernaum, will you be lifted up to heaven?" (11:23)

Formally, the first triad consists of two subunits: 11:2–19 and 11:20–24. The first subunit is framed by an inclusio: deeds (11:2 and 19) and Jesus's coming (11:3 and 19). Thematically, it consists of 11:2–6 (Who is Jesus?); 11:7–15 (Who is John?); and 11:16–19 (What response do Jesus and John get?). The second subunit (11:20–24) is a prophetic oracle of woe against Chorazin, Bethsaida, and Capernaum because of their negative response to Jesus's mighty works.

11:2–6. Matthew 11:2–6 (cf. Luke 7:18–23) is a dialogue between the Baptist and Jesus mediated through John's disciples. The evangelist provides the setting. **John, having heard in prison about the works of the Christ, sending his disciples, said to him, "Are you the coming one** (Matt. 3:11; 21:9; 23:39; Acts 19:4; Heb. 10:37), **or should we expect another?"** (11:2–3). Given the expectation of the Baptist voiced in 3:11 (the coming one is the judge of the end time), John's perplexity is understandable.

Jesus's answer is for the disciples of John to go and tell the Baptist what they hear and see (11:4). **The blind see and the lame walk, lepers are cleansed and the deaf hear, and the dead are raised and the poor hear good news** (11:5). Jesus then adds, **Blessed is the one who does not find a stumbling block in me** (11:6). There is no use of titles by Jesus for himself. The evangelist has already introduced him as the Christ/messiah (11:2). Jesus appeals instead to his deeds.

These are the very things that Jesus has done in chapters 8–9. They are also the types of things that were expected in the messianic times (Isa. 26:19: dead raised; Isa. 29:18–19: deaf hear, blind see, poor hear good news; Isa. 35:5–6: blind see, deaf hear, lame walk, dumb speak; Isa. 42:7: blind see, prisoners freed; Isa. 61:1: good news to the oppressed, release of prisoners).

Some Jewish traditions associated the messiah with miracles. At Qumran, 4Q521 (frag. 2, col. 2) is a messianic apocalypse that associates the messiah (line 1) with the poor receiving the Spirit (line 5); with freeing prisoners, giving sight to the blind, and straightening the twisted (line 8); with healing the badly wounded, making the dead live, proclaiming good news to the meek, and enriching the hungry (line 12). This indicates that the Isaianic passages cited above were interpreted by at least some Jews of Jesus's time as deeds of the messiah in the end time (Wise and Tabor 1992; Falcetta 2003). In *2 Bar.* 70.9–10, salvation in the end time comes to those who are in the hands of God's servant, the anointed one (note the use of "servant" and "anointed one" as synonyms; cf. Matt. 12:17–18; 3:16–17; 17:5). In *2 Bar.* 73.1–2, when the

Miracle Lists in Early Christianity

A number of early church fathers cite lists of Jesus's miracles that reflect a common tradition. Justin Martyr says:

> *"Concerning the prophecy that our Christ should cure all diseases and raise the dead to life, hear what was spoken. Here are the exact words of the prophecy: 'At His coming the lame shall leap like a stag, and the tongue of the dumb shall be clear; the blind shall see, and the lepers shall be cleansed, and the dead shall rise and walk about.'"* (*1 Apol.* 48.1–2, trans. Falls 1948, 85)

Cyprian says Jesus

> *"drove out from men the demons by His word, . . . nerved up the paralytics, cleansed the leprous, enlightened the blind, gave power of movement to the lame, raised the dead again, compelled the elements to obey Him . . . , the winds to serve Him, the seas to obey Him, the lower regions to yield to Him."* (*Idol.* 13, ANF 5:468)

Tertullian says Jesus was

> *"expelling devils from men by a word, restoring vision to the blind, cleansing the leprous, reinvigorating the paralytic, summoning the dead to life again, making the very elements of nature obey Him, stilling the storms and walking on the sea."* (*Apol.* 21.17, ANF 3:35)

Such lists were presented as signs of messianic legitimacy.

messiah sits on the throne of his kingdom, then rest will appear, health will descend, illness will vanish, fear will pass away, and joy will encompass the earth. In this milieu, Jesus would be saying to the Baptist that the messianic times have indeed arrived (cf. Matt. 12:28), but the time of judgment is still in the future (cf. 25:31–46). Who is Jesus? He is the messiah/Christ. How do we know? He is known by his deeds.

11:7–15. In 11:7–15 (cf. Luke 7:24–28; 16:16), the focus shifts to the question, Who is the Baptist? First, there is a statement about who he is not (11:7–8). John is not one who like a reed is blown this way and that by the changing winds; nor is he an elegantly clad court lackey. These two negatives may very well be veiled references to Herod Antipas (Theissen 1991, 26–39). Second, there is a statement about who John is (11:9–15). He is **a prophet, . . . yes, and more than a prophet. This is the one about whom it is written, "Behold, I am sending my messenger before your face, who will prepare your way before you"** (11:9–10; cf. Mal. 3:1). In 11:14 the point is clearly stated. **If you are willing to receive it, this is Elijah who is to come** (cf. 17:12). What is his place in God's salvific history? He stands on the cusp of two eras. He is the last and greatest of the prophets, whose task is to prepare for the coming of the one in and through whom the times of fulfillment are inaugurated, but his stature is less than anyone who belongs to the time of fulfillment (11:11, 13; cf. Heb. 11:39–40). **From the days of John the Baptist until now, the kingdom of the heavens suffers violence, and violent ones lay hands on it** (11:12). This difficult saying, in context, probably refers to the violent treatment of the Baptist by Herod Antipas (cf. 4:12; 14:1–12; 17:12; Cameron 1984, 214–46). Those associated with the kingdom suffer violence, including Elijah who prepares for the coming of the Lord (cf. 17:11–13). This was, after all, the fate of the prophets (cf. 2 Chron. 36:15–16).

11:16–19. What kind of response do John and Jesus receive from their contemporaries? This is the issue addressed in 11:16–19 (cf. Luke 7:31–35). Formally this pericope follows an ABB′A′ pattern:

A playing the flute (11:17a)
  B wailing (11:17b)
  B′ John came (11:18a)
A′ the son of man came (11:19a)

Here A and A′ refer to Jesus, B and B′ to John. The order of the parable (playing the flute before wailing) reflects the order within the preceding material (Jesus in 11:2–6; John in 11:7–15). The order of the interpretation reflects the chronological order (John before Jesus). The parable runs: **To what shall I compare this generation? It is like children sitting in the marketplace who call to others, saying, "We played the flute for you and you did not dance, we wailed and you did not mourn"** (11:16–17). The interpretation follows. **For**

John came neither eating nor drinking, and they say, "He has a demon." The son of man came eating and drinking, and they say, "Behold, a glutton and a drunkard (cf. Deut. 21:20, a rebellious son), a friend of tax collectors and sinners" (11:18–19; cf. 9:11). The commentators follow one of two readings. Either John and Jesus are the children who refuse to play (they refuse to conform to the wishes of this generation; Linton 1976) or John and Jesus are the children who criticize their playmates for not joining in their games (they will not join in because they want neither an ascetic nor a world-affirming religious reform; Schweizer 1975, 264). The major objection to the second reading is that the introduction in 11:16a explicitly compares this generation to the children speaking. This objection reflects a misunderstanding of the relation of introductions to the parables they introduce. The kingdom of God is not like a grain of mustard seed, nor is it like a merchant in search of pearls, nor is this generation like children calling to their playmates. The parables reflect a process that makes the point. So the kingdom is like "a mustard seed that when planted turns into a full-grown shrub that shelters birds," and like "a merchant who found the greatest gem and sold all for it," and likewise this generation is like kids who just do not want to play. Once it is recognized that the process reflected in the parable is its point, the objection no longer carries weight. Then context takes over and lends decisive weight to the second reading. This generation is like children who just will not play any game (a commonplace in antiquity; cf. Epictetus, *Diatr.* 24.20, who speaks of children who say, "I won't play any longer," when the thing does not please them). John and Jesus both have met rejection from their contemporaries. The issue is unreasonable rejection.

This pericope ends with Jesus's statement, **Wisdom is justified by her works** (11:19b). The issue here is whether this text identifies Jesus with wisdom (*sophia*). A number of scholars have argued that Matthew identifies Jesus with wisdom, yielding a wisdom Christology of incarnation: wisdom incarnate (Suggs 1970; Christ 1970; D. Smith 1970). Others oppose this reading (Pregeant 1996; Gench 1997; and Macaskill 2007). The strength of the latter scholars is their determination to read 11:19b in light of the overall context. The focus in chapter 11 so far has been on the rejection of John and Jesus by their contemporaries. So, in context, wisdom's deeds are the ministries of John and Jesus that manifest the righteousness of wisdom. If one expands the context to include chapter 10, then wisdom's deeds also include those of the twelve disciples, who have met rejection. Read in context, then, 11:19b refers not to Jesus as the incarnation of wisdom but to the ministries of John, Jesus, and Jesus's disciples. Their deeds vindicate God's salvific plan, showing God to be faithful to his relationship with the people of God.

11:20–24. Matthew 11:20–24 (cf. Luke 10:13–15) is a pericope consisting of two prophetic oracles of woe (11:21–22 against Chorazin and Bethsaida; 11:23–24 against Capernaum), each following the pattern: address, indictment, verdict (cf. Num. 21:29–30; Jer. 13:27; 48:46; Rev. 8:13; Matt. 23:13, 15, 16, 23, 25, 27, 29). These Jewish cities are indicted because if Jesus's deeds of power had been done in gentile cities like Tyre and Sidon, or in a notoriously wicked city like Sodom, the gentile/wicked auditors would have repented. (*T. Ash.* 7.1 exhorts right living by saying, "Do not become like Sodom, which did not recognize the Lord's angels and perished forever" [*OTP* 1:818].) There is no excuse for these Galilean, Jewish towns. Their position at the judgment will be dire. With this note, the first cycle in 11:2–12:50 is finished.

Jesus the Son: Conflict and Withdrawal (11:25–12:21)

The second of the three cycles in 11:2–12:50 comes in 11:25–12:21. Here Jesus is depicted as son of the Father, the revealer, and the giver of rest (11:25–30). In 12:1–8 and 12:9–14, two conflict stories convey the negative reactions. Both are set on the Sabbath; both have Pharisees as the opponents; both depict Jesus as the object of criticism. In response to a plot against him, Jesus withdraws (12:15–16). A quotation from Isa. 42:1–4 then transitions into the next cycle.

11:25–30. The presentation of who Jesus is opens the cycle (11:25–30; cf. Luke 10:21–22). This pericope is composed of three ingredients: a thanksgiving for revelation (11:25–26), a declaration about the medium of revelation (11:27), and two invitations and two promises (11:28–29). Verses 25–26 are a thanksgiving by Jesus for God's revelation (cf. 1QH^a 7.26–33). **I give thanks to you, Father, Lord of heaven and earth, because you have concealed these things from the wise and understanding and have revealed them to little children. Yes, Father, because such was pleasing to you.** What are **these things**? In 13:11 what has been revealed to the disciples are the "mysteries of the kingdom of heaven," which surely would include the secret of Jesus's messiahship (Schnackenburg 2002, 108). In the Qumran hymns is similar thanksgiving for God's revelation to the elect (e.g., 1Q35, frag. 1: "[I give you] thanks, Lord, because you have taught me your truth, you have made me know your wonderful mysteries" [trans. García Martínez 1996, 361]).

Matthew 11:27 is a declaration about the medium of revelation. **All things are delivered to me by my Father and no one knows the Son except the Father, nor does anyone know the Father except the Son and to whomever the Son may wish to make a revelation** (cf. John 3:35; 13:3; 10:14–15; 17:25). It is out of the mutual knowledge between Father and Son that the Son's revelation is possible. Similarities may be found in the relation between Moses and God (cf. Deut. 34:10: "Moses, whom the Lord knew face to face"; Num. 12:8: "with him I speak face to face"; Exod. 33:12–23: reciprocal knowledge; Sir. 45:1–5: out of the face-to-face knowledge, Moses was able to teach the people; Allison 1988).

Matthew 11:28–30 concludes with two invitations (A and A′) and two promises (B and B′).

A Come to me all those who are tired and weighed down;
　B and I will give you rest.
A′ Take my yoke upon you and learn from me, because I am meek and
　　lowly in heart
　B′ and you will find rest in your souls, for my yoke is pleasant and my
　　burden is easy to bear.

The term "rest" is often a synonym for salvation (cf. Heb. 3:11; 4:1, 3, 5, 10–11; Rev. 14:13). The image of the yoke comes from the practice of porters who would lay the heavy wooden bar on their neck and shoulders as they carried the burdens of others. Some burdens were heavy (Lam. 5:5: "With a yoke on our necks we are hard driven; we are weary, we are given no rest"). The image is used in Matt. 23:4 for the scribes and Pharisees' imposition of rigorous religious duties on the people. By contrast, the Matthean Jesus's burdens are easy to bear. "Jesus . . . invites persons to enroll in his school, . . . where he is both the teacher and the core curriculum" (Garland 2001, 135). Although parallels between Jesus's words here and statements about wisdom in Jewish sources are sometimes referenced to argue that the Matthean Jesus sees himself as wisdom incarnate, this seems unlikely. The word "wisdom" is not used here; son is preferred. Moreover, the two most distinctive features of the Jewish *sophia* (wisdom)—preexistence and mediator in creation—do not appear in this text (Gench 1997, 119). Furthermore, the image of taking the yoke upon oneself was used of torah (*m. Avot* 3.5) and the commandments (*m. Ber.* 2.2) as well as of wisdom (Sir. 51:26). When the image is used with wisdom, wisdom is understood as the equivalent of torah. The yoke of Jesus, as Matthew understands it, is not fidelity to a code but dedication to a person (Maher 1975).

12:1–8. The first conflict story in this section, 12:1–8 (cf. Mark 2:23–28), follows the pattern of occasion (12:1), criticism (12:2), and response (12:3–8). The occasion: **At that time Jesus was proceeding on the Sabbath through the grainfields. His disciples were hungry and began to pick the grain and to eat** (12:1). Deuteronomy 23:25 says, "If you go into your neighbor's standing grain, you may pluck the ears with your hand." The criticism: **Now the Pharisees, seeing**

Jesus's Claim to Uniqueness as a Stumbling Block

The Jewish rabbi Jacob Neusner has written a book in which he imagines himself accompanying Jesus, listening to him, and then deciding not to become a disciple (2000). At one point in the process, Neusner imagines himself going to the local rabbi to debrief after a day of hearing Jesus teach. The local rabbi asks, "What did Jesus leave out (of Torah teaching)?" Neusner responds, "Nothing." The rabbi then asks, "What did he add (to Torah teaching)?" Neusner responds, "Himself" (107–8). This was *the* obstacle, then and now.

it, said to him, "Look, your disciples are doing what is not lawful to do on the Sabbath" (12:2). Work on the Sabbath was forbidden (Exod. 20:10; Deut. 5:14). Harvesting on the Sabbath was considered to be working on the Sabbath (Exod. 34:21; *m. Shabb.* 7.2). The Pharisees in 12:1–8 apparently regard picking the grain heads as harvesting and hence as unlawful work.

The readings of Jesus's response take one of two directions. Either the argument of 12:1–8 aims to highlight Jesus's authority to define appropriate Sabbath behavior, or the unit functions to depict Jesus's discernment of the Sabbath's intent. To decide between them, one must focus on Jesus's reply in 12:3–8. Formally, Jesus's response consists of two examples from Scripture (12:3–4; 12:5–6) followed by the basis for his position (God's words, 12:7) and ending with his summation of the argument (12:8; J. Hicks 1984).

The first example comes in 12:3–4: **Have you not read what David did when he and those with him were hungry? How he entered into the house of God and ate the bread of the presence that was not lawful for him and those with him to eat, but for the priests only?** First Samuel 21:1–6 tells of David being on a secret mission for the king during which his physical need and that of his associates is met by the holy bread (Lev. 24:5–9). What is the point of the comparison of David and his men with Jesus's disciples? It is not that both take place on the Sabbath. David's act was not on the Sabbath. What the two events have in common is that hunger trumps legal rules (note that Matthew adds "hungry" to Mark in 12:1). Surely the Davidic precedent applies (Hillel's rule 2: argument from an equivalent regulation or situation; Evans 1992, 116–18). Human need takes precedence.

The second part of the defense is found in 12:5–6: **Or have you not read in the law that on the Sabbath the priests in the temple violate the Sabbath and have no guilt? I say to you, a greater thing than the temple is here.** According to Num. 28:9–10, priests perform their duties in the temple even on the Sabbath. The temple service takes precedence over Sabbath observance (e.g., *m. Eruv.* 10.11–15; *t. Shabb.* 15.16). What is the point of 12:5–6? Just as temple trumps Sabbath, so does the inbreaking kingdom of God. In Jesus, the kingly activity of God is at work (something greater than the temple sacrifices), making him and his ministry trump Sabbath observance (Hillel's rule 2: equivalent regulation or situation).

Why include verse 7? (Mark does not have it.) The basis of the defense appears in 12:7. It consists of a quotation from Hosea 6:6 (cf. Matt. 9:13). **If you knew what "I desire mercy and not sacrifice"** (God's words) **means, you would not have condemned the innocent.** The two examples, then, are illustrations of Hosea 6:6. If David and his men acted as they did because they were hungry, it was in line with the law's intent: mercy. If the temple sacrifices take precedence over Sabbath observance, and if mercy trumps sacrifices, then mercy takes precedence over Sabbath guidelines. In 12:8 one finds the Matthean Jesus's summation of the overall argument: **For the son of man is lord of the**

Figure 8. View looking south onto the Sea of Galilee.

Sabbath. What does 12:8 mean in context? In the Jewish scriptures, the son of man was used in at least three ways: of an insignificant creature valued by God (Job 25:4–6; Ps. 8:3–6); of a spokesman for God, a prophet (Ezek. 3:1–3, 4, 17); and of a heavenly figure who is to come at the end-time judgment (Dan. 7:13–14). Here in 12:8 "son of man" refers to the human creature so highly valued by God that securing the creature's welfare (mercy) trumps ritual and thereby Sabbath observance. Although Matt. 12 does not use Mark 2:27's "The sabbath was made for man, not man for the Sabbath" (RSV), Matthew's use of Hosea 6:6 affects the understanding of 12:8 in the same way.

12:9–14. The second conflict story is located in 12:9–14 (cf. Mark 3:1–6). The location changes from the grainfields to the synagogue. It is still the Sabbath. The opponents are still the Pharisees. The issue is still proper Sabbath observance. Formally, a healing story is shaped into a conflict story. There are four components: the setting (12:9–10a), the question (12:10b), the response (12:11–12), and the reactions (12:13–14).

The setting: **And leaving there he came into their synagogue. And behold, a man having a withered hand** (12:9–10a).

The question: **And they asked him, saying, "Is it lawful to heal on the Sabbath?" in order that they might accuse him** (12:10b). In the rabbinic tradition, there is a consistent forbidding of anything resembling healing on the Sabbath (*m. Shabb.* 14.3–4; *b. Shabb.* 18a, 53b, 75b, 108b, 111b, 128a, 140a, 147b–48a). In *m. Shabb.* 22.6, it is expressly forbidden to straighten a dislocated hand or foot on the Sabbath. Of course, if a life is in danger, this overrides the Sabbath (*m. Yoma* 8.6).

The response: **Which of you who has one sheep, and if it should on the Sabbath fall into a pit, will not lay hold of it and get it out? How much more valuable is a person than a sheep. So it is lawful on the Sabbath to do good** (12:11–12). In the rabbinic tradition (*b. Shabb.* 128b) an animal that falls into a pit on the Sabbath could be assisted (e.g., by feeding it or by supplying devices that would help it climb out), but it should not be lifted out. At Qumran regulations were more severe: do not lift the animal out (CD 11.13–14). Jesus's question seems to assume an average person's pragmatic response to such a situation, not that of the rigorous Pharisees or Essenes. Of course the animal would be lifted out. Then comes the comparison: how much more. The conclusion is that the Sabbath is a time to do good.

The reactions are twofold. On the one hand, Jesus says to the man, **Stretch out your hand** (12:13a). When the man stretches out his hand, it is restored as good as the other. Note that Jesus does not touch or lift the man. The man stretches out his hand, and God does the healing (cf. John 5:2–17). Here God's act of healing on the Sabbath reinforces mercy as Scripture's intent. (Tacitus, *Hist.* 4.81–82, and Dio Cassius, *Rom. Hist.* 65.8, tell of Vespasian healing a man with a useless hand.) On the other hand, the Pharisees go out and plot about how to kill Jesus. The rejection here is more than academic.

12:15–21. Knowing what they were plotting, **Jesus withdrew from there** (12:15; cf. 2:13, 22; 4:12). Many followed him, and he healed them all but told them not to make him known (12:16). According to 12:17–21, he did this **in order that the word through Isaiah the prophet might be fulfilled** (12:17). What follows is a transitional quotation (Isa. 42:1–4, only in Matthew) that links up with what has come before and what will follow:

> **Behold my child** (*pais*) **whom I have chosen,**
> **my beloved in whom my soul takes delight** (cf. Matt. 3:17; 17:5).
> **I will put my *Spirit* upon him**
> **and he shall announce judgment to the nations.**
> **He will *not quarrel* nor cry out loudly**
> **nor will anyone hear his voice in the streets.**
> **A bruised reed he will not break**
> **and a smoldering wick he will not quench**
> **Until he brings judgment to victory;**
> **And in his name the gentiles will hope.** (Matt. 12:18–21)

Early in this quotation there is a reference to the gift of the Spirit bestowed on the one spoken about. This ties Isa. 42:1–4 to Matt. 12:28 ("If by the Spirit of God I am casting out demons") that follows. Later in the quotation, the servant/child who is not publicly contentious links with what precedes (Jesus's withdrawal [12:15] and the command not to make him known [12:16]). So the first of the quotation has ties with what follows, and the last of the quotation has links with what precedes. This chain-link device ties the second and third cycles together (11:25–12:21 and 12:22–50; Neyrey 1982).

Jesus, the Spirit-Anointed Servant (12:22–50)

The third cycle follows the same pattern as the first: Jesus is the Spirit-anointed servant/child whose exorcisms show the kingdom inaugurated in his ministry. He meets rejection in two lengthy conflict stories (12:22–37; 12:38–45). This rejection meets warnings of judgment. A concluding pronouncement story tells about true family (12:46–50).

12:22–37. The initial conflict story in 12:22–37 is pieced together from a variety of traditions (cf. 12:22–24 with Luke 11:14–15; cf. 12:25–26 with Mark 3:23–26; cf. 12:27–28 with Luke 11:18b–20; cf. 12:29 with Mark 3:27; cf. 12:30 with Luke 11:23; cf. 12:31 with Mark 3:28–29; cf. 12:32 with Luke 12:10; cf. 12:33 with Luke 6:43–44; cf. 12:34–35 with Luke 6:45; 12:36–37 is unique to Matthew). It consists of a concise miracle story expanded into a conflict narrative (Repschinski 2000, 116–31).

Matthew 12:22–24 is a concise miracle story with the expected components: the problem (**Then they brought to him a demon-possessed man who was blind and could not speak** [12:22a]); the cure (**and he healed him so that he could speak and see** [12:22b]); and the reactions, which are twofold (**All the crowds were amazed and were saying, "Is this not the son of David?" The Pharisees, on hearing this, said, "This one casts out demons by Beelzebul, the ruler of the demons"** [12:23–24]). This was a charge leveled against Jesus elsewhere (Matt. 9:34; 10:25; cf. John 7:20; 8:48, 52; 10:20; Justin Martyr, *Dial.* 69; Stanton 2004). In the ancient Mediterranean world, miracle workers faced a variety of accusations: they used their power for evil purposes, to harm people; they used their power to gain riches or other power for themselves; they subverted the established order (Kolenkow 1976). In the Synoptic tradition, another charge is added. The miracle-worker Jesus is acting out of demonic power. (At Qumran, Beelzebub was used as a synonym for Satan; Penney and Wise 1994.) Other stories of the healing of mutes circulated in antiquity. (In *b. Hag.* 3a, a rabbi prays for two mute men, and they are healed; at Epidauros, stele 1.5 says that Asclepius healed a mute boy.)

What follows is Jesus's response to the Pharisees. It consists of three arguments (12:25–26; 12:27–28; 12:29) and three warnings (12:30; 12:31–32; 12:33–37; Carter 2000, 273).

The first argument (12:25–26) runs as follows: **Every kingdom divided against itself will fall, and every city or household divided against itself will not stand. And if Satan is casting out Satan, he is divided against himself. How then will his kingdom stand?**

The second argument (12:27–28) runs as follows: **If I by Beelzebul am casting out demons, by whom are your sons casting them out? Because of this, they will be your judges. If I by the Spirit of God am casting out demons,**

then the kingdom of God has come upon you. David had success in driving out the evil spirit that plagued Saul (1 Sam. 16:14–23). Solomon, a son of David, was associated in Jewish lore with power over demons (Josephus, *Ant.* 8.45–49; Pseudo-Philo, *L.A.B.* 60.3: one from David's loins would rule over evil spirits). Does **your sons** refer to these Davidic figures or to Jewish exorcists generally? It is probably the latter. (The practice of exorcism was prevalent in ancient Judaism. Compare the following texts: *T. Mos.* 10.1–3; *T. Dan* 5.10–13; 1QM 6.5–6; 14.8–10; 4Q510, frag. 1, 1–8; 4Q511, frag. 10, 7–12; 11Q11 [= 11QApPs^a] 1.2–6; 28.1–11; 1QapGen ar [= 1Q20] 20.16–32; 4Q242; Josephus, *Ant.* 8.42–49; 18.47; Pseudo-Philo, *L.A.B.* 60.)

The third argument (12:29) runs as follows: **How is one able to enter the household of a powerful person and take his things unless he first binds the strong one? Then he can plunder his household.** This surely is an allusion to the Jewish belief that the evil powers will be bound in the end time by God or his agent(s) (e.g., *Jub.* 5.6; 10.7, 11; *1 En.* 10.4; 13.2; 14.5; 18.16; *2 En.* 7.1; *2 Bar.* 56.13).

The flow of thought starts with the fact that Jesus casts demons out of people. The question raised is, by what power? The Pharisees say the power is itself demonic. Jesus says that it makes no sense for the demonic to destroy itself. Rather, the power is that of the Spirit. That exorcisms occur means that Satan has been bound and that Jesus is now plundering his realm. Since this was something that was expected in the end time (*1 En.* 10.4, 11–13; 55.4; *T. Mos.* 10.1; *T. Zeb.* 9.8), then the kingdom of God is breaking in.

The argument now moves to three warnings.

The first warning (12:30) runs as follows: **The one who is not with me is against me, and the one who does not gather with me scatters.**

The second warning (12:31–32) includes two sayings that are formally similar:

> **Every sin and blasphemy will be forgiven humans,**
> **but the blasphemy against the Spirit will not be forgiven.**

> **Whoever speaks a word against the son of man, it will be forgiven,**
> **but whoever speaks against the Holy Spirit will not be forgiven**
> **either in this or the coming age.**

The third warning (12:33–37) says, **Either you make the tree good and its fruit good, or you make the tree bad and its fruit bad. For by the fruit you will know the tree. You brood of vipers, how are you able to speak good things when you are evil? For from the overflow of the heart the mouth speaks. The good person from good treasure brings forth good, and the evil person from evil treasure brings forth evil. I tell you that at the last judgment humans will**

155

have to give an account for every foolish word they speak. For from your words you will be justified, and from your words you will be condemned.

The logic of the warnings begins with an either-or. You are either with me or against me. It continues by saying that the only sin that will not be forgiven is blasphemy against the Spirit. The second of the two parallel statements makes sense if once again (cf. 12:8) son of man here is taken to mean "human being" (Bauckham 1985). Then the contrast is between humans and God. Criticizing a human being is one thing, but confusing the Spirit's work with that of Satan is unpardonable. Why? To call good (God) evil (Satan) is to put oneself beyond the pale of redemption (Schnackenburg 2002, 116). The warnings end with the claim that whatever is said (i.e., about Jesus's exorcisms and their link with Satan or the Spirit) reflects the inner character of those speaking. By such words (and the implied character) one will be judged. With this the complex conflict story is at an end. It is to be followed, however, by yet another.

12:38–45. The second conflict story (cf. Luke 11:29–32; 11:24–26; Repschinski 2000, 133–42) begins with some of the scribes and Pharisees demanding a sign (12:38). Of course, already in Matthew people have been asking for healing from Jesus (e.g., 8:2, 6, 8; 9:18, 27). How is this different? "There is a difference between a request for a miracle out of some need, to which Jesus responds in a compassionate manner, and a request for a miracle to prove something about one's self" (Witherington 2006, 248). The demand for a sign here is the same as that in 16:1 and echoes the second temptation in 4:5–7. The demand is satanic. Jesus's response is given in two stages (12:39–42; 12:43–45).

Stage 1 begins with a recognition of the source of the demand. **An evil and adulterous generation seeks a sign** (objective, external proof, 12:39a). Then what will be given is specified. **No sign will be given to it except the sign of the prophet Jonah** (12:39b). And what might that be? In Matt. 12 it is twofold. In Luke 11:29–32, as in Matt. 12:41, the sign of Jonah is Jesus's preaching of repentance. In Matt. 12:40 an additional explanation is provided. **Just as Jonah was in the belly of the fish for three days and three nights, so the son of man** (here probably a prophetic figure who speaks God's message and suffers and dies for doing so) **will be in the heart of the earth for three days and three nights** (cf. Luke 16:31b).

Stage 2 (12:43–45) speaks about an unclean spirit going out of a person and then returning with seven more spirits worse than itself. The parallel material in Luke 11:24–26 consists of teaching about what must follow deliverance if the person is not to be worse off than before. "It is not adequate, however, to cast out a demon if there is no acceptance of the Kingdom of God whose power is attested by its expulsion. Only God's rule of human life prevents the return of demonic activity, hence those are blessed who 'hear the word of God and keep it'" (Talbert 2002, 143). "In order to benefit permanently from this divine power, however, one must respond properly" (Talbert 2002, 144). In Luke 11, therefore, the material refers to the experience of an individual who has been delivered. In Matthew, however, this experience of an individual who has been delivered and has been reinvaded by demons is used as an analogy/parable of a generation that has experienced the inbreak of God's reign, rejected it, and finds its end state worse than before Jesus's ministry. The parable is christological in import. The opponents' last state will be worse than their first because they refuse to acknowledge what God is doing in Jesus (cf. John 9:35–41; 2 Pet. 2:20). Once again, in the Matthean plot, Jesus comes out on top in his conflict with the scribes and Pharisees.

12:46–50. The chapter ends with the pronouncement story in 12:46–50 (cf. Mark 3:31–35). **While he was speaking to the crowds, behold, his mother and brothers stood outside seeking to speak to him** (12:46). Jesus's response to this news is a question and an answer: **Who is my mother and who are my brothers?** (12:48). **Stretching his hand out toward his disciples he said, "Behold my mother and my brothers. For whoever does the will of my Father in the heavens, this one is my brother and sister and mother"** (12:49–50). Here the community of Jesus's disciples replaces the natural family. (Philo knows the distinction between a kinship of blood and a kinship based on a relation to God. Cf. *Spec.* 1.317–18; 3.126; 3.155b; 4.159; *Abr.* 67; 167–99. Matt. 3:7–10 and 10:34–37 already reflect the concept.) The ending pericope of this thought unit (11:2–12:50), which has sketched Jesus's rejection by Israel—led by scribes

---

The Brothers and Sisters of Jesus

In Christian history there have been three different ways of reading references to Jesus's brothers and sisters.

1. They are true siblings (i.e., half brothers and half sisters with one common biological parent, Mary). This was a position taken early by Hegesippus (Eusebius, *Hist. eccl.* 2.23.4; 3.19.1–3.20.1), Irenaeus (*Haer.* 3.21.10; 3.22.4), and Tertullian (*Marc.* 4.19; *Carn. Chr.* 7; *Mon.* 8.1–2; *Virg.* 6.6). It was represented by Helvidius in the fourth century.

2. They are stepbrothers and stepsisters (i.e., children of Joseph by a previous marriage and thus legally but not biologically linked). An early representative of this position is the *Prot. Jas.* 9.2; 11.4; 19.3–20.1. It remained dominant in the East (so Epiphanius, *Pan.* 1.29.3–4; 2.66.19; 3.78.7, 9, 13).

3. They are cousins. This reading became dominant in the West. Jerome, *Against Helvidius*, is a late fourth-century advocate.

As a result of a careful study of the evidence, John P. Meier (1992), a Roman Catholic scholar and priest, concludes that if the historian is asked to render a judgment on the NT and patristic texts viewed simply as historical sources, then the most probable reading is that the brothers and sisters of Jesus were true siblings.

and Pharisees—makes clear that out of Israel has come a community of disciples that is a new family, the community that does God's will.

Functions of the Unit as a Whole

The use of the Matthean narrative to compose an encomium for Jesus continues into chapters 11–12. In order to praise a person, attention could be called to the individual's ascribed honor (e.g., the respect that comes from being a member of a certain family) or achieved honor (i.e., what is earned). In a shame-and-honor setting like ancient Mediterranean culture, most forms of competitive behavior consisted of challenges to another's reputation. Such challenges demanded a defensive riposte. Conflict stories are expressions of this Mediterranean competitive practice. They involve a challenge and a defense. Whoever comes out on top in the exchange achieves honor; whoever loses acquires shame. When the evangelist tells of Jesus's exchanges with the scribes and Pharisees, he relates the stories in such a way that Jesus wins and

---

Conflict Stories

Conflict stories all contain an objection and a riposte. They are found in Greco-Roman and Jewish settings in antiquity. Note these brief examples:

"Being once reproached for giving alms to a bad man, he [Aristotle] rejoined: 'It was the man and not his character that I pitied.'" (Diogenes Laertius, *Vit. phil.* 5.17, trans. R. Hicks 1925)

"Once when a tax-collector behaved insolently to him in the law court, and said: 'Stop barking at me,' Nicetes replied with ready wit: 'I will, by Zeus, if you too will stop biting me.'" (Philostratus, *Vit. soph.* 1.19, trans. Wright 1921, 65)

"A Roman general . . . questioned R. Johanan b. Zakkai. 'In the detailed record of the numbering of the Levites, you find the total is 22,300, whereas in the sum total one only finds 22,000. Where are the remaining 300?' He replied to him: 'The remaining 300 were Levite first-born, and a first-born cannot cancel the holiness of a first-born.'" (b. Bek. 5a, trans. Epstein 1948)

The conflict stories in Matthew are much longer and more complex than these parallels from their milieu. Not all conflict stories were so simple. Xenophon (*Mem.* 3.13.3) presents a conflict story in which Socrates and his unnamed opponent are involved in five exchanges. In *Gen. Rab.* 28.3.2, a conflict story involving Hadrian and Rabbi Joshua consists of three exchanges. It is also possible that Matthew's stories have been expanded by analogy with ancient "contests in dialogue" (Repschinski 2000, 292). If so, this allows the evangelist to portray Jesus as an exceptional adversary, which, of course, redounds to his praise.

---

acquires greater honor. Such honor is worthy of the readers' praise (Neyrey 1998, 15–20).

Theological Issues

In Matt. 11:27, Jesus makes a claim to be *the one mediator* of a knowledge of God. In fact, in the First Gospel the Matthean Jesus makes other audacious claims. For example, he claims to know how the last judgment will turn out (5:3–10; 8:11–12; 10:14–15; 11:22–23; 18:35; 19:28), what criteria will be in effect (5:3–10, 20; 7:21–23; 25:31–46), and who will be the judge (7:21–23); he claims to be the true expositor of God's will in Israel's scriptures (5:21–48; 19:3–9); he claims to be able to mediate God's forgiveness to sinners (9:2–8); he claims that one's relation to him determines one's fate at the last judgment (10:32–33); he claims to be greater than Jonah and Solomon (12:41–42); he predicts his death and resurrection (16:21; 17:22; 20:18–19; [26:2]); he predicts the transfer of leadership over God's people (21:43) based on reactions to him (21:44); he predicts the destruction of the temple (23:38; 24:2); he predicts his betrayer (26:21, 24), his denier, and his deserters (26:31–35); he claims to be the eschatological judge (26:64); he claims to have been given all authority in heaven and earth (28:18). The claim to be the one mediator of a knowledge of God is in character with how Jesus speaks and acts in the rest of Matthew.

These claims made by Jesus in Matthew are not out of line with those made by and for him elsewhere in the NT. John 10:7–9 ("I am the door of the sheep. All who came before me are thieves and robbers" [RSV]); 11:25–26 ("I am the resurrection and the life. . . . Whoever lives and believes in me shall never die" [RSV]); and 14:6 ("I am the way, and the truth, and the life. No one comes to the Father except through me") have Jesus speak with the same audacity as the Matthean Jesus. Acts 4:12 has Peter make such a claim for Jesus ("There is no other name under heaven given among mortals by which we must be saved"). In 1 Tim. 2:5 the same claim is made ("For there is one God, and there is one mediator between God and men, the man Christ Jesus" [RSV]). In 1 John 2:23 the same theme is expressed ("No one who denies the Son has the Father; everyone who confesses the Son has the Father also"). Revelation 5 provides a scene in heaven in which the book of destiny, sealed with seven seals, cannot be opened by anyone except the Lamb who was slain. In Rev. 3:21 the risen Christ says to the church in Laodicea, "To the one who conquers I will give a place with me on my throne, just as I myself conquered and sat down with my Father on his throne." Such references within the NT could be multiplied. The depiction of Jesus in the First Gospel is at one with that in the rest of the NT writings.

Such claims face at least two challenges from some within as well as without the church. First, there is a discomfort arising out of the postmodern aversion to universal claims. Postmodernism denies universals. There are no values that are universally valid for all peoples in all times and places. Hence, truths that are held, whether by individuals or by cultures, are valid only within their respective cultures but not beyond them. When such truths presume to be metanarratives, they become oppressive. Postmodernists do make truth claims. The statement "Jesus Christ is the savior *for us*" is acceptable to a postmodernist (cf. Ariarajah 1985). The statement "Jesus Christ is savior *of the world*" is, however, untenable for a postmodernist. Hence, faith claims tend to become personal or cultural preferences (J. Edwards 2005, 166–71). This rejection of universal truth leads one to espouse soteriological pluralism. There are many ways to attain salvation. To claim the uniqueness of Christ, it is said, is to reflect the assumed superiority and arrogance of the West. It is divisive; it is elitist. It would seem that the only universal allowed by post-modernists is that there are no universals, a self-contradiction that undermines the entire argument.

Second, there are the objections arising out of the Jewish-Christian dialogue in the period after the Holocaust. Some argue that such a Christology is the root of anti-Semitism (Reuther 1974) and call for a two-covenant approach (e.g., the Jews [Rosenzweig 1971] and the Christians [Stendahl 1976; Gaston 1987; Gager 1983; 1990]). The advocates of this stance contend that there is one way of salvation for the Jews and another for gentiles. For Israel, their covenant relationship with God, never abrogated, guarantees their salvation. The gentiles, who do not enjoy this covenant relationship, are saved through Christ. Therefore, the gentiles will be saved through Christ, and the Jews will be saved without him. The Jews, then, are not saved by turning to Christ through missionary efforts of gentiles who have been saved through Christ. Although this position has no substantial support from NT texts, its appeal is that it offers a possible way to avoid the persecutions of the past. James Edwards poses the problem succinctly:

> Indeed, universal religious claims, especially as they appear in the West, are not obviously compatible with the many and diverse cultures, nations, and social systems of the world. Can people who profess one God, one way of salvation, and one moral code live responsibly, respectfully, and non-coercively among peoples who believe none of those things? And if so, how? (J. Edwards 2005, 183)

Can any religious group believe it is *the* religion and not be harmful to others?

Consider two issues. First, it is a fact that certain adherents of modern rabbinic Judaism, like ancient rabbinic Judaism, consider themselves *the* religion. Orthodox rabbi Henry Siegman writes:

> Traditional Jews affirm that Judaism is the "truest" religion. . . . They do not expect Christians to be offended by it. Conversely, Jews cannot be offended by parallel affirmations of faith made by Christians—or by Muslims, for that

matter. Furthermore, a Jewish "demand" that Christian theology recognize the validity of Judaism for Jews is problematical in that it implicitly grants a Jewish legitimacy to Christian theology. Judaism constitutes a denial of the central Christian mystery and its notion of salvation; it cannot at the same time demand that Christianity be reformulated to accommodate the "equality" of Judaism. (Siegman 1978, 256)

The gist of such a statement is that adherents of universal religions regard pluralism as a betrayal of their religion. Do their claims to normativity endanger others?

There is certainly the potential for danger to others. In ancient Judaism, forced conversion of gentiles was practiced. In Christian history in the West, forced conversion of Jews was practiced. In India, an anticonversion law passed in 2003 allows Hindu extremists to harass Christians with spurious arrests and incarceration. In Russia, a state church has government power behind it to close evangelical Protestant worship centers. In Muslim countries, non-Islamic religions are persecuted by state law, and religious leaders call for the deaths of non-Muslims. What is the answer? The solution is not a universal religion's embracing soteriological pluralism. It is rather the recognition that power must never be used for or against the conscience of any human being in the area of religion. The separation of church and state is a place to begin. Religions' embracing the concept of religious liberty and the freedom of conscience is a crucial step. Persuasion must always be the only tool used for or against a religion. If this rule is granted, then each religion's claim to normativity may be granted. Each religious community can maintain its theological integrity and still agree on the necessity to guarantee all people their full civil liberties—including but not limited to their religious freedom. If all religions could agree on the principle of religious freedom, then there would be no danger from the one against the claims of the others.

Matthew 13:1–53

Discourse 3:
Jesus Reflects on the Divided Response

Introductory Matters

Matthew 13:1–53 is the third big discourse in the First Gospel. Note the typical concluding refrain in 13:53. It is held together by a thematic inclusio (12:46–50 and 13:53–58; Ewherido 2006, 65, 69–70). It is composed of seven or eight parables plus a theory of Jesus's parable usage. Using a series of parables was a literary convention (e.g., *Lev. Rab.* 2.4–5 has a series of five parables). This discourse follows a narrative (11:2–12:50) that highlights various reactions to Jesus (crowds, religious leaders, family, disciples), mostly negative, and that reflects the difference between disciples and all others. The discourse of 13:1–53 is also followed by a narrative that assumes this difference between disciples and everyone else (13:54–16:20). Building on this difference, 13:1–53 reflects on the two groups and their conflicting responses to Jesus and tries to explain why this is so.

How to Read Gospel Parables

Matthew 13 consists of a collection of seven or eight parables. To facilitate their reading, a brief word about the history of interpretation of parables is first necessary (Gowler 2000 provides an informative overview).

We may begin by noting two trajectories in parable interpretation. On the one hand, many scholars have detached the parables from their Gospel contexts in order to interpret them. Using a historical-critical approach, scholars have often used the detached parables to reconstruct a picture of the historian's Jesus

(Jeremias 1955 is a classic example). Scholars who use a literary approach have sometimes regarded the parables as autonomous, polyvalent aesthetic objects that may be detached from their Gospel contexts and read within a different belief system (Via 1967 and Wittig 1975 are obvious examples). On the other hand, there are readers who concentrate on the meaning of the parables in their Gospel contexts (e.g., Gerhardsson 1991; Kingsbury 1969; Carter and Heil 1998; Münch 2004; Snodgrass 2008). The order and connection of the Matthean context is regarded as the carrier and control on the meaning of the parables. In this commentary, the interpretative task is understood to be reading the parables in their Matthean context as part of the overall plot of the First Gospel.

If the parables are read in their Gospel context, there are both external and internal controls on one's reading (Crossan 1992). External controls include commentary (e.g., Matt. 13:3–8 is interpreted by 13:18–23; and 13:24–30 is interpreted by 13:36–43; and 13:47–48 is interpreted by 13:49–50) and context (e.g., Matt. 18:12–13 in context reads differently from the same parable in Luke 15:3–6 read in its context). Internal controls consist of the very details

An Old Testament Parable

In 2 Sam. 12:1–7, the prophet Nathan is sent to David the king. Nathan said:

"There were two men in a certain city, the one rich and the other poor. The rich man had very many flocks and herds; but the poor man had nothing but one little ewe lamb, which he had bought. He brought it up, and it grew up with him and with his children; it used to eat of his meager fare, and drink from his cup, and lie in his bosom, and it was like a daughter to him. Now there came a traveler to the rich man, and he was loath to take one of his own flock or herd to prepare for the wayfarer who had come to him, but he took the poor man's lamb, and prepared that for the guest who had come to him." (vv. 1b–4)

When David was angry (v. 5) and demanded justice (v. 6), Nathan said to him, "You are the man!" (v. 7). This is a story plus an interpretation used to confront an immoral situation.

A Parable Ascribed to Socrates

Aristotle offers a saying of Socrates as an example of a parable. Socrates said, "If one were to say that magistrates should not be chosen by lot, . . . this would be the same as choosing as representative athletes not those competent to contend, but those on whom the lot falls or as choosing any of the sailors as the man who should take the helm, as if it were right that the choice should be decided by lot, not by a man's knowledge" (*Rhet.* 2.20.4, trans. Freese 1975). This is a simple comparison.)

A Rabbinic Parable

This passage from *Exodus Rabbah* 20.5 shows how a parable was used to interpret Scripture.

"Another interpretation of: AND IT CAME TO PASS, WHEN PHARAOH HAD LET THE PEOPLE GO. It is written: 'Thy shoots are a park of pomegranates' (Song of Songs IV, 13). It is like one who had a field in which there was a heap of stones. This he sold to another man who removed the heap and discovered running water beneath it. He then planted therein rows and rows of vines, and various kinds of spices and pomegranates. . . . He also built a tower wherein he placed a keeper, with the result that all who passed by the field stopped to praise it. When its former owner happened to pass by and saw it teeming with all good things, he exclaimed, 'Woe is me, that I should have sold and let out of my hands such a field!' Israel, likewise, were but a heap of stones in Egypt, . . . but no sooner did they depart than they became a park of pomegranates." (trans. Freedman and Simon 1939, 3:246)

embedded in the story itself (e.g., in Matt. 22:1–14 the addition of the material about the man without a wedding garment makes the story read differently from Luke 14:16–24, which lacks this incident).

It is important next to note the recent concern with the functions of parabolic language. Parables do not so much provide new information for their auditors as they function performatively (Hagner 1993, 1:364–65). For example, questions can function as requests for information (e.g., Are you married? To which one replies yes or no as appropriate) or as catalysts for existential self-examination (e.g., Are you happily married? In response to which, one must reflect and engage in self-examination before answering). If the parables in Matt. 13 function performatively, they could do so in several ways: to deconstruct a world, to construct a new world, and/or to reinforce a new world already partially constructed. When addressed to nondisciples, the parables function as questions that are catalysts for existential self-examination. This can lead to the deconstruction of one's old world (by altering normal seeing) and as a guide to the construction of a new world (by enabling a new way of perceiving). Parables cause the hearer to see things differently, that is, in terms of Jesus's view of reality. When addressed to disciples, parables can lead to a reinforcement of their newly constructed world. Their seeing things differently is reinforced. Interpretations of parables that provide information often serve to reinforce the new world of disciples (Carter and Heil 1998, 60–63). Insofar as parables alter the auditors' perceptions, and thereby their dispositions and motivations, they enable character formation.

In Matt. 13, if it is assumed that the parables function performatively, then there is a further question: To whom is the performative parabolic language addressed? John Paul Heil (Carter and Heil 1998, 64–95) rightly recognizes the performative function of the parables in Matt. 13. His terminology for this function is alternately "pragmatically," "pragmatics," "pragmatic message," "pragmatic model." His interest is in how these parables perform in relation to the First Gospel's *audience* (disciples and nondisciples *outside* the Gospel who are listening to its narrative). In this commentary, however, the concern is for the performative function of the parables in relation to the *characters* being addressed by them *within* the Matthean narrative world and plot (e.g., how the crowds and the disciples *in* the First Gospel would have been affected). This type of reading would then control the way Matthew's audience would be expected to understand and react to the parables.

The Structure of Matthew 13:1–53

There are three major suggestions for understanding the organization of 13:1–53. The first sees two parts with a division at 13:36 (e.g., Kingsbury 1969, 12; Hagner 2000; Roloff 2005). Part 1 (13:1–35) is set outside the house; part 2 (13:36–52) takes place inside the house. There cannot be any doubt that the schema "outside the house, inside the house" controls the discourse. It cannot be defended, however, that part 1 (outside the house) is addressed only to the crowds while part 2 (inside the house) is addressed to disciples. Matthew 13:10–23 is clearly spoken to disciples. The second suggestion argues for three parts: 13:1–23, 24–43, and 44–52 (e.g., Davies and Allison 1991, 2:370–72; Boring 1995, 8:301). It is true that the First Evangelist often uses triads. It is also true that there may be an inclusio holding each of the triads together (sower/sower; tares/tares; treasure/treasure), although perhaps not as decisively as it first appears. This structure, however, ignores the shift from outside to inside (13:1, 36) and the distinction between crowds and disciples. The third proposal argues for four divisions: 13:1–9, 10–23, 24–35, and 36–52 (e.g., Carter and Heil 1998, 65–66; Patte 1987, 185). This arrangement observes the distinction between crowds (13:1–9, 24–35) and disciples (13:10–23, 36–52) and recognizes the break between outside the house (13:1–35) and inside the house (13:36–52), although perhaps not as strongly as does Matt. 13. The arrangement that will be used in this commentary on Matt. 13:1–53 is a combination of the two-part and four-part schemas.

Matthew 13:1–53 in the Narrative Flow

Birth narratives (1:1–2:23)

Jesus's ministry begins (3:1–8:1)

Jesus's authority is revealed (8:2–11:1)

Jesus's ministry creates division (11:2–13:53)

Narrative: Jesus encounters a divided response (11:2–12:50)

▶ *Discourse*: Jesus reflects on the divided response (13:1–53)

Outside: To the crowds and to the disciples (13:1–35)

Inside: Teaching the disciples (13:36–53)

Tracing the Narrative Flow

The arrangement of 13:1–52 is in terms of the audiences addressed: crowds, disciples, crowds, disciples.

Outside: To the Crowds and to the Disciples (13:1–35)

In the first part of the discourse, delivered outside, the parable of the sower and the soils (13:1–9) poses the question to the crowds: Will you be part of the great harvest? (Isa. 55:10–11). Jesus explains to his disciples (13:10–23) that he speaks in parables because the people are obdurate. The disciples must continue being good soil. Then, again addressing the crowds (13:24–35), Jesus uses three parables. The parable of the wheat among the weeds asks, which seed are you? The following double parable (mustard seed and leaven) assumes a link between Jesus's ministry and God's eschatological triumph and asks, will you be part of it? The summarizing quotation from Ps. 78:2 in Matt. 13:34–35 indicates that Jesus's parables are a means of revelation.

An Outline of Matthew 13:1–35

Outside: To the crowds and to the disciples (13:1–35)

To the crowds: The sower (13:1–9)

To the disciples (13:10–23)

1. Why parables? (13:10–17)
2. Interpretation of the parable of sower (13:18–23)

To the crowds: Three parables (13:24–35)

1. Weeds among the wheat (13:24–30)
2. Double parable: Mustard seed and leaven (13:31–33)
3. Parables as revelation of mysteries (13:34–35)

13:1–9. The parable in Matt. 13:1–9 (cf. Mark 4:1–9), the first unit, is addressed to the crowds in the hearing of the disciples on the same day as the rejection in 12:24–45. The setting is outside the house and beside the sea (13:1). Because of the number of people, Jesus sits in a boat while the people stand on the shore (13:2). He teaches them many things in parables (13:3). Verses 3–9 are provided as one example of the many parables. It is about a conventional topic: types of listeners or pupils. The topic was addressed by Jews (e.g., Philo, *Congr.* 64–70, speaks about four types of listeners to philosophers' teaching; *m. Avot* 5.12–15 says there are four types of disciples, distinguished by their responses to the master's teaching) and by Greco-Roman writers (e.g., Plato, *Phaedr.* 61, gives a parable of Socrates that uses the imagery of a farmer sowing seed in different types of soil as an analogy of a teacher sowing his words in his students; Seneca the Younger, *Ep.* 38.2, says, "Words should be scattered like seed; no matter how small the seed may be, if it once has found favorable ground, it unfolds its strength and from an insignificant thing spreads to its greatest growth" [Gummere 1970–79]). The conventional use of this analogy about hearers' responses to teaching fits the Matthean context perfectly. Matthew 11–12 has shown a variety of responses to Jesus's ministry. Matthew 13 is Jesus's reflection upon the types of responses.

The parable of the sower and the soils begins the reflection. There are four kinds of soil with four different results. First, some seed **fell beside the path,** with the result that **when the birds came, they devoured it** (13:4). Second, other seed **fell on stony ground,** where a thin layer of soil covers the rocky ledge. The twofold result was that the seed germinated quickly but then withered when exposed to the sun (13:5–6).

Third, still other seed **fell among thorns,** with the result that the thorns grew up and squeezed out the seedlings (13:7). Fourth, other seed **fell on good soil,** with the result that it produced fruit, as much as a hundredfold (13:8; a sign of God's blessing, as in Gen. 26:12; see also Pliny the Elder, *Nat.* 18.21.94–95). The parable assumes that there will be a blessed harvest (cf. Isa. 55:11 regarding God's word: "It shall not return to me empty, but it shall accomplish that which I purpose, and succeed in the thing for which I sent it"). It also says that not every soil/auditor will be good soil (cf. 2 Esd. [*4 Ezra*] 8:41: "Just as the farmer sows many seeds in the ground, . . . yet not all that have been sown will come up . . . ; so also those who have been sown in the world will not all be saved"). **Those having ears, let them hear** (13:9). This parable, in its cultural and Matthean contexts, poses questions to its auditors: Are you good soil? Will you be a part of the eschatological harvest? It is performative language that tries to deconstruct the auditors' old world and open them to a new way of seeing.

13:10–23. The second part of 13:1–52 is addressed to the disciples who have overheard Jesus's first parable to the crowds. It comes in verses 10–23 and consists of two subunits: (1) why teach in parables (13:10–17; cf. Mark 4:10–12) and (2) the interpretation of the sower/soils parable (13:18–23; cf. Mark 4:13–20).

1. Matthew 13:10–17, the first subunit, opens with a question asked by the disciples: **Why are you speaking to them in parables?** (13:10b). To which Jesus responds, **Because to you it has been given to know the mysteries of the kingdom of the heavens, but to those it has not been given. For whoever has, it will be given to them and they will have a lot; but whoever does not have, even that which they have will be taken away from them** (13:11–12). This is proverbial language. (Cf. *b. Ber.* 40a: A rabbi says that God is different from humans because whereas a human can only put something into an empty vessel, God puts more into a full vessel but does not fill an empty one. A similar view is found outside Judaism. Lucian, *Nigr.* 37, says that only those respond positively to a philosopher's teaching who previously have in their nature some secret bond of kinship with philosophy.) In this context, what the disciples have is faith in Jesus. What they are given beyond this is a deepening understanding of Jesus's teaching. (Philo, *Cher.* 48, says, "These thoughts, ye

initiated, whose ears are purified, receive into your souls as holy mysteries" [trans. Colson 1929–62]) **Because of this I speak to them in parables, *because* (*hoti*) seeing they do not see, and hearing they do not hear nor understand, and the prophecy of Isaiah (Isa. 6:9–10 LXX) is fulfilled in them, that says:**

> In listening you will hear and not understand,
> And seeing you will see and not know.
> For the heart of this people has grown dull,
> And with their ears they hear with difficulty,
> And they have closed their eyes
> Lest they should see with their eyes and hear with their ears
> And understand with their hearts and turn back,
> And I should restore them. (13:13–15)

In Mark 4:12 the critical word is *hina* (in order that); in Matt. 13:13 it is *hoti* (because). The difference is striking. In Mark, the parables are given in order that (for the purpose that) the people may not see, hear, and understand. The parables are intended to obscure the message. In Matthew, they are given because the people are hard hearted, dull of hearing, and spiritually blind. Parabolic speech is used because of (as a result of) the people's inability to understand (Evans 1989, 107–13; Kingsbury 1969, 49). Indeed in 13:35, the citation from Ps. 78:2 indicates that Jesus's speaking in parables is aimed at making known the mysteries of the kingdom. The parables are performative language with a benign intent, to restore the people, not to shut them out. **But blessed are your eyes because they see and your ears because they hear. For truly I say to you that many prophets and righteous people have wanted to see what you are seeing and have not, and to hear what you are hearing and have not** (13:16–17; cf. Heb. 11:39; *Pss. Sol.* 18.6: "Blessed are those born in those days, to see the good things of the Lord which he will do for the coming generation" [*OTP* 2:669]). Congratulations to the disciples for their privileged position (a reinforcement of their new world)!

2. The second segment of the address to the disciples comes in 13:18–23. It consists of Jesus's interpretation of the parable of the sower/soils in 13:3–9. He calls for the disciples to understand the parable's different kinds of soil (13:18). Why give the disciples this interpretation? Because they have, more is being given to them. **To all who hear the word of the kingdom and do not understand it, the evil one comes and seizes what was sown in their heart. This is what was sown beside the path** (13:19). (In *Jub.* 11.10–12, Prince Mastema sends crows and birds to pick the seed off the surface of the earth before the seed is plowed in.) **That which was sown on stony ground, these are the ones who hear the word and immediately receive it with joy but do not have root within themselves but are temporary, and when there is tribulation or persecution because of the word, immediately they are scandalized** (13:20–21). **Now those sown among the thorns, these are the ones who hear the word,**

but the cares of the age and the desire for wealth choke the word, and they become unfruitful (13:22). **But those sown on good soil, these are those who hear the Word and understand, who bear fruit and make some a hundredfold, some sixtyfold, and some thirtyfold** (13:23). The interpretation of the parable focuses on the reception of the word (Jesus's message) by his auditors. This didactic language, directed to disciples who have been told they are good soil, functions to reinforce their new world brought into existence by their faith in Jesus. Continue being good soil!

13:24–35. In 13:24–35 the focus shifts back to the crowds, with the disciples overhearing what is said. In these verses are three parables, each beginning with the phrase "another parable": (1) the parable of the weeds among the wheat (13:24–30) and (2) a double parable featuring the mustard seed and leaven (13:31–33). Then comes (3) a summarizing comment on parables as revelation of mysteries (13:34–35).

1. The first parable, the weeds among the wheat (13:24–30) is unique to Matthew. The scenario of weeds and wheat competing in the field was a conventional analogy for God's people among the nations (cf. *Ag. Ber.* 23). The Matthean parable is about two sowings and their outcomes. **The kingdom of the heavens is like a man sowing good seed in his field. But while the men slept, his enemy came and sowed** *zizania* (darnell, a weed that resembles wheat as it comes up) **in the midst of the wheat and went away** (13:24–25). When the weeds came up amid the wheat, the servants asked if they should go and pull up the weeds (13:26–28). The master replied, **No, lest when you pull up the darnell you also disturb the wheat. Leave both to grow together until the harvest. At that time I will say to the harvesters, "First pull up the darnell plants and bind them in bundles in order to burn them, but collect the wheat into my barn"** (13:29–30). Addressed to the crowds, this parable is performative language. It asks them: Which sowing do you represent? What outcome can you expect? The aim of such questions is to shatter their old world and point toward a new way of seeing through Jesus's eyes. Because of their hardness of heart, provocative language is needed.

2. The next two parables, the mustard seed (13:31–32; cf. Mark 4:30–32) and the leaven (13:33; cf. Luke 13:20–21), form a double parable and should be taken together. Both are parables of contrast. In both the contrast is between a tiny beginning and a very sizable ending. On the one hand, the mustard seed was famous for its minute size. From no other small seed, however, did the fully grown plant attain the size of the mustard plant. The shrub could reach a height of ten to twelve feet. On the other hand, the leaven referred to was a small piece of fermented dough. When put within three measures of flour (enough to feed a hundred people at a single meal), it leavened the whole, a sizable outcome (cf. 1 Cor. 5:6). The contrast between the small amount of leaven and the large mass of bread is the same as that between the tiny mustard seed and the fully grown shrub. The two parables possess an assumed

confidence about the link between Jesus's ministry, which is small in scope, and God's eschatological triumph in the entire creation. Given the link, the double parable poses a question to the crowds: Will you be a part of God's cosmic victory? This is performative language, posing an existential question that aims to shatter their old world and point toward the creation of a new one. Given the link, the way to be a part of the grand end result is to align oneself with Jesus and his small movement in the here and now.

3. The conclusion to this half of 13:1–53 comes in 13:34–35. **All these things Jesus spoke in parables to the crowds, and without a parable he spoke nothing to them. So the word through the prophet might be fulfilled, saying, "I will open my mouth in parables, I will announce things hidden from the foundation of the world"** (Ps. 78:2). This quotation makes clear the evangelist's understanding of parables as vehicles for the revelation of mysteries. In the parables addressed to the crowds to this point, Jesus has confronted them with a series of questions: What type of soil are you? To which planting do you belong? What outcome do you expect? Will you be a part of God's end-time triumph? All of these questions, raised by the parables, aim to shatter their old world and create a new one based on faith in Jesus.

Inside: Teaching the Disciples (13:36–53)

In the second part of the discourse, delivered inside, all attention is focused on the disciples. Teaching on the last judgment functions to reinforce the disciples' understanding of themselves as good seed: they must continue to be who they are (13:36–43). The double parable of the treasure in the field and the pearl of great price (13:44–46), focused on the incalculable value of the kingdom, for which all else is to be abandoned, reinforces the decisions the disciples have made already: they have done the right thing. The parable of the net (13:47–50), which repeats the message that good and evil are mixed together until the last judgment, again reinforces the disciples' world: they are to continue to be righteous ones. The concluding dialogue (13:51–53) tells the disciples that because they understand their instruction, they are like a householder who brings old and new from his treasure.

13:36–43. At 13:36 the location and audience change. Thus far Jesus has been outside; now he moves inside the house, leaving the crowds and focusing exclusively on the disciples. **And his disciples came to him, saying, "Explain to us the parable of the darnell of the field"** (13:36). Since to those who have, more will be given, Jesus proceeds to interpret the parable. **The one who sows the good seed is the son of man** (cf. 9:6; 10:23). **The field is the world** (not the church, because the context here has nothing to do with church discipline; that comes in Matt. 18; here the issue is still Israel's unbelief, not that of the church [Davies and Allison 1991, 2:428, 430; Luomanen 1998a]). **The good seeds are the children of the kingdom. The darnell plants are the children of the evil one. The enemy who sowed them is the devil. The harvest is the**

end of the age; the harvesters are the angels (for angels as agents of judgment, cf. *1 En.* 53.3–5; 63.1). Just as the darnell is gathered and cast into the fire, so it will be at the end of the age. The son of man (Matt. 16:27; 24:30; 25:31–46) will send his angels, and they will collect from his kingdom (cf. 1 Cor. 15:24–25, 28) all the stumbling blocks and those doing lawlessness, and they will cast them into the furnace of fire. . . . Then the righteous will shine as the sun in the kingdom of their father (13:37–43). Once again, to those who have, more will be given. In this case, traditional apocalyptic information is given, information that the disciples would have known

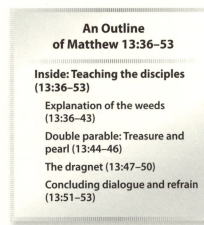

**An Outline
of Matthew 13:36–53**

Inside: Teaching the disciples (13:36–53)

Explanation of the weeds (13:36–43)

Double parable: Treasure and pearl (13:44–46)

The dragnet (13:47–50)

Concluding dialogue and refrain (13:51–53)

already. The interpretation, then, serves to reinforce and confirm their new identity. Continue as children of the kingdom of the son of man.

13:44–46. Jesus then proceeds to tell another double parable: the treasure in the field (13:44) and the pearl of great price (13:45–46), both unique to Matthew. This time the double parable is addressed to disciples, not to the crowds. In the first parable, a man finds, by accident, a treasure hidden in a field (not an uncommon thing in antiquity; cf. Josephus, *J.W.* 7.114–15; *Songs Rab.* 4.12.1; Horace, *Sat.* 2.6.10–13). In the latter parable, a pearl of great value is located by earnest seeking (parables about pearls were commonplace; cf. *Midr. Teh.* 28.6; *Mek.* 20.2.9; *b. Shabb.* 119a). The focus is twofold. First, the exceptional value of the objects is highlighted. Second, the extraordinary sacrifice made in each case to possess the valuable object (sells all) concludes each story. (The theme of sacrificing relative goods for an ultimate good was conventional. Philo [*Prov.*, frag. 2.21–22] says that Socrates considered "that there is nothing good or excellent save acquiring virtue, for which he labored neglecting all the other goods. And who with the thought of the genuine before them would not disregard the spurious for its sake?" [trans. Colson 1929–62]) These two little parables are addressed to disciples who have left everything to follow Jesus (cf. Matt. 4:18–22; 19:27). They are not, therefore, aimed to deconstruct their auditors' worlds. The disciples have already been deconstructed and reformed around the object of great value, Jesus. The parables in this context, then, function to reinforce and confirm the disciples' new world. You have done exactly the right thing!

13:47–50. The final parable, the seventh, is found in 13:47–50 (unique to Matthew), unless 13:52 is an eighth. In this case the parable (13:47–48) and its interpretation (13:49–50) come together. **Again the kingdom of the heavens is like a dragnet cast into the sea, and it collects every kind of fish, which when**

Figure 9. Remains of an ancient fisherman's boat discovered in the shore of the Sea of Galilee.

it is full is pulled up on the shore, and sitting down they put the good fish into a basket, but the bad they throw away (13:47–48).

This type of net had one end attached to the shore. The other end was taken out by boat in a wide circle and then back to land. The upper part of the net was held up by corks; the lower was weighted. Since this method caught all kinds of fish, the fishermen, once back on shore, had to sort them. This meant that some were kept and some were discarded (Kingsbury 1969, 119). **So it will be at the end of the age. The angels will come and take the evil ones from the midst of the righteous and will cast them into the furnace of fire** (13:49–50a). Like the interpretation of the parable of darnell among the wheat, this parable and its interpretation speaks about the last judgment, when there will be a separation of good from evil. This traditional apocalyptic teaching is addressed to disciples who are, therefore, understood as belonging to the righteous. The parable and its interpretation function as a reinforcement of their new identity based upon their faith in Jesus. Continue as those who at the last judgment will be kept.

13:51–53. The discourse comes to an end in 13:51–53, a portion unique to Matthew. In 13:36–50 Jesus has been directing his teaching exclusively to his disciples. Now, having finished his discourse, he asks them, **Have you understood all these things?** They answer, **Yes** (13:51). (They will demonstrate later that they understand a lot less than is apparent here. Cf. 14:17, 28–31; 15:16, 33; 16:5–8, 22–23; etc.) To this Jesus's reply is given in parabolic form. **Because of this** (your understanding), **every scribe discipled in the kingdom of the heavens is like a householder who brings forth from his treasure new and old** (13:52). The image is that of a storeroom where the master of the house keeps provisions of every kind to meet the needs of the household. Christian scribes (cf. 23:34), as reflected in chapter 13, draw on the old (the scriptural tradition) and the new (Jesus's role in it all) to meet needs just as the master

---

Metaphors of Judgment in Matthew

Fishing (with a net) for humans was a metaphor often used in Mediterranean antiquity for final judgment by God/a god. In the Jewish world, there are several examples. In Scripture are Hab. 1:14–16 (humans are like fish that God drags out with his net) and Ezek. 32:3–4 (God's dragnet is a metaphor of God's judgment on Pharaoh). In rabbinic literature, the final fishing activity of God is manifest at the end of history. In the Greek world, gods could be said to fish for humans as a metaphor of judgment. For example, Hades is the god of retributive justice and the punisher of wrongdoers; to be caught in his net is to be brought to justice by trial, whose outcome is either vindication or condemnation. In the ancient Near East, the net of Shamash is for the Semites what the net of Hades is for the Greeks. In Matt. 13:47–50, the same net metaphor is used for the last judgment. In Matt. 13:24–30, 36–43, however, the metaphor for the last judgment is the harvest. In 25:31–46, the separation of the sheep and goats is yet another metaphor for the final tribunal (Wuellner 1967).

---

of a household would. This was an expected practice (e.g., *b. Sanh.* 99a: a rabbi says, "Whosoever studies the Torah and does not revise it is likened unto one who sows without reaping" [trans. Epstein 1948]; *b. Eruv.* 21b: a rabbi asks his student the meaning of "new and old." Upon receiving what he regards as a wrong answer, he suggests that the "old" are the commandments derived from the Torah, while the "new" are those derived from the words of the scribes). Having finished this segment of teaching, Jesus goes away (13:53).

Functions of the Unit as a Whole

The encomiastic intent of the First Gospel is, of course, continued. As Quintilian (*Inst.* 3.7.15) said, in praising a person, the encomium should cover the whole course of his life, words as well as deeds. Plutarch (*Cat. Maj.* 7.2) said, "Men's characters are revealed much more by their speech than, as some think, by their looks" (trans. Perrin 1916). This large discourse, like the other four, contributes to the acquired honor of Jesus as his wisdom is displayed in the chapter on parables (Neyrey 1998).

In addition, chapter 13's discourse fits perfectly within the overall Matthean plot. In chapters 5–7, Jesus has given a powerful teaching. Chapters 8–9 have noted his powerful deeds. Chapters 11–12 focused on the varied responses to Jesus, mostly negative but not entirely. A new family of disciples emerged of those who do the will of God. Chapter 13's parable collection reflects on the two kinds of auditors. Because their hearts are hard, the crowds do not perceive who Jesus is. Still, through his provocative parables, he tries to provide

Scribes in Antiquity

The NT frequently mentions scribes (e.g., Mark 2:16; Acts 23:9: scribes of Pharisees; Mark 3:22: scribes from Jerusalem; Mark 11:27; 14:43; 15:1: chief priests, elders, scribes; Acts 4:5; 6:12: rulers, elders, scribes). The roots go back into the OT period. For example, Ezra was said to be a scribe skilled in the law of Moses (Ezra 7:6), who set his heart to study the law, to do it, and to teach it in Israel (7:10).

Sirach 38:24–39:11 discusses the vocation of an ideal scribe. It includes devoting himself to the study of the law and seeking out the wisdom of the ancients (39:1), preserving the sayings of the famous, and penetrating the subtleties of parables and proverbs (39:2–3).

Enoch was called a scribe (*1 En.* 12.3–4; 15.1; 92.1; *2 En.* 36.3 [shorter recension]), and Moses is called a scribe par excellence (*Tg. Onq.* at Deut. 33:21). Although regarded as a scribal community, Qumran does not refer to its members with the label "scribe." Scribes appear throughout the First Gospel, sometimes portrayed neutrally (e.g., 2:4; 17:10) but more often unfavorably (e.g., 5:20; 7:28–29; 9:3; 12:38; 23:2–3, 13, 23, 25, 27, 29; 26:57; 27:41) and only rarely favorably (e.g., 8:19[?]; 13:52; 23:34). The reference to scribes in 13:52 and 23:34 has usually been interpreted to mean that the Matthean community had scribes within its membership. Matthew 13:52 has sometimes been taken to mean that Matthean apocalyptic scribes shaped the scriptural and dominical traditions, including the First Gospel, to meet the community's needs (Orton 1989).

a catalyst for the deconstruction of their old world and for the construction of a new world. The disciples, however, already have a new world under construction. Hence, they can understand more and more what Jesus's message is saying. Here in the middle of chapter 13, Jesus turns to his disciples alone and begins to instruct them in ways that reinforce their new world. The people's lack of receptivity is due to their hard hearts and to the devil's machinations. No matter; God's purposes will ultimately be accomplished. In the meantime, there is a new community being built around Jesus. As the plot develops in chapters 14–16, the gap will widen between the two communities.

Theological Issues

Why Read Parables in Their Gospel Contexts?

Susan Wittig (1975, 177) poses the problem in modern guise. She grants that the original teller of the Gospel parables had a meaning system in mind and that, from the evangelist's perspective, advancing multiple meanings of parables would be wrong. At the same time, she argues, "From another, more objective point of view [i.e., other than the Gospel author's], what is demonstrated here is the ability to semantically alter a parabolic sign by embedding it within another belief-system and validating the new significance by reference to those beliefs." That is, by detaching a parable from its Gospel context, one can make it say something other than what it means in that context.

In the ancient church, a similar problem may be noted, together with its answer (Talbert 1988, 62–63). Irenaeus complains about gnostics who try to adapt the Jesus tradition to their own position by disregarding the order and connection of the Gospels, thereby dismembering and destroying the text: "By transferring passages and dressing them up anew, . . . they succeed in deluding many through their wicked art in adapting the oracles of the Lord to their opinions." They "endeavour, by violently drawing away from their proper connection, words, expressions, and parables whenever found, to adapt the oracles of God to their baseless fictions" (*Haer.* 1.8.1, *ANF* 1:326). Irenaeus's defense against the heretical violations of context is to appeal to the Scripture's actual order of presentation (*Haer.* 1.9.1). In contrast to the heretics, when the orthodox Christian "has restored every one of the expressions quoted to its proper position, and has fitted it to the body of the truth, he will lay bare, and prove to be without any foundation, the figment of these heretics" (*Haer.* 1.9.4, *ANF* 1:330).

Tertullian reflects a similar position. Analogous to the way the heretics treat the Jesus tradition is the handling of Homer and Virgil in Tertullian's time. "You see in our own day, composed out of Virgil, a story of a wholly different character." In like manner, certain collectors of Homeric odds and ends "stitch into one piece, patchwork fashion, works of their own from the lines of Homer, out of many scraps put together from this passage and from that (in miscellaneous confusion)" (*Praescr.* 39, *ANF* 3:262). The Gospels offer an opportunity for the same type of behavior. In response, Tertullian contends that "no divine saying is so unconnected and diffuse, that its words only are to be insisted on, and their connection left undetermined" (*Praescr.* 9, *ANF* 3:247). Context or order is important. The argument from order or context is a major weapon in the arsenal of the antiheretical writers of the early church in order to prevent gnostic subversion of the individual parts of the Jesus tradition.

It is possible to detach individual Jesus traditions, like parables, from their Gospel contexts and to embed them in another belief system. When this is done, however, one is no longer interpreting the parables of the Matthean Jesus (Snodgrass 2000, 22, 26, 27). "When the parables are taken out of their contexts within the gospels, there always lurks the danger of making them what one will in the way of hermeneutical experiments. . . . Or the interpreter will tend to place them within a preconceived notion of what their function 'really was'" (Hultgren 2000, 17). Why does this commentary insist on interpreting the parables within their Matthean context? It is because the aim of the commentary is to interpret Matthew's Gospel and that

Gospel's portrait of Jesus (the Matthean Jesus). The question is not, What did the historian's Jesus mean by this parable? Nor is it, What is the Jungian or Freudian meaning of this parable? The question must always be, What did the Matthean Jesus, within the context of the overall plot of the First Gospel, mean by this parable?

PART 4

Matthew 13:54–19:2

Jesus Focuses on His Disciples

This fourth large cycle of material in the First Gospel is composed of a narrative (13:54–17:23) and a discourse (17:24–19:2). The narrative is broken into two parts (13:54–16:20 and 16:21–17:23), each with its own pattern of organization.

Matthew 13:54–19:2 in Context

Birth narratives (1:1–2:23)

Jesus's ministry begins (3:1–8:1)

Jesus's authority is revealed (8:2–11:1)

Jesus's ministry creates division (11:2–13:53)

▶ **Jesus focuses on his disciples (13:54–19:2)**

Narrative: Jesus's disciples understand more (13:54–16:20)

Narrative: Jesus's disciples understand even more (16:21–17:23)

Discourse: Jesus tells disciples how to relate to insiders and outsiders (17:24–19:2)

Jesus and judgment (19:3–26:1a)

Passion and resurrection narrative (26:1b–28:20)

Matthew 13:54–16:20

Narrative 4, Part 1:
Jesus's Disciples Understand More

⌘

Introductory Matters

The fourth narrative falls into two parts: 13:54–16:20 and 16:21–17:23. The two parts complement one another, following the principle enunciated in 13:12: "Those who have, more will be given to them." Each of the two parts reflects a different pattern of arrangement. In this segment of the commentary, the focus will be on 13:54–16:20.

The major matter of introduction for this section is the material's organization. Matthew 13:54–19:2 is organized into narrative (13:54–17:23) and discourse (17:24–19:2). The various suggestions about the material's arrangement require a survey of those that deal with both narrative and discourse and those that focus on a more limited segment of the material.

D. W. Gooding (1978) suggests that 13:53–18:35 contains four sequences of five paragraphs each, but his analysis misses the major break between 16:20 and 16:21 recognized by most scholars, so his results are thrown off center. Paul Gaechter (1965, 468–584) suggests that 14:1–17:27 falls into two chiastic patterns. The thing to note here is the recognition that 16:20 is the end point for the first part of the narrative. Jerome Murphy-O'Connor (1975) proposes a threefold organization in which 13:53–14:12 hangs together and functions as an introduction. A. G. Van Aarde (1982) proposes dividing the first half of the narrative into triads, with each of the three subunits ending with Peter. This arrangement ignores the Peter narrative in 16:21–23 that begins the alleged third subunit, raising questions about the entire proposal. Nevertheless, note here again the recognition that 16:20 is a breaking point in the narrative.

Table 10
Proposed Analyses of the Part 4 Narrative

Gooding 1978	Gaechter 1965	Murphy-O'Connor 1975	Van Aarde (1982)
1. 13:53–14:36	1. 14:1–16:20	Intro. 13:53–14:12	1. 13:53–14:33
13:53–58	A 14:1–12	1. 14:13–15:20	2. 14:34–16:20
14:1–12	B 14:13–15:20	2. 15:21–16:4	3. 16:21–17:27
14:13–22	C 15:21–28	3. 16:5–17:27	
14:23–33	B′ 15:29–16:12		
14:34–36	A′ 16:13–20		
2. 15:1–16:12	2. 16:21–17:27		
15:1–20	A 16:13–20		
15:21–28	B 16:21		
15:29–39	C 16:22–28		
16:1–4	D 17:1–9		
16:5–12	C′ 17:14–21		
3. 16:15–17:20	B′ 17:22–23		
16:15–20	A′ 17:24–27		
16:21–28			
17:1–13			
17:14–19			
17:19–20			
4. 17:22–18:35			
17:22–23			
17:24–27			
18:1–14			
18:15–20			
18:21–35			

Since none of these suggestions has gained a consensus among scholars, some commentators conclude that there are no clear structural divisions in this section. Matthew simply follows the Markan order, with every pericope based on Mark except the concluding 17:24–27 (e.g., Davies and Allison 1991, 2:451; Hare 1993, 159–60; Boring 1995, 316). If there is a signaled break, it is at 16:21. However, such pessimism may not be warranted.

A helpful proposal offered by X. Léon-Dufour (1965, 231–54) sees three divisions, each beginning with an occasion that serves as a catalyst for Jesus's withdrawal: (1) 14:1–36; (2) 15:1–39; (3) 16:1–20. These withdrawals of Jesus are peculiar to Matthew and seem to be predominantly literary in character.

Léon-Dufour's suggestion has been endorsed and supplemented by David Verseput (1992), who argues that after the provocation and Jesus's withdrawal, Jesus continues to pursue a ministry of mercy. This pattern yields a studied oscillation between hostile reactions to Jesus and his ongoing ministry. If one adds to Léon-Dufour's and Verseput's suggestions the additional note that Jesus's ongoing ministry of mercy elicits faith in some, then this adjusted schema provides a workable understanding of the arrangement of the evangelist's material, as exhibited in the accompanying outline.

Table 11
The Structure of Matthew 13:54–16:20
(following Léon-Dufour 1965 and Verseput 1992)

1. Provocation	13:54–14:12	15:1–20	16:1–4a
2. Jesus withdraws	14:13a	15:21	16:4b
3. Jesus continues a mission of mercy that elicits faith from some	14:13b–36	15:22–39	16:5–20

Tracing the Narrative Flow

First Cycle (13:54–14:36)

In the structural arrangement of the material adopted here, the first triad is found in 13:54–14:36. It has three components: provocation, withdrawal, and continuing ministry that elicits faith among some.

13:54–14:12. In this first triad, the provocation is composed of two pericopes: (1) the mother and brothers of Jesus (13:54–58) and (2) the death of John the Baptist (14:1–12).

1. The first pericope functions in two different ways. On the one hand, this story about Jesus (13:54–58; cf. Mark 6:1–6), mentioning both his mother, brothers, and sisters (13:55–56), functions together

Matthew 13:54–16:20 in the Narrative Flow

Birth narratives (1:1–2:23)

Jesus's ministry begins (3:1–8:1)

Jesus's authority is revealed (8:2–11:1)

Jesus's ministry creates division (11:2–13:53)

Jesus focuses on his disciples (13:54–19:2)

▶ *Narrative*: Jesus's disciples understand more (13:54–16:20)

First cycle (13:54–14:36)
  Provocation (13:54–14:12)
  Withdrawal (14:13a)
  Continuing ministry (14:13b–36)
Second cycle (15:1–39)
  Provocation (15:1–20)
  Withdrawal (15:21)
  Continuing ministry (15:22–39)
Third cycle (16:1–20)
  Provocation (16:1–4a)
  Withdrawal (16:4b)
  Continuing ministry (16:5–20)

with 12:46–50 (which also mentions Jesus's mother and brothers) as a frame around the parable discourse of 13:1–53. On the other hand, 13:54–58 functions together with 14:1–12 as a provocation that will elicit Jesus's withdrawal in 14:13. The pericope falls into an ABCB'A' pattern (Davies and Allison 1991, 2:51):

A hometown (*patris*; 13:54a)
B where did he get this? (*pothen toutō*; 13:54b)
C three questions, each with "not" (*ouch, ouchi*; 13:55a, 55b, 56a)
B' where did he get this? (*pothen toutō*; 13:56b)
A' own country (*patris*; 13:57)

> **An Outline of Matthew 13:54–14:36**
>
> **First cycle (13:54–14:36)**
> **Provocation (13:54–14:12)**
> 1. Mother and brothers (13:54–58)
> 2. Death of John the Baptist (14:1–12)
>
> **Withdrawal (14:13a)**
> **Continuing ministry (14:13b–36)**
> 1. Healing and feeding (14:13b–21)
> 2. Walking on the water (14:22–33)
> 3. Summary statement (14:34–36)

The story is that of Jesus's rejection by his hometown (cf. Jer. 12:6; 11:21). The three questions posed by his hometown aim to reduce the extraordinary to the ordinary. This story is linked to the one that follows in 14:1–12 by the word "prophet" (13:57; 14:5). In 13:53–58 the prophet (Jesus) suffers rejection. In 14:1–12 the prophet (John the Baptist) suffers arrest, imprisonment, and death.

2. Matthew 4:12 has already told the auditor that when Jesus heard that the Baptist had been arrested, he withdrew to Galilee. In 12:14–15, when Jesus learns that the Pharisees are plotting his death, he withdraws. In 14:1–12 (cf. Mark 6:17–29), John's death comes on the orders of Herod Antipas. The cause

The Carpenter in Antiquity

Is not this the carpenter's son (Matt. 13:55)? Mark 6:3 has, "Is not this the carpenter, the son of Mary?" Xenophon describes the role of a carpenter in a village. "In small towns the same man makes couches, doors, ploughs, and tables, and often he even builds houses, and still he is thankful if only he can find enough work to support himself" (*Cyr.* 8.2.5, trans. Miller 1914). Lucian calls carpenters unlettered men and lists them among tanners, fishermen, and money changers (*Vit. auct.* 11). The *Childhood Gospel of Thomas* (Greek text A, 13) says that Joseph was a carpenter who made plows and yokes and a bed. The boy Jesus sometimes helped him.

was the Baptist's statement to Herod about Herodias: **It is not lawful for you to have her** (14:4). Herodias was the wife of Philip, also a son of Herod (Josephus, *Ant.* 18.135). So Antipas was married to the wife of a living brother (Josephus, *Ant.* 18.109–12), in violation of Lev. 18:16; 20:21 (Matt. 14:3). Through the machinations of Herodias, Herod was forced to have John beheaded. (For other examples of a king at a banquet offering a queen or princess up to half of his kingdom, cf. Esther 5:6; 7:2; Herodotus, *Hist.* 9.109–11.) This Gospel account is a bit different from that of Josephus (*Ant.* 18.116–19), who says Herod had John put to death because he feared an insurrection due to John's influence on the people. Regardless of which account one prefers historically, the issue is the Baptist's martyrdom at the instigation of Herod.

14:13a. The withdrawal element of the first triad comes when John's disciples tell Jesus about John's death: **Jesus withdrew from there in a boat into a wilderness place alone.**

14:13b–36. Jesus then continues his mission of mercy and finds a response of faith in some (14:13b–36). There is (1) a feeding story (14:13b–21), (2) a sea story (14:22–33), and (3) a summary of various healings (14:34–36).

1. Matthew 14:13b–21 (cf. Mark 6:30–44) tells how the crowds have followed Jesus so that when he goes ashore, he finds a large group of people. There is nothing in the Matthean text to indicate that the feeding is for gentiles. Rather, Jesus here continues his ministry to the lost sheep of the house of Israel (cf. 10:5; also 15:24). Matthew changes Mark 6:34's "and he began to teach them many things" to **he healed their sick** (14:14b). The feeding follows the healings. Jewish visions of the future often associated abundant food and healing with the time of fulfillment (e.g., *Jub.* 23.29; 2 Esd. [*4 Ezra*] 7:123; 8:53; *2 Bar.* 29.7). After Jesus's directive to the disciples to feed the crowd, they reply, **We have nothing here except five loaves and two fish** (14:17). So Jesus says, **Bring them here to me** (14:18). **Taking the five loaves and two fish, looking up into heaven, he gave a blessing, and breaking the loaves, he gave to the disciples and the disciples to the crowds. And all ate and were satisfied. And they took up the excess of what was broken, twelve baskets full. Now those who ate were five thousand men, not counting women and children** (14:19b–21).

The basic interpretative issue concerns the background against which the feeding story is to be read. On the one hand, some note that Moses fed the Israelites in the wilderness with manna (Exod. 16; Num. 11; Wis. 16:20–21). In the messianic age, moreover, a return of the manna was expected (*2 Bar.* 29.3, 8; *Eccles. Rab.* 1.28). This was the way John 6 interpreted the feeding. Others point to 2 Kings 4:42–44, where Elisha tells a man with twenty loaves and some fresh ears of grain to set the food before a hundred people. After protests that this food is not sufficient to feed that many people, the prophet says, "Give it to the people and let them eat, for thus says the LORD, 'They shall eat and have some left.'" And so it happened. The detail about having some food left over is striking. In the Deuteronomic history, Moses prophesies that God will raise up a prophet like him from among the people (Deut. 18:15–19). In the narrative that follows, a series of figures are raised up that reflect the expectation of a prophet like Moses (e.g., Joshua, Elijah, Elisha). This feeding story in 2 Kings 4, therefore, has Mosaic overtones. These first two options are basically the same: the background of the feeding story in Matthew is Mosaic, as it is in the Fourth Gospel. This is entirely possible given the Mosaic typology that begins in the birth narratives and continues throughout the First Gospel.

On the other hand, still others point to Ezek. 34, where Yahweh indicts the shepherds of Israel (their leaders) because they have not healed the sick (34:4) or fed the sheep (34:3). Instead, they have fed themselves and have not fed the sheep (34:8). Then God promises that he will feed the people on the mountains of Israel (34:13). Finally, Yahweh says, "I will set up over them one shepherd, my servant David, and he shall feed them: he shall feed them and be their shepherd" (34:23). In Mic. 5:4 the ideal Davidic king of the future time of salvation will feed his flock (Heil 1993; Hare 1993, 166; Carter 2000, 305). In Ps. 72 the ideal king of Israel provides abundant food (72:3, 16). The general image of the ideal king in Mediterranean antiquity, moreover, is also of one who provides abundant food (Statius, *Silv*. 5.1.79–107; 1.6.39–42). The Davidic echoes are entirely possible given the son-of-David motif that runs through the entire course of the First Gospel's plot. Perhaps the best alternative is to hear multiple echoes (Mosaic, Davidic, and ideal king) that flow into Jewish hopes for the end times (e.g., *2 Bar.* 29.4–6 says that when the messiah is revealed, there will be a time of abundant food). These hopes, the story says, are fulfilled in Jesus as he carries out his mission of mercy. Note the ending. Twelve baskets full are taken up from the leftovers of Jesus's mission to Israel (see 15:27).

2. The second component of Jesus's continuing mission of mercy is a sea story (14:22–33; cf. Mark 6:45–52). John Nolland (2005, 597) sees a chiastic arrangement in this pericope:

A separation (14:22–23)
  B danger (14:24)
    C first miracle (14:25–26)
      D who Jesus is (14:27)
    C′ second miracle (14:28–29)
  B′ danger again (14:30)
A′ reunion (14:31–33)

Section A (14:22–23) says that Jesus makes the disciples embark in the boat and go before him to the other side, until he disperses the crowds. And leaving the crowds, he goes up into the mountain alone to pray. When evening comes, he is alone. There is separation. Section B (14:24) continues: **The boat was** already a long way from land, being battered by the waves, for the wind was against them. There is danger. Section C (14:25–26) tells of the first miracle. **Between 3:00 and 6:00 AM he comes to them, walking on the sea. Now when the disciples saw him walking on the sea, they were frightened, saying it was a ghost, and they cried out from fear.** In antiquity some believed that the spirits of those drowned at sea wandered endlessly above the waters (e.g., Achilles Tatius, *Leuc. Clit.* 5.16.1–2). In section D (14:27), the center point in the pattern, Jesus immediately speaks to them: **Have courage. I am** (*egō eimi*). **Do not be afraid.** The disciples experience an epiphany. The normal reaction to such an event is fear. The expected heavenly response is, "Do not be afraid." Then the heavenly figure identifies himself (cf., e.g., Rev. 1:10–16: epiphany; 1:17a: fear reaction; 1:17b: do not be afraid; 1:17c–18: Christ identifies himself). The question is then, How does the Matthean Jesus identify himself? What does *egō eimi* mean in this context?

Normally, one would translate *egō eimi* as "It is I." That is, it is not a ghost but it is I, Jesus. Since, however, it is part of an epiphany, it could be translated

Walking on Water: Cultural Context

In the ancient Mediterranean world, walking on the water is above all something that a god or God can do, as is stilling a storm at sea. Examples include Job 9:8 LXX, where God walks on the waves of the sea; Ps. 77:16, 19, where Yahweh is both ruler of the waves and able to traverse the sea; Hab. 3:15; Homer, *Od.* 5.54, where Hermes' sandals carry him over the water; Virgil, *Aen.* 1.147, where Neptune glides over the waters, and 5.1057–59, where Neptune says he has often checked the frenzy of the sea.

It is also a gift that a god can give to his son. Examples include Homer, *Od.* 11.281–86; Apollonius of Rhodes, *Argon.* 1.179–84, where Poseidon gives his son Orion the ability to travel over the sea unharmed; Apollodorus, *Bibl.* 1.4.3; and Hyginus, *Astronom.* 2.34.

Moreover, it is a practice that a powerful man who is not inferior to the gods would be able to do (Dio Chrysostom, *Or.* 3). For example, Iamblichus (*Vit. Pyth.* 28) tells how Pythagoras performed signs, including calming waves and walking on water. Jewish stories with some similarities include that about Elisha, who split the Jordan River by rolling up his mantle and striking the river with it (2 Kings 2:8). Sometimes a ruler, overcome with hubris, thought he was capable of such a feat. For example, at 2 Macc. 5:21, after robbing the temple in Jerusalem, Antiochus Epiphanes "hurried away to Antioch, thinking in his arrogance that he could sail on the land and walk on the sea, because his mind was elated." So popular were such stories that Lucian could satirize the claims by telling of men with cork feet walking on the water (*Ver. hist.* 2.4; *Philops.* 13–14). A Jewish text titled the *Sword of Moses* provides a magical spell to enable one to walk on the waters of the sea (Gaster 1971, 1:331). (For further discussion and examples, see Nicholls 2008; A. Collins 1994.)

as it is in John 8:58 ("Very truly, I tell you, before Abraham was, I am [*egō eimi*]"). In this place in John, *egō eimi* (I am) makes no sense if translated either "It is I" or "I am he." What does make sense is a reading of *egō eimi* as the equivalent of the divine self-predication in Deutero-Isaiah and Deut. 32:39. In the LXX of Isa. 41:4; 43:10, 25; 46:4; 51:12, God speaks of himself as *egō eimi*, which functions there as the divine name of the one God besides whom there is no other (Talbert 2005, 163). In Matthew, it seems to fit the context best to understand "I am" as the pronouncement of the divine name. This choice is supported by comparative material (see the sidebar). The associations of walking on the water and stilling storms were such that the event could only be described as an epiphany during which the one being manifest speaks his name: I AM.

Section C' (14:28–29) offers the second miracle. **Peter said, "Lord, if it is you, command me to come to you on the waters." So Jesus said, "Come." And leaving the boat, Peter walked around on the waters and came toward Jesus.** Section B' (14:30) notes danger once again. **But seeing the wind, he became frightened, and when he was beginning to sink, he cried out, saying, "Lord, save me."** Section A' (14:31–33) describes the reunion of Jesus and his disciples. **Now straightaway, Jesus, extending his hand, pulled him up and said to him, "Little-faith one, why did you doubt?" As they were getting into the boat, the wind stopped. Those in the boat worshiped him, saying, "Truly, you are the son of God."** It is significant that whereas Mark 6:52 concludes the episode with a statement that the disciples did not understand and that their hearts were hardened, Matt. 14:33 has the disciples worship Jesus and profess that he is the son of God, a foreshadowing of Peter's confession in 16:16. In the First Gospel's plot, Jesus's continuing mercy extends to people even after his rejection sometimes results in faith. The disciples are so portrayed as a result of the epiphany at sea.

3. The first triad concludes with a summary statement about Jesus's healings at Gennesaret (14:34–36). **The people of that place sent into all of the surrounding region, and they brought to him all those having illness, and they begged him that they might only touch the fringe of his clothing; and as many as touched it were healed** (14:35–36).

Second Cycle (15:1–39)

The second triad, 15:1–39, has the same three components as the first: provocation, withdrawal, and continuing ministry.

15:1–20. Matthew 15:1–20, the provocation (cf. Mark 7:1–23), is held together by an inclusio (15:2: question; 15:20: answer). The material falls into three parts: (1) words addressed to scribes and Pharisees regarding Scripture and tradition (15:1–9), (2) words to the crowds regarding the irrelevance of ritual dietary restrictions (15:10–11), and (3) words addressed to disciples (15:12–20). Taken as a whole, it is one of Matthew's long conflict stories.

(*Pesiq. Rab.* 21.2/3 has a structure similar to Matt. 15:1–20. There is a controversy followed by a teacher's explanation to his disciples.)

1. The issue in 15:1–9 is the relation of Scripture and tradition. The Pharisees ask Jesus, **Why do your disciples violate the tradition of the elders? For they do not wash their hands when they eat bread** (15:2). There were no biblical instructions requiring the washing of hands by everyone before eating. Only priests had such requirements (Exod. 30:17–21; Lev. 22:4–7). The Pharisees, however, believed that if one's hands were unclean, then the food was defiled; and if the food was defiled, when it entered the mouth, the whole body would be unclean. On this assumption, washing of hands was authoritative tradition. Jesus responds with a question of his own. **Why do you violate the commandment of God because of your tradition? For God said, "Honor your father and mother"** (Exod. 20:12; Deut. 5:16) **and "The one who speaks evil of father or mother, let him be put to death"** (Lev. 20:9). **But you say, whoever says to one's father or mother, "Whatever you may be owed by me is a gift"** (to God), **may not honor his father or mother. And you cancel the word of God because of your tradition** (15:3–6). The practice assumed here was allowed by Pharisaic tradition. A child owed parents certain care in their old age. If, however, the child did not want to spend the wealth of the estate on their care, he could give the wealth to the temple as a gift (*corban* means "devoted to God"). In this case, the child did not have to spend the wealth on the parents. As apparently happened, when the parents had died, all or a portion of the wealth could be returned to the child. Such a tradition, Jesus argues, violates the clear words of Scripture (Fitzmyer 1959). Such behavior, says Jesus, fulfills a prophecy of Isaiah (29:13; used also in *Pss. Sol.* 4.1 and *Tg. Isa.* 29.13 as a rebuke to the hypocrisy of religious leadership). **This people honors me with their lips, but their hearts are distant from me; in vain are they worshiping me, advocating the teachings of humans as commandments** (15:8–9).

The Pharisaic view was that there were two laws, both from Moses (*m. Avot* 1). One was the written Torah, the other was the oral torah (certain regulations handed down by former generations but not recorded in the law of Moses; so Josephus, *Ant.* 13.297). The conflict reflected here is over the Pharisees' alleged violation of the written law because of their oral law. Sometimes the rabbinic tradition indicates the oral was valued over the written Torah (*m. Sanh.* 11.3:

An Outline of Matthew 15:1–39

Second cycle (15:1–39)

Provocation (15:1–20)

1. Scripture and tradition (15:1–9)
2. Dietary restrictions (15:10–11)
3. Words to disciples (15:12–20)

Withdrawal (15:21)

Continuing ministry (15:22–39)

1. Healing a Canaanite woman (15:22–28)
2. Healing and feeding great crowds (15:29–39)

"Greater stringency applies to the observance of the words of the Scribes than to the observance of the works of the written Law" [trans. Danby 1933, 400]; *b. Eruv.* 21b: "My son, be more careful in the observance of the words of the Scribes than in the words of the Torah. . . . Whoever transgresses any of the enactments of the Scribes incurs the penalty of death" [trans. Epstein 1948]; cf. *b. Shabb.* 31a). That is what is assumed here. In *t. Ned.* 1.6.4 a vow is said to take precedence over a biblical commandment. In *m. Ned.* 9.1, however, in a rabbinic debate, the view that wins out holds that honor of parents takes precedence over a vow. Jesus was not alone in manifesting hostility toward Pharisaic tradition before AD 70 (cf. Josephus, *Ant.* 13.296–98, 408: Sadducees reject the oral tradition of the Pharisees; *t. Hag.* 3.35: Sadducees ridicule Pharisaic traditional practice; *Avot R. Nat.* 5: Sadducees criticize Pharisaic tradition and its practice). The Matthean Jesus's interactions here would therefore fit an anti-Pharisaic milieu in first-century Palestine.

2. Matthew 15:10–11 is addressed not to the Pharisees but to the crowd. Jesus says, **It is not what enters into the mouth that defiles a person; but what comes out of the mouth, this defiles the person** (15:11). Here Jesus simply says that the Pharisees are wrong. It is customary for commentators to say that unlike Mark 7:19b, Matthew does not nullify the laws of ritual defilement, such as food laws. Instead, he declares the relative importance of inner over outer (e.g., Boring 1995, 8:333). The text, however, like the explanation that follows, does not say one is more important than the other; rather, it says one is irrelevant while the other is crucial. Although Mark's explicit "Thus he declared all foods clean" is missing in Matthew, the implication is the same. There was at least a minority opinion among the rabbis that in the time to come God will again permit the eating of the flesh that he has forbidden (*Midr. Teh.* on Ps. 146:7). Does the Matthean Jesus's position show this was as early as the first century? If so, then this is another testimony to Jesus's inaugurated eschatology.

3. Matthew 15:12–20 is addressed to the disciples. There are two parts: 15:13–14 offers an evaluation of the Pharisees to the disciples; 15:15–20 provides an explanation of 15:11 to the disciples. **Then coming over, the disciples said, "Did you know that when the Pharisees heard your word, they were scandalized?"** (15:12; cf. 13:57). Jesus's response runs, **Every plant that my heavenly Father did not plant will be pulled up** (cf. 13:24–30, 36–43). **Disregard them. They are blind guides of the blind. If a blind person guides a blind person, both will fall into a ditch** (15:13–14). The language and concept are proverbial (e.g., Plato, *Resp.* 6.484d: Shall we, then, appoint these blind souls as our guardians?). In 15:15, Peter asks Jesus, **Explain the parable to us.** (An example of a controversy followed by an explanation for disciples may be found in *Pesiq. Rab.*, Piska 21.2/3.) This means that 15:11 is understood by Matthew to be a parable that was in need of explanation (cf. 13:36). Jesus explains: **Do you not know that everything that enters into the mouth goes into the**

stomach and is eliminated in excrement? The things that come out of the mouth come from the heart; such things defile the person. For out of the heart come forth evil thoughts, murder, adultery, fornication, stealing, false witness, blasphemy. These are the things that defile the person; but to eat with unwashed hands does not make the person unclean (15:17–20). Jesus here focuses on moral rather than cultic defilement (cf. 9:13; 12:7). Note how many of the items in the vice list are from the Decalogue (cf. 19:18–19).

15:21. Jesus's withdrawal comes in response to Pharisaic hostility: **And going out from there, Jesus withdrew into the region of Tyre and Sidon** (cf. 12:14–15). This locates Jesus in gentile territory and sets the stage for the story that follows.

> **Vice Lists in Antiquity**
>
> One way that both Jewish and pagan teachers instructed their audiences was through the use of vice lists. Undesirable behavior would be summarized in terms of a list of specific vices. Avoidance of such would be enjoined. Examples of such lists may be found in Wis. 14:25–26; 1QS 4.9–11; Philo, *Sacr.* 32; *T. Levi* 17.11; Epictetus, *Diatr.* 2.8.23. From the earliest time, the followers of Jesus used this form of instruction (e.g., Rom. 1:29–31; 1 Cor. 6:9–10; Gal. 5:19–21).

15:22–39. Jesus then once again continues his ministry of showing mercy, meeting with faith in some. (1) He heals a Canaanite woman (15:22–28; cf. Mark 7:24–30) and then (2) heals and feeds great crowds (15:29–39).

1. In gentile territory, Jesus is confronted by a gentile woman (15:22–28) who sees him as the genealogy does (1:1; son of David) and asks for mercy, four times in Matthew as opposed to twice in Mark. **And behold, a Canaanite woman from that region as she was coming cried out, saying, "Be merciful to me, Lord, son of David. My daughter is possessed with an evil demon"** (15:22). What follows has evoked multiple interpretations among scholars. The responses to the woman are four. First, Jesus **did not answer her a word** (15:23a). She is ignored. Second, **his disciples asked him, saying, "Send her away because she is crying out after us"** (15:23b). Third, Jesus says, **I was not sent except to the lost sheep of the house of Israel** (15:24; cf. 10:6). Not rebuffed, the woman responds by worshiping him and saying, **Lord, help me** (15:25). Fourth, Jesus responds by saying, **It is not good to take the bread of the children and to throw it to the dogs** (15:26). Not rebuffed, the woman responds by saying, **Even the dogs eat from the scraps that fall from the table of their masters** (15:27; cf. 14:20, which indicates that there were plenty of leftovers). After the woman's persistence in spite of four rebuffs, Jesus replies, **O woman, great is your faith. May it be to you as you wish** (15:28a). The story concludes with the result. **And her daughter was healed from that hour** (15:28b). (In Philostratus, *Vit. Apoll.* 3.38, a mother asks the philosopher for the exorcism of her child.)

Two examples of approaches to the story help to clarify issues. On the one hand, there are those who regard Jesus's behavior as "morally offensive," "insulting," and reflecting prejudice (Theissen 1991, 61, 80). Sharon Ringe (1985), for example, depicts the woman as an aggressive single parent who defies cultural taboos and acts to free Jesus from his sexism and racism by catching him in a bad mood with his compassion down, besting him in an argument, and thereby becoming a vehicle of his liberation and the deliverance of her daughter. On the other hand, Glenna Jackson (2002) notes that in the Jewish scriptures people argue with God (Jacob, Moses, Joshua, Elijah). The Hebrews persisted in their requests for God's assistance. In Ps. 6 LXX, for example, there are four petitions: (1) "O Lord, rebuke me not in your wrath nor chasten me in your anger" (v. 1); (2) "Have mercy on me, Lord, for I am weak" (v. 2a); (3) "Heal me, O Lord" (v. 2b); (4) "O Lord, deliver my soul, save me for your mercy's sake" (v. 4). These are followed by answered prayer: The Lord has listened to my petition, he has accepted my prayer (v. 9). This pattern carried over into the making of a proselyte. *Ruth Rabbah* 2.16 relates that a would-be proselyte is told three times to turn back, but if he persists after that (a fourth time), he is to be accepted. On the basis of such data, Jackson concludes that Jesus is following the Jewish custom for testing a prospective proselyte, and the Canaanite woman is a convert to Judaism.

The Importance of Being Earnest

In Jer. 29:13 God says, "When you search for me, you will find me; if you seek for me with all your heart." Teachers in Mediterranean antiquity practiced a similar rule. There is a famous story of a gentile coming to Shammai and asking to be taught the whole law while he stood on one foot (i.e., give me just the bottom line and quickly). In response, Shammai drove him away. He was not seeking with his whole heart (*b. Shabb.* 31a). The same mind-set is reflected by Dio Chrysostom (*Or.* 35.10). His advice to the true sage is that if someone follows at his heels, the teacher should drive him away, even pelting him with stones if necessary. This is the principle behind the resistance shown by Jews to one who desired to become a proselyte. Given this practice, it should be no surprise that there are accounts of unsuccessful attempts to become disciples. Diogenes Laertius, *Vit. phil.* 6.36, tells of someone wanting to study philosophy under Diogenes of Sinope. Diogenes gave him a fish and commanded him to follow him. The man threw the fish away and left. He did not have the commitment to be a disciple. In Matt. 8:19–22 two individuals approached Jesus about discipleship. In each case Jesus responded in a way to test their commitment. We are not told whether they persisted. In Matt. 19:16–22 a rich young man came to Jesus. Jesus's response was not encouraging: you do not know who is good; keep the commandments; sell your possessions and give to the poor; come and follow me. Not having the wholehearted commitment, the young man went away. It is within the context of such behavior that Matt. 15:21–28 should be understood.

If the first thesis substitutes ideology for interpretation of the text, the second reading seems plausible until the conclusion. In this story the woman does not become a Jewish proselyte; she either is or becomes a devotee of Jesus. The four responses of Jesus and the disciples are a test of her sincerity/faith in Jesus after the analogy of the treatment of would-be proselytes (Tagawa 1966, 120). That this is the issue is evident from the conclusion: **O woman, great is your faith** (15:28a). The similarities with 8:5–13 are striking. In both cases, Jesus, who is sent at this point in his ministry to the lost sheep of the house of Israel, is approached by a gentile who asks for healing of a child (or servant). Through conversation, the faith of both gentiles is laid bare, evoking wonder on Jesus's part and resulting in the petitioned healing.

2. Jesus's ministry of mercy continues in the summary of 15:29–31 (cf. Mark 7:31–37?) and the second feeding story (15:32–39; cf. Mark 8:1–10), which because of setting and characters should be taken as a unity (on a mountain in Galilee [15:29]; association with the crowds [15:30, 32]). Just as 14:13–21, so here in 15:29–39 Jesus heals the sick before he feeds the crowd. The crowd that witnesses the healings are amazed, and **they gave glory to the God of Israel** (15:31b). The crowd sees in Jesus's healings the activity of Israel's God, unlike the Pharisees who saw demonic power (12:24). Jesus's concern for the crowd goes beyond healing their diseases. He is also concerned that they be fed. He says to the disciples, **I have compassion on the crowd** (cf. 9:36) **because they have been with me already three days, and they do not have anything to eat, and I do not wish to send them away hungry lest they faint on the way** (15:32). The disciples ask, **Where in the wilderness is enough bread for such a crowd to eat?** (15:33). As it turns out, they have only seven loaves and a few fish (15:34). The crowd sits down on the ground, and Jesus **took the seven loaves and the fish and having blessed them, he broke and gave to the disciples, and the disciples to the crowds. And all ate and were filled, and the leftovers of what was broken were seven baskets full. And those who ate were four thousand men, not counting women and children** (15:36–38). The triad ends with the note that after dismissing the crowds, Jesus got into a boat and went to the region of Magadan (15:39, an unknown site).

© Stephen von Wyrick

Figure 10. Bread-and-fish mosaic before the altar in the church at Tabgha commemorating Jesus's feeding of the five thousand. This church to the west of Capernaum is on the opposite side of the Sea of Galilee from where Matt. 14:13–34 places the feeding. This is likely due to an accommodation to later pilgrimage needs.

Jesus here continues his ministry to Israel. Both feeding stories have that same function. W. D. Davies and Dale Allison (1991, 2:566–67) argue that the background of this story is a Zion eschatology. (1) Mount Zion was regarded as the eschatological gathering place of scattered Israel (Jer. 31:10–12; Isa. 35:10; Mic. 4:6–7). (2) Zion was regarded as an eschatological place of healing (Isa. 35:5–6; Jer. 31:8; Mic. 4:6–7). (3) Zion was regarded as the place of an eschatological feast (Isa. 25:6; Jer. 31:12–14). Viewed against this backdrop, Matt. 15:29–39 has Jesus on a mountain in Galilee, healing the sick and feeding the multitudes of Jews. Read in this way, Jesus replaces the mountain in Jerusalem and its temple. His person has supplanted that place. In him is seen the fulfillment of the ancient hopes of eschatological healing and nourishment. In Ezek. 34 one also finds eschatological hopes that relate to the feeding story (Heil 1993). God indicts the shepherds of Israel (their leaders) because they have neither fed nor healed the sheep (the people). So God will feed them on the mountains of Israel and will shepherd them with a son of David. Either way, Jesus is depicted as the fulfillment of Israel's hopes. Here again, after Jesus has fed Israel, there are many leftovers. Are they a foreshadowing of his benefits to the gentiles (cf. 15:27)?

Third Cycle (16:1–20)

The third triad (16:1–20; cf. Mark 8:11–13, 14–21, 27–30) also contains the three components found in the previous two triads: provocation, withdrawal, a continuing mission that meets with faith in some.

16:1–4a. The provocation comes: **Pharisees and Sadducees, testing Jesus, asked him to show them a sign from heaven** (16:1; cf. 12:38). In 19:3 and 22:18, 35, religious leaders again test Jesus. All of these occasions are, in the Matthean view, an expression of the devil's testings in 4:1–11. In particular, 4:5–7 (cast yourself down from the pinnacle of the temple) is analogous to this testing. Both ask Jesus to perform a spectacular work to demonstrate his position. In ancient Judaism some expected that a messianic figure would perform an authenticating sign (cf. the "sign prophets" mentioned by Josephus). In *b. Sanh.* 98a, Rabbi Jose ben Qisma (ca. AD 100) prophesies that when the messiah comes, he will authenticate his words with a sign (the water of the caves of Paneas will change to blood). This, in Matthew's point of view, is demonic. Jesus is more than willing to heal those who ask out of faith in him, but to do a marvel in order to justify himself before others is out of the question. So he replies that this generation knows how to read the

---

An Outline of Matthew 16:1–20

Third cycle (16:1–20)

Provocation (16:1–4a)

Withdrawal (16:4b)

Continuing ministry (16:5–20)

1. The leaven of the Pharisees and Sadducees (16:5–12)

2. Peter's confession (16:13–16)

3. The rock and the keys (16:17–20)

weather signs but cannot interpret the signs of the times (Jesus's ministry). **An evil and spiritually adulterous generation seeks a sign, and no sign will be given to it except the sign of Jonah** (16:4a). In 12:38–41, a doublet of this pericope, the sign of Jonah is interpreted in two different ways: Jonah's preaching of repentance (12:41) and the three days and nights that Jonah and Jesus share in the depths of sea and earth (12:40). Although its meaning is not provided here, one would assume that the two interpretations of 12:40–41 also apply here.

16:4b. Confronted by a demonic request that he must reject, Jesus withdraws: **And leaving them, he went away** (cf. 12:15).

16:5–20. Jesus's ministry continues through further interaction with his disciples: (1) warning of the leaven of the Pharisees (16:5–12), (2) eliciting Peter's confession of him as messiah (16:13–16), and (3) commenting on Peter's confession (16:17–20).

1. Just as in 15:1–20, after his confrontation with the Pharisees and Sadducees, Jesus teaches his disciples (16:5–12). The intent of this segment is to show the dangers of the mind-set of the religious leadership. In this pericope the disciples and Jesus begin by operating on two different levels (much like what occurs in the Fourth Gospel). **And when they came to the other side, the disciples had forgotten to bring bread** (16:5). This is one level. Jesus says to them, **Look out and be on guard against the leaven of the Pharisees and Sadducees** (16:6). This is a second level. The disciples say that **it is because we did not bring bread** (16:7). Here the thought shifts back to level one. Jesus responds, **Why are you discussing among yourselves, little-faith ones, that you have no bread? Do you not yet know, nor remember the five loaves of the five thousand and how many baskets you took up, nor the seven loaves of the four thousand and how many baskets you took up?** (16:8–10). Given this past history, if you are worried about bread to eat, would I not be able to meet your needs? This is a response at level one. Then comes the response that moves back to level two. **Watch out for the leaven of the Pharisees and Sadducees** (16:11b). Finally the disciples arrive at the right level of understanding. **Then they understood that he did not speak about leaven of bread but of the teaching of the Pharisees and Sadducees** (16:12; cf. 15:14).

2. Matthew 16:13–20 (cf. Mark 8:27–30) closes the third triad and the first part of the fourth narrative. In it Jesus's continuing mission meets faith in some, especially Peter (16:13–16). The site is the region of Caesarea Philippi (16:13a), a place where Herod the Great had built a temple to Caesar Augustus. The central issue of the narrative from 13:54 to 16:20 is whether or not people are able to discern from Jesus's ministry who he is (Carter 2000, 332). In 14:33 the disciples confess that Jesus is truly "son of God"; in 15:22 the Canaanite woman confesses that Jesus is "son of David"; in 15:31b the crowds praise the God of Israel for his work through Jesus. Now the pericope 16:13–20 focuses the issue for the disciples once again. It begins with a series of questions and answers. Jesus asks them, **Who do the people say the son of man is?** (16:13b).

Here "son of man" is merely a circumlocution for "I" (cf. Mark 8:27: "Who do people say that I am?"). Their reply is that **some say John the Baptist** (cf. Matt. 14:2), **others Elijah** (Mal. 4:5; Sir. 48:10; John 1:21; Matt. 11:13–15; 17:3), **others Jeremiah** (2 Macc. 15:11–16) **or one of the prophets** (16:14). Jesus then asks the disciples for their opinion. **Who do you say I am?** (16:15). Simon Peter speaks for the group: **You are the Christ** (cf. 1:1; 2:4; 11:2), **the son** (cf. 2:15; 3:17; 4:3, 6; 11:25–27) **of the living God** (16:16). A Qumran Aramaic apocalypse (4Q246, col. 2) refers to one who will be called son of God and son of the Most High, whose kingdom will be eternal, and his paths will be in truth and uprightness. This son of God is probably a messianic figure (so J. Collins 1993; contra Fitzmyer 1993). If so, then Peter's confession that joins messiah and son of God makes sense in its Jewish context.

3. Peter's confession evokes an extended response from the Matthean Jesus in 16:17–20 (unique to Matthew). There are three sentences to Jesus's reply (16:17, 18, 19), each of which has three parts (Meier 1979, 110). The first (16:17) runs as follows:

> **Blessed are you, Simon son of Jonah,**
> **because flesh and blood did not reveal this to you**
> **but my Father who is in the heavens.**

Matthew uses a blessing for those who have received a revelation (cf. 13:11, 16–17). Recognition of Jesus's identity is something that the Father gives because only he knows the Son (11:27). Peter has been given this blessing (cf. Gal. 1:11–12 for Paul's similar situation).

The second sentence (16:18) runs as follows:

> **I say to you, you are** *Petros* **(a stone),**
> **and upon this** *petra* **I will build my** *ekklēsia,*
> **and the gates of Hades will not win a victory over it.**

This has been a battleground of interpreters for centuries. The *ekklēsia*, usually translated "church," refers to the people of God (cf. LXX of Deut. 9:10 and 1 Macc. 2:56; also Acts 7:38, where *ekklēsia* is used for the congregation of Israel in the wilderness). The Matthean Jesus is building a renewed people of God. Against Jesus's congregation, death will not prevail (cf. Rev. 1:18). This renewed people of God will be built upon *petra,* a ledge of rock that makes a firm foundation (cf. Matt. 7:25). This general idea of a new eschatological community established on a rock foundation is found at Qumran (1QH[a] 6.25–26 [col. 14]; 7.8–9 [col. 15]). Identification of this Matthean ledge of rock is disputed (see Luz 1994, 57–74 for a concise survey). Among the options, a few are the most favored: (1) the rock is Jesus or his teachings (cf. 7:24; Gundry 1982, 334); (2) the rock is Peter's confession of faith (Caragounis 1990; Garland

2001, 173–74); (3) Peter is the rock (Davies and Allison 1991, 2:603), precisely in the act of confessing Jesus as Christ (Nolland 2005, 669). At the end of a detailed history of research, Joseph Burgess (1976, 168) concludes that opinion has shifted toward identification of Peter, not Christ or Peter's faith, with the *petra* in 16:18. The name *petros* is masculine because Peter is male (Hare 1993, 190). The decisive argument seems to be that in certain Jewish circles, Abraham was regarded as the rock on which Yahweh built the old congregation (cf. Isa. 51:1–2: "Look to the rock from which you were hewn. . . . Look to Abraham your father"; *Yalqut Shim'oni* 1.766 on Num. 23:9: a parable tells about a king who planned to build a palace, digging to solid rock for a foundation; just so, God saw Abraham who was to arise and said that he was the solid rock on which to build the world).

The third sentence (16:19) runs as follows:

> I will give to you the keys of the kingdom of the heavens
> and whatever you may bind on earth will have been bound in the heavens

---

The Name Cephas (Aramaic)/ Peter (Greek)

Widespread opinion holds that *kepha* is not a proper name in Aramaic and that the name *Petros* has not been discovered to be a proper name during the time of Jesus. James Charlesworth (1993) contends that both opinions are wrong. First, in an Aramaic papyrus dated to 416 BC, one does find the proper name (Aqab, son of Kepha). Second, in 4QM130, an abecedary (a fragment on which the alphabet and occasional words or names are penned), one finds *pytros*. If Charlesworth's reading is correct, then the Cephas/Petros tradition fits into an appropriate Jewish context.

Who or What Is the Foundation?

In Matt. 7:24–27, the words of Jesus are the foundation for disciples; Matt. 16:18 says that Peter is the foundation for the church. Ephesians 2:20 calls the apostles and prophets the foundation of the church. First Corinthians 3:10–11 specifies Jesus as the church's foundation. Doing good and being generous and ready to share constitute a good foundation for believers in 1 Tim. 6:18–19.

The word of truth is God's firm foundation in 2 Tim. 2:15, 19. Hebrews 6:1–2 describes the foundation as the basic teaching about Christ: "repentance from dead works and faith toward God, instruction about baptisms, laying on of hands, resurrection of the dead, and eternal judgment." Revelation 21:14 says that the twelve apostles are the foundation of the church. The one image (foundation) is used in a variety of ways, depending on the needs of the context.

and whatever you may loose on earth will have been loosed in the heavens.

The keys of the kingdom are usually associated with Isa. 22:22, where the person responsible for managing the king's household is said to have the key or keys of the house of David, so that he shall open and no one shall shut, and he shall shut and no one shall open (*2 Bar.* 10.18 associates keys with priests). Jesus here promises Peter the supervisory role in the son of Abraham's and son of David's new congregation (*ekklēsia*). The second and third lines describe what that role will be. Binding and loosing in their Jewish context refer to the practice of determining the application of scriptural commandments for contemporary situations (Powell 2003). In the context of Matthew, it seems to mean the same thing as 13:52 ("bringing forth what is new and what is old" from the scribe's treasure). It is an interpretative task of saying what is appropriately relevant and what is not. The sentiment is expressed by Rabbi Yehuda: "Whoever translates verbally a verse of the Bible is a falsifier; whoever adds anything is a blasphemer" (*t. Meg.* 3.21, trans. Neusner and Sarason 1977–86). Elsewhere in Matthew this discernment function is extended to all disciples (18:18; 13:11, 52).

> ### The Gates of Hades
>
> The expression "gates of Hades" was used by Jews and pagans to refer to the realm of death. For Jewish usage, see Pss. 9:13; 107:18; Job 38:17; Isa. 38:10; Wis. 16:13; 3 Macc. 5:51; *Pss. Sol.* 16.2; 1QH[a] 6.24. For pagan usage, see Homer, *Od.* 14.156; Hesiod, *Theog.* 773; Euripides, *Hipp.* 56–57; Diogenes Laertius, *Vit. phil.* 10.126. The realm of the dead could be portrayed concretely as a castle in front of which stand a huge gate and pillars of solid adamant that neither man nor sons of heaven could uproot (e.g., Virgil, *Aen.* 6.552–53).

In lines two and three of 16:19 the very tenses have created debate. The translation **will have been bound/loosed in heaven** represents in Greek a periphrastic future perfect passive. Traditionally this has been interpreted to mean not that heaven ratifies Peter's judgment but that Peter's judgment reflects what God has already determined (Gundry 1982, 335; Chamberlain 1957, 80). Stanley Porter (1989) has tried to overturn this reading. He argues that Greek tenses carry no inherent temporal dimension (76–83). Instead, there are three aspects (257): perfective (reflected in the aorist tense), imperfective (reflected in the present and imperfect tenses), and stative (reflected in the perfect and pluperfect tenses). Only context can determine the temporal dimension. The basic problem with this contention is that Greek contains both imperfect and pluperfect tenses. Why these extra tenses if Porter's thesis is correct? Furthermore, the traditional reading accurately reflects the theological context of the First Gospel (cf. 13:11; 16:17). Like the prophet Nathan (2 Sam. 12:13), the prophet Jesus pronounces God's forgiveness of sin (Matt. 9:6). Like their master Jesus (Matt. 9:6), Peter (16:19) and the other disciples (18:18) reflect the discernment that God has given to them (13:11–12). It is with the traditional reading that this commentary sides. When Peter interprets, it is a reflection of what has been revealed to him.

Functions of the Unit as a Whole

Once again the encomiastic function of the Matthean narrative continues. Quintilian (*Inst*. 3.7.15) says that sometimes it is good to treat a praiseworthy person in terms of the course of his life and at other times to treat his deeds under the individual virtues. In Matt. 13:54–16:20 the two are conjoined. This segment of narrative is a true part of the development of Jesus's career. At the same time certain virtues stand out in the narrative. In both cases the dictum of Aristotle is fulfilled. In *Poetics* (1452a, 1454b–55a) the philosopher says that the best recognition of a person is based on "that which arises from the actions alone." In this part of the Matthean narrative, Jesus withdraws rather than being threatening or confrontational. Quintilian regarded this as deeds of courage. Jesus's deeds, moreover, are always done for others (e.g., healings, feedings) and out of compassion (14:14; 15:32). These Quintilian grouped with deeds of magnanimity. On the basis of all that this narrative reflects, Jesus is certainly to be praised.

The previous narrative has presented Jesus as teaching and working miracles in Israel (Matt. 5–10), running into opposition (Matt. 11–12), and reflecting on the division into two groups, pro-Jesus and contra-Jesus (Matt. 13). In Matt. 14–16 three cycles of material show that division continuing to the point that there occurs a focus on the new community (ecclesiology). Disciples, Jewish and gentile, recognize Jesus as son of God, son of David, and Christ. Then Jesus announces the formation of a new congregation and promises Peter a role in it as interpreter. Peter functions here as a new Abraham, standing at the head of a new people. Like Abraham, Peter is a rock. He is given a unique role in salvation history. His faith is the means by which God brings a new people into being (Davies and Allison 1991, 2:643). This means that Peter is not only the first disciple chosen (4:18; 10:2) in salvation history (Kingsbury 1979) but also the disciple entrusted with the scribal interpretative task (but not to the exclusion of other disciples; see 18:18; 13:11, 52; Nau 1983).

Theological Issues

How should one view the relevance of Peter for non-Matthean and post-Matthean Christians? A context for the answer must be provided first.

Each branch of the church has its own story of origins. Greek Orthodox Christians, for example, regard themselves as the one unreformed church with an unbroken succession stemming from the apostles (from whom Roman

Peter as a Rock

Is Peter really a rock? There are at least three accounts in Matthew that make the name *Petros* (stone) seem ironic in 16:18. In 14:28–31, Peter asks to come to Jesus by walking on the water, becomes frightened, starts to sink, and must be delivered by Jesus. At this point, Jesus's appraisal of Peter is that he is a person of little faith, a doubter. In 16:21–23, when Jesus speaks of his coming suffering and death, Peter rebukes him, saying that it will never happen. To this Jesus responds with a rebuke of his own, classing Peter's perspective with that of Satan. Jesus, moreover, calls him a stumbling block (a rock to stub one's foot on, causing a fall). In 26:31–35, when Jesus predicts that all his disciples will become deserters when he is arrested, Peter responds indignantly that the others may do so but he certainly will not. Then in 26:69–75, Peter denies Jesus three times out of fear.

Prior to Jesus's resurrection, Peter's behavior does not seem to reflect his name, if by "stone" one means a firm foundation. If, however, one means that Peter sinks like a stone or trips people like a stone or rolls downhill at the slightest nudge like a stone, then Peter lives up to his name. If Jesus's designation of Peter as a new Abraham in 16:18 is to be taken in a nonironic sense, then it must be viewed as a prolepsis (a foreshadowing of a future reality; Stock 1987).

Even looking at the postresurrection period, Peter does not seem to be the foundation of the church in general. He was not the head of the Jerusalem church. In Acts 10–11 he is examined by the Jerusalem church, and in Acts 15 he is obviously under James's authority. In Gal. 1–2 he is but one of the three pillars. He was not the founder of the Roman church. In 1 Pet. 5:1, he designates himself as one of the elders. If Peter is the chief interpreter of the Jesus tradition for Matthew's church, it is obvious that he is not that for the church at large (Witherington 2006, 313).

Catholics broke away in 1054). Roman Catholic Christians regard themselves as the church in unbroken succession from Peter (from whom the Orthodox broke away in 1054 and Protestants in the sixteenth century). Protestants regard themselves as a reform movement that broke away from a decadent Roman Catholic Church in the sixteenth century, returning to either the church before the Middle Ages or the church of the first four ecumenical councils or the pre-Constantinian church or the church of the first and second centuries. In the mid-twentieth century, the Bultmann School (e.g., Rudolf Bultmann and Ernst Käsemann) located the church's fall away from apostolic faith already in the NT. This decadence they called "Early Catholicism." For them, Early Catholicism is recognized in a certain church order (officers/bishops who by ordination become leaders of a sacramental cultus), right doctrine (determined by the authorized bearers of the tradition/bishops appointed by the apostles), legalistic soteriology, and moralistic piety (where sin is understood moralistically). For Bultmann, the gospel can be found only in Paul and the Fourth

Gospel (the latter in a precanonical form). The rest of the NT reflects Early Catholicism (a fall away from apostolic faith). This has produced a "canon within the canon" (Bultmann 2007).

In connection with Vatican II, Hans Küng critiques Käsemann's canon within the canon (Küng 1963). He says that Käsemann uses the lack of unity in the canon to make a selection from the canon (Paul), abandoning the wholeness of the NT. This is heresy (an absolutizing of a part instead of the whole). In contrast, the Catholic attitude strives to preserve an openness toward the whole of the NT. "Only a Catholic can do justice to the Catholicism of the New Testament" (181). "If this New Testament, in its latter parts, leads on to early Catholicism, then the Catholic exegete will strive to show that what is happening here is not . . . a perversion of the true and original thing, but a genuine and valid development" (188). The important thing to note here is that Küng claims that only a Catholic can affirm the whole of the NT over against a Protestant reduction of the canon to one stream of its thought. Is there any carryover in one's reflection on the role of Peter for later Christians?

In the apostolic and postapostolic periods, a number of forms of church polity existed. In the genuine Pauline Epistles one finds a charismatic form of ministry (e.g., 1 Cor. 12–14; Rom. 12; cf. also the post-Pauline Eph. 4). Acts 14:23; 20:17, 28 mentions ruling elders patterned after the synagogue (cf. Titus 1:5, 7). In 1 and 2 Timothy, bishops are functioning as an incipient monarchial episcopacy, with succession from an apostle (in this case, Paul). In the Revelation to John, the churches seem to be led by prophets (cf. also *Did.* 11–15). In the Johannine Epistles (and Papias), the churches are supervised by a teaching elder whose authority is derived from his personal link with the earlier apostles. If one affirms both the normative status of the whole canon and the differing positions taken by the diverse documents, then what should be said about polity? Peter is *the* leader for the Matthean community/Gospel although he is one among all the apostles (Matt. 18). For the other writings, however, he is not *the* apostle who teaches and passes on true tradition. In the Pastorals, Paul is. In the Johannine Epistles, the teacher is an unnamed teaching elder with links to unnamed apostles. In Revelation, John the prophet apparently supervises prophets who head up the churches in Asia Minor. In churches mentioned in Acts, ruling elders act as overseers. In the Fourth Gospel, the Beloved Disciple functions as the source of normative tradition for that community. If one follows Küng and affirms the normative character of the whole NT, then one is not going to absolutize the position that Peter holds in the Matthean community/Gospel. That would be heresy (absolutizing a part at the expense of the whole). Rather, Peter may be recognized as only one teaching authority among a host of canonical others who function in the apostolic and postapostolic periods.

Michael Crosby (2008), a Roman Catholic, contends that Roman Catholics' selective use of Matt. 16:17–19 at the expense of Matt. 18:17–20 reflects a fundamentalist (proof-texting) approach to the Bible's interpretation in the Roman Catholic Church. It is an approach that is rejected by the Pontifical Biblical Commission's own document on the Interpretation of the Bible in the Church in 1994, whose preface was written by then-Cardinal Joseph Ratzinger. This argument is a reinforcement of the previous one (the danger of absolutizing a part of the whole, in this case, a part of Matthew, instead of considering the whole of the First Gospel).

Matthew 16:21–17:23

Narrative 4, Part 2:
Jesus's Disciples Understand Even More

Introductory Matters

The principle of organization for 16:21–17:23 is rarely discussed. This is the central matter of introduction for the second part of the fourth narrative. Of the several proposed analyses of the entire fourth cycle described at the beginning of the preceding unit (13:54–16:20), that of Gaechter (1963, 468–584) is helpful in connection with this second part of the narrative. Gaechter proposes a chiastic pattern for 16:13–17:27. It runs as follows:

A Peter (16:13–20)
   B first passion prediction (16:21)
      C Peter critiqued (16:22–28)
         D transfiguration (17:1–9)
      C′ disciples critiqued (17:14–21)
   B′ second passion prediction (17:22–23)
A′ Peter (17:24–27)

This pattern has possibilities, except for its A and A′ components. Section A in the pattern misses the break between 16:20 and 16:21, and section A′ detaches 17:24–27 from the discourse in chapter 18.

If one were to accept these critiques of Gaechter's proposal and limit the material to 16:21–17:23, held together by an inclusio (Garland 2001, 181, notes that 16:21–17:23 is framed by two predictions of the passion), then there does seem to be a concentric pattern for the material.

Tracing the Narrative Flow

Matthew 16:21–28 (cf. Mark 8:31–9:1) is a narrative unit that reflects sections A (16:21) and B (16:22–23, 24–28) in the pattern. Verses 21–23 constitute a simple conflict story with the required three parts: Jesus's prediction of his passion (16:21); Peter's rebuke of such a thought (16:22); Jesus's response to Peter (16:23; Davies and Allison 1991, 2:653).

(A) Predicting the Passion (16:21)

In 16:21 occurs the first of four passion predictions in Matthew (cf. 17:22–23; 20:17–19; 26:2; also 17:12b?): **Then Jesus Christ began to show his disciples that it was necessary (*dei*) for him to go up to Jerusalem and to suffer many things from the elders and chief priests and scribes and to be killed and on the third day to be raised.** To those to whom it has been given to understand the mysteries of the kingdom, more is being offered (cf. 13:11–12). Note that the prediction contains neither "in accordance with the scriptures" nor "for our sins" (1 Cor. 15:3; Schnackenburg 2002, 161). There is only the *dei*, indicating that Jesus's sufferings, death, and resurrection are a part of the divine plan. How so? Prophets who confronted God's people suffered and often died (cf. 17:12).

Ancient auditors would have understood this prediction. Cicero (*Div.* 1.66) states the principle: "The human soul has an inherent power of presaging or of foreknowing infused into it from without and made part of it by the will of God" (trans. Falconer 1923). Natural divination has its roots here. It included oracles uttered under divine inspiration (e.g., passion predictions). Regarding predictions about death, there are three trajectories in ancient sources. First, there are predictions of another's death. For example, in Esther 6:13 the villain's wife predicts his death. Josephus (*J.W.* 1.78–80) tells of an Essene who predicted an individual's death to the exact time and place. Astrologers predicted the time and manner of Domitian's death when he was still a young

---

Matthew 16:21–17:23 in the Narrative Flow

Birth narratives (1:1–2:23)

Jesus's ministry begins (3:1–8:1)

Jesus's authority is revealed (8:2–11:1)

Jesus's ministry creates division (11:2–13:53)

Jesus focuses on his disciples (13:54–19:2)

Narrative: Jesus's disciples understand more (13:54–16:20)

▶ *Narrative*: Jesus's disciples understand even more (16:21–17:23)

  (A) Predicting the passion (16:21)

  (B) Critiquing Peter, instructing disciples (16:22–28)

  (C) Up the mountain with three disciples (17:1–8)

  (C′) Down the mountain with three disciples (17:9–13)

  (B′) Critiquing and instructing disciples (17:14–21)

  (A′) Predicting the passion (17:22–23)

---

man (Suetonius, *Dom.* 15). Mardonius's death at the hand of a Spartan who crushed his head with a stone was foretold by the oracle of Trophonius long before the event (Plutarch, *Arist.* 19.1–2). Second, one might have foreknowledge that one was not going to die at present. For example, Iamblichus says that Pythagoras knew he was not going to die at the hand of the tyrant Phalaris (*Vit. Pyth.* 217). Philostratus says Apollonius knew he would not die at that time at the hand of the emperor (*Vit. Apoll.* 7.38; 8.5, 8). In John 7:6, 30 Jesus knows his time is not yet.

Third, individuals predict their own deaths. For example, Suetonius tells of an astrologer's prediction of his own death, and so it happened (*Dom.* 15.3). Plutarch tells how heaven gave to Dion and Brutus an intimation of their approaching death (*Dion* 2.1). Furthermore, he says Sulla not only foresaw his own death but also wrote about it (*Sull.* 37), and Alcibiades had a premonition of his own death (*Alc.* 39.1–2). Suetonius says that Domitian predicted his death the day before he was killed (*Dom.* 16). Philostratus says Apollonius predicted that he and Nerva would die soon (*Vit. Apoll.* 8.27). Philo says that Moses knew and wrote about his death before it happened (*Mos.* 2.291). Simeon the Just is said to have predicted his own death (*b. Yoma* 39b). That an individual might have foreknowledge of his own death and speak about it to others was therefore taken for granted in Mediterranean antiquity, pagan and Jewish. In 2 Macc. 7:9, 14 are also predictions of resurrection. What was provocative about the Matthean Jesus's prediction of his passion was that someone confessed as "the Christ, the son of the living God" (16:16), someone who accepted this designation as "the Christ" (16:20), and someone called by the narrator "Jesus Christ" (16:21a) should speak about *his* suffering and death. Ancient Judaism looked for a triumphant messiah (cf. *Pss. Sol.* 17.32).

(B) Critiquing Peter, Instructing Disciples (16:22–28)

Peter recoils from the very idea of his messiah's suffering and death: **Mercy be to you, Lord. This will never happen to you** (16:22). The little conflict story ends with Jesus's retort: **Go behind me, Satan** (cf. 4:10). **You are a stumbling block to me, because you are not thinking the things of God but the things of humans** (16:23). A demonic mind-set is unable to receive the additional revelation. The disciples need assistance to accept this new teaching. That will come in 17:1–8.

After the conflict story comes additional revelation to and for disciples (16:24–28). There are no crowds, as in Mark 8:34. The unit is held together by link words: **wish** (*thelei*), 16:24, 25; **his life**, 16:25, 26; **will give**, 16:26, 27; **son of man**, 16:27, 28. It begins with a general statement in 16:24: **If any wish to come after me, let them deny themselves and take up their crosses, and let them follow me.** The hated punishment, crucifixion, was known to Palestinian Jews. The Jew Alexander Jannaeus, prior to Jesus, crucified eight hundred Jews at one time. The Roman governor of Syria, shortly after the

Would an Ideal King Suffer?

Dio Chrysostom presents a portrait of the king as a solitary, poor, and suffering figure. The model for this type is Heracles. In *Or.* 1.59–65 is a summary of the important themes: (1) the king abases himself, (2) he is reviled, (3) he must endure physical suffering, (4) he must engage in the most severe moral struggle, (5) he is a king disguised as a slave. For all of this, Heracles was the son of Zeus and worthy of kingship (cf. Epictetus, *Diatr.* 3.26, 32). At least some non-Jews would not have been surprised that the ideal Jewish king must suffer (Höistad 1948, 195).

death of Herod the Great in 4 BC, was forced to move into Jewish territory to put down an insurrection. After finishing the work and restoring order, he crucified two thousand Jews (Josephus, *Ant.* 17.295). Nearer to the time of the First Gospel, during Titus's attempts to end the revolt of AD 66–70, on a number of occasions he crucified Jews in front of Jerusalem's walls to frighten the defenders within the city (Josephus, *J.W.* 5.289, 449–51). Jesus's words would have conveyed a vivid image to auditors of his time and of the time of the First Gospel. **To deny oneself** and **to take up one's cross** reflect aorist verbs; **let them follow me** reflects a present-tense verb. Hence, the saying envisions a decision and a process (Davies and Allison 1991, 2:671).

This general statement is unpacked in the following explanatory comments that fall into an ABB'A' pattern. (A) **Those who lose their lives on account of me will find them** (16:25b). (B) **For what will people gain if they acquire the whole world and lose their lives?** (16:26a). (B') **Or what will people give in exchange for their lives?** (16:26b). (A') **For the son of man is about to come in the glory of his Father with his angels, and then he will give to everyone according to their behavior** (16:27; cf. Ps. 62:12b; Rom. 2:6). Discipleship may involve the same kinds of suffering and death that Jesus has predicted for himself. To lose one's life for Jesus's sake, however, will be gain at the parousia, when the son of man comes. This is the promise of 16:27. The **behavior** referred to is that of loyalty to Jesus (cf. 10:32–33, 37–39). The last saying in this grouping also constitutes a promise (16:28): **Truly I say to you all that there are certain of those standing here who may not taste death until they see the son of man coming in his kingdom.**

Matthew 16:28 has been variously interpreted in Christian history. Many early fathers, including Clement of Alexandria (*Exc.* 4.3), Origen (*Comm. Matt.* 12.31), John Chrysostom (*Hom. Matt.* 56–57), and Augustine (*Cons.* 2.56), saw this as a promise of the transfiguration. Rudolf Schnackenburg (2002, 164) and David Turner (2008, 416) are modern advocates of this position. Both 16:28 and 17:1–9 involve only some disciples, deal with vision, and contain eschatological motifs. The one objection is that the son of man's coming refers most naturally to the parousia (Davies and Allison 1991, 2:677–78). If one then takes 16:28 to be a reference to the parousia (e.g., Gundry 1982,

341; Boring 1995, 351; Carter 2000, 346), then the inference is that Jesus was mistaken about the timing. This type of mistaken imminent expectation was certainly true of early Christians who expected the end while they were still alive (e.g., 1 Thess. 4:15: "we who are alive, who are left until the coming of the Lord"; 1 Cor. 15:52). In this case, the logion has been preserved because it is a Jesus tradition, even if it is mistaken about the time of the end. A major problem for this reading is that, properly interpreted, Matthew contains no logia elsewhere that speak of an imminent end. For those who find neither of these first two interpretations appealing, other options have been suggested: 16:28 refers to the resurrection (cf. 28:16–20; Garland 2001, 183), to Pentecost (but Pentecost is nowhere mentioned in Matthew), or to the fall of Jerusalem in AD 70. In this commentary, 16:28 is taken to refer to the transfiguration, which is understood as a vision of the disciples in which they see Jesus proleptically in his parousia glory. The verse may be better paraphrased by taking the verb **see** as an ingressive aorist (begin to see). The transfiguration does not

---

The Meaning of Taking Up One's Cross

There are three different forms of the cross-bearing saying in the early church: (1) Mark 8:34//Matt. 16:24//Luke 9:23; (2) Q: Matt. 10:38//Luke 14:27; (3) Coptic *Gospel of Thomas* 55. The meaning of these logia has been a matter of dispute. Consider three possible options: (1) Bearing one's cross means patiently enduring the various trials of everyday life (Küng 1976, 570–81). (2) Taking up one's cross means nonviolent resistance to or subversion of the political order (Yoder 1994). (3) Taking up one's cross is a virtual synonym for denying oneself (Davies and Allison 1991, 2:670–71).

The third option is supported by references in the letters of Paul. In Rom. 6:6, Paul says, "Our old self was crucified with him so that the body of sin might be destroyed, and we might no longer be enslaved to sin." In 6:10, "The death he died, he died to sin," clarifies the meaning. To be crucified with Christ is to die to sin. In Galatians are three passages that shed light on the subject. In 2:19b–20, we read: "I have been crucified with Christ; and it is no longer I who live, but it is Christ who lives in me." Here crucifixion with Christ means death to the old ego, the false self. In 5:24, Paul says, "Those who belong to Christ Jesus have crucified the flesh with its passions and desires." Here crucifixion with Christ means death to the orientation to life that makes the created order one's ultimate value. In 6:14, we read, "our Lord Jesus Christ, through whom the world has been crucified to me, and I to the world" (NRSV marg.). Here crucifixion means death to the created order organized in independence from God. In Ign. *Rom.* 7.2, the same usage is found. What is crucified is false love for the world. When the Matthean Jesus called for would-be disciples to deny themselves and take up their crosses, it was a call for a death to everything that competed with following him, that is, death to idolatry.

exhaust the disciples' vision of Jesus's parousia, but its vision gives them an initial, parousia preview.

(C) Up the Mountain with Three Disciples (17:1–8)

Matthew 17:1–8 (cf. Mark 9:2–8) is C in the concentric pattern (going up the mountain). **And after six days Jesus took Peter and James and John his brother and led them into a high mountain alone** (17:1). What happens next is described by Matthew as a *horama* (17:9; cf. Acts 10:17; 16:9; Exod. 3:3). This means that Matthew views the transfiguration as a visionary experience of the three disciples, like a dream-vision (Hanson 1980, 1422). In the First Gospel, the transfiguration is not presented as a specific, definite event in the life of Jesus. Apart from the introduction about going up into the mountain and the conclusion about going down the mountain, the narrator reports only what the disciples see and hear (R. Edwards 1997, 80). The transfiguration narrative clearly reflects a typology of the events of Moses on Mount Sinai in Exod. 24 and 34, such as six days later (24:16), a mountain (24:12, 15–18; 34:3), a select group (24:1), shining face/skin (34:29–35), a bright cloud (24:15–18; 34:5), a voice from the cloud (24:16), and fear of the bystanders (34:29–30). Another echo, **Listen to him** (17:5), is from Deut. 18:15 (Carter 2000, 348). Since Hellenistic Judaism understood Moses's ascent into Sinai as a mystical experience, Jewish disciples would naturally think in these cultural-religious categories. If they had a vision, it would reflect their primary categories for such experiences (Exod. 24:9–11: a vision of God by Moses, Aaron, Nadab, Abihu, and seventy elders).

The story itself, however, belongs to the genre of dream-vision narratives: (1) scene setting, (2) the dream-vision proper, (3) the responses of the dreamer-visionary to the experience (Dodson 2006, 291–308). (1) Matthew 17:1 provides the dream setting. The recipients are named (Peter, James, and John), they are alone, the place is given (a high mountain), and the time is specified (after six days). (2) The dream-vision proper combines visionary (the appearance of Moses and Elijah; the transfigured Jesus) and auditory components (the voice from the cloud). The vision is for the disciples (17:3, **and behold Moses and Elijah appeared *to them***). (3) The disciples' response to the experience is twofold. On the one hand, in response to the vision of Moses and Elijah talking with Jesus, Peter says to Jesus in the vision, **It is good for us to be here. If you wish, I will make here three tents, one for you and one for Moses and one for Elijah** (17:4). Matthew omits any negative statement about Peter's reaction (contrast Mark 9:6; Luke 9:33). The evangelist seems to find Peter's reaction appropriate.

Peter's proposal is to commemorate the event, behavior regarded as culturally appropriate. He offers to do what is normally expected. On the other hand, the disciples' reaction to the overshadowing cloud and voice from heaven (**This is my Son, the beloved, in whom I take delight. Listen to him** [17:5]) is **they fell**

Figure 11. Mount Tabor was originally one of several sites suggested for the transfiguration. Mount Hermon and the Mount of Olives were other possibilities. In 348 Cyril of Jerusalem decided on Tabor. Supported by Epiphanius and Jerome, the Tabor tradition was established.

on their faces and were exceedingly fearful (17:6). This is the type of response that one expects from those who have experienced a theophany (e.g., Rev. 1:17a; Num. 22:31–35; Josh. 5:13–15; 2 Macc. 3:22–34). Both responses are deemed appropriate by Matthew. After a person experiences a theophany and falls down and is afraid, the reaction from the heavenly visitant is normally, **Do not be afraid** (17:7; cf. Rev. 1:17b; Luke 1:30). This is an expected conclusion to a theophany or angelophany. It is so here. At the end of the vision, the disciples, back to their normal state of consciousness, see only Jesus (17:8).

If Matt. 17:1–8 is to be understood as an account of a dream-vision in which the three disciples see the glorified Jesus, certain issues must be settled. First, according to Artemidorus Daldianus (*Onir.* 1.2), a vision (*horama*) sometimes pre-enacts a future event (cf. Acts 10:9–10, 19). Jewish tradition claimed that

Commemorating Epiphanies

Ancient Egypt shows the deep roots of the practice of erecting some structure in response to an epiphany (Thutmose IV [reigned 1400–1390 BC] received an epiphany while he was still prince and commemorated it later by erecting a granite stele [Pritchard 1955, 245–47]). Greek and Roman authors speak of individuals who have experienced a vision responding by dedicating a temple or setting up an altar (Plutarch, *Them.* 30.3: because Themistocles was amazed at the epiphany of the goddess, he built a temple in her honor; Pausanias, *Descr.* 3.14.4: a priestess of Thetis, after being taken to Laconia as a prisoner of war, established the cult in that city because of a vision. Cicero, *Rep.* 2.20 and *Leg.* 1.3 say that Romulus appeared to the Alban farmer, Julius Proculus, ordering the temple of Quirinus to be built on the spot of the epiphany. For inscriptional evidence, see Dodson 2006, 52–54; Renberg 2003, 169, 175). Jewish tradition knows the same type of response (Gen. 28:10–22: after Jacob had a vision and an audition at Bethel, he took a stone and set it up for a pillar to commemorate his encounter with God; 26:23–25: after Isaac experienced a vision and an audition, he built an altar at Beersheba).

certain ancient noteworthies were given visions of the end times (e.g., Abraham: 2 Esd. [*4 Ezra*] 3:14; Isaiah: John 12:41). So the disciples' vision could easily have been understood as a preview of Jesus's parousia (the end time).

Second, in antiquity it was believed that more than one person could have the same visionary experience simultaneously (e.g., P.Oxy. 11.1381.91ff.: the same divine figure is experienced in exactly the same way by two people in an altered state of consciousness simultaneously [Pilch 1995, 58]; Epidaurian inscriptions, stele 2.21: a mother and daughter see the same dream; Pausanias, *Descr.* 10.38.13: a shared waking vision; Exod. 24:9–10: Moses, Aaron, Nadab, Abihu, and seventy elders "went up and they saw the God of Israel"; Acts 9:3–6, 7: both Saul and the men traveling with him hear the voice that is part of the christophany). So a Mediterranean auditor would have had no problem with a story that said three disciples had the same visionary-auditory experience simultaneously.

Third, it was a part of at least one stream of Jewish apocalyptic expectation that Moses and Elijah would come together as part of the eschatological windup of history (e.g., *Deut. Rab.* 3.17 on Deut. 10:1: a saying attributed to Rabbi Johanan ben Zakkai; Rev. 11:3–6; cf. 2 Esd. [*4 Ezra*] 6:25–26; Moses was regarded by some Jews as one who was taken up, as were Elijah and Enoch, cf. Josephus, *Ant.* 4.323–26; *Sifre* 357 on Deut. 34:5; Clement of Alexandria, *Strom.* 6.15.132: Joshua saw Moses ascend with the angel; Jerome, *Comm. Amos* 9.6: Moses ascends like Enoch and Elijah).

Fourth, the transfiguration of Jesus includes things (shining face, clothes dazzling white) that are regarded as typical of the end times (e.g., *2 Bar.* 51.1–6: at the end the righteous will be transformed into light; Matt. 13:43; *2 En.* 22.9–10: garments of glory). It would seem, then, that Matthew's telling of the transfiguration narrative speaks about a visionary experience of three disciples. They see Jesus's eschatological glory, a parousia preview (Witherington 2006, 323), and in addition hear both God's second declaration of Jesus's sonship (3:17 is the first) and the divine command to listen to Jesus (i.e., his teachings about his own passion and the cross-bearing of his disciples).

Finally, this reading of the transfiguration narrative agrees with 2 Pet. 1:16–18, where the transfiguration is regarded as proof of Jesus's power and coming (parousia). This could only be if it is interpreted as an anticipatory vision of the

The Function of the Transfiguration

Matthew 17:1–8 presents a particular religious experience of the three disciples. It was a peak experience, unique and unrepeatable. It has limits, however. It is preparation for the return to ordinary life (17:14–21). These three disciples participated in both the mountaintop and the valley experiences. Without suffering, peak experiences become illusory. Without peak experiences, suffering becomes devoid of hope (Luz 1995, 103–4). For a defense of the authenticity of such experiences in human life, see William Alston (1991).

Elijah as a Preparer Figure

Elijah's role in God's plan for the shift of the ages was variously understood in Middle Judaism. (1) Sometimes Elijah alone was depicted as a preparer figure, either as a forerunner of the day of the Lord (e.g., Mal. 4:5–6; Sir. 48:9–10; *Sib. Or.* 2.187–89) or as the forerunner of the messiah (e.g., *1 En.* 89.52; 90.31; Justin Martyr, *Dial.* 8.4 and 49.1; *b. Eruv.* 43a–b; *Tg. Ps.-J.* of Deut. 30:4; *Pesiq. Rab.* 35.3; *Pirqe R. El.* end of chap. 4). The issue for M. M. Faierstein (1981) is whether these sources are too late to be useful for NT study. Methodologically, if early Christian Jewish sources show knowledge of a tradition that appears later in rabbinic materials, the former establishes the existence of a form of the latter in NT times. (2) At other times Elijah and Enoch together were depicted as preparer figures, as forerunners either of the day of the Lord (e.g., 2 Esd. [*4 Ezra*] 6:26) or of the messiah (*Apoc. El.*). (3) On still other occasions, Elijah and Moses together served as preparer figures of the day of the Lord (e.g., *Deut. Rab.* 3.17 on Deut. 10:1).

In the NT, Elijah fulfills two functions. First, two of the Synoptics view Elijah as the forerunner of the messiah within history (e.g., Matt. 3:4; 11:14; 17:11–12: the Baptist is Elijah who prepares for the messiah; Mark 1:6; 9:13: John is Elijah; Luke 1:76; 7:27: John is the prophet who prepares the way, while the name of Elijah is not mentioned; cf. John 1:21, 25: the Baptist denies that he is Elijah). This function is one that is carried out in history, prior to the public ministry of Jesus. Second, in Rev. 11 the two witnesses seem to be Elijah and Moses. Their function is performed prior to the day of the Lord.

In later Christian thought, Elijah is portrayed in two broad ways: one dependent on Rev. 11:3–13 and the other rooted in Mal. 3:23–24 LXX (4:5–6 Eng.). The first way depicts Elijah, sometimes with a second figure like Enoch, as coming to witness against the Antichrist (e.g., Ethiopic *Apoc. Pet.*; Tertullian, *An.* 50). The second way sees Elijah functioning as herald of the parousia (e.g., Augustine, *Civ.* 20.29), often connected with the conversion of the Jews before the judgment (John Chrysostom, *Hom. Matt.* 55; J. Weaver 2007).

---

parousia (Neyrey 1980). Matthew 17:1–8 is, then, a fulfillment of the promise made by Jesus in 16:28. Three disciples have seen the parousia of Jesus, if only in a vision.

(C′) *Down the Mountain with Three Disciples (17:9–13)*

Section C′ is a dialogue between Jesus and the three disciples as they descend from the mountain. First, Jesus issues a command. **Speak to no one about the vision** (*horama*) **until the son of man has been raised from the dead** (17:9). Then the disciples ask their question: **Why do the scribes say that Elijah must** (*dei*) **come first?** (17:10).

Jesus's response is, **Elijah is coming, and he will restore all things. And I say to you that Elijah has already come, and they did not recognize him, but they** did to him whatever they wished. So also the son of man is about to suffer at their hands (17:11–12). The narrator concludes, **Then the disciples understood that he spoke to them about John the Baptist** (17:13; cf. 11:14; 3:4). Again, the disciples who have understanding are given further insight (cf. 13:11–12). This dialogue functions in two ways. On the one hand, it is apologetic. Against the charge that Jesus could not be the Christ because Elijah has not yet come (Justin Martyr, *Dial.* 49), this pericope says that Elijah has indeed already come in the person of John the Baptist. On the other hand, the Baptist is set forth as the prototype of the suffering that Jesus will also have to endure (Nolland 2005, 709). The voice from heaven has told the disciples to listen to Jesus. Now Jesus speaks once again about his coming suffering. To this the three disciples must listen.

(B') Critiquing and Instructing Disciples (17:14–21)

Section B' is a drastic reshaping of the miracle story in Mark 9:14–29. The focus has shifted from the details of the exorcism in Mark to the issue of the faith of the disciples. Jesus's words are both a rebuke of the disciples' faithlessness and instruction about faith. This radical reshaping is what makes 17:14–21 a parallel to 16:22–23, 24–28.

When Jesus and the three disciples reach the crowd at the foot of the mountain, a man comes to Jesus and kneels before him, saying, **Lord, have mercy on my son. He is an epileptic and . . . often falls into the fire, often into the water. I brought him to your disciples, and they were not able to heal him** (17:15–16). To which Jesus responds with a rebuke: **O faithless and perverse generation, how long will I be with you? How long can I endure you? Bring him here to me** (17:17). Jesus casts the demon out, and the child is healed immediately (17:18). (Oribasius [*Collections medicae* 45.30.10–14] tells of Asclepius's healing of one with epilepsy; *b. Me'il.* 17a–b recounts how Simeon ben Yohai commanded a demon to leave the emperor's daughter.) This is the occasion for the disciples to come to Jesus with their question: **Why were we not able to cast it out?** (17:19). To which Jesus replies with further instruction: **Because of your little faith. Truly I say to you all, if you should have faith like a grain of mustard seed, you would say to this mountain, "Move over there," and it would move, and nothing would be impossible for you** (17:20; cf. 21:21). Several observations need to be made about this story. First, the language about moving mountains is conventional speech for doing the impossible. Second, the NT speaks about different types of faith, such as saving faith (Phil. 1:29) and miracle-working faith (1 Cor. 12:9–10). Both are enabled by God. Remember Matt. 10:1 for the latter. The power to work miracles is a gift from Jesus. Here the context indicates that it is miracle-working faith that is in view (Davies and Allison 1991, 2:727). Third, Eugene Boring (1995, 369) says correctly that "this is not a saying about the power of faith but about the power of God, even if God language is not used in either place. . . . God is the one who acts, not an attitude called 'faith.'"

(A′) Predicting the Passion (17:22–23)

Section A′ (cf. Mark 9:30–32) is a second major passion prediction (cf. 16:21). **The son of man is about to be delivered into others' hands, and they will kill him, and on the third day he will be raised** (17:22–23a). Whereas in Mark 9:32 and Luke 9:45 the disciples do not understand the saying, in Matt. 17:23b **they were exceedingly grieved.** In Matthew, the disciples understand certain things (13:11). Yet they have had difficulty with the teaching about Jesus's suffering and death (16:22–23). After the vision and audition on the mount of transfiguration (17:1–7), here they are portrayed not as failing to understand but as grieving. This is the type of behavior that an auditor in the Mediterranean world would expect. Xenophon (*Symp.* 4.48) has Hermogenes express the cultural perspective:

> Greeks and barbarians believe that the gods know everything both present and to come. . . . They know the results also that will follow any act; and so they send to me as messengers omens of sound, dreams, and birds, and thus indicate what I ought to do and what I ought not to do. And when I do their bidding, I never regret it. (Marchant and Todd 1923)

The disciples have made progress, however small.

Functions of the Unit as a Whole

The praise component of Matthew's narrative continues. Two things stand out in 16:21–17:23. In the first place, Quintilian (*Inst.* 3.7.15) says that an encomium often involves a focus on the various virtues displayed in the person being praised. For example, when faced with death, the person displays deeds of courage. This the Matthean Jesus does as he announces, without blinking, his upcoming suffering and death (16:21; 17:22–23). In the second place, an encomium often included the testimony of God or the gods to the person's greatness. This testimony could be shown in various ways. Sometimes divine oracles proclaimed the person's greatness (cf. 17:5: "This is my Son, the beloved. . . . Listen to him"). Sometimes the deity communicated through visions. The divine oracle attesting Jesus's identity and authority comes in a vision in 17:2–8. The disciples are granted a vision (*horama*) in which they behold Jesus's eschatological status and authority (cf. Cicero, *Top.* 20.76–77). Matthew's encomium thus continues in 16:21–17:23.

The apologetic dimension of Matthew's narrative, protecting Jesus against attack, also continues. Against the charge that Jesus cannot be the messiah because Elijah has not yet come (cf. Justin Martyr, *Dial.* 49), Matt. 17:12 says that Elijah has already come and 17:13 says that John the Baptist has fulfilled that role.

In Matt. 13:54–17:23, the fourth narrative, there has been steady progress in the emergence of a new community gathered around Jesus. It is a community that recognizes his messiahship. It is also a community that has, through divine intervention, come to accept, however imperfectly, his impending suffering and death. The community's identity is derived from that of Jesus. Now that the existence and identity of Jesus's *ekklēsia* (people of God, church) is clear, it is time for the fourth discourse, 17:24–19:2, which deals with the life of the community in its relations to outsiders and insiders.

Theological Issues

Matthew 16:21–17:23 opens and closes with passion predictions (16:21; 17:22–23). In the middle of the narrative (17:12), Jesus indicates the meaning of his coming suffering and death. Just as John the Baptist suffered and was killed, so the son of man (prophetic figure who speaks God's word to the people) will suffer at their hands. This places Jesus, along with the Baptist, within the rejected prophet motif.

The background for this motif is found in the deuteronomistic view of history. It may be described in seven steps. (1) Israel's history is one of disobedience. (2) Yahweh sends prophets who call for repentance. (3) Israel rejects these prophets, often killing them. (4) Yahweh punishes Israel. (5) A new call for repentance is issued. (6) If Israel repents, then Yahweh will restore them. (7) This restoration will involve judgment on Israel's enemies. This perspective permeates other authors as well, especially as it relates to the role and fate of prophets.

The people did not listen to the prophets (Jer. 7:25–26; 35:15). Rather, they mocked and scoffed at them (2 Chron. 36:15–16) and sometimes killed them (Neh. 9:26–30). A violent fate came to be an expected part of a prophet's role (e.g., 1 Kings 18:4, 13; 19:10, 14; 22:26–27; 2 Kings 9:7; 2 Chron. 16:10; 24:20–22; Jer. 2:30; 26:20–23; *Jub.* 1.12–13; Josephus, *Ant.* 10.38–39). National sin was viewed as the cause of the exiles of both the northern and southern kingdoms (e.g., 2 Kings 23:26–27; *Pss. Sol.* 9.1–3; cf. *Pss. Sol.* 17.1–18, which says Pompey's capture of Jerusalem was due to the same thing). There was a hope that Jerusalem would be restored under the leadership of a righteous king and messiah (*Pss. Sol.* 17.21–46).

This perspective was taken over by the First Evangelist. In the parable of the wicked tenants, the servants who were sent and who were beaten and killed are the prophets of Israel (21:34–36). In the parable of the marriage feast, the servants sent to Israel with invitations to the banquet are seized and treated shamefully (22:6). In Matt. 23, Jerusalem is characterized as killing the prophets and stoning those sent to them (23:37). The First Gospel, moreover, views the Baptist, Jesus, and Jesus's disciples as rejected prophets. John the Baptist is regarded as a prophet (3:4, cf. 2 Kings 1:8; Matt. 11:9, 14; 14:5; 17:12) who is rejected and suffers violence (3:7; 11:12, 18; 14:3–11; 17:12). Jesus is also portrayed as a rejected prophet (13:57; 14:1–2; 16:13–14; 17:12; 21:11). Jesus's disciples' suffering is compared to that of the prophets (5:11–12; 23:34). This is a calling they share with Jesus (16:24–26). As in the deuteronomistic theology, so also in Matthew the fall of Jerusalem is attributed to the rejection of God's messengers (23:34–36), especially Jesus (23:37–39; 24:1–2). Matthew interprets the fall of Jerusalem in AD 70 within a deuteronomistic framework. It is due to the rejection of God's prophets (Knowles 1993).

Matthew 17:24–19:2

Discourse 4: Jesus Tells Disciples How to Relate to Insiders and Outsiders

Introductory Matters

In this discourse, whose close is signaled by the customary formula in 19:1–2 ("And when Jesus finished these sayings"), the focus is on the community's relationships with those outside and inside the fold. Proportionately, the emphasis is greater on the latter.

The Beginning of the Fourth Discourse

Where does the fourth discourse begin? In this commentary the unit begins with 17:24. There are several reasons for taking this position. First, the locale is the same for all of 17:24–18:35: Capernaum. Second, the entire unit is bracketed by material about Peter (17:24–27 and 18:21–22). Third, the theme (on not giving offense to others, 17:27 and 18:6–9) ties the material of 17:24–27 together with that in 18:1–9. Fourth, the form (question-answer + pronouncement) is the same in 17:24–25a, 25b–26a + 26b–27a and in 18:1–2 + 3–4 and in 18:21–22 + 23–35.

The Addressees

To whom is the discourse addressed? Either it is spoken to church leaders (e.g., Meyer 1994, 91; cf. 18:12–14, where the image of a shepherd evokes a community leader; also Meier 1979, 94–135) or to disciples as a whole (most scholars). There does not seem to be any necessary reason to narrow the

214

audience to community leaders. Indeed, when Matthew wants to make sure that leaders are involved, he is very clear (cf. 10:1; 24:45–51). In this commentary, the fourth discourse is taken as addressed to disciples in general.

The Function of the Fourth Discourse's Language

How does the language in the fourth discourse function? What kind of language is one reading? Is it law? If so, what kind of law: apodictic (e.g., Exod. 20:13, 14, 15, 16, 17) or casuistic (e.g., Exod. 21:12, 15, 16, 17, 18–19)? Or is it performative language? If so, is it in the form of a promise (e.g., Matt. 5:3–11), a verbal icon (e.g., Matt. 5:21–48), or an existential question (e.g., Matt. 13:3–9, 24–30, 31–32, 33)? Any reading of the fourth discourse must discern what kind of language is being used. For example, 18:3, 6, 8–9, 15–17 are casuistic law, while 18:10–14, 21–22, 23–35 are either verbal icons or existential questions, and 18:18–20 is a promise. What is the significance of distinguishing these types of language in the discourse? Casuistic language provides rules for actions in a specified circumstance: if you do this, then that will be the result. This type of language aims to control those actions. Performative language aims either to provoke (serve as a catalyst for the destruction of an old world and the construction of a new one) or to reinforce a new world already espoused. It is aimed at developing character. A proper reading of the fourth discourse, therefore, requires attention to the function of the language encountered in it.

The Organization of the Fourth Discourse

How is 17:24–19:2 organized? Dominique Hermant (1996) proposes an arrangement of chapter 18 into six periods, each with three components:

1. 18:1–4 (1–2, 3, 4)
2. 18:5–9 (5–6, 7, 8–9)
3. 18:10–14 (10, 12–13, 14)
4. 18:15–17 (15–16, 17a, 17b)
5. 18:18–20 (18, 19, 20)
6. 18:21–35 (21–22, 23–34, 35)

(Cf. also Bonnard 1963, 267–79, who differs only at 18:1–5, 6–9.) Others suggest four (18:1–5, 6–14, 15–20, 21–35) or five paragraphs (18:1–5, 6–9, 10–14, 15–20, 21–35). The differences are minimal. The subunit 18:1–5 is held together by a repetition of *paidion/paidia* (child/children); 18:6–9 by *skandalizō/skandalon* (cause of stumbling); 18:10–14 by an inclusio ("one of these little ones" [18:10 and 14]); 18:15–20, 21–22, 23–35 by the key word *adelphos* (brother). More important, the chapter breaks into two parts (18:1–14 and 18:15–35), each ending with a parable (18:12–14, 23–35) whose last verse includes *houtōs*

... *patēr* ("so ... Father"; Davies and Allison 1991, 2:750–51) The accompanying outline shows the result if one takes 17:24–27 as part of the whole.

Tracing the Narrative Flow

Relations with Outsiders: The Temple Tax (17:24–27)

Matthew 17:24–27 (unique to Matthew) is concerned with how Jesus's disciples relate to those *outside* their community (cf. 1 Cor. 9:19). The pericope consists of two question-and-answer scenes: 17:24–25a; 17:25b–27. Relations of Jesus's disciples with those outside the community are to be governed by the principle of not using one's freedom in a way that would give offense to outsiders.

17:24–25a. In the first question-and-answer scene, the players are tax collectors and Peter. **When they came to Capernaum, those who receive the didrachma came to Peter and said, "Does your teacher pay the didrachma?" Peter said, "Yes."** The tax referred to is a pre–AD 70 tax intended for the upkeep of the temple in Jerusalem. Payment was a custom (Josephus, *Ant.* 18.312) allegedly rooted in Exod. 30:11–16. If 4Q159, frag. 1, col. 2.7, is any indication, then at Qumran the tax was paid only once in a lifetime. Priests thought they did not have to pay it, but some like Rabbi Johanan ben Zakkai said that if a priest did not pay it, he committed sin (*m. Sheqal.* 1.3–4). Philo (*Spec.* 1.76–78) said everyone, beginning in his twentieth year, should make an annual contribution. It was collected locally and sent to Jerusalem. Since Jesus and Peter reside in Capernaum (4:13; 8:5, 14), this is where their payment would be collected. Philo (*Spec.* 1.77) says the tax was given cheerfully and gladly. The tax of one-half silver shekel was paid in Greek coinage (two drachmas, hence the term *di*drachma). After the war of AD 66–70 and the destruction of the Jerusalem temple, Vespasian imposed a tax of two drachmas on all Jews for support of the temple of Jupiter at Rome (Josephus, *Ant.* 7.218). This pericope in Matthew's plot is pre-70, so the issue is a Jewish religious tax, not a Roman one.

17:25b–27. In the second scene the characters are Jesus and Peter. **When Peter came to the house, Jesus spoke to him first, saying, "What do you think, Simon? From whom do the kings of earth receive taxes, from their children or from others?" And when Peter said, "from others," Jesus said to him, "Then the children are free** (cf. 1 Cor. 9:19). **Now in order that we may not be a stumbling block for them, when you go to the sea, cast a hook in and take the first fish you pull in, and opening its mouth, you will find a stater** (equaling two didrachmas). **Take that and give it to them for me and you."** The point of the story is not to be a stumbling block to outsiders (cf. 1 Cor. 9:19–23; Gal. 5:13; 1 Pet. 2:12–16). Jesus models such behavior. (Similar fish stories are found across cultures, ancient and modern. E.g., Herodotus, *Hist.* 3.39–42, tells of Polycrates, who throws his ring in the sea to appease fate, and then a week later it comes back to him at dinner in a fish; cf. also *b. Shabb.* 119a.)

Relations with Insiders (18:1–35)

This section first gives a general norm for relations with fellow disciples (18:1–4), then provides specific guidelines. These latter fall into two parts (18:5–14 and 18:15–35), each ending with a parable.

18:1–4. The general norm of behavior—relating to other disciples with the humility of a child—is found in 18:1–4 (cf. Mark 9:33–36; also Phil. 2:3). The disciples want to know who is the greatest in the kingdom of heaven. Jesus stands a child in their midst and says two things. First, **Unless you turn and become as children, you will not enter into the kingdom of the heavens** (18:3). This is a startling logion because children were not highly regarded in Mediterranean culture. Second, **Those who humble themselves as this child, they are the greatest in the kingdom of the heavens** (18:4). Humility is the condition both for entering and for having status in the kingdom (cf. *T. Jos.* 17.8: "I did not exalt myself above them arrogantly, . . . but I was among them as one of the least" [*OTP* 1:823]).

18:5–14. After a statement of the general norm, part 1 (18:5–14) follows with the point, Do not be the cause of offense to others. There are two subunits: (1) The first (18:5–9; cf. Mark 9:37; 9:42–48) urges

An Outline of Matthew 18:1–35

Relations with insiders (18:1–35)

The behavioral norm (18:1–4)

Specific guidelines, part 1 (18:5–14)

1. Warning against causing offense (18:5–9)
2. Restoring the straying little one (18:10–14)

Specific guidelines, part 2 (18:15–35)

1. Seeking repentance (18:15–20)
2. Forgiving repeatedly (18:21–35)

disciples not to cause a little one to sin. (2) The second (18:10–14) warns against failing to restore a little one who has strayed.

1. In 18:5–9, the exact identification of the little ones is unsettled. Possibilities include disciples, weaker disciples, simple believers, new believers, ordinary church members. A contrast begins the unit. On the one hand, **Whoever receives one such child in my name receives me** (18:5). "Child" here refers to an adult who has become as a child (18:3) and who has humbled oneself as a child (18:4), that is, a disciple. To receive such a disciple is to receive Jesus (cf. 10:40, 42). On the other hand, **Whoever becomes a stumbling block** (cf. 17:27) **for one of these little ones** (disciples) **who believe in me** (this is the only logion in the Synoptic tradition that speaks of having faith in Jesus), **it would be better for them if great millstones were fastened about their necks and they were drowned in the sea's depths** (18:6; cf. 1 Cor. 8:9, 12–13; 10:32; Rom. 14:13, 21). There will be stumbling blocks, of course, but **woe to those through whom they come** (18:7b). To make sure that they do not become stumbling blocks, it is necessary for disciples to eliminate aspects of the self that are stumbling blocks for them, whether it be part of the outer or inner self (18:8–9; cf. 5:29–30). The only way to avoid being a corrupting influence in someone else's life is first to deal with the corruption that is within oneself (cf. 7:3–5).

Figure 12. A typical view of a shepherd and his sheep amid the mountains.

A Textual Variant in Matthew 18:15

There are two possible readings for Matt. 18:15. On the one hand, the verse can be translated, "If your brother should sin, go and speak to him between you and him alone." This reading is supported by Sinaiticus and Vaticanus, some versions, and several early church fathers, such as Origen. On the other hand, the verse can also be translated, "If your brother should sin *against you,* go and speak to him between you and him alone." This variant is supported by D, K, L, X, numerous minuscules, some versions, and a number of church fathers like Cyprian. In both NA[27] and UBS[4] the words *against you* are in brackets. What difference does the variant make in one's interpretation? If the variant *against you* is accepted as the original reading, then what follows is a disciplinary procedure to be used when one is sinned against by a fellow disciple. If the variant is omitted, then what follows is speaking about the responsibility disciples have for holding straying members accountable. The textual witnesses for the omission of the variant are so strong that in this commentary *against you* is omitted (in agreement with, e.g., REB; NAS; JB; Harrington 1991, 268; contra, e.g., NRSV; RSV; TEV; Turner 2008, 444). This means that Matt. 18 falls into an ABB′A′ pattern. Sections A (18:5–9) and A′ (18:21–35) deal respectively with the issues of not causing another disciple to sin (A) and with forgiving a fellow disciple who sins against you (A′). Sections B (18:10–14) and B′ (18:15–20) treat the matter of the reclamation of straying believers. Section B tells disciples what to do; section B′ outlines how to do it.

2. The second subunit (18:10–14; cf. Luke 15:3–7) says disciples must not neglect to restore a little one (a disciple) who has strayed (cf. Gal. 6:1). This pericope is held together by an inclusio (**one of these little ones,** 18:10, 14). A warning opens the unit: **Watch out that you do not despise one of these little ones** (disciples). Why? Because **their angels in the heavens always see the face of my Father in the heavens** (18:10). These are usually taken as guardian angels (Tob. 12:11–15; Acts 12:15; Herm. *Vis.* 5.1–4). These angels are in close contact with God. The little ones, therefore, are valuable to God. Then follows a parable (18:12–13) and its interpretation (18:14). A similar parable is found in Luke 15:3–7. There it functions to defend Jesus's eating and drinking with tax collectors and sinners (15:1–2) by asking the Pharisees whether or not they are able to rejoice over a saved sinner like heaven does. Here the parable has another function. It is about the reclamation of straying disciples. **What do you think? If a man has one hundred sheep and one of them strays, will he not leave the ninety-nine on the mountain and go to seek the one that strayed? And if he should find it, truly I tell you, he rejoices over it more than over the ninety-nine others that did not go astray** (18:12–13). Note the repeated use of "stray" (not "lost" as in Luke 15).

The use of the same parable in different contexts yielding different meanings can be found also in rabbinic writings (e.g., *Sifre* 19 and 356 on Deuteronomy). The interpretation concludes the section: **So it is not the will of your Father in the heavens that one of these little ones** (here, straying disciples) **should perish** (18:14). (In *Mek.* on Exod. 19:21 God says, "If only one of them [Israelites] should fall, it would be to me as though all of them fell. . . . Every one of them that might be taken away is to me as valuable as the whole work of creation" [trans. Lauterbach 1961]). In Luke's parable, Jesus is the seeker. In Matthew's, the church is the seeker (cf. Prov. 24:11; Ezek. 34:4, 6). Here the parable with its hyperbole functions as a verbal icon through which disciples can see into God's will and, with that perception, have their

---

The Context of Reproof and Correction

The exhortation to engage in reproof and correction has roots in Israel's scriptures. Leviticus 19:17b reads: "You shall reprove your neighbor, or you will incur guilt yourself." In 2 Sam. 12, Nathan's reproof of David brings acknowledgment of sin and repentance. In Ezek. 33:8, Yahweh says, "If . . . you do not speak to warn the wicked [within the people of God] to turn from their ways, the wicked shall die in their iniquity, but their blood I will require at your hand." Sirach 19:13–17 urges readers to check with the alleged offending party before making a judgment. If the other did actually do wrong, then he may not do it again. In 20:2–3, Sirach encourages readers to rebuke an erring one. If that one admits the fault, he may be kept from future failure. Paul says in 1 Cor. 5:12 that it is those inside the community of faith that the Corinthian believers are to judge. In Gal. 6:1 he says, "If anyone is detected in a transgression, you who have received the Spirit should restore such a one in a spirit of gentleness." James 5:19–20 reads: "If anyone among you wanders from the truth and is brought back by another, you should know that whoever brings back a sinner from wandering will save the sinner's soul from death and will cover a multitude of sins." In 1 John 5:16 is a clear statement of the principle: "If you see your brother or sister committing what is not a mortal sin, you will ask, and God will give life to such a one." In *2 Clem.* 15.1 one hears that "it is no small reward to turn to salvation a soul that is wandering"; 17.2 reads: "Let us then help one another, and bring back those that are weak in goodness, that we may all be saved, and convert and exhort one another" (trans. Lake 1975, 1:153, 157). Among the meritorious works on behalf of the community that *Barn.* 19.10 lists is "striving to save souls by the word" (trans. Lake 1975, 1:405). Finally, *Ep. Apos.* 39.10–11 says, "Now if his neighbor has admonished him and he returns, he will be saved; and the one who admonished him will receive a reward" (trans. James 1924). In the Jewish heritage and in the early Christian congregations, there was present a conviction that God's people were accountable to each other and that believers held each other accountable.

new world—built around doing God's will—reinforced. At this point, part 1 (18:5–14) is formally finished.

18:15–35. In part 2 (18:15–35), the point is, If a fellow community member sins, do what is necessary to help heal the situation. There are two subunits: (1) an exhortation to seek the repentance of those who sin (18:15–20) and (2) an exhortation to forgive repeatedly (18:21–35).

1. The first of these subunits, 18:15–20 (cf. Luke 17:3), says that disciples should not fail to seek the repentance of another disciple who has sinned, following proper procedure. There is in 18:15–17 a multistep procedure for dealing with problems of holding disciples accountable. (1) **If your** (sg.) **brother should sin, go and speak to him between you and him alone. If he should heed you, you have gained your brother.** (2) **If he should not heed you, take with you one or two others, in order that "by the mouth of two or three witnesses every word may be established"** (Deut. 19:15; cf. 2 Cor. 13:1; 1 Tim. 5:19). (3) **If he should refuse to heed them, speak to the church** (*ekklēsia*). (4) **If he should refuse to heed the church, let him be to you** (sg.) **as a gentile and a tax collector.** The passage is about the practice of reproof and correction. One disciple sees another sinning and, holding that one accountable, tries to evoke repentance from the guilty party (cf. CD 9.7–8: "You shall reproach your fellow so as not to incur sin because of him" [trans. García Martínez 1996, 40]). The problem being addressed, then, is that mentioned in James 5:19–20. "My brothers and sisters, if anyone among you wanders from the truth and is brought back by another, you should know that whoever brings back a sinner from wandering will save the sinner's soul from death and will cover a multitude of sins." This passage is a follow-up to the previous section (18:10–14) about bringing back the straying. This is how to do it. If there is no repentance by the straying one, then treat the sinner as a gentile and tax collector (a nondisciple who must be evangelized, following the example of Jesus [11:19] and in response to his commission [28:19]; Carter 2000, 368; however, Fenton 1978, 297, is representative of those who contend that the discipline is punitive, with no chance of restoration).

There follow three promises by Jesus in 18:18–20 to the community engaged in reproof and correction. Matthew 18:18 repeats 16:19 except that the verbs are plural. **Truly I say to you** (pl.), **whatever you** (pl.) **may bind upon the earth will have been bound in heaven, and whatever you** (pl.) **loose upon the earth will have been loosed in heaven.** The disciples as a whole are here given the same promise given to Peter in 16:19. They have the same interpretative gift of discernment. As in 16:19, the verbs **will have been bound** and **will have been loosed** are periphrastic future perfect passives. This means that what the disciples decide about sin and repentance and bringing back the straying is a reflection of what God has revealed to them. It is a promise that the community will be given discernment in its process of reclaiming the straying (cf. 7:6–12; James 1:5). In 18:19, the second promise, the setting is again that

Similarities between Matthew 18 and Qumran

The early Jesus movement and Qumran represent two versions of Judaism outside the mainstream. Both were centered on a figure who was believed to possess the true interpretation of Scripture. At Qumran, as in the First Gospel, Lev. 19:17 ("You shall reprove your neighbor, or you will incur guilt yourself") and Deut. 19:15 ("Only on the evidence of two or three witnesses shall a charge be sustained"; cf. Deut. 17:6) were combined to produce a procedure for reproof and correction. First, reproof is meant for those inside, not those outside the group (1QS 9.16–17; Matt. 18:15; cf. Prov. 9:7–9; 1 Cor. 5:12–13). Second, the initial step is individual to individual (1QS 5.24–6.1; Matt. 18:15). Third, if the individual-to-individual reproof does not produce repentance, then reprove the erring one before witnesses (CD 9.9; Matt. 18:16). Fourth, if the previous step has not reclaimed the sinning member of the group, then take it to the whole body for action. This may include casting out the sinner (CD 20.2–3; Matt. 18:17). This should not stop the reproof, because there is hope that such a one might return (CD 20.2–3; Matt. 18:17 in the context of the whole Gospel). Such similarities do not indicate borrowing but rather a similar interpretation of two Scripture texts.

of reclaiming a disciple who has strayed: **Truly I say to you, if two of you shall agree upon the earth concerning anything about which you ask, it will be done for them by my Father in the heavens.** In its Matthean context, this logion is addressing the same thing mentioned in 1 John 5:14, 16: "And this is the boldness we have in him, that if we ask anything according to his will, he hears us. . . . If you see your brother or sister committing what is not a mortal sin, you will ask, and God will give life to such a one—to those whose sin is not mortal." Matthew says that God's will is that not one straying disciple should be lost. Hence, if the disciples pray for a straying disciple's restoration, God will hear.

The third promise comes in 18:20: **For where two or three are gathered together in my name, there I am in the midst of them.** If this is a postresurrection saying, then it is similar to 28:20 ("I am with you always, to the end of the age" [NRSV]; Witherington 2006, 352). If this is a pre-Easter saying, then it must mean something similar to 1 Cor. 5:4–5 ("When you are assembled, and my spirit is present with the power of our Lord Jesus, you are to hand this man over to Satan"). Either way, the presence of Jesus empowers the disciples to accomplish their task of holding one another accountable. (A rabbinic version of a similar saying attributed to Rabbi Hanina ben Teradion [early second century AD] goes as follows: "If two sit together and words of the Law are [spoken] between them, the Shekinah rests between them" [*m. Avot* 3.2, trans. Danby 1933].) The logic of the argument so far in chapter 18 has been: (A) do not cause another disciple to stumble; (B) if a fellow disciple has gone astray, do not look down on that one but know that God desires reclamation; (B′) A step-by-step process for holding a straying disciple accountable is given; plus, Jesus promises to enable the community in its pursuit of the necessary accountability and reclamation.

2. The final logical step in the fourth discourse (A′) comes in 18:21–35, a two-part sequence of thought dealing with forgiveness. The first subunit (18:21–22; cf. Luke 17:4) consists of a brief exchange between Peter and Jesus: **Then, coming over, Peter said to him, "Lord, how many times shall my brother sin against me and I forgive him? Until seven times?" Jesus said to him, "I say unto you not until seven times but until seventy-seven times."** This episode is a verbal icon through which one sees into God's will. What is it? "Whoever counts has not forgiven at all" (Boring 1995, 8:380). Be a forgiving person.

> ### Limiting Forgiveness
>
> A disciple's forgiveness of another disciple is rooted in God's behavior. *Avot R. Nat.* 40: If a human says, "I will sin and then repent," God forgives up to three times but no more. Also in *b. Yoma* 86b: If a person commits a transgression, that one is forgiven three times but not the fourth. So in *t. Yoma* 4.13: If a person sins two or three times, they (others in the people of God) forgive him but not on the fourth occasion.

A lengthy parable (18:23–35, only in Matthew) addressed to disciples (18:35) reinforces the point. It grounds forgiveness in the nature of God. The story has usually been regarded as an allegory about relations between God and Christians (e.g., the king is God; slaves are disciples; the unpaid loan is our debt; the fate of the unforgiving servant is damnation; etc.; de Boer 1988). This is problematic. Not everything in the story has parallels outside the parable: for example, God would not be ignorant of the first servant's behavior until told by fellow slaves (18:31); God would not be involved in torture (18:34); the first slave would never have been able to pay his debt, either before or after prison (18:26, 34). The king, then, is not a univocal picture of God, nor are all of the relationships between king and servants exact replicas of Christian reality. Parables mirror only certain aspects of reality. They are not straightforwardly equivalent, as if parable and reality were connected by equals signs. In reading a parable, one needs to know the limits of the analogy in each case. One also needs to know the function of the analogy. Parable interpretation is about correspondences between two processes (Snodgrass 2008, 66–75). How does this apply to the parable at hand?

Act 1: A king wants to make a reckoning with his servants. One owes him ten thousand talents (an impossible sum). When he does not have enough to settle, the lord orders the servant, his wife, and his children, and all he has to be sold and the account settled. The servant asks for patience so he can pay everything. The lord feels compassion, turns him loose, and forgives the loan.

Act 2: The forgiven servant goes out and finds a fellow servant who owes him one hundred denarii (one hundred days' wages). When he cannot pay, he is thrown into prison until he repays everything.

Act 3: The fellow servants report all this to the king. The lord then says, **"Evil servant! All that debt I forgave you because you begged me. Should you not have shown mercy to your fellow servant as I showed mercy to you?"** (18:32–33). He then delivers the evil servant to the jailers until he repays his debt. Concluding interpretation: **So my heavenly Father will do to you** (pl.) **if you do not forgive, each his brother, from your** (pl.) **heart** (18:35; cf. 6:14–15).

The parable's analogy may be reduced to its simplest form as follows. Just as a king who mercifully forgave a loan would expect his servant to do likewise, so God mercifully forgives and expects his people to do the same and holds them accountable if they do not. The parabolic language functions, together with 18:21–22, to enable disciples to *see* that being a forgiving person is rooted in the nature of God. The parable does not depict God as an oppressor; it does not aim to separate forgiveness from holding the offender accountable (cf. 18:15–17); it does not say that one can earn God's forgiveness by forgiving others. It does say that forgiveness of others is rooted in God's forgiveness. Pass it on! (Cf. Sir. 28:2–4: "Forgive your neighbor the wrong he has done, and then your sins will be pardoned when you pray. . . . If one has no mercy toward another like himself, can he then seek pardon for his own sins?") "Salvation in Matthew is by sheer mercy apart from any prior condition of good works, as this parable classically shows. But this salvation, when it is true, produces mercy" (Bruner 2004, 2:240). The provocative parable aims to shock the auditors (disciples) into realizing the seriousness of failing to show mercy to other disciples.

The second half of this fourth discourse, dealing with relating to insiders, has combined two concerns: holding the other accountable and forgiving the other. The two concerns are also conjoined in Lev. 19:17–18 and *T. Gad* 6.3–4.

Concluding Formula (19:1–2)

The fourth discourse comes to the typical conclusion (cf. 7:28; 11:1; 13:53; 26:1): **And it happened when Jesus finished these sayings that he went away from Galilee and came into the region of Judea beyond the Jordan. And great crowds followed him, and he healed them there.**

Functions of the Unit as a Whole

In the fourth discourse, as in all of the discourses that have come before, Jesus is depicted as a forceful speaker. In the rhetorical categories of the day, this would have been regarded as an example of deeds of wisdom (e.g., Quintilian, *Inst.* 3.7.15). The encomium continues (Neyrey 1998).

Theological Issues

Reconciliation of Various Logia

If Matt. 18:15–17 speaks to the responsibility of a disciple to reprove and correct another disciple who is engaged in sin, even to the point, if there is no repentance, of finally treating the offender as a gentile and tax collector, can this be reconciled with what Jesus says elsewhere in the First Gospel? Two passages come to mind: 7:1–5 (judge not) and 13:24–30 (do not pull up the weeds).

In Matt. 7:1 Jesus says, "Do not judge, in order that you may not be judged." Does not this contradict Matt. 18:15's "If another member of the church sins, go and point out the fault when the two of you are alone" (NRSV marg.)? No. Why? There are two reasons why there is no contradiction. First, 7:1–5 is not about judging (in the sense of making moral judgments) in and of itself. It is rather about judging (condemning) before taking care of the same or a worse problem in oneself. Listen to the text. "Why do you see the speck in your neighbor's eye, but do not notice the log in your own eye? Or how can you say to your neighbor, 'Let me take the speck out of your eye,' while the log is in your own eye? You hypocrite, first take the log out of your own eye, and then you will see clearly to take the speck out of your neighbor's eye" (7:3–5 NRSV). Second, 7:6–12 enjoins the task of judgment (in the sense of discernment). For a full treatment of this text, see earlier in this commentary on 7:1–12. Verse 6 calls for discernment between the holy and the profane. Verses 7–11 promise that God will supply the wisdom to do so if one but asks. Verse 12 calls on the one who is making a moral judgment to respond humanely (in terms of the golden rule). Taken together, 7:1–12 expects moral judgments to be made, with God's wisdom, about others but only after one has first remedied one's own plight and then in line with the golden rule. There is no contradiction between 7:1–12 and 18:15–17. The former deals with the credentials of the one who is making the moral judgment about another. The latter warns against "winking at sin" (Bruner 2004, 233).

What about the parable of the weeds and the wheat in 13:24–30, 36–43? This parable and its interpretation deal with when a separation should be made between Jesus's disciples and those of the evil one. For a treatment of this material in its context, see earlier on Matt. 13. The Noah stories in Gen. 6–9 reflect the experience of ancient Israel. Israel believed that the Babylonian exile took place because of the people's sins. It was a chastisement for their deviating from the right way. When God finally delivered them from exile and allowed them to return to Palestine, not everyone went home. Only the truly faithful returned to the homeland. When these faithful arrived, they found that they were not without the sin that had driven them into exile. Good and evil were inextricably intertwined even in the righteous. The Noah stories illustrate this reality. Only the righteous were saved from the flood, but when the flood receded and the righteous emerged, the righteous sinned. This parable in Matt. 13 explains that the separation between righteous and unrighteous will not take place until the last judgment. In the meantime, they grow up together, side by side. This in no way forbids moral distinctions being made in the world, nor does it decry reproof and correction in the community of Jesus's disciples. It rejects only a permanent separation before the last judgment. Again, there is no contradiction here.

Boundary Maintenance

Early followers of Jesus recognized that their community had boundaries, and they dealt with it in different ways. The available texts vary depending on whether it is the church or the leader who acts and whether it is the individual or the church that is seen to benefit from the disciplinary actions taken. We begin with the two passages that offer the most detailed accounts. In 1 Cor. 5 Paul confronts the problem of incest in the church, a problem about which the community seems unconcerned. When the apostle offers reproof, it is a sign that the individual belongs to the church (5:11–13). If the reproof is ineffective, then have nothing to do with sexually immoral persons (5:9). The church is to hand over the individual to Satan (cast him out [5:5]), following Paul's example (5:3–4). The intent of such removal is redemptive ("so that his spirit may be saved in the day of the Lord" [5:5b]). In 2 Thess. 3:6–15 the problem is that some believers are refusing to work and are living in idleness. The apostle offers and calls for reproof, a sign of the offenders' belonging (3:15). If the reproof is ineffective, then the church is to have nothing to do with the offenders (3:14). The intent is clearly redemptive, both for the church and the individual. There are similarities and differences between these two Pauline texts and Matt. 18. They all share the view that reproof is necessary for correction and that reproof refused is grounds for separation from the community. They all have a redemptive intent. Neither Pauline text has the elaborate process for removal that Matt. 18 does.

The remaining examples are less detailed yet reflect the practice of separation from those who are deemed to be outside community boundaries. In 2 Cor. 12:20–13:4, Paul confronts misbehavior in the church at Corinth. He reproves the guilty ones (12:20–21; 13:2). He warns that if there is no repentance, then when he comes he will act with the power of the risen Christ to deal with the situation (12:21; 13:2–4). The beneficiary of such action will be the church, not the individuals involved (13:10). What exactly Paul meant by his authoritative actions may be reflected in 1 Tim. 1:19–20: "By rejecting conscience, certain persons have suffered shipwreck in the faith; among them are Hymenaeus and Alexander, whom I have turned over to Satan, so that they may learn not to blaspheme." Here an individual leader separates deviants from the flock. In Titus 3:10–11 a leader is exhorted so to act: "After a first and second admonition, have nothing more to do with anyone who causes divisions, since you know that such a person is perverted and sinful, being self-condemned." The church is the beneficiary. Within the Johannine literature, similar trajectories may be seen. Revelation 2:20–21 refers to a female false prophet, Jezebel, who is teaching Christians to practice fornication and to eat food sacrificed to idols. The risen Christ says through the prophet, "I gave her time to repent, but she refuses." Now the risen Christ says through his prophet John, "I am throwing her on a bed, and those who commit adultery with her I am throwing into great distress, unless they repent of her doings; and I will strike her children dead" (2:22–23). This also apparently refers to the power of the risen Lord that will be exercised through the prophet. The aim is that all the churches will know that Christ "will give to each of you as your works deserve' (2:23). The benefit of the disciplinary action is aimed at the churches.

In 2 John the elder exhorts his audience, "Do not receive into the house or welcome anyone who comes to you and does not bring this teaching; for to welcome is to participate in the evil deeds of such a person" (vv. 10–11). In 3 John the elder and the churches that support him are the objects of a similar shunning. Diotrephes "refuses to welcome the friends, and even prevents those who want to do so and expels them from the church" (v. 10). Community boundaries are important to both the elder and Diotrephes alike. The boundaries protect the churches. A final example is from Rom. 16: "I urge you, brothers and sisters, to keep an eye on those who cause dissensions and offenses, in opposition to the teaching that you have learned; avoid them" (16:17). The motivation of such avoidance is its benefit to the church. "For such people do not serve our Lord Christ, but their own appetites, and by smooth talk and flattery they deceive the hearts of the simple-minded" (16:18). Boundary maintenance was clearly a concern of the earliest churches reflected in the NT. Matthew 18 fits within this larger concern and makes its own contribution by elaborating a process for its readers to follow when engaged in reproof and correction (Forkman 1972).

PART 5

Matthew 19:3–26:1a

Jesus and Judgment

The last of Matthew's five big cycles consists of the customary narrative (19:3–24:2) and discourse (24:3–25:46), with the usual closing formula (26:1a). The two are linked by the theme of judgment: on Israel's leaders, the temple, inauthentic disciples, and the nations. The judgment is both within history and at the end of history. The narrative segment (19:3–24:2) falls into two main parts: 19:3–20:34 (from Galilee to Jerusalem, actually beginning with 19:1b) and 21:1–24:2 (into and in Jerusalem). The second (21:1–24:2) is the segment that, along with the discourse (24:3–26:1a), focuses on judgment.

Matthew 19:3–26:1a in Context

Birth narratives (1:1–2:23)

Jesus's ministry begins (3:1–8:1)

Jesus's authority is revealed (8:2–11:1)

Jesus's ministry creates division (11:2–13:53)

Jesus focuses on his disciples (13:54–19:2)

▶ **Jesus and judgment (19:3–26:1a)**

Narrative: Jesus teaches about household behavior (19:3–20:34)

Narrative: Jesus pronounces about judgment in the present (21:1–24:2)

Discourse: Jesus teaches about final judgment (24:3–26:1a)

Passion and resurrection narrative (26:1b–28:20)

Matthew 19:3–20:34

Narrative 5, Part 1:
Jesus Teaches about Household Behavior

Introductory Matters

The first part of the fifth narrative continues the emphasis of 17:24–19:2 on the behavior of true disciples. Whereas 17:24–19:2 concentrated on the community's relations with outsiders (17:24–27) and with church life, that is, relations among members inside the community (Matt. 18), 19:3–20:34 is concerned with the everyday life of disciples within the basic unit of ancient society, the household (Nolland 2005, 767). This section is held together by an inclusio (went away from Galilee, followed, healing [19:1b–2]; went out of Jericho, healing, followed [20:29–34]).

Household Management as the Key to Unity

The first introductory issue has to do with that which holds 19:3–20:34 together as a unit. Although a concentric structure has been proposed for 19:1–20:34 (Doyle 1994), Warren Carter (1994, 9) rightly contends that chapters 19–20 include the four standard subjects of household management in antiquity: (1) husbands and wives, (2) parents and children, (3) masters and slaves, and (4) wealth. He cites the first-century BC writer Arius Didymus (*Epitome*) as representative of the concerns of household management (Carter 1994, 73): "Rational household management, which is the controlling of a house and of those things related to a house, is fitting for a man. Belonging to this are fatherhood, the art of marriage, being a master, and moneymaking" (cf. Josephus

[*Ag. Ap.* 2.207–8], who discusses wealth after marriage [2.199–203] and children and parents [2.204–7], as do Philo [*Hypoth.* 7.3–4] and Pseudo-Phocylides [153–227]). These are precisely the topics addressed in Matt. 19:3–20:28. In the evangelist's discussion of these four conventional topics of household management, the aim is to subvert the values found in the culture generally. This segment of the narrative is designed to say what true discipleship looks like in the four areas normally associated with household management in Mediterranean antiquity. Matthew 20:29–34 then ends the unit with a general statement about the essential nature of discipleship.

Arrangement

Once the matter of the unity of the narrative section is settled, the question of the unit's arrangement is easily answered. There are four pericopes. All four involve topics related to ancient households. An alternative value system is proposed for Jesus's disciples in their own households. These four pericopes are followed by a concluding section on the nature of true discipleship: discipleship means being healed of blindness so one can follow Jesus.

**Matthew 19:3–20:34
in the Narrative Flow**

Birth narratives (1:1–2:23)

Jesus's ministry begins (3:1–8:1)

Jesus's authority is revealed
(8:2–11:1)

Jesus's ministry creates division
(11:2–13:53)

Jesus focuses on his disciples
(13:54–19:2)

Jesus and judgment (19:3–26:1a)

▶ Narrative: Jesus teaches about
  household behavior (19:3–20:34)

  Marriage, divorce, and celibacy
  (19:3–12)

  Children (19:13–15)

  Wealth (19:16–20:16)

  Servants (20:17–28)

  The essence of discipleship
  (20:29–34)

Tracing the Narrative Flow

Marriage, Divorce, and Celibacy (19:3–12)

Matthew 19:3–12 (cf. Mark 10:2–9 with Matt. 19:3–8; cf. Mark 10:10–12 with Matt. 19:9; 19:10–12 is unique to Matthew) deals with marriage. It consists of three exchanges: 19:3–6 (Pharisees and Jesus); 19:7–9 (Pharisees and Jesus); and 19:10–12 (disciples and Jesus).

19:3–6. In the first exchange, Pharisees ask Jesus, **Is it lawful to divorce one's wife for any cause?** (19:3b). The question is not the legality of divorce. That was assumed by Jewish culture at large. The question is, On what grounds is divorce permitted? This was a debate between the schools of Hillel and Shammai. The school of Shammai said divorce was possible only if the wife was unfaithful; the school of Hillel said divorce was possible even if she spoiled a dish for her husband (*m. Git.* 9.10; Sir. 25:16–26 says since evil wives are terrible to live with, "If she does not go as you direct, separate her from yourself" [25:26]; Josephus, *Ant.* 4.253, sides with Hillel). Jesus is asked on which side of the debate he stands. His answer takes the form of an appeal to Genesis: **Have you not read that the one who created from the beginning "made them male and female"** (Gen. 1:27) and said **"on account of this a man will leave his father and mother and will be joined to his wife**

> **An Outline
> of Matthew 19:3–12**
>
> **Marriage, divorce, and celibacy
> (19:3–12)**
>
>   Jesus and Pharisees (19:3–6)
>
>   Pharisees and Jesus (19:7–9)
>
>   Disciples and Jesus (19:10–12)

and the two will become one flesh"? (Gen. 2:24). **So they are no longer two but one flesh. That which God has united, let a man not separate** (19:4–6).

19:7–9. In the second exchange, the Pharisees ask, **Why then did Moses command "to give a writ of divorce" and "to put her away"?** (19:7; cf. Deut. 24:1). The essential formula of the writ of divorce was "You are free to marry any man" (*m. Git.* 9.3). Jesus's response is, **Moses allowed you to divorce your wives because of the hardness of your hearts. But from the beginning it was not so.** (Hillel's rule 7: interpretation derived from context [Evans 1992, 117–18].) **I say to you, whoever divorces his wife, except for unfaithfulness, and marries another commits adultery** (19:8–9). The word here translated "unfaithfulness" (*porneia*) cannot be incest (as Witherington 2006, 362, claims) because in that case there would have been no need for a divorce certificate. The marriage would have been considered invalid from the start (Lev. 18:18; *m. Qidd.* 2.7). Matthew 19:9 adds to 5:32's statement of consequences ("makes her commit adultery; and whoever marries a divorced woman commits adultery") by saying that if the divorcing husband remarries, he commits adultery. Jesus allows formalizing the break between husband and wife that has already occurred due to faithlessness, but he does not allow the husband to remarry (Gundry 1982, 377; Carter 2000, 379). In the two exchanges between Jesus and the Pharisees, Jesus appeals to creation (cf. *Jub.* 2.1, 17, where creation is the basis for human behavior regarding the Sabbath). He views the chronological priority of Genesis over Deuteronomy's concession to human sinfulness as decisive (cf. Paul's similar argument from chronological priority in Gal. 3:15–20. For a Jewish argument against having two wives [polygamy] during one's lifetime based on Gen. 1:27, see CD 4.21). What is the nature of the language used here? Jesus identifies his position with God's intention in creation. He considers the practice of divorce in Jewish life to be an accommodation to human fallenness. To see things that way enables character to be formed.

19:10–12. In the third exchange, the disciples react to Jesus's stringent position about divorce. If there is no door of escape, then **it is better not to marry** (19:10; cf. 1 Cor. 7:1, the very position of certain Corinthian ascetics but from a dualistic

Celibacy in Ancient Judaism

Among men in the OT, we know only of Jeremiah as being unmarried (Jer. 16:1–4). Moses was transformed into a celibate after his revelation from God by Philo (*Mos.* 2.68–69; cf. *Exod. Rab.* 46.3). The pre-Christian Rechabites, known from the narrative of Zosimus, were a group of Jewish ascetics. Philo knew of the Therapeutae, who were celibate Jews in his time (*Contempl.*). John the Baptist, Jesus, and Paul (1 Cor. 9:5; 7:7), in a category similar to Jeremiah, fit this mold as well. Josephus knew of the hermit Bannus (*Life* 11). At least one group of Essenes was celibate (Josephus, *J.W.* 2.120; cf. 2.160, so at least two groups; Philo, *Hypoth.* 11.14; Pliny the Elder, *Nat.* 5.15, 73). Rabbi Shimon ben Azai (early second century AD) never married. When criticized for it, he responded, "What can I do? My soul thirsts for Torah. Let other people keep the world going" (*t. Yevam.* 8.7; *b. Yevam.* 63b). At the same time, he urged his followers to marry (*b. Yevam.* 63a; van der Horst 2002). The normal Jewish attitude toward sex and marriage was positive (Gen. 2:18; Tob. 8:6). Rabbi Johanan said, "He who is twenty years old and not married spends all of his days in sin" (*b. Qidd.* 29b). Jewish men felt a strong obligation to marry. Mishnah *Yevam.* 6.6 says, "No man may abstain from keeping the law, 'Be fruitful and multiply.'"

motivation). That it was better for a man not to marry was a position widely advocated in Mediterranean antiquity. Quintilian (*Inst.* 2.4.24–25) lists the topic "whether marriage is desirable" as one that aspiring orators needed to handle. The ancient Greek tradition was divided between those who were for marriage (e.g., Socrates, Xenophon) and those against it (e.g., Thales, Epicurus, Diogenes of Sinope). To this negative contention by his disciples, Jesus responds with a qualification uttered in an ABA′ pattern. (A) **Not all can receive this word** (the disciples' comment in 19:10; so Nolland 2005, 776) **but only those to whom it has been given** (19:11; cf. 1 Cor. 7:7, 17, where Paul says celibacy is for those with that gift). (B) **For there are eunuchs who were born such from their mother's womb, and there are eunuchs who have been made such by humans, and there are eunuchs who have made themselves such because of the kingdom of the heavens.** (A′) **The one who is able to receive, let him receive it** (19:12). The unit 19:3–12 has made three points. First, marriage is the expected behavior. Second, divorce, except for unfaithfulness, is a negative. Third, celibacy for those who have that gift is an option for Jesus's disciples (cf. Isa. 56:4).

Children (19:13–15)

The second category in household management materials in antiquity was that of parents and children. In Matt. 19:13–15 (cf. Mark 10:13–16; also Matt. 18:2–4) the topic of children is treated. The brief unit is best seen in terms of a concentric pattern (a modification of Ostmeyer 2004):

Eunuchs for the Kingdom's Sake

Eusebius (*Hist. eccl.* 6.8) says Origen, taking Matt. 19:12 literally, castrated himself. Such a practice was sometimes found in pagan religions. In the worship of Cybele and Attis, on the one hand, and of Artemis, on the other, worshipers sometimes engaged in self-mutilation (Catullus, *Attis*; Lucian, *Syr. d.* 19–20). The metaphorical interpretation has dominated Christian history (e.g., Athenagoras, *Leg.* 33). Clement of Alexandria said that the true eunuch is not the one who cannot but the one who will not indulge himself (*Paed.* 3.4.26). According to the First Council of Nicaea, canon 1, those who have castrated themselves cannot be priests. To become a eunuch for the sake of the kingdom means to live a celibate life. (For early Christian references about castration, see Hanson 1966.)

A Children are brought to Jesus (19:13a)
 B that Jesus might lay his hands on them (19:13b)
  C The disciples rebuke the parents (19:13c; cf. 2 Kings 4:27)
  C′ Jesus rebukes the disciples (19:14)
 B′ Jesus laid his hands on the children (19:15a)
A′ Jesus goes on his way (19:15b)

Children here are not a paradigm for the disciples' attitude, as in 18:2–4. Here they represent a group within the household of whom special care must be taken (Schnackenburg 2002, 186; not limited to children in church, as Boring 1995, 8:387). Elsewhere in the First Gospel, Jesus has manifested his concern for the young. He heals children (9:18–26; 15:21–28; 17:14–18); he feeds children (14:13–21; 15:29–39); he holds them up as a model for disciples (18:3); he prays for them (19:13–15); he receives their praise with appreciation (21:15). So now here he admonishes, **Let the children come to me** (19:14). Contrary to the common cultural attitudes, Jesus is depicted as caring for children (*m. Avot* 3.11: Children's talk is one of the things that put people out of the world. It may be compared with oversleeping, overdrinking, or sitting in the assembly of the vulgar; *Avot R. Nat.* [A] 21: Children's prattle causes one to neglect the study of torah; vulnerability was the general situation of

Virginity/Celibacy in the Early Church

Celibacy was known in earliest Christianity (e.g., Acts 21:9; 1 Cor. 7:1; 1 Tim. 4:3; Ign. *Smyrn.* 13; Justin Martyr, *1 Apol.* 15; *Acts Paul* 5, 11; *Acts Thom.* 12, 14–15; *Acts Andr.* 5; *Acts John* 113; Athenagoras, *Leg.* 32; Tatian, *Orat.* 32.3). Warnings were issued against the pride of virgins in *1 Clem.* 38.2 and Ign. *Pol.* 5. Paul (1 Cor. 7) and Matt. 19 put limits on celibacy. It is only for Christians with that gift—that is, those who are abstainers for the sake of the kingdom.

Jewish children in antiquity [Tropper 2006]). His disciples are to learn the value of children from Jesus's behavior.

Wealth (19:16–20:16)

The third topic characteristic of ancient household management that is covered in this part of Matthew's narrative is the matter of wealth. Matthew 19:16–20:16 (with 19:16–30; cf. Mark 10:17–31; Matt. 20:1–16 is peculiar to Matthew) deals extensively with this issue. This segment is comprised of a recognition story (19:16–22), an explanation of what has just happened (19:23–26), a question-and-answer sequence (19:27–30), and a parable (20:1–16). All are connected with wealth.

19:16–22. Matthew 19:16–22 is a recognition story in which a person recognizes something about himself that he did not know before (Karris 1977, 207). It should be read against the background of the Talmud's discussion of the seven types of Pharisees (*b. Sotah* 22b). One type is the Pharisee who says, "What further duty is there for me that I may perform it," as though he had fulfilled every obligation. So in our story, one comes to Jesus, asking, **What good thing shall I do that I may have eternal life?** (19:16). Jesus responds, **If you wish to enter into life, keep the commandments** (19:17b). The questioner asks, **Which ones?** Jesus replies, **Do not murder** (Exod. 20:13), **do not commit adultery** (Exod. 20:14), **do not steal** (Exod. 20:15), **do not bear false witness** (Exod. 20:16), **honor your father and mother** (Exod. 20:12), **and love your neighbor as yourself** (Lev. 19:18). The young man says, **All these I have kept. What do I still lack?** Jesus replies, **If you want to be perfect** (*teleios*), **go and sell your possessions and give them to the poor, and you will have treasure in the heavens, and come and follow me** (19:18–21). At Qumran, perfection meant complete obedience to the law as understood by a community (1QS 8.1–2, 10b; 9.6, 8, 19) that designated itself a house of perfection (1QS 8.9). In Matt. 5:48, it is understood as loving enemies as well as friends, that is, completeness like that of God in the scope of one's love. **And hearing this word, the young man went away sorrowfully, for he had many possessions** (19:22). What he discovers is that he loves his things more than he loves either his neighbor or Jesus (cf. 6:24). He leaves with this dawning recognition.

This failed discipleship story is similar to one told of the Cynic Diogenes of Sinope by Diogenes Laertius (*Vit. phil.* 6.36): "Someone wanted to study philosophy under him. Diogenes gave him a fish to carry and commanded him to

> **An Outline of Matthew 19:16–20:16**
>
> **Wealth (19:16–20:16)**
> The wealthy young man (19:16–22)
> The eye of a needle (19:23–26)
> What disciples will get (19:27–30)
> Workers in the vineyard (20:1–16)

follow him. But the man threw it away out of shame and departed. Some time later Diogenes met him and laughed and said, 'Our friendship was broken by a fish'" (trans. R. Hicks 1925). In both stories someone approaches a teacher and wants to become a disciple. He fails to attain his goal because the cost of discipleship is too great. In both cases the demand functions to determine whether or not the individual is a worthy candidate for discipleship (cf. 15:21–28).

19:23–26. After the young man has gone, Jesus explains to his disciples what has just happened (19:23–26). **With difficulty a rich person will enter into the kingdom of the heavens. . . . It will be easier for a camel to go through the eye of a needle than for a rich person to enter the kingdom of God** (19:23–24). Jesus's words are compatible with those of philosophers who contend that wealth prevents the study of philosophy (e.g., Plutarch, *Cupid. divit.* 7 [526]; Seneca the Younger, *Ep.* 17.3). The disciples, however, are stunned and ask, **Who then is able to be saved?** Jesus's response is, **With humans this is impossible, but with God all things are possible** (19:25–26). Jesus uses hyperbole to make his point (cf. 7:3–5). Camels cannot go through a needle's eye! This is impossible (cf. the rabbinic saying about one never imagining an elephant going through the eye of a needle [*b. Ber.* 55b; *b. B. Metzi'a* 38b]). The disciples' astonishment is due to the widely held belief that wealth was a sign of righteousness and virtue.

For the pagan world, note Seneca the Elder's claim that wealth reflects a person's virtue (*Con.* 2.1.17). From the Jewish side, see Deut. 28:1–14, which says that if Israel is loyal to the covenant with Yahweh, the Lord will make them abound in prosperity (see also Ps. 112:3; Prov. 3:13–16; 8:12–18; *Pss. Sol.* 5.16–18; Philo, *Migr.* 18.104). No text is clearer than Job. The book says that Job is righteous (1:8) and his household's wealth a divine blessing (1:10). When Job loses his wealth, his friends Eliphaz, Bildad, and Zophar interpret his loss of wealth as punishment for his sin. If one is virtuous or righteous, so the assumption goes, then one will be wealthy. If wealth is a mark of righteousness, then the disciples' question makes sense: **Who then is able to be saved?** Jesus responds, **With humans this** (being saved) **is impossible; with God all things are possible.**

19:27–30. The third component of 19:16–20:16, on wealth, is a question-and-answer sequence between the disciples and Jesus (19:27–30). Peter starts with a question. Unlike the rich young man, **we have left everything and followed you** (cf. 4:18–22); **what will there be for us?** (19:27). That is, will we gain eternal life? Jesus's response covers both his immediate disciples (19:28) and everyone who acts like them (19:29). To the immediate disciples, Jesus says, **You** (pl.) **who have followed me, in the new age** (*palingenesia*) **when the son of man will sit upon a throne of his glory** (cf. *1 En.* 62.5; 69.29), **you will sit upon twelve thrones judging the twelve tribes of Israel.** This saying envisions the golden future with the re-creation of the cosmos: the new age (2 Pet. 3:5–7; Sim 1993b). The thrones for the son of man and the twelve disciples may be either thrones of judgment or thrones of ongoing rule. On the one hand, in Dan. 7:13–14 the son of man is given permanent rule; in Dan. 7:27 rule is given to the people Israel (cf. Wis. 3:8). In Rev. 3:21 both the risen Christ and his people are given thrones that involve rule. The same combination is found also in Luke 22:28–30 for Jesus and the Twelve. Matthew 20:20–21 assumes that Jesus's disciples will rule in his kingdom.

On the other hand, in *1 En.* 37–71 the son of man sits on the throne to judge at the last day. In *1 En.* 108.12–15 the saints are seated on thrones at the last judgment. Likewise, 1QS 8.10 says the saints will decide the judgment of the wicked (cf. *T. Ab.* 13.6); 1 Cor. 6:2 reflects an early Christian statement of the same position. Scholars are divided, some opting for rule over an extended period (e.g., Davies and Allison 1997, 3:56–57), most, however, for judgment at the last day. To disciples in general whose behavior is like that of Peter and the other immediate disciples, Jesus says, **Everyone who has left houses or brothers or sisters or father or mother or children or fields on account of my name will receive many times as much and will inherit eternal life** (19:29). The blessings of the age to come far exceed anything sacrificed in the here and now (cf. Rev. 21:1–22:7).

The conversation closes with a generalization in 19:30. **Many who are first will be last, and the last first** (cf. Mark 10:31). This proverb has been read in two very different ways. Some take it as the conclusion to 19:16–29. If so, then it offers congratulations to the disciples. The rich young man, the one with status in a society that associated wealth and virtue, is the first (one with status); the disciples who have left all to follow Jesus are the last (those without status). Yet in the age to come the situation will be reversed, as 19:28–29 has made clear (Carter 1994, 127). The last will be first, the first will be last. So, congratulations to those who follow Jesus. The parable in 20:1–16, then, is an illustration of the principle (the *gar* [for] in 20:1 makes the parable of 20:1–16 interpret the saying of 19:30; Gundry 1982, 395). Others, however, think that 19:30 goes with what follows in 20:1–16 and is a warning to disciples against thinking that they are among the first (Garland 2001, 207; Davies and Allison 1997, 3:61; Hare 1993, 231; Morris 1992, 498–99). In this case, the disciples consider themselves first because they are the first to have left all and followed Jesus and to have received from him promises of future status. Lest they think their future status depends on their achievements, the parable functions as a caution that all is dependent on God's generosity. The former reading fits the context better and will be the one employed in this commentary. The evangelist therefore follows the principle verbalized by Quintilian (*Inst.* 5.11.5–6): fables/parables are useful not only as embellishments but also as proofs in an argument. There are also similarities to haggadic midrash, where a scriptural text (here, a saying of Jesus) is interpreted by a story (often a parable).

20:1–16. William Herzog (1994, 79–97) treats the parable of 20:1–16 as an allegory in which the vineyard is Israel or the church, the owner is God, the denarius is salvation, the workers hired first are Jews or Jesus's disciples, and the workers hired last are gentiles or recent converts. Klyne Snodgrass (2008, 372–73) contends, however, that parables and reality are not connected by equals signs. Parables mirror only certain aspects of reality. There are, therefore, limits to the analogy. A parable is concerned with the correspondences between two processes. The question to ask is, what is the function of the analogy? The function of 20:1–16 is exposed both by what is within the parable and by the context of the story. Look first at what is within the parable. It is organized into two parts: 20:1–7, the hiring, and 20:8–15, the paying. Verse 16, echoing 19:30, focuses the point. In the verses devoted to the hiring, the reader is led from the first hired early in the morning to those hired at 9:00 AM, at noon, at 3:00 PM, and finally to the last hired at 5:00 PM. The details in 20:1–7 are irrelevant. The hiring from first to last is the focus of the story. In the verses covering the paying of the workers (20:8–15), the crucial note comes in verse 8. **When evening came** (cf. Lev. 19:13; Deut. 24:14–15), **the lord of the vineyard said to his manager, "Call the workers and give them their wages, beginning from the last until the first."** There is more to the story, namely, the unhappiness of those who have worked all day and have received the same wages as those who went to work only late in the afternoon. The conclusion, 20:16, however, keeps the reader's/auditor's attention focused on the desired point. **Just so, the last will be first, and the first last.** This, then, is a story about a process of reversal that runs contrary to common social norms.

Looking to the context for additional assistance, one finds that 19:16–30 has been about this precise point. Although social conventions equate wealth, righteousness, and status (the first), at the last judgment or in the new age it will be those who have left all to follow Jesus—resulting in their being poor and of no social status (the last)—who will receive eternal life and blessings beyond all that was sacrificed. Truly, then, the last will be first and the first last. Judging from the context on the one hand and the structure and conclusion of the story on the other, 20:1–16 is a parabolic proof/illustration of the process described in 19:16–30. One's status in the kingdom is tied not to wealth but to devotion to Jesus. This unit, 19:16–20:16, dealing with wealth, uses the imaginative story of 20:1–16 as a catalyst to enable disciples to see wealth differently. If they have already understood its lesson, then it functions as a reinforcement of their new world. If they have not yet understood, then it functions to shatter their old world and to call them to form a new one around Jesus's values.

Servants (20:17–28)

In 20:17–28 the evangelist's attention turns to servants/slaves, another topic treated in ancient household management (cf. Matt. 20:17–19 with Mark 10:32–34; Matt. 20:20–28 with Mark 10:35–45). There are two components in this subunit: another passion prediction (20:17–19) and the episode of

> **An Outline of Matthew 20:17–28**
>
> Servants (20:17–28)
>
> Predicting the passion (20:17–19)
>
> Seeking special status (20:20–28)

disciples' wanting special status in the kingdom (20:20–28). The two components are held together by an inclusio (20:17–19: Jesus's example; 20:28: Jesus's example).

20:17–19. On the way to Jerusalem, probably as part of a festal group of pilgrims, Jesus takes his disciples aside and speaks to them again about his coming passion in the holy city. The details of the passion prediction are a preview of the passion narrative. The son of man will be

handed over to the chief priests and scribes (26:47–56)
condemned to death (26:57–68)
handed over to the gentiles (27:1–14)
mocked (27:29, 31, 41)
flogged (27:26)
crucified (27:33–50)
raised on the third day (28:1–20)

This pericope is both preparatory and paradigmatic for 20:20–28.

20:20–28. Matthew 20:20–24 reflects a lingering misunderstanding among the disciples about the nature of the kingdom. **The mother of the sons of Zebedee** (cf. 27:56) **came with her sons and asked something from Jesus. . . . "What do you want?" . . . "Tell me that these two sons of mine** (James and John, 4:21–22; 17:1) **will sit one at your right hand and one at your left hand in your kingdom"** (20:20–21). In 19:28 the Twelve had already been promised thrones in the kingdom. This request, then, is for top status among the Twelve. According to Josephus (*Ant.* 6.235), the eldest son sat on the king's right hand and the commander of the army on his left. **"You do not know what you are asking. Are you** (pl.) **able to drink the cup** (cf. 26:39, Jesus's death; cf. *T. Ab.* 1.3) **that I am about to drink?" They said to him, "We are able"** (cf. Matt. 26:31–35). **Jesus said to them, "You will drink my cup** (cf. Acts 12:2 for James), **but to sit at my right hand and at my left hand is not mine to give, but it is for the one for whom it has been prepared by my Father"** (20:22–23). If 19:16–20:16 addressed the issue of status and wealth, now the need is attention to status and power. The other ten disciples are no better. In 20:24 we read, **And when the ten heard about it, they were incensed toward the two brothers.** Competition reigns for the top spots. This is but a reflection of their culture (cf. 1QSa 2.11–17, which says that the men of renown will sit in the presence of the messiah, "each according to his rank").

This leads to Jesus's teaching about status, power, and service in 20:25–28. **You know that the rulers of the gentiles lord it over them and the great exercise** authority over them. **It is not so among you. Whoever wishes to become great among you, let him be your servant** (*diakonos*), **and whoever wants to be first, let him be your slave** (*doulos*; 20:25–27). (Cf. *T. Jos.* 17.8: "I did not exalt myself above them arrogantly because of my worldly position of glory, but I was among them as one of the least" [*OTP* 1:823]; in Dio Chrysostom's fourth oration on kingship, which is a lengthy discourse between a young Alexander and the Cynic philosopher Diogenes of Sinope, the Cynic says to Alexander that he will become a true king only if he dons a slave's tunic and serves [*Or.* 4.46–51, 65–70].) These are the precepts. Their point: "The way to make it to the proverbial top as a disciple is to get down low as a slave" (Garland 2001, 212). Now comes the example. **Just as the son of man did not come to be served but to serve and to give his life a ransom** (*lytron*) **for many** (20:28; cf. 1 Tim. 2:6). Jesus's example defines greatness and status for his disciples: service for others.

The term translated "ransom" has been the object of overinterpretation by many who wish to find a highly developed soteriology here (e.g., Keener 1999, 487–88; cf. the theological issues section for Matt. 26:1b–28:20). Examples of Jewish usage show the type of meaning associated with ransom. In Jer. 15:20–21 LXX, Yahweh says to Jeremiah, "I am with you to save you and to deliver you, . . . and I will ransom you." In the parallelism, save, deliver, and ransom are synonyms. In Jer. 27:34 LXX (50:34 Eng.), when Yahweh says he is the one who ransoms Israel, it is in the context of his defeat of Israel's enemies (deliverance). In Jer. 38:11 LXX (31:11 Eng.), when the Lord has ransomed Jacob, it means that Yahweh has delivered him out of the hands of stronger foes (return from the exile). Ransom is, then, synonymous with salvation and deliverance. In Ps. 129:8 LXX (130:8 Eng.) this is certainly so (Yahweh "will redeem Israel from all his lawlessness"). There is nothing in the term that demands an elaborate soteriological theory. It simply means that Jesus is acting on others' behalf in his ministry, which will include his death and resurrection. In this context, "ransom" is used as part of his example as a servant and slave. If 20:28 gives Jesus's example for disciples to follow, it cannot include more than disciples can follow. The position taken here by the Matthean Jesus, moreover, would have called to mind the linking of rule and servanthood in the Hellenistic tradition of the ideal king. The ideal king was servant of his people (Plato, *Resp.* 1.347d; 7.540b; Dio Chrysostom, *Or.* 1.12–34; Musonius Rufus 61–65). Cynics used the tradition to depict the ruler as one who shares in Zeus's reign over humans by ruling, serving, and giving his life for his subjects (Epictetus, *Diatr.* 3.22.54–61, 77–85; 4.30–32). John Nolland (2005, 826) is on target when he says, "What exactly is thought to be involved in the son of man giving his life as a ransom for many remains quite imprecise."

The Essence of Discipleship (20:29–34)

This part of Matthew's narrative closes with 20:29–34 (cf. Mark 10:46–52; also Matt. 9:27–31), an illustration of the essential nature of discipleship. Two blind men, sitting beside the road, call out to Jesus as he comes out of Jericho (cf. 8:28, two demoniacs; 9:27, two blind men). **Lord, have mercy on us, son of David** (20:30b). The crowd tells them to be quiet. The blind cried out again. **Lord, have mercy on us, son of David** (20:31b). The address to Jesus as Lord implies that the blind men are believers (Boring 1995, 8:399). If so, then taken in context, they are believers whose blindness about household relationships needs to be healed so that they can follow Jesus. Jewish tradition regarded David (1 Sam. 16:14–23) and his son Solomon (Josephus, *Ant.* 8.25; *T. Sol.* 20.1) as having power over evil spirits. After a critique of the false shepherds of Israel because they had not fed or healed the people, Ezek. 34 has God say that he will give Israel one shepherd, a Davidic king, to do what has been lacking. There was, then, a hope associated with the Davidic king connected to healing. The two blind men reflect this expectation. Jesus stops, calls the men, and asks, **What do you wish that I should do for you?** Their answer is, **That our eyes should be opened.** Jesus, moved with compassion (cf. 9:36; 14:14; 15:32), **touched their eyes, and immediately they could see and they followed him** (20:32–34). The saga of the two blind men provides a model for the essence of discipleship: from blindness to sight resulting in following Jesus (cf. John 9). In Matt. 19:3–20:28 Jesus has given teaching that subverts the common values of Mediterranean households. This has, hopefully, opened his disciples' eyes. Now they are to follow him in their everyday experience lived in their households.

Functions of the Unit as a Whole

Once again the Matthean Jesus demonstrates his embodiment of the virtues valued by Mediterranean society (as verbalized by Quintilian, *Inst.* 3.7.15). When faced with honor challenges (e.g., Matt. 19:3), Jesus exemplifies courage; when dealing with issues of right behavior in society, he manifests wisdom; when confronting the temptations of sex and wealth and power, he reflects temperance; when human hurt calls for his compassion, he manifests magnanimity. The behavior of Jesus, judged by the conventional norms for an encomium, is worthy of praise.

© Stephen von Wyrick

Figure 13. Excavations at New Testament Jericho. Ancient Jericho dates back to at least 7000 BC. During the Hellenistic-Roman period, a new settlement emerged not far to the west. Herod the Great died at this new site.

Uses of Household Codes in Early Christianity

The common components of household management in Mediterranean antiquity were relations between husband and wife, parents and children, and masters and slaves and how to build and preserve wealth. Early Christians used the common cultural materials in different ways depending on varying circumstances. Ephesians and Colossians address the question of whether the equality of the worshiping community carries over into the conduct of family business. The answer of these two letters is that in a Christian household a division of labor with a hierarchical structure still governs the operation of household affairs. In 1 Peter, where Christian wives and slaves find themselves in non-Christian households, they are encouraged to act in such a way that will win their non-Christian husbands and masters to Christ. In Matthew, where the household is assumed to be Christian, the normal patterns of behavior are largely overturned by values derived from Jesus.

Theological Issues

Matthew 19:21 ("Go sell your possessions and give to the poor, and you will have treasure in the heavens, and come and follow me") has historically raised a serious question for would-be disciples of Jesus. Is this a general command applicable to all who would be disciples of Jesus? Three types of answers characterize interpreters. The first takes the command of Matt. 19:21 to be applicable to everyone. Certain individuals in church history have understood Jesus's words to be a general command and, as a result, have given away all of their private possessions: e.g., Origen (so Eusebius, *Hist. eccl.* 6.3), Anthony of Egypt (so Athanasius, *Vit. Ant.* 2), Cyprian (so Jerome, *Vir. ill.* 67), and Francis of Assisi (so Bonaventure, *Leg. maior* 33). The evidence of the First Gospel makes it unlikely that this is a general command applicable to everyone. It is true that Peter, Andrew, James, and John left everything to follow Jesus (4:18–22; 19:27), as did Matthew (9:9), but Joseph of Arimathea (27:57) was both a disciple and a rich man. Further, those who have given up everything cannot give alms (6:2–4). Moreover, one can no more generalize 19:21 than turn 8:22 into a general order to neglect the deceased.

Such arguments have led interpreters to try a second type of reading. Jesus's ethical teachings are to be divided into two groups: precepts and counsels. Obedience to the precepts is essential for salvation; obedience to the counsels is essential for perfection. The former are teachings obligatory for all disciples; the latter are designed for those who have made a total commitment by separating themselves from the common life of the laity. This distinction is based on Matthew's wording. In 19:17 Jesus says, "If you wish to enter into life, keep the commandments." In 19:21 he says, "If you wish to be perfect, go and sell your possessions and give to the poor." This has been taken to mean that obedience to the Decalogue and Lev. 19:18 leads to salvation while obedience to the demand for poverty is essential for perfection (cf. *Did.* 6.2–3: "If you are able to bear all of the yoke of the Lord, you will be perfect; but if you are not able, do what you are able to do" [trans. Lake 1975]). This view is fully developed in Thomas Aquinas: "The difference between a counsel and a commandment is that a commandment implies obligation, whereas a counsel is left to the option of the one to whom it is given" (*Summa* q. 108, art. 4; Thomas Aquinas 2009).

The difficulty with this reading is threefold. First, there was no clergy-laity split in Jesus's time. Second, as has been noted in the earlier section, "perfect" does not refer to a state above and beyond keeping the law. It rather refers to the quality of one's obedience. In modern terms, perfection refers to radical rather than formal obedience. Third, the promise for perfection is "and you will have treasure in heaven" (19:21). This is a synonym for "entering into life" (19:17). Note *t. Pe'ah* 4.18, where a king gives away a great deal of wealth in order to have treasure in heaven (inherit eternal life).

The third option for reading 19:21 holds that whereas Jesus's ethical teachings apply to everyone who would be a disciple, certain particular demands are tailored to a specific individual's situation. They address what Jesus regards as the particular problem standing in the way of this or that person's becoming a disciple. In the case of the rich young man, it is obvious that his problem is idolizing his possessions. Hence, the young man is asked to give up his idol (sell his possessions). This reading is currently the dominant one among interpreters.

Matthew 21:1–24:2

Narrative 5, Part 2:
Jesus Pronounces about Judgment in the Present

Introductory Matters

The first part of the fifth narrative (19:3–20:34) dealt with Jesus's movement from Galilee to Jerusalem; the second part (21:1–24:2) focuses on Jesus's entry into and ministry in Jerusalem. This segment consists of Jesus's entry into Jerusalem (21:1–11), followed by two days of Jesus's entering and leaving the temple (21:12–24:2). The unit is held together by two inclusios: Mount of Olives (21:1 and 24:3); "Blessed is the one who comes in the name of the Lord" (21:9 and 23:39). After the entry (21:1–11), there are two days that Jesus ministers in the temple (beginning at 21:12 and 21:23). The entire narrative (21:1–24:2) presents Jesus's confrontation with the religious leaders in Jerusalem.

The basic issue of introduction is how the material is arranged. An understanding of the material is conditioned by one's view of the organization of the whole. The overall key is that on two days Jesus enters and leaves the temple. On day 1 (21:12–22), Jesus enters the temple at 21:12 and leaves at 21:17. On day 2 (21:23–24:2), he enters the temple at 21:23 and leaves it at 24:1. On both days, Jesus's departure from the temple is associated with a pronouncement of judgment (21:19 and 24:2). The best help for understanding the organization of day 2 comes from Eugene Boring (1995, 8:409; cf. also Martens 2000). The motif of judgment that runs throughout ties 21:1–24:2 together with the discourse in 24:3–25:46.

Tracing the Narrative Flow

Jesus's Entry into Jerusalem (21:1–11)

The second part of the fifth narrative is introduced by the pericope of Jesus's entry into Jerusalem (21:1–11; cf. Mark 11:1–10). The story reflects the form of a celebratory welcome of a visiting king/general. At the approach of the dignitary, a band of municipal officials and other citizens, including the social, religious, and political elite, would proceed some distance from the city in order to meet the celebrity well in advance of the city walls. Enthusiastic expressions of welcome would be laced with extreme flattery as they escorted the dignitary back to the city. He would enter and, in some cases, would go to the city's holy place for some type of action, positive or negative. For example, Alexander the Great was met outside the city of Jerusalem, greeted and escorted into the city, and then taken to the temple, where he was involved in cultic activity (Josephus, *Ant.* 11.325–39). Marcus Agrippa was welcomed in Jerusalem, having been met by Herod and brought into the city amid acclamations, and there offered sacrifice (Josephus, *Ant.* 16.1–15). Cicero says that he was accorded this type of treatment wherever he traveled throughout the world on Rome's behalf (*Att.* 5.16). If this type of welcome was not accorded the visitor, the consequences were dire, usually the destruction of the city. For example, when Judas Maccabeus was refused a welcome by the city of Ephron, he and his party razed and plundered the city and destroyed every person in it (1 Macc. 5:45–51). Also, the chief priests urged the crowds to meet the troops of Florus, the Roman governor, with customary regard, so that he would have no excuse for further destruction of the city (Josephus, *J.W.* 2.318–24; Talbert 2002, 209–10; Davies and Allison 1997, 3:112, provide a list of examples; Carter 2000, 414, analyzes the form of such stories). Note that the people of Jerusalem do not go out to welcome

Jesus. He instead is celebrated by the crowds that have come with him to the city (20:29; 21:8–9).

Against the background of such social conventions, Jesus's actions make sense. The initiative is his. He sends two disciples to bring a donkey and a colt. This takes place to fulfill Isa. 62:11 (**Say to the daughter of Zion**) and Zech. 9:9 (**Behold, your king is coming to you, meek and seated upon a donkey and upon a colt, the offspring of a donkey** [Matt. 21:5]). The Matthean Jesus's initiative, an act of prophetic symbolism, is a claim to be the coming ruler of Israel (Nolland 2005, 832). He rides into Jerusalem on a donkey, as Solomon rode to be acclaimed king (1 Kings 1:32–40). A conqueror would ride a warhorse (*Pss. Sol.* 17.23–27, 37), so this is not his mission. The cloaks of the disciples are thrown over the two animals, as in modern Palestine both the mother donkeys and their unridden colts trotting after them have garments put across their backs (Gundry 1982, 410). Cloaks are spread across the road, as when Jehu was proclaimed king (2 Kings 9:12–13; Josephus, *Ant.* 9.111). Branches, like those used as part of the celebration when Simon liberated Jerusalem from the gentiles (1 Macc. 13:42, 51) and when Judas rededicated the temple (2 Macc. 10:7–9), were spread on the road. The crowds shout, **Hosanna to the son of David! Blessed is the one coming in the name of the Lord! Hosanna in the highest!** (21:9). The acclamation echoes Ps. 118:26, a fragment of a royal psalm recited on the enthronement of the king. The crowds coming to the festival (not Jerusalem's citizens) shout praise to the Davidic king (cf. 20:30–31). Here Jesus's claim is acknowledged by the arriving crowds. It presents a challenge to the city. Who is this Jesus? **As he entered Jerusalem, the whole city was shaken, saying, "Who is this?" And the crowds were saying, "This is the prophet, Jesus from Nazareth of Galilee"** (21:10–11). This episode controls what follows in 21:12–24:2. Who is Jesus? What will be the city's response to this question?

First Day (21:12–22)

21:12–16. Frequently in ancient celebratory welcomes, after entering the city the celebrity goes to the city's holy place. So in Matt. 21:12–16 (cf. Mark 11:15–17) on the first day Jesus enters the temple. There he drives out those who are buying and selling in the temple, overturns the tables of the money changers, and overturns the seats of those who sell doves. He then says, **My house will be called a house of prayer** (Isa. 56:7), **but you are making it a den of robbers** (Jer. 7:11; Matt. 21:3).

Two very different ways of understanding what follows have been advanced. The basic issue is whether Jesus's act of prophetic symbolism aims to purify the place where bandits do their robbing or to pronounce judgment on the place where they come after committing their crimes. On the one hand, some read Matt. 21:12–16 as Jesus's protest against bad behavior in the temple: failure to actualize Isaiah's description of God's house as a place of prayer

© Stephen von Wyrick

Figure 14. The Wailing Wall is the place where Jews come to pray and lament the destruction of the temple. The great stones formed part of the retaining wall to support the temple built by Herod the Great and destroyed by the Romans in AD 70.

for the outcasts of Israel (Isa. 56:8) and for foreigners (56:6). Rather, it has become a center of commercialism. If so, Jesus was not the only one so to protest. In *m. Ker.* 1.7, on one occasion Simeon ben Gamaliel (ca. AD 10–80) protested within the temple precincts because the price of a pair of doves (the poor person's sacrifice; Lev. 5:7; 12:8) had been raised to one golden denar, a price some twenty-five times the proper charge. In *t. Menah.* 13.18–22 we hear that the destructions of both the worship center at Shiloh and the first temple were because of bad behavior (e.g., love of money, greed). Jesus's actions that stopped the commercial transactions and his subsequent healing of outcasts symbolized a recovery of the temple's scriptural purpose. The son of David has purged Jerusalem (*Pss. Sol.* 17.30).

On the other hand, others read Matt. 21:12–16 as Jesus's pronouncement of judgment on the temple because of bad behavior outside the temple. Stopping the selling and money changing in effect caused the sacrificial system to shut down. This is not purification; it is abolition. Its reason may be discerned from the context of the Jeremiah quotation. Jeremiah's protest is against the unethical behavior outside the temple of those who came to worship in the temple, thinking the temple was their protection. Jeremiah then pronounced the coming destruction of the temple.

The same sort of protest was made by Apollonius of Tyana (Philostratus, *Ep.* 65) against the practices of those who worshiped in the Ephesian temple

---

Entering the Temple

In ancient celebratory welcomes, the celebrity often goes to the city's holy place after entering the city. The Hellenistic novel titled *An Ethopian Tale* reflects this practice when it narrates the entry into Syene of King Hydaspes.

> *"He himself also with picked men of his army entered the town, and all the citizens of every rank and age came to meet him and cast upon him and his soldiers garlands and such flowers as grow about the Nile, and commended him greatly for his notable victory. As soon as he came within the walls, riding upon an elephant instead of a chariot, he busied his mind about the service of the gods and sacred things, and asked of the origin of the Nile feast, and if they could show him anything worthy to be looked at."* (Heliodorus, *Aeth.* 9.22.1–2, trans. Underdowne 1923)

In the course of the king's conversation with the priests, they address him as "our savior and god" (9.22.7).

---

of Artemis. These worshipers were thieves, kidnappers, and all sorts of sacrilegious rascals. He charges, "Your temple is just a den of robbers." Given the context in which Jesus's acts and words occur (destruction of the temple in Jerusalem), it is more likely that the second reading is the proper one. Either way, this second act of prophetic symbolism protests a cultic center that has lost sight of its purpose.

And as the blind and lame, outcasts in Israel (Lev. 21:18–19; 2 Sam. 5:8 LXX; 11QT^a 45.13; *m. Hag.* 1.1), come to him in the temple, **he healed them** (21:14). Jesus's behavior in the temple evokes praise from the children present. **Hosanna to the son of David** (21:15). In antiquity, utterances of small children were often regarded as oracular (e.g., Plutarch, *Is. Os.* 356: especially when children are playing in holy places and happen to cry out whatever comes into their minds). The chief priests and scribes react with anger: **Do you hear what these are saying?** (21:16a). To this Jesus responds with a quotation from Ps. 8:2 LXX: **Out of the mouths of babies and nursing infants you have perfected praise** (21:16b). Jesus accepts the children's praise as appropriately prophetic.

21:17–22. Then he went out of the city to Bethany, and there he spent the night (21:17).

Matthew 21:18–22 takes place on the next morning as Jesus returns to the city. It has two components: a third act of prophetic symbolism (21:19) and a teaching on faith (21:20–22). The prophetic symbolism consists of the cursing of a fig tree that has nothing on it at all except leaves. **May no fruit ever again come from you** (21:19b). The tree withers at once. In context, this can only be construed as a pronouncement of judgment on the temple, which

Jesus the day before found to have lost sight of its purpose (cf. Hosea 2:12; 9:10, 16, where a withering fig tree is a metaphor for the judgment of Israel; cf. Jer. 19:10–11 for a symbolic act of judgment). In this, the Matthean Jesus is similar to other Jewish sources near AD 100 that attribute the demise of Jerusalem and the temple in AD 70 to Jewish religious failings (e.g., 2 Esd. [4 Ezra] 3:25–27; 2 Bar. 1.1–5; 13.4; Apoc. Ab. 27.1–7). The First Gospel stands apart in its claim that the particular Jewish failing is Jerusalem's failure to recognize and accept Jesus, the son of David.

The disciples who witness the act wonder only at the marvel: **How did the fig tree wither so quickly?** (21:20). This leads to a teaching on faith and prayer. Using hyperbole, Jesus says that a prayer of faith can accomplish the humanly impossible (cf. 19:26; 17:19–21).

Second Day (21:23–24:2)

At 21:23 the long second day in the temple begins. The first section corresponds to his entering the temple (21:23–23:39). The brief conclusion (24:1–2) records the judgment he pronounces on the Pharisees and on Jerusalem.

21:23–23:39. The material covering Jesus's second-day entry into the temple falls into two subsections: (1) controversy regarding his authority to teach (21:23–22:46), and (2) his pronouncement of judgment on the Pharisees and the city of Jerusalem (23:1–39).

1. The controversy over Jesus's teaching authority (21:23–22:46) unfolds in an ABB′A′ pattern.

Section A (21:23–27) is held together by an inclusio ("by what authority," 21:23, 27). When Jesus enters the temple and is teaching, the chief priests and elders come to him, asking a twofold question: **By what authority are you doing these things? Who gave you this authority?** (21:23; cf. 9:33–34; 12:23–24). This challenge to Jesus's authority provides the occasion for all that follows in 21:24–23:39. Jesus responds to the twofold question with a question of his own: **The baptism of John, whence was it: from heaven or from men?** (21:25a). This places the leaders in a quandary. **If we say from heaven, he will ask us, "Why, then, did you not believe him?"** If we say, from men, we must be afraid of

---

An Outline of Matthew 21:23–22:46

1. The authority of Jesus (21:23–22:46)

(A) **Jesus's question (21:23–27)**

(B) **Three parables of judgment (21:28–22:14)**

Two sons (21:28–32)

Tenants (21:33–44, 45–46)

Marriage feast (22:1–14)

(B′) **Three controversies (22:15–22:40)**

Taxes (22:15–22)

Resurrection (22:23–33)

Great commandment (22:34–40)

(A′) **Jesus's question (22:41–46)**

the crowd, for all hold John to be a prophet (21:25b–26). So they say to Jesus, **We do not know.** Jesus replies, **Neither will I tell you by what authority I am doing these things** (21:27). The stage is set. Jesus's opponents have already begun to characterize themselves as people of poor character.

Section B consists of three parables of judgment (21:28–32; 21:33–46; 22:1–14). The collection of three is usually regarded as due to the hand of the evangelist (Olmstead 2003, 20). (Cf. *b. Avod. Zar.* 54b for a series of controversies involving multiple parables.)

The first parable in section B (21:28–32) is unique to Matthew. This unit continues the previous discussion. **What do you** (the chief priests and elders; cf. 21:27b) **think?** (21:28a). The form of the parable that follows (21:28b–30) is that of the NRSV (based on NA[27] and UBS[4]). An alternate reading that reverses the order of the sons is found in the REB. In the form assumed here, the first son, when asked to go work in the vineyard, initially refuses but later goes. The second, when asked to go and work in the vineyard, agrees to go but never goes. This is little more than an expanded proverb: better the son who repents and obeys his father than the son who promises obedience but does not obey. Jesus then asks, **Which of the two did the will of the father?** (21:31a). The religious leaders reply, **The first** (21:31b). They are convicted by their own mouths. Jesus's interpretation of the parable follows: **Truly I say to you, the tax collectors and sinners are going before you into the kingdom of God. For John came to you in the way of righteousness, and you did not believe him. But the tax collectors and the sinners believed him. Now when you saw this, you did not change your position to believe him** (21:31c–32; cf. 7:21; 12:50; 23:13). This is a parable of judgment on the chief priests and elders for their treatment of the Baptist (cf. Luke 7:29–30). The negative characterization of the leaders continues. (Similar stories may be found in Seneca the Younger, *Ben.* 6.11.1–2; *Exod. Rab.* 27.9.)

The second parable in section B (21:33–46; cf. Mark 12:1–12) is tied to the previous parable by their common structure (Jesus's introductory word [28a and 33a]; the parable [28b–30 and 33b–39]; Jesus's question [31a and 40]; opponents' response [31b and 41]; Jesus's pronouncement of judgment [31c–32 and 42–44]) and their common theme of the authorities' fear of the crowds, who regard John and Jesus as prophets (21:26, 46). The pericope probably reflects haggadic midrash, a rabbinic pattern of synagogue address (Davies and Allison 1997, 3:175). How so? It begins with a biblical text in 21:33 (Isa. 5:1–2 LXX), followed by an exposition by means of a parable (21:33–41), and concludes with another biblical text (Ps. 118:22 in 21:42). Because the story's characters and their behaviors resemble salvation history, this is usually taken to be an allegory about faithlessness and judgment related to Israel's leaders and Jesus. In this schema the vineyard is Israel (cf. Isa. 5:2); the tenant farmers are the religious leaders (cf. Ezek. 34); the servants sent to get the fruit are the prophets, probably including the Baptist (cf. Jer. 7:25–26; 2 Chron. 24:17–19;

36:15–16; Acts 7:51–53); the son who is cast out and killed is Jesus, not John the Baptist (cf. Heb. 13:12; contra Stern 1989, 65; and Lowe 1982); and the builders who reject the stone are the religious leaders.

Jesus asks the leaders, **When the lord of the vineyard comes, what will he do to those tenants?** (21:40). The religious leaders reply, **He will kill the evil ones and will let out the vineyard to other tenants who will give him the fruits in their season** (21:41). Again, the leaders are convicted by their own words (cf. *2 Bar.* 10.18). The opponents' conclusion does not implicate Jesus in a violent depiction of God. Jesus's interpretation in 21:43 pronounces judgment, but a nonviolent one: **Because of this, I say to you that the kingdom of God will be taken from you** (cf. 1 Sam. 15:28) **and will be given to a people** (*ethnei*) **producing the fruits of it.** Two terms in this logion require attention. First, **kingdom of God** here refers not to the new age, as elsewhere, but to a special relationship of the religious leaders to Israel. Through them God's rule has historically been effective. This rule of God through them is what is being taken away (cf. Ezek. 34:10; Carter 2000, 429). Second, **a people producing the fruits of** God's rule refers to the twelve disciples of Jesus who will rule/judge the twelve tribes in the end time (19:28; cf. Luke 22:28–30).

The parable and Jesus's interpretation of it are not about Israel being replaced by the church (as they are usually read). Rather, they are about the Jewish leadership being replaced by the Twelve (Milavec 1989, 107). Note 21:45: **And when the chief priests and Pharisees heard his parables, they knew he was speaking about them.** (Gundry 1982, 430; Davies and Allison 1997, 3:188–89; and Olmstead 2003, 117, correctly see that it is the Jewish leaders who are replaced but wrongly regard the people who replace them as the church rather than the twelve disciples.) If the first parable of judgment relates to the leaders' rejection of the Baptist, this second parable is concerned with the leaders' rejection of Jesus. Arresting Jesus is unsuccessful, however, because the leaders fear the crowds, who held Jesus to be a prophet (21:46). (For a similar parable, cf. *Sifre* on Deut. 3:12.)

The third of section B's three parables of judgment comes in 22:1–14 (cf. Luke 14:16–24 for Matt. 22:1–10; 22:11–14 is unique to Matthew). It concerns a wedding banquet that a king was giving for his son. After the invitation went out, the king sent servants to call the guests. When they would not come, the king sent other servants to tell the invited guests that the time was ready. Come! They, however, again would not come. Some actually seized the messengers, mistreating and killing them. **And the king was angry, and sending his soldiers he killed those murderers and burned their city** (22:7). Then the king sent his servants out into the streets with an invitation for everyone to come to the feast (cf. *y. Hag.* V.[I]). Both good and bad filled the wedding hall. This first half of the story is like the kingdom of heaven. Two processes are analogous. Just as the king invited guests who turned him down, so God's invitation to Israel has met with rejection. Just as the king then invited everyone, good and bad, to the feast, so Israel's rejection has resulted in an invitation to everyone, good and bad. Scholars usually hear overtones of the destruction of Jerusalem in AD 70 in 22:7. The temple was in fact burned (*2 Bar.* 7.1; 80.3; Josephus, *J.W.* 2.395–97; 6.249–408). Nonmessianic Jews also believed that Rome's destruction of Jerusalem in 70 was due to God's punishment of the city (2 Esd. [*4 Ezra*] 3:28–36; 4:23–25; 5:21–30; *2 Bar.* 1.1–5; 4.1; 6.9; 32.2–3; Josephus, *J.W.* 4.386–88; 5.559; 6.96–103, 409–11; 7.323–36, 358–60). Rome, it was believed, functioned as God's agent (*Pss. Sol.* 2.1–10), as did the Assyrians (Isa. 10:4–7), Babylonians (Jer. 25:1–11), and Persians (Isa. 44:28; 45:1–13) earlier. Jesus's followers saw the punishment as christologically based. It was due to the rejection of Jesus, the son of David.

The second part of the parable (22:11–14) shifts God's judgment from the Jewish elite to those brought in, both bad and good. Scholars usually see the inclusion of these folk as analogous to the inclusion of Jewish outcasts and gentiles in the Christian mission. **Now when the king entered to see those reclining at table, he saw there a man not clothed in a wedding garment. He said to him, "Friend, how is it that you have entered here without a wedding garment?" And he could not speak. Then the king said to the servants, "When you have bound his feet and hands, throw him into the darkness outside, where there will be weeping and gnashing of teeth"** (22:11–13). The evangelist concludes, **For many are called but few are chosen** (22:14).

This part of the parable shows that judgment falls not only on the unresponsive elite but also on disciples who do not manifest "evidential works of righteousness" (Gundry 1982, 439). God is inclusive but expects change (Nolland 2005, 885). So what happens to the elite can also happen to disciples. (A similar parable in *Eccles. Rab.* 9.8.1 tells of a king, a banquet, guests with splendid attire and some with dirty garments, and of the exclusion of the latter from the feast. This would imply that the missing wedding garment is newly washed.) Taken as a whole, the parable speaks of judgment both on those of the religious elite who refuse the invitation offered by God through his servants and on those who, when invited, accept but do not respond with appropriate seriousness.

Section B′ shifts to three controversy stories (22:15–22; 22:23–33; 22:34–40). It is still set in the temple on day 2. (For examples of a series of conflict stories, cf. *b. Sanh.* 90b–91a; *b. Hul.* 60a).

The first conflict story in section B′ comes in 22:15–22 (cf. Mark 12:13–17). The issue is whether or not Jews should pay taxes to the Romans. **Then the Pharisees took counsel how they might entrap him in something he said** (22:15). In rabbinic writings someone who was enticing others to idolatry needed to be entrapped (*m. Sanh.* 7.10; *t. Sanh.* 10.11). If such a person was finally caught, he would be held until a festival for execution, to fulfill Deut. 13:12, "Then all Israel shall hear and be afraid" (*t. Sanh.* 11.7; *b. Sanh.* 89a; Schwartz 1995). Something like this seems to underlie the Pharisees' attempt to entrap

Jesus. After flattery intended to soften up the culprit, they ask their question: **Is it lawful to give taxes to Caesar or not?** (22:17b). The issue of taxes was critical. Since Rome had gained control of Judea in 63 BC, Jews paid taxes to their overlords. Early in Jesus's lifetime (ca. AD 6–9), a Galilean named Judas revolted against the Romans over the issue of paying taxes to Rome (Josephus, *J.W.* 2.117–18; *Ant.* 20.102) on the grounds that it was idolatry. This resulted in his death and the crucifixion of his sons. In a revolt against Florus in AD 66, Agrippa told the people that not to pay the tax was an act of war against Rome.

Herein lay the trap. If Jesus answers no, the Romans will get him; if he answers yes, certain Jews will reject him. Jesus responds: **Show me the coin used for the tax** (22:19a). When they bring him a denarius, he asks, **Of whom is this image and inscription?** (22:20). This particular coin bears an image of the emperor's head and, if current, probably the inscription, "Tiberius Caesar, son of the divine Augustus." They answer, **Caesar's** (22:21a). Jesus then says, **Give the things of Caesar to Caesar and the things of God to God** (22:21b). Unsuccessful, the disciples of the Pharisees and the Herodians go away. Jesus's words in 22:21b indicate that the state has limited legitimate claims (cf. Prov. 8:15; Dan. 2:21, 37–38; Wis. 6:1–3; Rom. 13:1–7; 1 Pet. 2:13–17) but that the total self of a human belongs to God (Deut. 5:7; 6:4–5). When the state oversteps its proper bounds, then it is demonic and under God's judgment (Wis. 6:4–5; Acts 12:20–23; Rev. 13).

The second conflict story in section B′ is 22:23–33 (cf. Mark 12:18–27). The same day the Sadducees try to ridicule Jesus around the issue of the resurrection. (For the use of catch-questions to trap a teacher, cf. Lucian, *Demon.* 15.) The Sadducees do not believe in resurrection from the dead (Josephus, *J.W.* 2.162; *Ant.* 18.11–17; Acts 23:8) and accept as their canon only the first five books of Moses (Josephus, *Ant.* 18.16). They first refer to a part of their authoritative Scripture, Deut. 25:5–6, which deals with levirate marriage: **Teacher, Moses said, "If one should die without having children, his brother should marry his wife and raise up offspring for his brother"** (22:24). This law was designed to preserve the childless dead brother's line and name (cf. Gen. 38:8–10; Ruth 3:9–4:10). The Sadducees then pose a trick question of interpretation that they believe will ridicule belief in the resurrection: **Now there were among us seven brothers. The first married and died and, not having had children, left his wife to his brother. Likewise also the second and the third, until the seventh. Last of all, the woman died. In the resurrection, then, of which one of the seven will she be wife? For all had her** (22:25–28). In other words, belief in the resurrection makes interpretation of Scripture ridiculous.

Jesus's response focuses on two issues: the nature of resurrected life (22:30) and how resurrection can be derived from the Pentateuch (22:31–32). Regarding the nature of resurrected life, he says, **In the resurrection, they neither** marry nor are given in marriage but are like angels in heaven (22:30). This reflects some Jewish thought about life after the resurrection (e.g., *1 En.* 15.7: angels do not marry; *1 En.* 51.4; 104.6; *b. Ber.* 17a: no begetting in the world to come; *Gen. Rab.* 8.11). Since the Sadducees did not accept as authoritative any books beyond the Pentateuch, it would have been pointless to appeal to Dan. 12:2 or Isa. 26:19. So, in regard to deriving belief in resurrection from the law, Jesus quotes God's words in Exod. 3:6: **I am the God of Abraham and the God of Isaac and the God of Jacob.** Jesus then interprets, **He is not the God of the dead but of the living** (22:32). This type of exegesis is typical of certain streams of ancient Judaism (e.g., *b. Sanh.* 90b, 91b; *Mek.* on Exod. 15:1; Philo, *Fug.* 55–58, says he attended lectures of a wise woman who argued for immortality from the Pentateuch: e.g., Deut. 4:4; 30:15, 20). The crowds are astonished that Jesus has silenced the Sadducees (22:33).

The third conflict story in section B′ is found at 22:34–40 (cf. Mark 12:28–34). Once again the Pharisees are involved. To test him, one of their number, a lawyer, asks Jesus, **What commandment in the law is the greatest?** (22:36). It was a cultural practice to attempt to reduce massive legislation to one or two principles. From the pagan world, Plutarch (*Cons. Apoll.* 28) says the two most indispensable inscriptions at Delphi are "Know thyself" and "Avoid extremes." In the Jewish world, a rabbi asks, "What is the smallest portion of scripture from which all essential regulations of the Torah hang?" (*b. Ber.* 63a, trans. Epstein 1948). Akiba's answer is that loving the neighbor is the greatest principle in the law (*Sifra* on Lev. 19:18). It is this type of question that is addressed to Jesus. His response is twofold. **You shall love the Lord your God with your whole heart and with your whole soul and with your whole mind** (Deut. 6:5). **This is the greatest and first commandment. A second is like it: You shall love your neighbor as yourself** (Lev. 19:18). **On these two commandments the law and the prophets hang** (22:37–40; cf. *T. Iss.* 5.2: "Love the Lord and your neighbor" [*OTP* 1:803]; *T. Iss.* 7.6; *T. Dan* 5.3: "Throughout all your life love the Lord, and one another with a true heart" [*OTP* 1:809]; Philo, *Spec.* 2.63). This is the Matthean Jesus's hermeneutical key to reading Scripture. No reactions to Jesus's remarks are recorded by Matthew.

Section A′ follows in 22:41–46, where Jesus asks his own question of the Pharisees. "He abandons his defensive posture for the offensive" (Davies and Allison 1997, 3:249). **What do you think about the Christ? Whose son is he?** They reply, **He is the son of David** (22:42; cf. *Pss. Sol.* 17.21–43; 18.7–9; also Matt. 1:1; 9:27; 12:23; 15:22; 20:30–31; 21:9, 15). Jesus says to them, **How then does David by the Spirit call him Lord, saying, "The Lord said to my lord, 'Sit at my right hand until I put your enemies under your feet'"?** (22:43–44). The text being quoted is Ps. 110:1 (cf. elsewhere at Acts 2:34–35; Heb. 1:13; 2:8; 10:13; 1 Cor. 15:25–27; *1 Clem.* 36.5; *Barn.* 12.10). Assumed is that David is the author of the psalm and that he speaks under divine inspiration (cf. 11Q5 27.2–11). Also assumed is that a son is never his father's lord; just the reverse.

The cultural convention is reflected in *Midr. Teh.* 1.18.29: in the time to come when the Holy One seats the messiah at his right hand, "as is said, The Lord saith unto my lord: 'Sit thou at my right hand' (Ps. 110:1)," and seats Abraham at his left, Abraham's face pales and he says to God, "My son's son sits at the right, and I at the left!" (Braude 1959, 1:261). Unthinkable! Jesus then levels his interpretative challenge: **If then David calls him lord, how is he his son?** (22:45). Of course, no one can give an answer, and from that point onward no one asks him any more questions. Might not the expected answer, given the Matthean plot, have been that David's son is also God's son (cf. 2 Sam. 7:14; Ps. 2:5–9; Matt. 2:15; 3:17; 11:25–30; 17:5; 28:19)? The messiah is more than, but not other than, a son of David.

2. Following Jesus's response (21:24–22:46) to the challenge to his authority (21:23), his teaching in the temple continues in 23:1–39. He has responded to various challenges to his honor made by priests (21:23, 45), Pharisees (21:45; 22:15, 34), and Sadducees (22:23, 34) with significant success (e.g., 22:22, 33, 34, 46). Presumably, his disciples have overheard all of these challenges and responses. Although Kenneth Newport (1995) argues that Matthew took chapter 23 from a Jewish-Christian polemical tract (23:2–31) and adapted it by adding 23:32–39, most scholars regard the chapter in its entirety as a Matthean composition. In Matt. 23 are three subunits: 23:1–12, addressed to the crowds and disciples (23:1); 23:13–36, addressed to the scribes and Pharisees; and 23:37–39, addressed to Jerusalem (following Garland 1979, 32). In 24:1–2 Jesus exits the temple at the end of this second day and pronounces judgment on the temple.

Matthew 23:1–12 has two foci: 23:1–7, a criticism of what the scribes and Pharisees do and do not do; 23:8–12, guidelines for disciples about what not to do and what to do.

In 23:2–7, the charges are two. First, 23:2–4 depicts the scribes and Pharisees as those who do not practice what they preach. **The scribes and Pharisees sit on Moses's seat** (either a literal seat at the front of the synagogue upon which teachers sat [Newport 1995, 85] or a metaphorical way of saying someone was Moses's successor [Garland 1979, 42]; either way, they are the people's instructors in matters religious). **Therefore everything they say to you, do and keep, but do not act according to their works** (23:2–3). The basic import is clear. It was a cultural commonplace to critique philosophers and other teachers for not practicing what they taught (e.g., Seneca the Younger, *Ep.*

An Outline of Matthew 23:1–39

2. Judgment on Pharisees and Jerusalem (23:1–39)

  Criticism of scribes and Pharisees (23:1–12)

    What Pharisees do (23:1–7)

    What disciples must do (23:8–12)

  Seven woes on Pharisees (23:13–36)

  Judgment on Jerusalem (23:37–39)

20: one's life should not be out of harmony with one's words; *Tranq.* 18.1: you talk one way, you live another; 19.3: no one of them practices what he preaches; 20.1: philosophers do not practice what they preach; also *t. Hag.* 2.1: those who preach but do not practice; contrast Jesus, who fulfills all righteousness before he speaks about righteousness). The difficulty lies in the words **Everything they say to you, do and keep.** Elsewhere it is clear that Jesus does not advocate doing whatever the Pharisees teach (e.g., 15:3–9, 14; 16:11–12). Various expedients have been tried to deal with this difficulty (e.g., "what they say" refers not to their interpretation of the law but their passing on of the Scriptures [Powell 1995a]). The easiest way would be to regard "doing what they say" as irony that dismisses "what they say" even as it apparently approves it. It was a part of prophetic style for the prophet to tell the people to perform an act that obviously was not approved (e.g., 1 Kings 18:27; Isa. 6:9; Jer. 44:25–26; Amos 4:4–5).

Second, 23:5–7 depicts the scribes and Pharisees as those who do things out of a wrong motive. The general indictment comes first: **They do all of their works in order to be seen by others.** Examples of this indictment follow: **They broaden their phylacteries and lengthen their fringes. They love the place of honor at dinner, and the chief seats in the synagogue, and being greeted in the marketplace, and being called rabbi by others.** In *b. Sotah* 22b, a section speaks about "the plagues of the Pharisees" under the rubric "There are seven types of Pharisees." One of those types is the Pharisee who does his religious duty from unworthy motives. The accusations of the Matthean Jesus echo those of the rabbis (cf. Matt. 6:2–6).

Josephus's View of the Pharisees' Status among the Jews

According to Josephus, the Pharisees are a sect of the Jews deemed most skillful in interpreting the Jewish laws (*Ant.* 17.41; *J.W.* 1.110; 2.162; *Life* 191). They have the support of the general populace. The Sadducees are able to persuade only the rich (*Ant.* 13.298). Whatever the Pharisees prescribe about worship, prayers, and sacrifices, the people do at their direction. In fact, if the Sadducees ever become magistrates, they must accept the views of the Pharisees because the people would not tolerate anything else (*Ant.* 18.15, 17). If the Pharisees ever say anything against the king or high priest, they are believed by the people (*Ant.* 13.288). They have great authority among the Jews, both to hurt and to help, because they are believed by the multitude even when they speak severely against others (*Ant.* 13.401–2). According to Josephus, then, Pharisaic dominance was a long-standing fact of Jewish life. This Josephus lamented (*Ant.* 13.400–402, 410; 17.41; *Life* 189–94). His unhappiness with them was due to their interference in political matters, which was not always from the purest motives (Mason 1990).

Phylacteries and Fringes/Tassels

Phylacteries are small leather boxes that contain passages of Scripture, usually Exod. 13:1–10, 11–16; Deut. 6:4–9; 11:13–21. They are worn on the left hand and forehead. The practice is based on a literal reading of Exod. 13:9, 16, and Deut. 6:8. The purpose of the practice is to provide a concrete reminder of one's obligations to what the law commands. The practice is spelled out in *Let. Aris.* 159 and in Josephus, *Ant.* 4.213. Fringes/tassels are blue cords on each corner of one's garment. They, likewise, are to remind the Jews to do the Lord's commandments (based on Num. 15:37–41; Deut. 22:12). Matthew 9:20 and 14:36 indicate that Jesus wore fringes on his garment.

The guidelines for disciples in 23:8–12 recall 18:1–4 and 20:25–28, where humility is set forth as a basic premise for the disciples' life together. There do seem to be special functionaries assumed by the First Gospel (e.g., scribes [13:52; 23:34], prophets [10:41; 23:34], sages [23:34], teachers [28:20; 5:19]). Those in such positions are warned against claiming titles like rabbi, father, and instructor (23:8–10; Ascough 2001). The comments are summed up in the saying **Those who exalt themselves will be humbled, and those who humble themselves will be exalted** (23:12, a proverb; cf. Diogenes Laertius, *Vit. phil.* 1.69: Zeus humbles the exalted and exalts the humble).

Verses 13–36 constitute the second subunit of Matt. 23. The unit consists of seven woes spoken against the scribes and Pharisees (23:13, 15, 16, 23, 25, 27, 29; cf. Isa. 5:8–23 for a series of six woes; Luke 11:42–52: six woes). The woes here are the reverse of the blessings spoken to disciples in 5:3–12. They are, like the woe in 11:21, expressions of proleptic condemnation (Haenchen 1951, 46). The woes are directed against the Pharisees because they are hypocrites (cf. Sir. 32:15; 33:2; *Pss. Sol.* 4.20, 22, where the essence of hypocrisy is understood as pretense). The charge of hypocrisy is a standard feature of ancient polemic (e.g., Plutarch, *Mor.* 1117d; Philo, *Legat.* 162; 1QS 4.14).

The first two woes (23:13–15) focus on the Pharisees' effect on others. They prevent others' entry into the kingdom of heaven (by turning them from Jesus). When the Pharisees do make a convert, the convert becomes a child of hell. Rabbi Eleazar of Modiim is alleged to have said, "God scattered Israel among the nations for the sole purpose that proselytes would be numerous among them" (*b. Pesah.* 87b, trans. Epstein 1948). What Jesus asks is, What good does this do a proselyte?

The third and fourth woes (23:16–22 and 23:23–24) are held together by an inclusio (blind guides in 23:16 and 24). They are illustrations of why the Pharisees are blind guides (cf. 15:14). Regarding oaths (cf. 5:33–37), the Pharisees think they can make a distinction between those that are binding and those that are not. This is impossible. Regarding tithing, they major on minors, neglecting the weightier matters of justice, mercy, and faith (cf. 9:13; *t. Pe'ah* 4.19: "Charity and deeds of loving-kindness outweigh all the other commandments in the Torah" [trans. Neusner 2002]).

The fifth and sixth woes (23:25–28) are held together by the common emphasis on outside-inside. The cup and plate provide the first example. The cleansing of utensils in keeping with the clean-unclean laws (cf. Mark 7:3–4; *m. Kelim* 25.1, 7–8) is used as a metaphor for the Pharisees' attention to religious externals at the expense of cleansing the heart (cf. 15:11, 17–20). The whitewashing of tombs that, while improved in exterior appearance, remain a source of ritual contamination is used as a second metaphor for the Pharisees' attention to religious externals at the expense of the inner self.

Jewish Missionary Activity/ Proselytism

"Although Judaism had no central sending agency and hence no 'missionaries' in the formal sense . . . , plenty of evidence, especially in Diaspora Jewish apologetics (e.g., Josephus, *Ant.* 20.17, 34–36; *Ag. Ap.* 2.210) and Gentile criticisms of Jewish conversions (e.g., Tacitus, *Hist.* 5.5; Dio Cassius, *Rom. Hist.* 57.18.5; 60.6.7; Horace, *Sat.* 1.4.141–44), testify to many Jewish people seeking Gentile converts in the course of their other work" (Keener 1999, 548, cf. 548n42).

The seventh woe (23:29–36) focuses on the Pharisees' reception of God's emissaries. By building tombs for and decorating the graves of past prophets, they hope to disassociate themselves from their ancestors who killed the prophets. The Pharisees are, however, true descendants of their ancestors. Witness how they treat the emissaries whom Jesus sends: **Behold, I send to you prophets and wise ones and scribes, some of whom you will kill and crucify, and some you will beat in your synagogues and persecute from city to city** (23:34; cf. 10:16–23). They will live up to what their ancestors have done by persecuting Jesus's envoys. This will complete the quota of evils that are allowed before judgment comes (cf. 1 Thess. 2:15–16; Rev. 6:9–11). The judgment is for the entire murderous history from Abel (Gen. 4:1–16) to Zechariah (probably the priest in 2 Chron. 24:20–22 whose dying words were, "May Yahweh hear and avenge."). If so, it would mean from beginning to end (since 2 Chronicles was the last book in the Hebrew Bible). Judgment is coming on these eminent religious leaders.

The third component in Matt. 23 is found in 23:37–39 (cf. Luke 13:34–35). The audience here has expanded beyond scribes and Pharisees to Jerusalem, the city. What is the character of the city? **Jerusalem, Jerusalem, that kills the prophets and stones those sent to her** (cf. Acts 7:51–52). What has been Jesus's intent? **How often have I wanted to gather your children together as a hen gathers her chicks under her wings** (cf. Ps. 17:8), **and you did not want it** (23:37). The Jewish scriptures use the image of God sheltering the people under his wings (Exod. 19:4; Deut. 32:11; Ps. 17:8; 36:7). Later Jewish teachers spoke of gentile conversion to Judaism as being brought under the wings of the Shekinah (*2 Bar.* 41.4; *Avot R. Nat.* [A] 12; *Gen. Rab.* 47.10). What are the consequences of not wanting shelter under Jesus's protection? They are two. First, **Behold, your house** (the temple [cf. 21:13; 24:2] or the city) **is abandoned** (by God's presence). Second, **You will not see me from now until you say, "Blessed is the one coming in the name of the Lord"** (23:38–39; Jerusalem left this up to the arriving pilgrims in 21:9). In Luke 13:34–35 this saying refers to the triumphal entry, but in Matthew it means that when his people bless him, the messiah will come (cf. Acts 3:19–21). The date of redemption for the Matthean Jesus, then, is contingent on Israel's acceptance of him (Allison 1983; cf. Acts 3:19–21). At this point ends the second day of Jesus's teaching in the temple.

24:1–2. In 24:1–2 (cf. Mark 13:1–2) Jesus leaves the temple for the final time. **As Jesus exited the temple and was departing, his disciples came to him to point out the buildings of the temple. And he said to them, ". . . Truly I say to you, there will not be left here a stone upon a stone that will not be cast down."** The Matthean Jesus here prophesies the destruction of the temple. In so doing, he is but one in a line of prophetic figures who have made such a prophecy. Micah 3:12; Jer. 7:1–15; and Jer. 20 were prior to Jesus. Johanan ben Zakkai (ca. AD 60; *y. Sotah* 6.3; *b. Yoma* 39b; *Lam. Rab.* 1.5 + 39), his disciple Rabbi Zadok (*b. Git.* 56a), and Jesus son of Ananias (an ignorant peasant who wailed for seven years and five months, a voice directed against Jerusalem and the sanctuary; Josephus, *J.W.* 6.300–309) were after Jesus. All predicted the fall of the city and the destruction of the temple. All understood the destruction as God's judgment on the people's sinfulness (cf. also *T. Levi* 15.1; 14.6; *T. Mos.* 5.4; 6.8–9). Jesus understands that sin as the city's rejection of the son of David, the last in a trail of shed righteous blood. A Christian tradition continued that claim (e.g., Justin Martyr, *Dial.* 16; *Gos. Pet.* 25; Melito, *Pascha* 99–100; Hippolytus, *Contra Jud.* 7; Origen, *Cels.* 8.42; Eusebius, *Hist. eccl.* 3.5.3; 2.6.3).

The key to understanding Matt. 24:1–2 is to recognize the connection between Jesus's departure and the prophecy of the temple's destruction. There was a broad-based belief in Mediterranean antiquity that before a city could fall, the deity that protected the city had to depart. Ezekiel 10:18 speaks of the glory of the Lord going forth from the temple in connection with the exile (also 11:23). In *1 En.* 89.56, God leaves their house of the Lord so that Judah can be taken into exile (586 BC). In *2 Bar.* 8.2, the Babylonian exile is made possible because the one who guards the house has left it. Prophecies after the exile speak of Yahweh's return to the city and to his house (Zech. 1:16; 2:10; 8:3). The evidence for Roman practice is similar. Pliny (*Nat.* 28.18–19) says, "Verrius Flaccus cites trustworthy authorities to show that it was the custom, at the beginning of a siege, for the Roman priests to call forth the divinity under whose protection the besieged city was, and to promise him the same or even more splendid worship among the Roman people" (trans. Rackham et al. 1938–63). An inscription discovered at Isaura Vetus in modern Turkey records such an evocation in around 75 BC.

In connection with the fall of Jerusalem and the destruction of the temple in AD 70, there is both Jewish and Roman testimony about the deity's departure from the temple before the city fell. In *J.W.* 6.290–300, Josephus reports a vision of celestial armies, and at the following Pentecost festival a commotion in the temple during which the priests heard a voice saying, "We are departing hence." In *J.W.* 6.127, he says Titus believed that any deity that had watched over the Jerusalem temple was now gone. Hence, Josephus could say that the deity has fled the holy places and has taken his stand on the side of the Romans (*J.W.* 5.412; 6.300). Tacitus (*Hist.* 5.13) says prodigies occurred prior to the destruction of the temple. For example, the doors of the inner shrine were suddenly thrown open, and a voice of more than mortal tone cried, "The gods are departing." That a temple could not be taken while the deities were present was assumed in both Jewish and pagan cultures (Kloppenborg 2005).

In Matt. 1:23 Jesus is said to be Emmanuel, meaning "God with us." If then Jesus leaves the temple, it is the presence of God departing. This is how 23:38 should be understood: "Your house is abandoned" means abandoned by the presence of the deity. According to 23:39b, the presence will not return until the city welcomes Jesus as the one who comes in the name of the Lord. With the divine presence departed, the temple and the city are vulnerable to their enemies. So according to Josephus (*J.W.* 7.1), Caesar ordered the whole city and the temple to be razed to the ground. With 24:1–2, the fifth narrative, parts 1 and 2, is ended.

Functions of the Unit as a Whole

In an honor-and-shame culture, such as the ancient Mediterranean, most competitive behavior was in the form of a challenge to a person's reputation. This consisted of four steps: first, a claim of worth or value; second, a challenge to that claim; third, a defense of that claim; fourth, a public verdict of success (Neyrey 1998, 19–20). The second part of the fifth narrative (21:1–24:2) consists of precisely this type of competition. It is between Jesus and the religious leadership in Jerusalem. By his entry (21:1–11) and his actions to purify the temple (21:12–16), Jesus claims to be messianic king and prophet. This claim is then challenged (in principle, 21:23; and in specific ways, 22:15, 23, 35). Jesus defends his claims (21:24–22:14; 22:18–21, 29–32, 37–40) and poses questions to the challengers that they cannot answer (21:24–27; 22:41–45). The reactions to this series of challenges and responses are all in Jesus's favor (21:46; 22:22, 33, 34, 46). Jesus has won the competition. He has gained acquired honor. This, of course, is all part of the construction of an encomium. Jesus is worthy of praise.

Theological Issues

Is Matt. 21:1–24:2, especially 21:33–44 and chapter 23, anti-Judaic? The answer must be, No. Why? A number of reasons have been given. First, the First Evangelist is a Jewish teacher in conflict with other Jewish teachers in the diverse Jewish community of the eastern Mediterranean at the end of the first century (Saldarini 2001, 167). With his polemics, Matthew's Jesus seeks to delegitimate the established leadership. He does not deny the fundamental legitimacy of Israel. To do so would destroy the basis for his own group. The critiques made by the Matthean Jesus are analogous to those of the classical prophets (e.g., Isa. 3:13–15), the Essenes (e.g., 1QpHab, col. 2; col. 9), Josephus (e.g., *Ant.* 13.400–402, 410; 17.41; *Life* 189–94), the pseudepigraphical writings (e.g., *Pss. Sol.* 4.1–12), the rabbinic writings (e.g., *b. Sotah* 22b, rabbinic critique of Pharisees), and the Pharisaic critique of the Jew, Jesus (e.g., demonic inspiration; Matt. 9:34; 12:24). What is found in Matthew is more of the same, namely, intra-Jewish polemic. From within Judaism, certain Jewish teachers critique other Jews. The debate is over religious issues. This is not anti-Judaism.

Second, Matthew's critique reflects Mediterranean conventions of dealing with opponents. Luke Timothy Johnson (1989) has shown that the slander in the NT in general and Matthew in particular is typical of that found among rival claimants to a philosophical tradition and is as common among Jews as among other Hellenists. The way Matthew talks about Jews is the way all opponents talked about each other in the ancient Mediterranean world. Compared to other polemic of the time, Matthew's language is a bit mild! Such vituperation signified that someone was an opponent. The purpose of the polemic was not the rebuttal of the opponent but the edification of one's own school. By vilifying the other, one defined oneself and one's group (Stanton 1992, 154–55). That the Matthean Jesus speaks in a way characteristic of the entire culture, including other Jews, does not make him anti-Judaic.

A third line of reasoning is that Matthew's language, while seeming to be directed to nonmessianist opponents, is really aimed at insiders within the Matthean community (R. Smith 1992; Garland 2001, 229). The evangelist is using the technique of covert allusion. This rhetorical device is explained by Demetrius of Phaleron (*Eloc.* 5.292). "Since great lords and ladies dislike to hear their own faults mentioned, we shall therefore, when counseling them to refrain from faults, not speak in direct terms; we shall rather blame some other persons who have acted in the same manner. For example, in addressing the tyrant Dionysius, we shall inveigh against the tyrant Phalaris and the cruelty of Phalaris. . . . The hearer is admonished without feeling himself censured" (Roberts 1965). If Matt. 23 reflects covert allusion, then the evangelist's aim is to deal with the shortcomings of the Matthean community, an internal issue. The warning for the church is that its members must not be like the scribes and

Pharisees, for if God did not spare Jerusalem, God will certainly not spare an unfaithful church. This argument, however, does not really deal with the issue of the polemical language, but that has been covered by the first two points. Whether or not covert allusion was an aim of the evangelist, it can surely be used for that purpose in later Christian history.

One may conclude that Matt. 23 is not anti-Judaic in its original context. However, this language designed for a specific historical context has the potential for misuse and has been so misused in Western history. This misuse is due not to the First Evangelist but to the fallenness of those who have misused it.

Matthew 24:3–26:1a

Discourse 5: Jesus Teaches about Final Judgment

Introductory Matters

In Matt. 24:3–26:1a one meets the final large discourse of the First Gospel. Its end is signaled by the typical refrain in 26:1a ("when Jesus had finished all these sayings"). The discourse falls into two parts: 24:3–36, phases of the ultimate future, and 24:37–25:46, exhortations to vigilance in light of the last judgment. Although the first four discourses in Matthew contain some references to judgment in their concluding sections (7:23b; 10:42; 13:49; 18:35), the fifth is focused almost totally on the final judgment and its accompanying events. This focus on judgment links 24:3–26:1a closely with the fifth narrative, second part (21:1–24:2).

Where Does the Fifth Discourse Begin?

A number of introductory questions demand attention. The first is, where does the fifth discourse begin: 24:1 or 24:3? An inclusio holds 21:1–24:2 together (Mount of Olives in 21:1 and 24:3). This is reinforced by the link between 23:38 and 24:1–2 (destruction of the temple because the divine presence has departed). There is also a shift from a public audience (23:1) to a private one (24:3), much like that in 13:1 and 13:36. The focus of the material shifts from judgment on Israel in chapter 23 to the events of the end in 24:3–25:46. For these reasons, the discourse should be seen as beginning in 24:3 (Burnett 1979, 21–25).

How Many Questions Do the Disciples Ask?

How many questions do the disciples ask Jesus in 24:3 ("Tell us, when will these things be, and [*kai*] what will be the sign of your parousia and end of the age?")? Is this one question, or are there two or three? Grammatically, it is possible to read it as one question. The *kai* can be read epexegetically ("Tell us, when will this happen, that is [*kai*], what will be the sign of your parousia and the consummation of the age?" [BDAG 495.1c]). If so, then the end of the question controls the beginning of the query. In that case, there is no reference to the destruction of the temple. The focus is only on the parousia and consummation of the age (so Burnett 1979, 207). The *kai* can also be understood more naturally as a simple connection between two topics: that of the first part of the question (destruction of the temple) and that of the last (the end of this age). The key is the phrase "these things." To what does the phrase refer? The most natural reference, given the context, is to the destruction of the temple that is mentioned in 24:2. If so, then there are two questions: "When will the temple be destroyed?" is the first, and the second is "What is the sign of the end of the age or parousia?" (Gibbs 2000, 167). The attempt to find three questions (the destruction of the temple, the sign of Jesus's coming, and the end of the age) is improbable given the fact that one article controls "sign of the parousia" and "end of the age." This commentary will assume the second option, that there are two questions.

How Is the Discourse Organized?

A third issue concerns the arrangement of the little apocalypse that constitutes Jesus's answer to the two questions posed by the disciples (24:4–36). This apocalypse presents occurrences commonly thought to precede the end of the world: events on earth (24:4–28) and in heaven (24:29). The inclusion of both earthly suffering and heavenly chaos is a convention in apocalyptic literature (e.g., Rev. 8:2–11:18: earth, sea, rivers, sun, moon, stars; 15:1–16:21: earth, sea, rivers, sun; Mark 13:24–25). This means that 24:29 belongs together with 24:4–28 as occurrences believed to precede the end. If so, then "immediately [*eutheōs*] after the suffering of those days" (24:29) means no more than that heavenly chaos will follow immediately after earthly suffering. The parousia, whose duration is unspecified (*tote*, "then," 24:30), happens after the heavenly chaos.

Tracing the Narrative Flow

Phases of the Ultimate Future (24:3–36)

24:3. Matthew 24:3–36 begins with two questions asked of the sitting Jesus (24:3 [the posture of a teacher]; cf. 5:1–2) by the disciples. **Tell us, when will**

these things be? What will be the sign of your parousia and end of the age? The first asks about the time of the destruction of the temple. The second seeks to know the sign of history's end. Such questions were common in antiquity (e.g., Dan. 8:13; 12:6; 2 Esd. [4 Ezra] 4:33; 6:7; 2 Bar. 21.19).

24:4–36. Jesus's answers are given in the form of a little apocalypse (24:4–36). The answer comes in two parts: (1) the components of the end time (24:4–31) and (2) the timing of the components of the end time (24:32–36).

1. The discussion in 24:4–31 of components of the end time addresses first the occurrences commonly thought to precede the end time (24:4–29) and then the parousia itself (24:30–31).

The former are twofold: tribulations on earth (24:4–28) and chaos in heaven (24:29).

The tribulations on earth (24:4–28) are presented in an ABA' pattern:

A False Christs and prophets (24:4–14)
    B Desecration of the temple (24:15–22)
A' False Christs and prophets (24:23–28)

In section A of the occurrences on earth, warnings about false Christs come in 24:4–5, 11. **Look out for anyone who might deceive you. For many will come in my name** (come as messiah), **saying "I am the Christ," and many will be deceived. . . . And many false prophets will arise and will deceive many.** (Apostasy was believed by Jews to be one of the signs of the end time: e.g., 1 En. 91.7; T. Iss. 6.1; 1QpHab 2.5–6; 2 Esd. [4 Ezra] 5:1–2; 14:16–18.) In this context it seems that "Christs" and "prophets" are interchangeable terms (cf. 21:9, 11, where the crowds use "son of David" and "the prophet" interchangeably; also Acts 3:17–26; John 6:14–15, 30–31; T. Levi 8.15: the messiah is the prophet of the Most High).

Beginning in the early first century, there was a succession of sign-prophets who made eschatological claims for themselves: a man in Pilate's time (AD 26–36) rallied Samaritans to go with him to Mount Gerizim, where he would locate the sacred vessels that Moses had buried (Josephus, *Ant.* 18.85–87); Theudas in Fadus's time (AD 44–46) claimed to be a prophet and to be able to part the waters of the Jordan River (Josephus, *Ant.* 20.97–99); an Egyptian false prophet in the time of Felix (AD 52–60) came with his followers to the Mount of Olives, aiming to enter Jerusalem, overpower the Romans, and set himself up as king (Josephus, *J.W.* 2.261–63; *Ant.* 20.169–72); in the time of Festus (AD 60–62) a certain figure promised salvation if people would follow him into the wilderness (Josephus, *Ant.* 20.188). Jesus warns that such figures must not deceive his disciples, because the end is not yet. And the gospel of the kingdom will be proclaimed in the whole world as a witness to all the nations, and then (*tote*) the end will come (24:14). The end's arrival is only after the world mission is complete.

Section B (24:15–22) sets the fall of Jerusalem in the midst of the tribulations on earth: **When you see the abomination**

An Outline of Matthew 24:3–36

Phases of the ultimate future (24:3–36)

  The disciples' questions (24:3)

  Jesus's answers (24:4–36)

  1. **Components of the end time (24:4–31)**

     Things thought to precede the end (24:4–29)

       Occurrences on earth (24:4–28)

       (A) False Christs and prophets (24:4–14)

       (B) Desecration of the temple (24:15–22)

       (A′) False Christs and prophets (24:23–28)

       Occurrences in heaven: sun, moon, stars (24:29)

     The parousia (24:30–31)

  2. **Timing of the components (24:32–36)**

     Beginning: In this generation (24:32–35)

     Ending: Only the Father knows (24:36)

End-Time Chaos

How would an ancient auditor have heard references to chaos on earth and in the heavens? Tacitus (*Hist.* 1.2, 3) gives the following description of the first century.

> "The history on which I am entering is that of a period rich in disasters, terrible with battles, torn by civil struggles, horrible even in peace. Four emperors fell by the sword, there were three civil wars, more foreign wars, and often both at the same time. . . . Italy was distressed by disasters unknown before or returning after the lapse of the ages. . . . Beside the manifold misfortunes that befell mankind there were prodigies in the sky and on the earth, warnings given by thunderbolts, and prophecies of the future, both joyful and gloomy, uncertain and clear." (C. Moore 1925–31, cited by Garland 2001, 242)

Matthew's description of the times of suffering and heavenly chaos is remarkably similar.

of desolation, spoken about through the prophet Daniel (Dan. 9:27; 12:11), set up in the holy place (let the one who reads understand), then let those in Judea flee to the mountains (where caves offered hiding places; 24:15–16). This desecration is almost certainly a reference to the Roman conquest in AD 70, when the Roman standards were set up in the temple (Lampe 1984, 162; but Hare 1993, 275–77, disagrees). *Genesis Rabbah* 10.7 says that "when the wicked Titus entered the Holy of Holies, he dragged down the veil, blasphemed and reviled God." Josephus (*J.W.* 6.316) says gentile sacrifices were made in the temple as it burned. It was a repetition of previous such events (e.g., Antiochus Epiphanes in the second century BC [1 Macc. 1:54]; Pompey in 63 BC [*Pss. Sol.* 2.1–2]; Caligula, who tried to have a statue of himself set up in the Jerusalem temple [Josephus, *J.W.* 2.184–203; Philo, *Legat.* 188–98, 207]). When this happens, flee! **For then there will be great suffering such as has not happened from the beginning of the world until now, and never will be. And if those days were not shortened, no one would be saved** (24:21–22a). When the disciples ask about *when* the temple will be destroyed, Jesus's answer is that it is part of the tribulation events that will transpire on the earth *before* the end time.

Section A′ (24:23–28) returns to the theme of false prophets and Christs. This theme is related to what has just occurred about the destruction of the temple. The unit opens with **Then** (*tote*, i.e., at the time of the desecration of the temple) **if anyone says to you, "Behold, here is the Christ, or here," do not believe it. For false Christs and false prophets will arise, and they will perform great signs and wonders in order to deceive, if possible, even the elect** (Jesus's followers). **Behold, I have told you beforehand. If anyone should say to you, "Behold, he is in the wilderness," do not go out; "Behold, he is in the inner rooms," do not believe it** (24:23–26). Why? Two illustrations make the point that the parousia will be public and obvious. **For just as the lightning comes from the east and shines to the west, so the parousia of the son of man will be** (24:27). Everyone can see it at once. **Wherever the dead body is, there the scavenger birds will be** (24:28). From the evidence, the parousia will be obvious to anyone. (Cornutus, *Nat. d.* 21, says the birds gather wherever there are many corpses.) The fall of Jerusalem and the desecration of the temple are not the end time. Among the occurrences on the earth that are part of the tribulation are suffering (of which the destruction of Jerusalem and its temple are one part) and deception.

Finally, 24:29 provides a brief statement about occurrences in the heavens that precede the end time: **Immediately after the tribulation of those days** (the sufferings on earth), **the sun will become dark, and the moon will not give off its light, and the stars will fall from heaven, and the constellations of the heavens will be moved** (Isa. 13:10). This means that 24:29 is not a description of an epiphany (so Nolland 2005, 982) but rather a sign of cosmic chaos. The outbreak of chaos in heaven matches that on the earth.

After the earthly sufferings and deceptions and the deceptions and the heavenly chaos, **then** (*tote*) **the sign of the son of man will be manifest in the heaven** (24:30a). (Note: the parousia occurs *after* the tribulation!) What is this sign? Of the various options, the two best alternatives are either the son of man himself (cf. Isa. 11:10, 12; so Schnackenburg 2002, 244) or the ensign, or standard, of the messiah. Perhaps they are two sides of one coin. In *1 En.* 62.5, when humans see the son of man sitting on his glorious throne, everyone will recognize him and be like women in travail. Matthew 24:30b is an expansion of the same point: **They will see the son of man coming on the clouds of heaven** (Dan. 7:13) **with great power and glory.** The throne of the son of man is the cloud chariot on which Yahweh rides (cf. Ezek. 1 and 10). The sign of the parousia is the son of man's appearing in heaven, riding on the throne chariot of Yahweh. The function of the parousia emphasized here is the gathering of the elect from the four winds (24:31). At this point, the first part of the Matthean Jesus's little apocalypse is finished. He has covered both the components of the events that precede the parousia and the coming of the son of man.

The Sign of the Son of Man

In the Jewish scriptures are two types of signs: the signs that legitimate prophets and the sign that heralds the beginning of a war. Matthew 16:1 echoes the former, Matt. 24:30–31 the latter. The latter was a totem set up on a hill to gather the peoples together for battle (e.g., Jer. 51:27; Isa. 5:26; 13:2–4; 18:3). In Isa. 11:10 the totem is said to be raised at the time of future salvation. It will be not a pole but a Davidic king. The results of the signal will be the gathering together of the dispersed people of God (11:11–12) and the judgment of the nations (11:13–15). This seems to be the background for understanding the sign of the son of man in Matt. 24:30–31. The son of man's coming in the heavenly throne chariot is the signal of the time of salvation. With it is associated the gathering of the elect and the mourning of the tribes of the earth (Draper 1993).

2. What is left to cover in this little apocalypse is the *timing* of the components of the end time (24:32–36). Matthew 24:32–35 consists of two basic promises: 24:32–33 and 24:34–35.

The first promise is in the form of a parable (24:32) and its interpretation (24:33): **From the fig tree learn the parable. When its branch is already tender and it puts forth leaves, you know that summer is at hand. So also, when you see all these things, you will know that he is at hand, at the gates.** In Palestine most trees are evergreen and keep their leaves throughout the winter. The almond and fig trees are exceptions. The almond tree loses its leaves in winter and sprouts early in the spring. The fig tree also loses it leaves in the winter but does not sprout until late spring. Its budding, then, signals the approach of summer (Gundry 1982, 490). Just as the budding of the fig tree signals that summer is near, so too the events of the tribulation and cosmic chaos (24:4–28, 29; Davies and Allison 1997, 3:366) signal that the parousia is at hand.

The second promise consists of a prophecy (24:34) and a guarantee (24:35). The prophecy runs, **Truly I say to you, this generation** (the generation then living; Matt. 11:16; 12:39, 45; 16:4; 23:36) **will not pass away until all these things begin to occur** (*genetai*). Three issues are raised by this translation. First, to what does **all these things** refer? Given the context, it must refer to the same things as those in 24:33, namely, the tribulation and cosmic chaos that precede the parousia (24:4–28, 29; Keener 1999, 589, says the desolation of the temple). It is not a reference to the parousia (Turner 2008, 586). Second, how should **this generation** be understood? The most obvious reference is to the generation to whom Jesus speaks (Turner 2008, 586). Third, how should the verb *genetai* be understood? This verb has been translated here as an ingressive aorist (where the stress is on the beginning of the action). So understood, this says that the events of the tribulation (including the fall of Jerusalem) have begun to happen in this generation. It does not say either that the parousia will occur in this generation or that the tribulation will have been completed in this generation. It prophesies that the tribulation events will begin within this generation's time span. The guarantee (24:35) runs, **The heaven and the earth will pass away, but my words will not pass away.** Jesus's words have a duration as great as or greater than the words of the law (cf. 5:18). Let the reader count on the certainty of Jesus's promises. This includes the start of the tribulation events in the lifetime of his audience.

Finally, 24:36 addresses the timing of the parousia and the end of the age. **Now concerning that day and hour, no one knows—neither the angels of heaven nor the Son—except the Father only.** The exact time of the parousia is known only to God the Father (cf. Mark 13:32; Acts 1:6–7). Verse 36 functions in a dual capacity. It is both the conclusion to the first part of the eschatological discourse (24:3–36: prediction, having to do with "those days") and the beginning of the second part (24:36–25:46: parenesis, having to do with "that day").

Exhortations to Vigilance (24:37–25:46)

Matthew 24:37–25:46 (which really begins with 24:36, as noted above) consists of parabolic material that is used to exhort vigilance in light of the last judgment. The pattern is ABA′B′C. The point of A and A′ is to *be ready* because the time of parousia and judgment is unknown. The point of B and B′ is to *be faithful* to your assigned task in the interval before the parousia and judgment. The point of C is to *be aware* of the criterion used at the last judgment.

(A) **24:37–44.** Section A (24:37–44; cf. Luke 17:26–27, 34–35; 12:39–40) is made up of several parabolic images: the people in the days of Noah (24:37–39; cf. *1 En.* 67.8–10; Josephus, *Ant.* 1.72–76), two working in the field and two grinding meal (24:40–42), and the house-holder and the thief (24:43–44). All speak of how judgment is coming: unexpectedly. In Noah's time, the people were eating and drinking, marrying and giving in marriage (common ventures of life), completely un-aware of the flood that came upon them. The two in the field and the two grind-ing meal are at work (common ventures of life), totally unaware that a separation is about to be made. The ones taken are those snatched away by judgment (With-erington 2006, 455; cf. Matt. 13:41–42: tares taken, wheat left). The householder is asleep (a common experience of life), unaware that the thief is about to break into his abode. The conclusion in 24:44 applies to all of the above: **Because of this, you must be prepared, because you do not know the hour in which the son of man is coming.** (In *b. Sanh.* 97a, Rabbi Zera says

> ### An Outline of Matthew 24:37–25:46
>
> **Exhortations to vigilance (24:37–25:46)**
>
> (A) Be prepared for the unex-pected coming of the Lord (24:37–44)
>
> (B) Be faithful in your tasks until the coming of the Lord (24:45–51)
>
> (A′) Be prepared for the unex-pected coming of the Lord (25:1–13)
>
> (B′) Be faithful in your tasks until the coming of the Lord (25:14–30)
>
> (C) The last judgment (25:31–46)

that three come when the mind is diverted: the messiah, a found article, and a scorpion.)

(B) **24:45–51.** Sections B (24:45–51; cf. Luke 12:42–46) and B′ (25:14–30) make the point: be faithful to your assigned tasks in the interval between Jesus's res-urrection and parousia. There are other parallels between the two parables. In 24:45–51 the characters are servants set over a household; in 25:14–30 they are servants entrusted with property. In both the master is gone for a long time. In both the outcome for faithlessness is dire. In both the reward for faithfulness is the granting of enlarged responsibility. Some scholars see the first parable as directed to leaders of communities (Gundry 1982, 495; Gnilka 1988, 2:345; Hare 1993, 283, claims this is the consensus reading; Schnackenburg 2002, 248, however, thinks it addresses all Christians). If it is directed to leaders, then this avoids the possible issue of legalistic soteriology that is found nowhere else in Matthew. The matter is rather akin to that in 1 Cor. 3:5–15, where the judgment has to do with ministers entrusted with a task of feeding the household. If they are found faithful, they receive a reward.

In B there is a contrast between two groups, similar to the wise and fool-ish maidens in A′ (25:1–13). On the one hand, the faithful and wise slave is assigned the task of making sure the other slaves are properly fed. When the master comes and finds him doing this, he is rewarded with more responsibil-ity. On the other hand, the evil slave, because his master is delayed, begins to mistreat his fellow slaves and to associate with the wrong people (cf. Ezek.

34:1–3 [shepherds who have not fed the people]; Amos 8:11–12; Jer. 5:30–31; 23:11–15; Ezek. 13:6–9 [false prophets]). The lord comes on a day and at an hour that are unexpected and finds this misbehavior. The slave's punishment is severe. This is not an allegory. The analogy is simply between faithful and unfaithful slaves and their Christian equivalents and between the principle of rewards and punishments that apply to certain types of behavior. There are limits to the analogy—the returning son of man does not cut anyone in two! Though there are similarities between the lord and Jesus, there is not a one-to-one equivalency. The point of the parable is to be responsible in the tasks assigned for the interim because one does not know the day or hour. Christian leaders, take note.

Imminence and Delay of the Parousia

Two eschatological trajectories run through earliest Christianity. One speaks about the nearness of the parousia. For example, in 1 Thess. 4:15 and 1 Cor. 15:52, Paul seems to believe that he will be alive when the Lord returns. First Peter 4:7 says the end of all things is near; James 5:8–9 says the Lord is near, the judge is standing at the doors; Heb. 10:36–39 claims that in a little while he will come; in Rev. 22:12, 20 the risen Christ says that he is coming soon; *Did.* 10.6 prays, "Lord, come quickly"; *1 Clem.* 23.5 promises the he will come quickly and not delay; *Barn.* 21.3 says the Lord is near, and 4.3 that the final stumbling block is at hand so the Beloved may make haste and come; Herm. *Vis.* 3.8.9 says that when the tower is finished, the end will come—it will quickly be built. Matthew 24:33 is closest to *Barn.* 4.3. Both seem to believe that the tribulation either has begun or is about to begin. The parousia follows the tribulation. In Matthew this does not, however, imply imminence of the parousia.

The other trajectory echoes concerns about the delay of the parousia: James 5:7 calls for patience until the parousia, which really is near; Heb. 10:36–39 urges the need for endurance because the coming really will be soon. Both *1 Clem.* 23.3 and *2 Clem.* 11.2 refer to the complaint that the promise about an imminent end was known to the forefathers, and now the complainers are old and nothing has happened. To this *1 Clem.* 23.5 says the coming really will be without delay, and *2 Clem.* 12.1, 6 says the parousia will occur when sexual differentiation is transcended. Second Peter 3:4, 8–10 quotes a complaining question about the delayed parousia and reassures readers that one day is as a thousand years to the Lord. Matthew 24:48–49; 25:5; and 25:19 all seem to refer to a delay in the Lord's return. The First Gospel does not promise imminence. It denies that anyone knows the day or the hour except the Father. The closest this Gospel comes to a promise of imminence is the statement in 24:33 that the tribulation will begin in this generation. There is no promise about how long the tribulation lasts. The parousia will come after the tribulation (24:33) and after the mission to the nations (24:14). Exactly when this will be, only the Father knows.

(A′) **25:1–13.** Section A′ (25:1–13 is only in Matthew; but cf. Luke 12:35–36; 13:25–27) is a parable directed to disciples (24:3–4). Verse 1 is the heading or introduction. Verse 13 reflects the evangelist's lens for reading the story. Perhaps the most difficult matter in the interpretation of this parable is discerning the cultural conventions assumed by the story. The most probable scenario runs like this. The bride is still at her house awaiting the bridegroom's arrival to take her to his parents' house. He is delayed by the final bargaining. The maidens are the bride's companions, who will accompany the couple to their destination, lighting the way. The trimmed lamps are rags wrapped around sticks dipped in oil and set aflame for the first time when the bridegroom arrives. These maidens go into the bridegroom's house, dance until their torches go out, and then retire to another room (Lambrecht 1991, 158–59). Within the introduction (25:1) and the conclusion (25:13), the story tells of five wise and five foolish maidens. The wise bring enough oil with them; the foolish do not. So when the bridegroom finally arrives, only the five wise maidens get to accompany the bride and bridegroom to the house and to enter into the feasting of the wedding celebration. This is usually taken as an allegorical parable in which the maidens represent rank-and-file disciples of Jesus who are waiting for the parousia; the bridegroom is Jesus (cf. 9:15); his delay is the delay of the parousia (cf. 24:48; 25:19); the oil stands for good deeds that are done in obedience to the Father's will, as found in Jesus's teachings (cf. 7:24–27; 12:50; 22:11–14; *Num. Rab.* 13.15–16 says study of the law must be mingled with oil [good deeds]); having sufficient oil echoes enduring to the end (cf. 24:13); the marriage feast is the life of the world to come (cf. 8:11–12); the shut door represents the finality of judgment (cf. 2 Esd. [*4 Ezra*] 7:102–5, 111).

The evangelist's conclusion (25:13) tells the reader how to view the story: **Watch, therefore, because you do not know the day nor the hour.** "For Matthew, then, this parable is exclusively a depiction of the end-time judgment, not a model for ethical or righteous behavior on the part of the 'wise' young women or the bridegroom" (Balabanski 2002, 93). The single focus in this context in no way relativizes the demand for justice in the present. Indeed, the call to watch in 25:13 is precisely that, a call to right behavior in the interim between Jesus's resurrection and parousia. "The parable is an allegory about spiritual preparedness, not a lesson on the golden rule" (Garland 2001, 240). Together with 24:37–44 (A), then, 25:1–13 (A′) makes the point that the unknown time of the parousia and last judgment calls for ongoing spiritual preparedness. Be ready because the time of judgment is unknown.

(B′) **25:14–30.** Section B′ (25:14–30; cf. Luke 19:12–27) is another parable calling for faithfulness in the interim. Although usually regarded as aimed at Christians generally, it is better seen as directed to disciples who have been given special gifts (Hare 1993, 286–88). For Matthew, the parable challenges disciples to make use of the gifts that God has entrusted to them. The matter is that reflected in 1 Pet. 4:10 ("Like good stewards of the manifold grace of

God, serve one another with whatever gift each of you has received"); Rom. 12:6 ("Having gifts that differ according to the grace given to us, let us use them" [RSV]); 1 Cor. 12:7; and Eph. 4:7. The story unfolds as the man entrusts his property to three slaves before he departs on a journey. To one he gives five talents (6000 denarii), to the second he gives two, and to the third he gives one, **to each according to his own ability** (25:15). Not all have the same gifts. While he is gone, the first doubles his money, as does the second, while the third digs a hole in the ground and hides his talent.

Certain customs are assumed. First, it is not odd for a master to entrust slaves with property or money. Second, if one accepts a deposit and buries it immediately, one is not liable for loss. Burial of treasure was regarded as the best security against theft (*m. B. Metzi'a*). Third, the first principle of business is to bring increase to the master's resources. When the man returns, he finds that the first two slaves have doubled their money. He praises them and promises to put them in charge of much more. The third, who buried his money, returns it intact. This brings condemnation from the master and removal of his one talent, which is now given to the one with ten talents.

The summary explanation offered in 25:29 is one heard earlier in 13:12: **To those who have, it will be given, and they will be abundantly enriched, but to those who do not have, even what they have will be taken away from them.** Many allegorical elements have been recognized in the story. The master is Jesus, the servants are Jesus's disciples, the talents are special gifts given to the disciples, the absence of the master is the interim between the first and second comings of Jesus, "after a long time" refers to the delay of the parousia, the settling of accounts is the last judgment, and the criterion of evaluation is active, responsible use of one's gifts. The point of the parable, then, is to be faithful in the use of the gifts given to you in the interim, while you await the return of the master.

(C) **25:31–46.** Section C (25:31–46; unique to Matthew) focuses on the last judgment. Some say this story is not a parable but a word picture of the last judgment (Davies and Allison 1997, 3:418), a typical judgment scene (Gnilka 1986–88, 2:367), a revelation discourse (Catchpole 1979), or an apocalyptic drama (Boring 1995, 8:455). Others regard it as an apocalyptic parable akin to the Similitudes of Enoch (*1 En.* 37–71, especially *1 En.* 62, called a parable in 58.1). Since such pictures of the last judgment involving the son of man (who is also called king) are labeled parables by *1 En.* 37–71, it seems natural to use the term "parable" for Matt. 25:31–46. **When the son of man comes in his glory and all the angels with him, then he will sit on the throne of his glory** (25:31; cf. 16:27; 19:28). The background for this image seems to be found in *1 En.* 45.3; 51.3; 55.4; 61.8; 62.2–3, where the son of man sits on the divine throne in order to carry out the last judgment. **And he will assemble all the nations before him, and he will divide them from one another, as the shepherd divides the sheep from the goats, and he will place the sheep on his right and the goats on the left** (25:32–33).

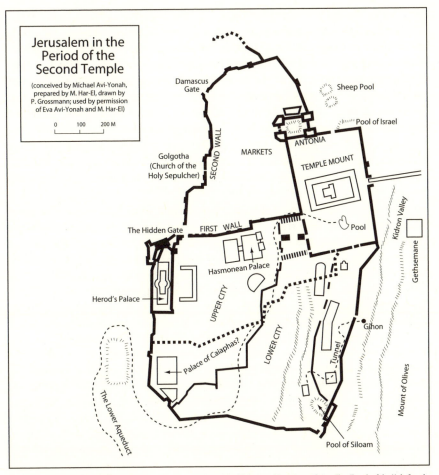

Figure 15. Map of Jerusalem showing the location of the temple and the likely site of Jesus's crucifixion. The Church of the Holy Sepulchre is outside the city walls of that time.

Who are **all the nations**? The simplest reading would be all humans who are not part of the elect (cf. 24:31 with 25:32). Keep in mind that instruction by parables does not necessarily give a total picture in a systematic theological fashion but rather focuses on one or another aspect of the total picture. Here the judgment of the people of God is not in view. That has been covered in 24:36–25:30. In view here is the judgment of the nations, those not of the people of God (cf. 28:19; 13:41, 43). What is the criterion of judgment at the last day for the nonelect? To the sheep the king says, **Come, blessed ones of my Father, inherit the kingdom prepared for you from the foundation of the world. For I was hungry and you gave me to eat, I was thirsty and you gave me a drink, I was a stranger and you gave me hospitality, naked and you clothed** me, I was sick and you cared for me, I was in prison and you came to see me (25:34–36). The righteous are perplexed and want to know when they have done all these things (25:37–39). Their perplexity is due to their failure to understand the link between Christ and his followers. This bond is clarified. The king answers, **Truly I say to you, inasmuch as you served one of the least of these my brethren, you served me** (25:40). The process is repeated with those on the left hand, the goats, who did not so act. They are also perplexed and want to know when they did not do these things for the judge. Again, the link between Christ and his followers is not perceived. The judge explains, **Truly I tell you, inasmuch as you did not serve one of the least of these, neither did you serve me** (25:45). On the basis of this criterion, the nations are separated for punishment or eternal life (25:46).

The key question here is the identity of **the least of these my brethren.** There are basically two traditions of interpretation. On the one hand, there are those who regard "the least" as everyone in need (cf. Prov. 19:17, but this refers to the poor of the in-group). If so, then the criterion at the last judgment is whether or not one has ministered to the universal host of needy. A passage from *Midr. Teh.* (5.17 on Ps. 118) illustrates this mind-set:

> *Open to me the gates of righteousness* (Ps. 118:19). When a man is asked in the world-to-come: "What was thy work?" and he answers: "I fed the hungry," it will be said to him: . . . Enter. . . . When a man answers: "I gave drink to the thirsty," it will be said to him: . . . Enter. . . . When a man answers: "I clothed the naked," it will be said to him: . . . Enter. . . . And David said: I have done all these things. Therefore let all the gates be opened for me. (Braude 1959, 2:243)

On the other hand, others see "the least" as Jesus's disciples, possibly missionaries to the nations (cf. *Did.* 12.1). If so, then the criterion at the judgment is how the nations have treated Jesus's emissaries. Any decision must be made on the basis of the evidence from the Matthean narrative world. "My brethren" is a term used in the First Gospel for a member of an in-group (12:50; 18:15, 21, 35; 23:8; 28:10 for the in-group of the community of Jesus's disciples; 5:22 for the in-group of Jews). In the context of Matt. 24:3–26:1, Jesus is addressing his disciples privately (24:3). The reference to brethren must be to Jesus's disciples as an in-group. "The least of these" is a superlative of "little ones." In Matt. 10:42; 18:6, 10, 14, the little ones are clearly disciples. In 10:42, they are missionaries who have suffered persecution. "Even the least of the little ones" most naturally refers to disciples, possibly missionaries (cf. 10:14–15). If this is the preferred reading, then the Matthean Jesus is saying that when the son of man comes, the criterion of judgment is how the nonbelievers have treated his in-group (e.g., Michaels 1965; Christian 1975; Lambrecht 1972, 309–42; Gundry 1982, 511; Gray 1989; Hagner 1993, 1:746; Garland 2001, 248; Witherington 2006, 466).

Why? Because Jesus is so identified with these little ones that any treatment of them is at the same time treatment of him and of the Father (10:40). It was a widespread belief in antiquity that how a deity's followers were treated was how the deity regarded himself/herself being treated. Two examples from the Greco-Roman world suffice. Euripides (*Bacch.* 784–95) says that any deity is injured if his followers are attacked. Achilles Tatius (*Leuc. Clit.* 8.2.2–3) tells that the goddess Artemis was so closely identified with her worshipers that when one of her suppliants was assaulted in the presence of her altar, it was like attacking Artemis herself (cf. also 7.14.6). Jewish examples are legion. Joel 3:1–3, 6–8, says that Yahweh punishes the nations because they have mistreated Israel. *First Enoch* 62.11 speaks about judgment on oppressors of God's children and elect ones. Philo (*Decal.* 119) says that the one who dishonors the servant dishonors the Lord. *Second Baruch* 72.4–6 says that every nation that did not mistreat Israel will be spared at the judgment (Stanton 1992, 164–65). The *Apocalypse of Abraham* 31.2 explicitly cites as the criterion of the last judgment how the nations treated God's people. Early Christian sources speak with the same voice. In Acts 9:4; 22:7; and 26:14, the risen Christ asks, "Saul, why are you persecuting me?" The risen Christ is so identified with his church that persecution of them is abuse of Christ (cf. Luke 10:16; 1 Cor. 8:11–12). How one treats Christ's followers determines one's outcome at the judgment (2 Thess. 1:6–7). This identification between Christ and his followers is so great that hospitality to God's people is regarded as a demonstration of faith (cf. Heb. 11:31 and James 2:25: Rahab; Acts 16:30–34: Philippian jailer; John 4:40–43: Samaritans).

The Concluding Refrain (26:1a)

At the end of the fifth discourse comes the customary refrain: **And it came to pass when Jesus finished all these sayings** (26:1a). The five big discourses are behind us. Now the passion narrative begins (26:1b–28:20).

Salvation by Works?

Does Matthew advocate salvation by works? The First Gospel's stance is that one enters the community of Jesus's disciples by grace. The Sermon on the Mount is addressed to those who are already disciples of Jesus. In Matt. 13:11 the disciples are told that their position is due to the fact that "to you it has been given to know the secrets of the kingdom of heaven" (NRSV). In Matt. 16:16–17 we hear that the Christian confession is due to God's revelation. In Matt. 20:1–16 grace, not works, is viewed as decisive. Also here in Matt. 25:31–46, properly interpreted, there is no support for works righteousness. Judgment is based on one's actions in response to the proclamation of the gospel, because that is a response to Jesus.

Functions of the Unit as a Whole

When Quintilian (*Inst.* 3.7.15) described ways of constructing an encomium (giving praise), he spoke of two paths. One was to trace a person's life, words, and deeds in chronological order from birth to death and after. The other was to bring together materials from different periods of the hero's life under key virtues. One such virtue included deeds of body and fortune. Although the evangelist is silent about the category of body, he does deal with matters of fortune, such as being a recipient of esoteric knowledge and unique power (e.g., 11:20–23; 13:54, 58; 14:2). Matthew 24–25 has Jesus speak about esoteric eschatological knowledge and claim unique power for himself in doing so. In this, as in other ways, Matt. 24–25 continues the First Gospel's presentation of an encomium of Jesus (Neyrey 1998).

Taken as a whole, 24:3–36 eliminates both an overrealized eschatology and a date-calculating imminent eschatology as options for Jesus's disciples. Taken as a whole, 24:36–25:46 draws out the practical implications of eschatology for Jesus's disciples. All disciples, since they do not know the day or hour of the son of man's return, have an incentive to live perpetually in a spiritually prepared state. If one is a leader in the congregation, it is important to feed the other servants and deny any tendency to self-indulgence. If one has spiritual gifts, then it is important to use them responsibly and profitably. What one does not use, one loses. All of Jesus's disciples should be aware that, because of their identification with Jesus, their reception by nondisciples is a determining criterion at the last judgment. From this, disciples may take encouragement and be bold.

Performative language includes promises, certain types of questions, and verbal icons. The First Gospel contains these types of performative language within its presentation of the teaching of Jesus. To these types must now be added both warnings and consolations. A warning not only conveys information but also is a catalyst for precautionary action. Consolation not only provides information but also is a catalyst for being comforted. In Matt. 24–25 both of these types (warning, consolation) are found as part of eschatological discourse. The dangers of the tribulation and the uncertainness of the end constitute a warning, sometimes expressed (watch [24:42; 25:13]; be ready [24:44]), sometimes inferred. The expressed or implied warnings function as catalysts for the disciples' spiritual wakefulness. The depiction of the last judgment in 25:31–46 is consolation for Jesus's followers who bear their witness in a hostile world. This consolation functions to provide comfort, assurance, and confidence of their ultimate vindication.

Theological Issues

In order to understand the eschatologies of early Christian messianists, one must begin with a sketch of non-Christian Jewish eschatologies. In ancient

278

Judaism, there were two very different eschatologies (views of the ideal future): the prophetic and the apocalyptic. In prophetic eschatology, the golden future was viewed as occurring on this earth within time and space as we know them and involving those who are alive when the golden age arrives (e.g., Jer. 16:14–15; 23:5–8; *Pss. Sol.* 17; 18; *T. Reu.* 6.10–12; *T. Sim.* 5.5; *T. Levi* 8.11–15; *Sib. Or.* 3.701–61, 767–95). A restored Davidic kingdom was often central to this hope. In this scheme, evil was regarded as a problem that could be corrected through proper discipline administered by God. Jeremiah serves as a good example. His message began, "Israel has sinned." The indictment was followed by "Judgment is coming." It was a this-worldly judgment. His message continued: "A foreign nation, Babylon, will come against Judah, defeat it in war, and take the chief citizens away into exile." There was also a word of hope: "After seventy years, those who are alive when the return from exile takes place will be allowed to return to their own land and live under their own king in peace and prosperity." Here in Jeremiah, evil is understood to be like a child's misdirection that can be corrected by proper judgment/discipline. This is an optimistic view of evil.

Apocalyptic eschatology took its character from the time of the Seleucid rule of the Jews in the second century BC. Antiochus Epiphanes structured life in such a way that to be a faithful Jew meant economic disaster and possible death. To be faithless to the law, however, enabled economic success and an untroubled life. Within this type of context, the apocalyptic writers' word about the present was that this present evil age is dominated by Satan, infected by sin, and infused with suffering and death. Because of this evil, judgment is certain. Since evil is so deep-seated and radical, it cannot be dealt with by this-worldly judgment. Rather, judgment takes the form of the end of the world. God simply wipes the slate clean and starts afresh. He will not allow evil to possess immortality, so he brings the entire historical process to an end. In apocalyptic literature, judgment takes the form of the last judgment, the end of the world. The golden future is seen in terms of new heavens and earth that are created by God and in which righteousness dwells. Only those whom God raises from the dead will have a share in this new world (e.g., Dan. 12; *T. Mos.* 10). This is a pessimistic view of evil. Evil is a mystery that only God can resolve in any ultimate way.

In some circles, there was an attempt to reconcile these two eschatologies. This synthesis treated the prophetic eschatology's vision of the future as a temporary messianic kingdom on earth prior to the eternal kingdom of God but beyond the resurrection from the dead (e.g., *1 En.* 91; 2 Esd. [*4 Ezra*] 7; *2 Bar.* 29–30; *2 En.* 3). When the Jesus movement appeared, these three forms of Jewish eschatology existed side by side. The latter two forms of Jewish eschatology had in common a belief in resurrection from the dead. From their perspective, there was only one resurrection: the general resurrection.

The early Christian form of Judaism confessed that Jesus had been raised from the dead (e.g., 1 Cor. 15:3–5). This forced a major shift in their eschatology. With the resurrection of Jesus, the general resurrection had begun. One man had been raised; the rest would be raised in the future. In the language of Paul, "Christ has been raised from the dead, the first fruits of those who have died. . . . Christ the first fruits, then at his coming those who belong to Christ" (1 Cor. 15:20, 23). The followers of the risen Jesus believed they lived where the ages overlapped. The new age had broken in with Jesus's resurrection; the old age continued until Jesus's parousia. Between Jesus's resurrection and his parousia, he reigns from heaven while defeating God's enemies (1 Cor. 15:24–26).

This early Christian Jewish apocalyptic perspective contained two forms of eschatology: the basic apocalyptic scheme (e.g., 1 Cor. 15) and the synthetic three-stage pattern, with a temporary messianic kingdom on earth before the eternal kingdom of God (found only in Rev. 20:1–6 in the NT). In Rev. 20:1–6 the thousand-year reign without the deceiver and with God's will for history made perfectly clear shows that God deals with humans to leave them without excuse. Earlier visions in Revelation show that the tribulation/judgment within history, designed to elicit repentance from humans, has failed (Rev. 9:20–21; 16:9, 11, 21). In vision seven, in which Rev. 20:1–6 is set, God goes to great lengths. He binds the deceiver and sets up a period of time in which his will is perfectly clear and obvious to all. The hope is that this will elicit the repentance of the nations. Alas, it is to no avail. When the deceiver is set free, he still finds the hearts of humans responsive to his seductions. The millennium, then, functions to prove that humans cannot blame their sinfulness on their environment or circumstances. The radical evil of the human heart is exposed. Humans are without excuse.

However, the earlier visions of the end time in Revelation have no millennium (4:1–8:1; 8:2–11:18; 11:19–13:18; 14:1–20; 15:1–16:21; 17:1–19:5). These visions reflect the basic apocalyptic eschatology in 1 Cor. 15. This means that in the Apocalypse to John, the two different forms of apocalyptic eschatology lie side by side. This is also found in non-Christian Jewish apocalypses. For example, 2 *Baruch* contains seven visions (1.1–9.2; 10.1–20.6; 21.1–34.1; 35.1–47.1; 47.2–52.7; 53.1–77.17; 77.18–87.1). Visions 3 and 4 contain a temporary messianic kingdom prior to the eternal kingdom of God, whereas visions 5 and 6 do not. Vision 5 reflects the basic apocalyptic pattern, and vision 6 reflects prophetic eschatology. The three types of Jewish eschatology lie side by side in one document. The diversity offered in the visions of the end is analogous to the diversity of the OT's portrayals of creation (e.g., Gen. 1:1–2:4; 2:4–24; Pss. 74:12–17; 104). Neither the biblical depictions of our origins nor those of our ultimate destiny reflect any uniformity in details. Poetic portrayals vary, as they emphasize first the one and then another theological aspect of the whole truth about our origins or destiny (Talbert 1994, 70–71, 93–97).

The eschatology of Matthew reflects the same basic apocalyptic pattern found in Paul and in the early visions of Revelation. The First Gospel knows nothing of a millennium. Its eschatology cannot be harmonized with Rev. 20:1–6. Nor does it know anything about a rapture.

Matthew 26:1b–28:20

Passion and Resurrection Narrative

Introductory Matters

The final large thought unit in the First Gospel is Matt. 26–28, the narrative of Jesus's passion and resurrection. In Matt. 26–28, assuming the two-source theory, the evangelist follows his principal source, Mark, closely. To Mark's narrative Matthew adds the following (Brown 1994, 1:59):

Judas's demise (27:3–10)

Pilate's wife's dream (27:19)

Pilate's washing his hands while the people accept responsibility for Jesus's death (27:24–25)

tombs opened and many bodies of holy ones raised (27:51–53)

the guard at the tomb (27:62–66)

an appearance to the women (28:9–10)

the report of the guard (28:11–15)

the appearance to the Eleven in Galilee, together with the Great Commission (28:16–20)

Matthew lacks only a few items from Mark's narrative: the naked flight of the young man (Mark 14:51–52), the second cock crow (14:30, 72), the names of the sons of Simon (15:21b), and Pilate's amazement that Jesus has already died (15:44–45). To convey his distinctive perspective, the First Evangelist often shapes the individual pericopes that he has taken over (e.g., Matt. 26:52: "All those taking a sword will perish by a sword"; 27:57: Joseph of Arimathea, "who was also a disciple of Jesus"). Matthew's passion-and-resurrection narrative is both based on an earlier tradition (Mark, assuming the two-source theory) and shaped by the evangelist to convey a distinctive message for another time and place.

The basic problem that must be settled before reading Matthew's passion narrative is how the evangelist has organized his material in these chapters. There are two basic views of the evangelist's organizational principle: first, the chronological, and second, the thematic cluster type. Eugene Boring (1995, 461–62; cf. also Senior 1998, 287–88) is an example of the former; John Nolland (2005, 1042–43, 1243) and John Paul Heil (1991a, 2–3) of the latter.

Boring sees a seven-day scheme governing Jesus's time in Jerusalem:

Day 1 (Monday; 21:1–17)
Day 2 (Tuesday; 21:18–25:46)
Day 3 (Wednesday; 26:1–16)
Day 4 (Thursday; 26:17–75)
Day 5 (Friday; 27:1–61)
Day 6 (Saturday; 27:62–66)
Day 7 (Sunday; 28:1–20)

The passion narrative comprises the last five days of the week in Jerusalem.

Nolland (2005; adapting Fiedler 1991) sees seven scenes (in **bold**) with frames:

Part 1:
    A Passover is near (26:1b–2)
      B Conspiracy to do away with Jesus (26:3–5)
        C **Anointing in Bethany** (26:6–13)
      B′ Judas's offer to betray Jesus (26:14–16)
    A′ Preparations for Passover (26:17–19)
Part 2:
    A Announcement of the betrayal (26:20–25)
      B **The Last Supper** (26:26–29 [30])
    A′ Announcement of the coming denial (26:[30] 31–35)
Part 3:
    A Jesus and disciples in Gethsemane (26:36–37)
      B **Three sessions of Jesus's private prayer** (26:38–44)
    A′ Jesus and disciples in Gethsemane (26:45–46)
Part 4:
    A The betrayal (26:47–56)
      B **Jesus before the council** (26:57–68; 27:1–2)
    A′ The denial (26:69–75)

Part 5:
  A The fate of the betrayer (27:3–10)
  B **Jesus before Pilate** (27:11–26)
  A′ The abuse of the soldiers (27:27–31)
Part 6:
  A The crucifixion by soldiers (27:32–38)
  B Ridicule of Jesus (27:39–44)
    C **Jesus's death on the cross** (27:45–53)
  B′ Affirmation of Jesus (27:54–61)
  A′ The soldiers secure the tomb (27:62–66)
Part 7:
  A What actually took place (28:1–10)
  B **Explanation of a false view** (28:11–15)
  A′ What actually took place (28:16–20)

Heil (1991a) sees Matt. 26–28 fashioned into three sections (26:1–56; 26:57–27:54; 27:55–28:20), each with three parts and following an ABA′ pattern:

Section 1: Jesus prepares for and accepts his death (26:1–56)

(1) A 26:1–5
   B 26:6–13
  A′ 26:14–16

(2) A 26:17–19
   B 26:20–25
  A′ 26:26–29

(3) A 26:30–35
   B 26:36–46
  A′ 26:47–56

Section 2: The innocent Jesus dies as true king and son of God (26:57–27:54)

(1) A 26:57–58
   B 26:59–68
  A′ 26:69–75

(2) A 27:1–2
   B 27:3–10
  A′ 27:11–14

(3) A 27:15–26
     B 27:27–44
  A′ 27:45–54

Section 3: The authority of the risen Jesus prevails through witnesses (27:55–28:20)

(1) A 27:55–56
     B 27:57–60
  A′ 27:61

(2) A 27:62–66
     B 28:1
  A′ 28:2–4

(3) A 28:5–10
     B 28:11–15
  A′ 28:16–20

The first thing that becomes apparent is that the chronological scheme of days does not match up well with the arrangement into scenes. The next thing that surfaces is that the chronological scheme does not match up well with Matthew's emphases. The amount of material relegated to a particular day or days may be extravagant or spare. The third thing is that whereas the scenes seem reasonable at points, at other places the material does not balance in the frames, and at times the center point/scene is clearly not where the evangelist's emphasis is to be found. This leads to another suggestion involving an editing of the two schemes of scenes.

There are, I suggest, seven units that make up the Matthean passion narrative: 26:1b–19; 26:20–35; 26:36–46; 26:47–27:2; 27:3–26; 27:27–61; 27:62–28:20.

Matthew 26:1b–28:20 in the Narrative Flow

Birth narratives (1:1–2:23)

Jesus's ministry begins (3:1–8:1)

Jesus's authority is revealed (8:2–11:1)

Jesus's ministry creates division (11:2–13:53)

Jesus focuses on his disciples (13:54–19:2)

Jesus and judgment (19:3–26:1a)

▶ Passion and resurrection narrative (26:1b–28:20)

  Scene 1: The approach of passover (26:1b–19)

  Scene 2: The final meal (26:20–35)

  Scene 3: Prayer in the garden (26:36–46)

  Scene 4: Betrayal and trial (26:47–27:2)

  Scene 5: Trial before Pilate (27:3–26)

  Scene 6: Crucifixion (27:27–61)

  Scene 7: Resurrection (27:62–28:20)

Tracing the Narrative Flow

Scene 1: The Approach of Passover (26:1b–19)

The first scene in Matthew's passion narrative is 26:1b–19. It falls into an ABCB′A′ pattern:

A Passover is near (26:1b–2)
    B Plot to arrest Jesus (26:3–5)
        C Anointing (proleptic preparation for burial; 26:6–13)
    B′ Judas joins the plot (26:14–16)
A′ Passover preparations (26:17–19)

(A) **26:1b–2.** Section A, the Passover prediction, differs from Mark (14:1a) and Luke (22:1) in presentation. In Mark and Luke, the narrator says Passover is at hand; in Matthew, Jesus speaks: **You** (pl.) **know that after two days Passover is coming, and the son of man is being delivered up to be crucified** (26:2, yet another passion prediction; cf. 16:21; 17:12b, 22–23; 20:18–19). This shift to first person makes Jesus's words a prophecy. He knows what is about to happen.

(B) **26:3–5.** In section B, the plot to arrest Jesus, the prophecy begins to be fulfilled. **Then the chief priests and the elders of the people** (*laou*) **were gathered together at the palace of the chief priest, called Caiaphas, and were planning how they might arrest Jesus by stealth and kill him** (26:3–4). Timing is crucial. As far as they can see, it cannot be during the feast without stirring up the people. No explicit motive is given for their desire to kill Jesus (contrast John 11:45–53).

(C) **26:6–13.** In section C, the anointing occurs while Jesus reclines at the table: **A woman with an alabaster jar** (alabaster containers provided good storage for perfumes; Pliny, *Nat.* 13.3) **of expensive ointment came to him and poured it on his head** (26:7). Anointing the head was the way to inaugurate a king (e.g., 1 Sam. 10:1); it was also a sign of hospitality for an honored guest at a banquet (e.g., Ps. 23:5b; Josephus, *Ant.* 19.239; Luke 7:46). The woman's act here appears to be the latter. Instead of using oil, however, she uses expensive perfume. The disciples are offended, thinking the perfume could have been sold to help the poor. Jesus defends the woman's actions. He then interprets its meaning in light of his foreknowledge: **By pouring this perfume on my body, she has prepared me for burial** (26:12). In that context such anointing was part of the burial ritual (e.g., 2 Chron. 16:14; Mark 16:1). In the First Gospel, however, no mention is made of anointing Jesus's corpse (cf. Matt. 28:1 with Mark 16:1). This proleptic preparation for burial would have to do, and the woman will be praised for it. Why will she be praised? Because in a Jewish context burying the dead surpasses almsgiving, extending hospitality, or visiting the sick (*t. Pe'ah* 4.9; *b. Sukkah* 49b). Her act will be viewed as meritorious because she is involved in the burial of the king, proleptically and according to Jesus's interpretation of her act.

(B′) **26:14–16.** In section B′, when Judas joins the plot, the authorities receive a windfall. **Then one of the Twelve, the one called Judas Iscariot, going to the chief priests, said, "What do you want to give me if I will deliver him to you?"** (26:14–15a). For this betrayal they pay him thirty pieces of silver (cf. Zech. 11:12). From that point onward, Judas seeks an opportunity to betray Jesus. The authorities' timing can now be moved up.

(A′) **26:17–19.** In section A′, Passover preparations, the disciples ask for directions about where Jesus desires to celebrate the Passover. Their query is **on the first day of Unleavened Bread** (26:17). Originally there were two separate festivals: the Passover and the Feast of Unleavened Bread. By the first century AD, the two had merged and their names were interchangeable. Josephus blends the two (e.g., *Ant.* 17.213; 18.29; 20.106–9): he calls Nisan 14 "the day of Unleavened Bread" (*J.W.* 5.98). So the reference in Matt. 26:17 to "the first day of Unleavened Bread" is to Nisan 14 (during the evening of which the Passover meal was celebrated). Jesus's directions again attest his knowledge of what is to come (cf. 26:2, 12): **Go into the city to so and so and say to him, "The teacher says, 'My time is near. I with my disciples will observe the Passover at your place'"** (26:18). Having settled on where, the disciples prepare for the meal. Scene 1 is complete.

Scene 2: The Final Meal (26:20–35)

Scene 2 falls into an ABA′ pattern:

A Prediction of betrayal (26:20–25)
  B Last supper (proleptic sealing of the covenant; 26:26–29)
A′ Prediction of desertion and denial (26:30–35)

(A) **26:20–25.** Section A focuses on Jesus's prediction of his betrayal: **When it was evening, he sat with the Twelve and, while eating with them, said, "Truly I say to you that one of you will betray me"** (26:20–21). The disciples' reaction is extreme grief (cf. 17:23). Each one asks, **Lord, it is not I, is it?** Jesus replies, **The one who has dipped his hand in the bowl with me, this one will betray me. The son of man goes as it has been written concerning him, but woe to that one by whom the son of man will be betrayed. It would have been a good thing if that man had not been born.** Judas, the betrayer, says to Jesus, **It is not I, is it, Rabbi?** Jesus's reply is, **You have said [it]** (26:22–25; cf. 26:64; 27:11). Jesus's knowledge of future events again stands out.

(B) **26:26–29.** Section B, the last supper, functions as a proleptic sealing of a covenant between God and the disciples. There are two different streams of last supper tradition in the NT: (1) 1 Cor. 11:23–25 and the long text of Luke 22:19–20; (2) Mark 14:22–25 and Matt. 26:26–29. The former is distinguished

Another Typological Fulfillment of Scripture

In Matt. 26:24, when the Matthean Jesus says the son of man goes as it has been written of him, where is the specific prophecy to which Jesus refers? None can be produced with certainty. If this happened to be another instance of a typological fulfillment of Scripture, it would make sense. In the scriptures of Israel are numerous texts that speak of a prophet's death due to his calling; there are also texts that refer to an innocent one's betrayal by a supposed friend. It is this type of situation that finds its fulfillment in Jesus's betrayal and death.

by its references to "new" covenant and the command "do this in remembrance of me." The latter sources agree in the omission of these two items. Matthew's shaping of Mark reflects two significant changes, one involving form and the other content. Formally, Matt. 26:27 has Jesus say about the cup, **Drink of it,** to parallel 26:26's word about the bread, **Take, eat.** In terms of content, Matt. 26:28 adds **for forgiveness of sins.** Within the context of a Passover meal that involves consumption of bread and wine with words spoken to interpret the

© Stephen von Wyrick

Figure 16. Since the fifth century, the traditional site of the upper room commemorating the last supper shared by Jesus and his disciples.

significance of the ingested ingredients, the Matthean Jesus offers new words, giving new meaning to the bread and wine.

> Jesus took bread, blessed it, broke it, and gave it to the disciples, saying,
> "Take, eat, this is my body." (26:26)
> He took the cup, gave thanks, and gave it to them, saying,
> "Drink from it, all of you, for this is my blood of the covenant poured out for many for the forgiveness of sins." (26:27–28)

Jesus himself does not partake. He says, **I tell you, from now** (cf. 26:64) **I will not drink of the fruit of the vine until that day when I am drinking it with you new in the kingdom of my Father** (26:29). It is a vow of abstinence; it is also a promise of a certain future for himself and for his disciples (Matthew adds "with you" to Mark 14:25) beyond his impending death.

How should this act of prophetic symbolism (like the triumphal entry and the cleansing of the temple) be interpreted? Jesus himself interprets the act by his words over the cup. Three parts of the logion demand attention. First, Jesus interprets his coming death in terms of a covenant sacrifice. **My blood of the covenant** calls to mind Exod. 24:4–8. There at Sinai, Moses took blood, dashed half on the altar and half on the people, and said, "See the blood of the covenant that the Lord has made with you" (cf. Zech. 9:11; Jer. 34:18; Gen. 15:17–21). A covenant sacrifice sealed a covenant. Jesus says that his death seals a covenant between God and Jesus's disciples. Second, his blood is **poured out for many.** The expression, "blood to be poured out," is a

The Meaning of "Is" in Matthew 26:26, 28

In Matt. 26:26 Jesus says, "This is my body." In 26:28 he says, "This is my blood." The meaning of "is" has been variously interpreted in Christian history. What does it mean in Matthew? Two types of evidence, both contextual, help to answer this question. First, in Matt. 26:17, 19, 20–29 the meal is described as a Passover celebration (cf. *m. Pesah.* 10). In Deut. 16:3 the unleavened bread that the Israelites were to eat at Passover to commemorate their hasty departure from Egypt is called "the bread of affliction." This unleavened bread is the bread of affliction. That means that the Passover bread represents the unleavened bread associated with Israel's departure from Egypt.

Second, Matt. 13:36–43 provides an explanation of the parable of the weeds in the field. Jesus says, "The field is the world," "The enemy who sowed the weeds is the devil," and "The harvest is the end of the age." Here the verb "is" means "represents." So when the Matthean Jesus says, "This is my body," and "This is my blood," the meaning is most likely that the broken bread and the wine poured out represent his anticipated self-sacrifice.

way of saying the person has been killed, often unjustly (cf. Matt. 23:35; Ps. 79:10; Gen. 4:8–11). The expression "for many" is a Semitism that refers to the collective that benefits from the act of the one who dies. If "many" echoes Isa. 53:11–12 LXX, the sense of the term would not be "some" as opposed to others but "all" (Carroll and Green 1995, 44n17). Elsewhere in Matthew's narrative, however, "many" refers to a large number but not all (e.g., 7:13; 8:11, 16; 24:5).

Third, **for the forgiveness of sins** poses the major problem of interpretation. This phrase has been read two very different ways. On the one hand, the dominant reading is that Jesus's death is an atoning sacrifice that brings forgiveness of sins. The dominant reading breaks into two streams. One contends that Jesus's death is an atoning sacrifice that makes possible the (new) covenant with God. It is related to entry into the covenant relation; it takes away prebaptismal sins (e.g., Kingsbury 1986, 90, 93; Senior 1990, 68; Heil 1991a, 37). The second stream argues that the forgiveness belongs exclusively to staying in the covenant. Jesus's blood grants forgiveness for postbaptismal sins to participants in the Eucharist (Luomanen 1998b, 229, 279, 283; cf. 1 John 2:1–2). On the other hand, the other way of reading **for the forgiveness of sins** regards Jesus's death as the sealing of the (new) covenant, which is based on God's prior act of forgiveness. In Ezek. 34:25 and 37:23–27 the prophet says that God cleanses the people as an accompaniment of his delivering and making a covenant with them. Jeremiah 31:31–34 says that God will make a new covenant with the people. Its presupposition is a prior act of God's forgiveness. This seems to be the way Heb. 8:12 understands Jer. 31:34; also Paul in Rom. 11:27 (where Isa. 59:21a, "This is my covenant with them," is linked to Isa. 27:9, "when I take away their sins"). In this reading, God's prior act of forgiveness is the presupposition or accompaniment of a new covenant. A covenant sacrifice might seal the relationship, but it is not the catalyst that causes God to forgive. God's forgiveness arises out of God's decision to forgive. The covenant sacrifice would function as the confirmation

Another Interpretation of Jesus's Death

Socinus raised a moral question about some traditional interpretations of Jesus's death. He argues that in humans there are things ethically higher than the strict exaction of civil satisfaction or penal justice. He points to the analogy of human forgiveness: "If any man can rightly freely pardon injuries inflicted upon himself, and avenge them in the smallest degree when the highest degree is possible; not only may he rightly do this, but is for that very reason extolled to the skies. Shall we dare to deprive God of that right and power?" (*De Jesu Christo servatore*, 3.1 [original Latin with English translation in Grensted 1962, 283]).

Jesus's Death and the Forgiveness of Sins

Matthew 1:21 says that Jesus will save his people from their sins. This prophecy does not explicitly connect saving from sins with Jesus's death. The subsequent narrative shows that Jesus offers salvation through various aspects of his ministry (e.g., 8:16–17; 9:2–8, 35; 12:15–21; Gurtner 2007, 128). Jesus's saving his people refers to his prophetic mission to Israel. "In Matthew's view, Jesus was not sent to die for his people but to heal their diseases, preach repentance and lead them into eternal life through his authoritative interpretation and proclamation of the law" (Luomanen 1998b, 226). The passion predictions of 16:21; 17:12, 22–23; 20:17–19; 26:2, 54 do not make explicit the atoning significance of Jesus's death (Luomanen 1998b, 230). It is said to be necessary (*dei*; i.e., part of God's plan) and it fulfills the Scriptures (part of God's plan). In 20:28 Jesus's giving his life as a ransom for many is unclear. "Ransom" may mean merely for the deliverance of the many. There is no clarity about how that may be (Gurtner 2007, 128, 133). Matthew 26:28's "blood of the covenant . . . for the forgiveness of sins" is equally imprecise. It does not explain "how" his death effects forgiveness (Filson 1960, 275). The most likely meaning is that Jesus's death sealed a covenant that is based on God's prior forgiveness. There is no text in the First Gospel that treats Jesus's death as an atoning sacrifice required to take away Israel's sins before the covenant can be established. Rather, Jesus mediates forgiveness toward a variety of individuals without waiting for an atoning death as a condition. This is analogous to Luke-Acts, where it is the living Jesus who mediates forgiveness (e.g., Luke 5:17–26; 7:36–50; 23:43; Acts 5:31).

---

of a covenant whose presupposition is God's prior forgiveness. The sealing of the covenant would thereby guarantee a prior forgiveness now available to all who are part of it.

(A′) **26:30–35.** Section A′, the prediction of denial, moves the disciples and Jesus from the place where they have eaten the Passover to a new location. **And having sung a hymn** (Pss. 113–18 were sung at the Passover meal: 113–14 near the beginning and 115–18 near the end), **they went out to the Mount of Olives** (26:30). Jesus had spent the previous nights in Bethany (21:17). On the basis of Deut. 16:7, Jewish tradition required that pilgrims spend Passover night within the district of Jerusalem. This accounts for their removal to the Mount of Olives. There Jesus predicts the disciples' desertion, citing Zech. 13:7 and possibly echoing Ezek. 34:5 (**I will strike the shepherd, and the sheep of the flock will be scattered** [26:31b]). Yet there will be hope beyond tragedy. **After my being raised, I will go before you into Galilee** (26:32). Peter is unable to accept such a description for himself. He protests, **If all stumble and fall because of you, I will never stumble and fall** (26:33). Jesus's response is yet another prophecy: **Truly I say to you, in this night before the cock crows, you will deny me three times** (26:34). Peter protests once again: **And if it is necessary**

© Stephen von Wyrick

Figure 17. Gethsemane, a garden at the foot of the Mount of Olives where Jesus went to pray before his arrest, is commemorated by the Church of All Nations and a garden with ancient olive trees.

for me to die with you, I will absolutely not deny you (26:35). And so say they all! With this the second scene comes to an end, with a stark contrast between Jesus's dependable word and the disciples' undependable promises.

Scene 3: Prayer in the Garden (26:36–46)

Scene 3 falls into an ABA′ pattern. It consists of one episode, Jesus's prayer in the garden. The scene opens and closes with Jesus's words to the disciples (A and A′). The heart of the episode is the threefold prayer of Jesus's surrender to God's will.

A Disciples addressed (26:36–38)
　　B Jesus's threefold prayer of surrender (26:39–44)
A′ Disciples addressed (26:45–46)

(A) **26:36–38.** In section A are two parts. In the first, Jesus tells the disciples to sit at a certain place in Gethsemane while he goes off to pray (26:36). In the second, Jesus goes off with Peter, James, and John until, being extremely sorrowful (Ps. 42:6), he withdraws from them as well (26:37–38).

(B) **26:39–44.** Section B tells us that **going a little further, he fell on his face, praying and saying, "My Father, if it is possible, let this cup** (Jesus's suffering and death; see 20:22–23; 26:27–28; cf. *T. Ab.* 16.11: the bitter cup of death) **pass away from me; nevertheless not as I wish but as you will**" (26:39). After finding the disciples sleeping, **going away a second time he prayed, saying, "My Father, if it is not possible for this to pass unless I drink it, let your will be done**" (26:42; cf. Phil. 2:8: obedient unto death). After finding the disciples still sleeping, Jesus returns yet a third time **saying the same word again** (26:44). Sleep could be used in antiquity for a kind of moral or philosophical laxity. For example, Socrates understood his vocation as rousing his fellow citizens from sleep (Plato, *Apol.* 31a).

(A′) **26:45–46.** Section A′ has Jesus addressing the disciples: **Behold, the hour is at hand, and the son of man will be delivered into the hands of sinners** (26:45b; perhaps the Romans or the Jerusalem establishment or both). Jesus not only knows what will happen but when. Here is the equivalent of yet another passion prediction: **Get up, let us go. Behold, my betrayer is at hand** (26:46). As in John 18, the Matthean Jesus is in control, both in his knowledge of what will transpire and in his willingness to participate in the events. Scene 3 is at an end.

Scene 4: Betrayal and Trial (26:47–27:2)

Scene 4 falls into an ABA′B′ pattern:

A Betrayal and desertion (26:47–56)
  B Before the council at night (26:57–68)
A′ Denial (26:69–75)
  B′ Before the council in the morning (27:1–2)

(A) **26:47–56.** Section A tells of Judas's betrayal: **Behold, Judas, one of the Twelve, came, and with him a great crowd with swords and clubs from the chief priests and elders of the people** (26:47). Those accompanying Judas are likely the Levite temple guard and the armed police who work with them. They come heavily armed, ready to take a *lēstēs* (bandit/revolutionary; cf. 26:55; 27:44). To these guards Judas has given a sign: **The one whom I kiss, this is he; seize him** (26:48). When Judas kisses him, what Jesus says in response is difficult to determine. It is an incomplete expression, needing words to be supplied. "Friend, why are you here?" or "I know what you are here for" or "Let what you are here for take place"—any of these would work (Nolland 2005, 1110–11). The statement or question probably lets Judas know that Jesus is ahead of the game. He knows! Jesus's address of Judas as "friend" is ironic. On the surface it points to an enduring relationship; in terms of Matthew's use of the address in 20:13 and 22:12, it refers to one unworthy of the kingdom of God (Matera 1986, 97). When the guards seize Jesus, **one of those with Jesus . . . struck the slave of the high priest and cut off his ear.** Jesus says, **Return your sword to its place.** He gives three reasons. First, **For all those taking a** sword will perish by a sword (this is a proverb; see, e.g., Rev. 13:10; *Syr. Men.* 18–19). Second, **Or do you suppose that I am not able to call on my Father, and he will send me now more than twelve legions of angels?** (a legion = about 6000 soldiers). Third, **How then would the Scripture be fulfilled, because it is necessary for it to be so?** (26:51–54).

How should these three statements be understood? The first basically says, put your sword up or you will get hurt. Recent history justifies this perspective. After the death of Herod the Great, civil violence broke out in Judea. Part of this was linked with three pretenders to the throne who led popular uprisings: Judas, son of Ezekias (Josephus, *J.W.* 2.39–79); Simon, a former slave (Tacitus, *Hist.* 5.9); and a shepherd named Athronges (Josephus, *Ant.* 17.254–98). The three probably were messianic pretenders in the ancient Davidic tradition of popular anointed kingship (Horsley 1984, 484–86). From the Roman point of view, they were rebels who had to be destroyed. Jesus's use of this proverb, then, is a reflection of his concern for the disciples' well-being (cf. John 18:8b–9): "Don't do something that will get yourselves killed" (not a principle of pacifism; so Stanley 1980, 184). The second reason Jesus gives is that if a defense against capture is desired, let God provide it.

> ### The Use of Force in Religious Matters
>
> The Matthean Jesus refuses the use of force, both human and angelic, in the advancement of his cause. This "is a grave caution to the Church against even condoning (much less employing) force in the propagation or defense of the Gospel" (Stanley 1980, 184).

The third reason claims that the arrest is just part of the divine will and plan, something that fulfills Scripture (though no specific text is noted; cf. John 18:11). As a result of the Gethsemane prayer time, Jesus's commitment is to the Father's will (unto death; cf. Phil. 2:8).

Then seeing that there was no defense by Jesus, **the disciples, all leaving him, were fleeing** (26:56b). The story is now into a time of fulfillment of Jesus's prophecies made earlier (26:20–25, 31–35).

(B) **26:57–68.** Section B deals with Jesus before the council at night. **Then those who had seized Jesus were leading him away to Caiaphas the high priest, where the scribes and elders were gathered together** (26:57). Peter followed at a distance, went into the courtyard, and sat with the guards. There are two basic readings of Matt. 26:57–68; 27:1–2. On the one hand, the predominant view holds that the time spent by Jesus before the council is a Jewish capital case. Central to this approach is highlighting the illegitimacy of the Jewish trial. A list of irregularities includes (1) a capital trial can only be held during the day (*m. Sanh.* 4.1); (2) it cannot be held on a Sabbath or feast day (*m. Sanh.* 4.1; *m. Betzah* 5.2); (3) no judgment can be rendered on the day of the trial (*m. Sanh.* 4.1); (4) blasphemy requires the use of the divine name (*m. Sanh.* 7.5); (5) the trial cannot be held in the high priest's house but is held in a gathering room for the council (*m. Sanh.* 11.2); (6) capital cases begin with a defense of the one charged (*m. Sanh.* 4.1; Lohse 1961, 96–97; Reinbold 1994, 252).

Criticisms are twofold. First, the Mishnah comes from a time near AD 200, much later than Matthew. One cannot be assured that the rules were the same in the two periods. Second, the Mishnah reflects Pharisaic practice, not the Sadducean that was probably in effect at the time of Jesus (Blinzler 1969, 216–29). Only two items can be traced back to the time of Jesus and/or Matthew: (1) false witnesses were abhorred (Josephus, *Ant.* 4.219), and (2) cross-examination of witnesses was required (Sus. 48–62). Neither of these seems to be observed in Matthew's scene. Therefore, most scholars conclude that a comparison of Jesus before the Sanhedrin with the Mishnah's procedures for a capital trial is a dead end. If Matthew is describing a capital trial, we have no comprehensive picture of what the required procedures were at that time.

On the other hand, a second reading is to regard the scene of Jesus before the Sanhedrin as a preliminary hearing looking for a cause with a political tinge (e.g., Bock 1998, 190–95). This is based on the belief that while a sentence of death was the privilege of the prefect (Josephus, *Ant.* 2.117; 18.2; John 18:31; 19:10), the local courts were kept intact and cooperated with the prefect (O. Betz 1992, 87–88). If this scene were viewed as a preliminary examination that was looking for a cause that would stand scrutiny before Pilate, then two items in Matthew's narrative make sense. First, if Jesus has spoken of the destruction of the temple, then he will be a danger to public order (cf. Acts 21). Second, if Jesus has claimed to be the messiah, a Jewish king, then he will be guilty of rebellion. Either or both would give Pilate a reason to act.

The examination begins on a somber note: **Now the chief priests and the whole Sanhedrin were seeking false testimony against Jesus so they might put him to death.** The best that they could do was to find two who claimed that Jesus said, **I am able to destroy the temple of God and to build it in three days** (26:59–61). Matthew has no such saying attributed to Jesus. Hence, he regards this as false testimony (cf. Acts 6:14; John 2:19). In the face of such accusations, **Jesus was silent** (26:63a; cf. Isa. 53:7). Finally, the high priest puts Jesus under oath and asks him, **Tell us if you are the Christ, the son of God** (26:63b). "Son of God" was a designation for the messiah (cf. 4QFlor 1.11–12). Jesus responds, **You have said** [it] (26:64a; cf. Mark 14:62: "I am"; Luke 22:70: "You say that I am"). The expression Jesus uses here is found in two other places in Matthew: first, in 26:25, where Judas asks if he is the betrayer; and second, in 27:11, when Pilate asks Jesus if he is the king of the Jews. If the phrase is to be taken as a definite yes, then Pilate would have sentenced Jesus immediately as a revolutionary. Since Pilate did not do so, the phrase must mean something like, "You are the one saying this." Or in this instance it could be a question, "Are you saying this?"

What Does *sy eipas* or *sy legeis* Mean?

At three places in the First Gospel Jesus uses the phrase *sy eipas* ("you said it"; see 26:25, 64) or *sy legeis* ("you are saying"; see 27:11; cf. also Luke 22:70; 23:3; John 18:37). The issue of meaning becomes acute in Matt. 26:64 because Mark 14:62 has Jesus respond to the high priest's question not with *sy eipas* ("you said it") but with *egō eimi* ("I am"), an affirmative answer. Given Mark 14:62's unequivocal yes and John 18:37's unequivocal no (Pilate asks if Jesus says he is a king; Jesus says, That is what you [Pilate] say"—*sy legeis hoti basileus eimi*; Jesus, however, says he came to bear witness to the truth), the question is what the Lukan Jesus means in Luke 22:70 (the council asks Jesus if he is the son of God; Jesus responds, "That is what you are saying"—*hymeis legete*) and 23:3 (Pilate asks Jesus if he is the king of the Jews; Jesus replies, "That is what you [Pilate] are saying"—*sy legeis*) and what the Matthean Jesus means in Matt. 26:64 and 27:11.

Are the responses to be taken as affirmative (like Mark) or negative (like John), or non-committal and ambiguous? The issue here is not what the historical Jesus might have said or intended but what the Lukan or Matthean Jesus communicates. Luke 23:3–4 clearly indicates that what Jesus says is not taken as affirmative because of Pilate's response. It is at least an ambiguous answer. The same is true for Jesus's response to Pilate in Matt. 27:11, again because of the governor's response. So, in Matt. 26:64 Jesus's answer to the high priest must be understood as a negative followed by a clarification of his identity in transcendent terms (cf. the same tactic in John 18:36). Mark 14:62 stands alone among the canonical four in having Jesus state openly that he is the Christ. The other Gospels all agree that Jesus does not give an affirmative response. Matthew and John have Jesus follow up with a redefinition of his self-identity and mission in transcendent terms (contra Catchpole 1971, who contends *sy eipas* and *sy legeis* are affirmative in content but circumlocutory in formation). Jesus's replies are noncommittal in their formulation. Their content must be determined by what the context demands.

Then, Jesus clarifies his position on two fronts. **From now** (the time of Jesus's crucifixion and resurrection; cf. 23:39; 26:29), **you will see the son of man "sitting at the right hand" of The Power** (Ps. 110:1) **and "coming on the clouds of heaven"** (Dan. 7:13; Matt. 26:64b). The first front involves the conflation of Ps. 110:1 and Dan. 7:13. In Matt. 22:41–45 Jesus asks his opponents how they would interpret Ps. 110:1 ("The LORD said to my Lord, 'Sit at my right hand until I put your enemies under your feet'"). In 26:64 the Matthean Jesus gives his own understanding of his role in the stages of salvation history that remain. To do that he interprets Ps. 110:1 by Dan. 7:9. The one at God's right hand (the messiah) is the son of man who comes on the clouds of heaven (God's chariot that had wheels; cf. Ezek. 1; 10; Dan. 7:9; Ps. 104:3) in judgment (cf. Matt. 24:30; Acts 1:9–11). Such a link would have been easy, given Jewish hermeneutics. In Ps. 80:17 (RSV) "the man of thy [God's] right hand" is used in parallel with "the son of man." Such an interpretation was not unique in a Jewish context. In the early second century, Rabbi Akiba is said to have taught that the "thrones" of Dan. 7:9 meant one was for God and one for David (*b. Hag.* 14a; *b. Sanh*. 38b). This would have been an interpretation of Dan. 7 by Ps. 110:1. Not later than the mid-first century, *1 En.* 37–71 identifies the Chosen One (45.3; 51.3; 55.4), the son of man (46; 62; 63; 69.27–29), and messiah (48.10; 52.4) and says that this figure sits on God's throne at the last judgment. This implicitly links Ps. 110 and Dan. 7. In Ezekiel the Tragedian's pre-Christian *Exagōgē*, Moses in a dream sees himself being seated on God's throne to judge (J. Collins 1995).

With this interpretation of his identity, the Matthean Jesus tells the high priest that he (Jesus), as the end-time judge, will be judging them (the council; cf. Matt. 7:21–23; 13:41–42). Here Jesus defines who the messiah is in terms of the authority he possesses. He will be the end-time judge. It is crucial that the reader hear the transcendent reference here. The First Evangelist uses the motif "heaven and earth" throughout the Gospel. It functions in much the same way that the language "from above" and "from below" does in the Fourth Gospel. When, therefore, the Matthean Jesus says he will be sitting at the right hand of The Power and will be coming on the clouds of heaven, he is casting his role in transcendent terms (cf. John 18:36: "My kingdom is not from this world"; Eusebius, *Hist. eccl.* 3.19.1–3.20.7). So understood, there is not any tinge of political rebellion present, whatever the authorities may have thought they heard.

The second front involves the claim that from Jesus's crucifixion and resurrection the authorities would "see" that to which he refers. In *1 En.* 62.3–5, on the day of judgment all the kings, governors, and high officials "will see" and recognize the son of man who sits on the throne of his glory. The rulers will

Matthew's Usage of "Heaven" and "Heavens"

Jonathan Pennington (2007) contends that Matthew distinguishes between "heaven" in the singular and in the plural. "Heaven" in the singular refers to the visible, created realm, the sky (e.g., 5:18, 34; 6:26; 8:20; 13:32; 16:2–3; 24:29, 35). "Heavens" in the plural refers to the invisible realm of God (e.g., 3:2, 16, 17; 5:3, 10, 12, 16, 19, 20, 45; 6:1, 9; 7:11, 21; 8:11; 18:10; 24:36). There is no question that the First Gospel has these two categories. What is lacking for an accurate reading of Matthew is a third category: occasions when "heaven" in the singular refers to the invisible realm (e.g., 6:10, 20; 11:25; 14:19; 16:1; 18:18; 21:25; 22:30; 28:2). The "heavens" refers to transcendence conceived of spatially; "heaven" sometimes also refers to transcendence when conceived of eschatologically (temporally). A classic example of this singular usage is 26:64, where "the clouds of heaven" (sg.) refers to God's chariot (Ezek. 1; 10; Dan. 7:13–16) and so to transcendence, not the sky.

be terrified when they "see" that son of man sitting on the throne (recognizing his exaltation by God to be judge at the last judgment). Although later rabbinic procedure limited blasphemy to use of the divine name (*m. Sanh.* 7.5; Lev. 24:10–23), Philo reflects a more comprehensive view. In *Somn.* 2.130–33, Philo describes blasphemy as daring to compare oneself to the all-blessed God; in *Decal.* 61–69, blasphemy is ascribing the same honor to creatures as to the Creator. John 10:31–39 shows that at the end of the first century, in some circles at least, blasphemy was equated with a human's making himself God (10:31, 33: "The Jews took up stones again to stone him; . . . 'we are going to stone you . . . for blasphemy, because you, though only a human being, are making yourself God'"; cf. also John 5:18: "For this reason the Jews were seeking . . . to kill him, because he . . . was . . . calling God his own Father, thereby making himself equal to God"). This explains the high priest's reactions in Matt. 26: **Then the high priest tore his garments** (a custom when the high priest heard blasphemy; *m. Sanh.* 7.5), **saying, "He has blasphemed. Why do we still have need of witnesses? See now, you (pl.) have heard the blasphemy. What is your opinion?"** The view of the group is, **He is deserving of death** (26:65–66). Mocking follows the decision, even though physical mistreatment of a prisoner was illegal. Jesus is spat upon (Isa. 50:6) and struck. Some taunt him, saying, **Prophesy to us, Christ; who is the one who struck you?** (26:68). After all, prophetic discernment was expected of the messiah (*Pss. Sol.* 17.37–51; *b. Sanh.* 93b).

(A′) **26:69–75.** Section A′ focuses on the denials of Peter (prior references to Peter include 4:18–19; 10:2; 14:28–33; 15:15; 16:17–19; 17:1, 4; 17:24–27; 18:21–22; 26:58). The nighttime trial of Jesus before the council (26:59–68) is sandwiched between two references to Peter sitting in the courtyard of the high priest (26:58, 69). While he is sitting there, a servant girl comes up to him and says, **You were with Jesus the Galilean.** And he denies it before all of them, saying, **I do not know what you are talking about.** When he goes out to the porch, another servant girl sees him and says to those there, **This one was with Jesus of Nazareth.** Again Peter denies it, this time with an oath: **I do not know the man.** After a while those standing around come over and say to Peter, **Truly you are of them, for your speech makes it clear.** Then, with cursing and swearing, Peter says again, **I do not know the man. And immediately the cock crowed. And Peter remembered the word of Jesus that before the cock crows, you will deny me three times. And he went out and wept** (26:69–75). This pericope must surely have functioned among the earliest auditors of the Gospel as a vivid illustration of the Pauline admonition in 1 Cor. 10:12: "If you think you are standing, watch out that you do not fall." The prophecies of Jesus are being fulfilled. Judas has betrayed him; all have fled; and Peter has denied knowing him. Jesus stands alone, a true prophet whose predictions have come to pass (Deut. 18:22).

(B′) **27:1–2.** Section B′ briefly treats Jesus's appearance before the council in the morning. **In the early morning all of the chief priests and the elders of**

Who Was Responsible for Jesus's Death?

In Matt. 26:2 Jesus predicts that he will be delivered up (*paradidōmi*) at Passover. In 26:21 he predicts that one of the Twelve will deliver him up (*paradidōmi*). In 26:46 he says the one who will deliver him up (*paradidōmi*) is near. Who delivered up Jesus? In Matt. 26:16, 25, 48 and 27:3, the narrator says it was Judas. In 27:4 Judas himself says he has sinned by delivering up innocent blood. The chief priests and elders of the people are said to deliver Jesus up (*paradidōmi*) in Matt. 27:2, 18. Finally, it is Pilate in Matt. 27:26 who delivers Jesus up (*paradidōmi*) to be crucified. Judas (27:3), the chief priests and elders (27:1–2), and Pilate (27:24) all try to shift the responsibility to someone else. The only ones who accept responsibility are "all the people" (27:25: not "the crowd"). From the narrator's perspective, all are complicit in the deed. Judas's judgment is a disgraceful suicide by strangling (27:5), that of the chief priests and elders is loss of their religious leadership (21:43), that of Pilate is to be found among the goats at the last judgment (25:46) or among the bad fish at the time of reckoning (13:47–50), and that of "all the people" will be the destruction of city and temple (23:37–38; 24:2). For the latter, if and when they recognize Jesus's rule (23:39), then his blood will cover their sins (26:28).

the people took counsel against Jesus (the official vote of either the preliminary examination or perhaps the capital trial) so that he should be killed. Binding him, they led him away and delivered him to Pilate the governor (27:1–2). It was necessary to involve Pilate because only the Romans had the power of life and death (John 18:31; Josephus, *J.W.* 2.117; cf. also Josephus, *Ant.* 20.200–203). Roman trials started at daybreak (Seneca the Younger, *Ira* 2.73). Keep in mind that, in Matthew's reckoning, this would have been Nisan 15, the day of the Passover. With this brief account of the events of the early morning, the fourth scene is finished.

Scene 5: Trial before Pilate (27:3–26)

Scene 5 focuses on the trial before Pilate. It falls into an ABA′ pattern with references to "blood" framing the trial:

A Judas says he betrayed innocent blood (27:3–10)
    B Jesus before Pilate (27:11–23)
A′ Pilate says he is innocent of this man's blood (27:24–26)

(A) **27:3–10.** Section A treats Judas's end. The segment is divided into two parts: 27:3–5 and 27:6–10. The first part begins, **Then when Judas, the one who betrayed him, saw that he was condemned, undergoing a change of mind** (*metamelētheis*), **he returned the thirty pieces of silver to the chief priests and** elders, saying, "**I have sinned by betraying innocent blood**" (27:3–4a; Deut. 27:25: "Cursed be anyone who takes a bribe to shed innocent blood"). The money is symbolic of responsibility (Senior 1990, 104). Returning it is his attempt to exempt himself from responsibility for Jesus's death. The change Judas undergoes, however, is not described with the usual word for repentance (*metanoeō*). The authorities' response is, "**What is that to us? You see to it.**" Judas throws the silver down in the temple (*naon*) and departs. **And going away, he hanged himself** (27:4b–5; Num. 35:33: "No expiation can be made for the land, for the blood that is shed in it, except by the blood of the one who shed it"). This episode is part of a *synkrisis* (an evaluative comparison) that includes Peter's denial (26:69–75). How do the denial and betrayal by these two disciples compare? In the Matthean narrative, Peter's response is repentance that leads to life, while Judas's change of mind leads to death (a perfect illustration of Paul's distinction between a godly grief that produces a repentance that leads to salvation on the one hand and a worldly grief that produces death on the other [2 Cor. 7:9–11]; Keener 1999, 656). Judas's death, moreover, is appropriate for one who has betrayed a king (cf. Ahithophel's suicide after his betrayal of David [2 Sam. 17:23]). As a hanging, it is an ignoble death (cf. Euripides, *Hel.* 298–303; Suetonius, *Aug.* 65; Esther 7:9–10; *Mart. Pol.* 6). (Heil 1991a, 68–69, however, contends that Judas repented and therefore may receive forgiveness.)

The second part of this pericope, 27:6–10, tells of the chief priests' reactions to Judas's return of the money: what they could not do and what they did do. They say, **It is not lawful to put it into the treasury, since it is blood money** (27:6). This is their acknowledgment that they are involved in the murder of an innocent man. They agree to use the money to buy the potter's field to bury strangers. The narrator says, **Therefore, that field has been called Field of Blood until today. Then the word of Jeremiah the prophet was fulfilled, which said, "And they took the thirty pieces of silver, the price set on one by sons of Israel, and gave them for the potter's field, as the Lord commanded me"** (27:8–10). The form of the prophecy cited is perplexing. The thirty pieces of silver and a reference to the treasury echo Zech. 11:12–13; the purchase of a field for silver (17 shekels) echoes Jer. 32:6–10; the references to a potter, the blood of the innocent, and burial may echo Jer. 18:1–3 and 19:1–13; and reference to the Lord's command may reflect Exod. 9:12 LXX. The Matthean quotation is a composite attributed to Jeremiah. The point is the same as all quotations in Matthew. What has happened is a part of God's plan.

(B) **27:11–23.** Section B presents the trial before Pilate. It opens with a simple statement: **Now Jesus stood before the governor. And the governor asked him, "Are you the king of the Jews?"** Jesus's reply was, **You are saying that.** When the chief priests and elders accuse him, **he did not give an answer.** Pilate then says to Jesus, **Do you not hear all the accusations made against you?** Again,

---

What Kind of Man Was Pilate?

Pilate is known to modern readers from the four Gospels, Christian sources; from Philo (*Legat.* 299, 302, 303) and Josephus (*Ant.* 18.55, 56, 60; *J.W.* 2.170), Jewish sources; and from Tacitus (*Ann.* 15.44) and an inscription discovered in Caesarea in 1961, Roman sources. Pilate was prefect, or governor, of Judea in AD 26–36. The only evidence about Pilate as judge comes from the NT accounts of Jesus's trial. Philo and Josephus give a very negative portrait of Pilate. He was a tough, cruel man who disregarded Jewish sensibilities. The Gospels, Matthew especially, tend to depict the Jews as the chief villains in Jesus's death and see Pilate as recognizing Jesus's innocence even though he did not protect an innocent man (cf. the similar pattern with Paul in Acts 21–26). The traits of indecision and ultimate weakness that are seen in the Matthean passion narrative are seen also in the matter of Pilate's introduction of iconic military standards into Jerusalem (Josephus, *J.W.* 2.169–74; *Ant.* 18.55–59). Matthew nevertheless shares with John (19:11) the view that Pilate's was the lesser guilt. Because of the Gospel's depiction of Pilate as recognizing Jesus's innocence, later Christians transformed him into a Christian (cf. the apocryphal *Letter of Pilate to Tiberius* and the *Letter of Pilate to Herod*; Callon 2006; McGing 1991).

Jesus answers not one charge (27:11–14). Pilate, a Roman, is amazed at this behavior. Plutarch's comment (*Inim. util.* 8) may explain why: "Nothing is more dignified and noble than to maintain a calm demeanor when an enemy reviles one." A similar notion is expressed by Epictetus (*Ench.* 48.2), who says that one of the signs that one is progressing in the philosophic life is that "if anyone censures him, he makes no defense." Jesus's silence impresses the Roman governor (Isa. 52:15?).

What follows next (27:15–23) is an attempt by Pilate to release Jesus. Verses 18 and 19 make it clear: **For he knew that they** (the religious authorities) **had delivered him up because of jealousy. While he was sitting on the bema** (judgment seat or tribunal; cf. Acts 18:12), **his wife sent a message to him, saying, "Have nothing to do with this righteous man, for I have suffered much today in a dream because of him."** In Matt. 2 dreams played a key part in protection for Jesus. Here it will not be so. Perhaps then the crowd would counteract their leaders' plot. So, assuming the custom of a governor's releasing any one prisoner they want at Passover (27:15), Pilate asks the crowd, **Whom do you wish that I release to you, Barabbas** (a notorious prisoner) **or Jesus, the one called Christ?** (27:17). Alas, it was not to be. The authorities have persuaded the crowd to ask for Barabbas. Again Pilate asks the crowd to decide whom he should release. And they say, **Barabbas.** Then he asks, **"What shall I do with Jesus, the one called Christ?" They all said, "Let him be crucified." Pilate said, "What evil has he done?" Now they were crying out even more, "Let him be crucified"** (27:22–23).

(A') **27:24–26.** Section A' returns to the theme of innocent blood. Faced with a riot (not untypical at a festival; cf. Josephus, *J.W.* 2.224), Pilate, like Judas, tries to divorce himself from the guilt associated with killing an innocent man.

> ### Releasing a Prisoner at Passover
>
> There is no non-Gospel evidence of this particular custom about which Pilate spoke. Nevertheless, such a practice is possible given Roman practice generally. The Romans sometimes deferred to local custom in forgiving a crime (Plutarch, *Quaest. rom.* 83), granted mass amnesties at the time of a local feast (Livy, *Hist.* 5.13.8), released prisoners due to public demand (Livy, *Hist.* 8.35.1–9), or freed captives in an exchange with terrorists (Keener 1999, 669).

Taking water, he washed his hands in the presence of the crowd, saying, "I am innocent of this blood (Deut. 21:6–7; Ps. 26:6; *Let. Aris.* 308; Homer, *Il.* 6.266–68; Virgil, *Aen.* 2.719). **You see to it."** And all the people (*laos*) say, **His blood be on us and on our children** (27:24b–25). That is, the people accept the responsibility and the guilt and the punishment (cf. Lev. 20:9–16). In the plot of Matthew, this locates the people within the indictment and the judgment of 23:29–39. The city and temple will be destroyed within the generation of their children. If, as some think, there is a double entendre here, then at a second level the evangelist relates their guilt to the possibility of forgiveness opened by Jesus's blood (26:28; Cargal 1991). Then Pilate releases Barabbas to them and, after a scourging (a practice that preceded execution: Livy, *Hist.* 8.20.7; Seneca the Younger, *Clem.* 9.2.6, 21; Dio Cassius, *Rom. Hist.* 78.9; 79.9.4; often inflicting near-mortal wounds: Josephus, *J.W.* 5.449; 6.304; 7.200–205), he delivers Jesus to be crucified. "Political expediency takes precedence over justice" (Keener 1999, 662). On this note we come to the end of the fifth scene.

Scene 6: Crucifixion (27:27–61)

Scene 6 follows an ABCDC'B'A' pattern whose center point is Jesus's death on the cross:

A   Soldiers abuse and crucify Jesus (27:27–38)
  B   Groups of mockers (27:39–44)
    C   A portent prior to Jesus's death (27:45)
      D   Death of Jesus on cross (27:46–50)
    C'   Portents after Jesus's death (27:51–53)
  B'   A group of confessors (27:54)
A'   Disciples watch and bury Jesus (27:55–61)

(A) **27:27–38.** Section A focuses on the Roman soldiers' behavior: mocking and crucifying Jesus. Verses 27–31 describe the mocking. In the praetorium (the governor's palace), they put a scarlet robe on him, a crown of thorns on his head, and a reed in his right hand (a parody of the trappings of a king). **And kneeling in his presence, they mocked him, saying, "Hail, king of the Jews"** (a parody of the reverence due royalty; 27:29). Then to show that it is all mockery, they spit on him (a severe expression of disgust; Num. 12:14; Isa. 50:6) and hit him with the reed (a demonstration of his powerlessness). **And when they had mocked him, they took off the robe and put on his own clothes and led him away to be crucified** (a mock enthronement; 27:31). The game of "playing king" was a means of mockery. It could, however, function in diverse ways. For example, Philo (*Flacc.* 36) tells how political dissidents dressed up a mentally ill man as king as a way of mocking Agrippa, who had just been appointed ruler. Dio Chrysostom (*Or.* 67–70) relates the practice to the Sacian feast of the Persians, where a prisoner was so indulged before his execution.

Normally the condemned prisoner would carry his own beam of the cross to the place of execution (Artemidorus, *Onir.* 2.56; Plutarch, *Sera* 9). Perhaps because Jesus is unable at this point to carry his cross (due to the scourging?), the soldiers force a man named Simon, chosen at random, to carry it (27:32; cf. 5:41). When they arrive at Golgotha, the soldiers offer Jesus **wine mixed with gall to drink** (27:34a; Ps. 69:21). This may reflect the practice referred to in *b. Sanh.* 43a ("When one is led out to execution, he is given a goblet of wine containing a grain of frankincense in order to benumb his senses" [trans. Epstein 1948]). Jesus refuses it (Why? cf. 26:29). **And having crucified him, they divided his garments by casting lots** (Ps. 22:18: naked crucifixion constituted the ultimate form of shame: cf. Epictetus, *Diatr.* 3.26.22); **and sitting down, they watched over him there** (so no one could come and take him down). They put over his head the charge against him: **This is Jesus, the king of the Jews** (27:35–37; cf. John 19:19), a continuation of the parody.

Then they crucify with him two criminals (*lēstai*), one on the right and one on the left (a parody of a king's chief associates; 27:38; cf. 20:20–21). In fact, the very act of crucifixion (being raised up) was a means of execution used for those who, in the Roman mind, tried to rise too high above their station (Marcus 2006). A person who claimed unusual status might be given the reward of a cross set up higher than the others (Suetonius, *Galb.* 9.1). The depiction of Jesus's crucifixion is, from the Roman and Jewish perspective, a parody of the enthronement of a royal figure. From the perspective of the Gospel's auditors, the depiction is dramatic irony. "In the very mode of the rejection, his true identity as king of Israel and king of the gentiles is paradoxically proclaimed" (Senior 1990, 124). The crucifixion of Jesus is in reality his exaltation (cf. 26:64; 28:18), a view shared with the Fourth Gospel.

(B) **27:39–44.** Section B gives a picture of three groups of mockers after Jesus has been crucified: the passersby (27:39–40); the chief priests, scribes, and elders (27:41–43); and the two criminals crucified with him (27:44). The narrative is again one of testing Jesus (Kingsbury 1986, 89; cf. 4:1–11). Romans usually crucified along a road so passersby could see and be warned. It is no surprise, then, that 27:39–40 mentions passersby. They take his name in vain (*eblasphēmoun*), wagging their heads (Ps. 22:7) and saying, **You who could destroy the temple and build it in three days** (26:61), **save yourself; if you are the son of God** (26:63), **come down from the cross** (27:40). The temptations of 4:1–11 and 26:53 present themselves again: to use his power for self-pres- ervation and self-authentication. The authorities cannot resist gloating. So the chief priests, scribes, and elders are a second group that mocks Jesus: **He saved others; he is not able to save himself. He is king of Israel; let him come down from the cross, and we will believe in him** (cf. the temptation of 16:1). **He trusted in God, let him come to the rescue now if he wants him** (Ps. 22:8), **for he said, "I am the son of God"** (cf. Wis. 2:16–20; Matt. 27:42–43). Even the criminals crucified with Jesus, a third group, revile him (27:44).

(C) **27:45.** Section C relates a portent before Jesus's death: **From the sixth hour** (noon) **there was darkness over all the earth until the ninth hour** (3:00 PM). Deaths of key figures were often accompanied by darkness: Romulus (Cicero, *Rep.* 2.10; 6.21–22), Julius Caesar (Virgil, *Georg.* 1.466–67, says the sun was moved to pity Rome on the day Caesar was murdered and so veiled its radiant face in gloom and darkness), Augustus (Dio Cassius, *Rom. Hist.* 56.29.3), and Enoch (*2 En.* 67.1–2). The significance of this period of dark- ness while Jesus hangs on the cross is reflected in a text from *Lamentations Rabbah* on Lam. 1:1 (Freedman and Simon 1939):

> R. Nahman said: The Holy One, blessed be He, asked the ministering angels: When a king of flesh-and-blood mourns, what is it customary for him to do? They said: He hangs sackcloth over his door. He said to them: I will do likewise, as it is said, "I clothe the skies in blackness. . . ." He again asked them: When a king mourns, what is it customary for him to do? They said: He extinguishes the lamps. He said to them: I will do likewise, as it is said, "Sun and moon are darkened."

God mourns at the death of his son, Jesus, with whom he is well pleased (3:17; 17:5); cf. also Isa. 13:6, 10 [the sun's darkness is a sign of the day of the Lord]; Amos 8:9; Joel 2:10).

(D) **27:46–50.** Section D speaks of Jesus's death on the cross. **Around the ninth hour** (3:00 PM), **Jesus cried out in a loud voice, "Ēli, Ēli, lema sabachthani?"** (meaning, **"My God, My God, why have you left me alone?"** [Ps. 22:1; Matt. 27:46]). Would the evangelist have expected his auditors to recognize that he did not use the verb *azavtani* (to forsake) but instead employed **sabachthani** (to leave alone; Marguerat and Bourquin 1999, 107)? Debate rages over whether this is an expression of abandonment (e.g., Hagner 1995, 2:844; Davies and Allison 1997, 3:625) or trust (e.g., Kingsbury 1986, 89; Keener 1999, 683).

Perhaps it is both. **My God** signals that a relationship exists. **Why** signals a sense of abandonment, but not despair. Note that Matt. 27:46 does not write "Eloi, Eloi" (as Mark 15:34 does) but rather Ēli, Ēli. Why? **Certain of those standing there, when they heard this, said, "He is calling for Elijah"** (27:47). The rabbis thought that Elijah, who had not died, would from time to time appear in order to rescue or aid the sages in need (e.g., *b. Ber.* 58a; *b. B. Qam.* 60b; *b. Avod. Zar.* 17b, 18b; *b. Sanh.* 98a). The cry Ēli, Ēli is apparently misunderstood as a call for Elijah to come to the rescue. When one of the onlookers tries to give Jesus some vinegar to drink (Ps. 69:21), the others say, **"Hold on, let us see if Elijah is coming to save him." Then Jesus, again crying with a loud voice, gave up his spirit** (27:49–50).

(C') **27:51–53.** Section C' lists a number of portents, at least one of which leads to a true confession (27:54). The verses, abbreviated into wooden English, look like this: "and the veil was split . . . and the earth was shaken and the stones were split and the tombs were opened and many bodies were raised and coming out . . . they entered the holy city and were manifest to many." How should this series of "and + passive verbs" be divided? English translations vary in their punctuation. They usually agree that a period goes after the veil of the temple being split (27:51a; so NIV, NRSV, TEV, REB, NAB). A number place a period after the earthquake and the rocks being split (27:51b; so NIV, NRSV); others include the tombs being opened (27:52a; so REB) and even the raising of the bodies (27:52b; so TEV, NAB) as part of the second portent. Grammar is of no help. Logically there are three events: (1) the veil is split (27:51a), (2) the earth is shaken (27:51b), and (3) many bodies are raised (27:52–53). The first two occur after Jesus's death and are consequences of that death. The third is located after Jesus's resurrection and is a consequence of it.

The first portent is given in 27:51a: **The curtain of the temple was split in two from top to bottom.** The reference is probably to the inner curtain (Exod. 26:33) that separated the holy of holies from the holy place. That the curtain is split from top to bottom means that God has done it. The exact meaning of the event is debated. It could mean that God's presence is departing from the temple in preparation for the destruction to follow (*Liv. Pro.* 12 [Habakkuk]: the destruction of the temple

To Which Curtain Does Matthew Refer?

There were two curtains in the Jerusalem temple. One curtain separated the holy of holies from the rest of the temple, and behind it only the high priest might enter and only on the Day of Atonement (Exod. 26:31–35; Lev. 16:2). The second curtain was at the main gate and separated the court of the Israelites from the outer parts of the temple (Exod. 26:36–37; 38:18). Since the Protestant Reformation, the preponderance of opinion has supported that Matthew refers to the former (Luz 2005, 3:565–66n56). This is certainly the way Heb. 6:19; 9:12, 24; and 10:19–22 understand it.

is signaled by the veil of the inner sanctuary being torn to pieces), or it could mean that God's presence is no longer confined to a particular location (*T. Benj.* 9.3: the temple curtain shall be torn and the spirit of God will move on to all the nations).

The second portent is provided in 27:51b. This is a two-part segment, each part with an identical structure.

> **And the earth shook** (cf. Isa. 2:19, 21; 13:13; Joel 2:10: an accompaniment of judgment; Virgil, *Georg.* 1.475: an earthquake occurs at the death of Caesar)
>
> **and the rocks were split** (cf. Rev. 6:12; 16:17–19: an accompaniment of judgment on the day of the Lord)

This second portent is linked to the first by the key word "split." (Some take "and the tombs were opened" [27:52a] as a third part of this segment [Baby 2003, 105; REB], perhaps because Matt. 28 associates an earthquake and the opening of a tomb and perhaps, like J. Wenham [1981], to avoid raised saints sitting in their tombs for three days before emerging.)

The third portent, 27:52–53, reads: **and the tombs were opened** (Ezek. 37:12–13 LXX: "I will open your tombs") **and many bodies of the saints who had fallen asleep were raised, and coming out of the tombs** (Ezek. 37:12–13 LXX: "and bring you out of your tombs") **after his** (Jesus's) **resurrection, they entered the holy city and were made manifest to many** (Ezek. 37:12, 14 LXX: "I will bring you back to the land of Israel. . . . I will place you on your own soil"). This leaves every event mentioned in 27:52–53 to take place after Jesus's resurrection. These events are not another portent connected to Jesus's death. They are rather associated with Jesus's resurrection. The unit, in brief, looks like this:

> Tombs were opened
> Bodies were raised
> > Coming out after his resurrection
> They entered the city
> They were manifest to many

Both the two assertions before and the two after the centerpiece are controlled by "after his resurrection." Why then is the third portent placed here? First, it does not fit into the theological tendency of Matt. 28. Second, it is characteristic of the First Evangelist to anticipate future events (e.g., 16:28–17:8; 26:12, 26–28), and so 27:52–53 functions proleptically. Third, the formal sequence of "earthquake/stone rolled away/Jesus raised" corresponds to that in Matt. 28. Matthew 27:52–53 is a homiletical/haggadic comment by the

306

Myth and/or Midrash in Matthew 27:52–53

It is difficult to find a modern scholar who does not regard 27:52–53 as something other than history. Either Matthew took over from tradition or himself created the theological statement presented as narrative. Its origins were in the fulfillment of OT prophecy (e.g., Ezek. 37) and/or a theological conviction of the church (e.g., Christ is the firstfruits of the general resurrection; 1 Cor. 15:20–28). This echoes D. F. Strauss's belief that the Gospel miracle stories were myths created by early Christians out of OT prophecies, sayings of Jesus, or theological convictions of the early church (cf. Strauss 1972, 694–96, for an interpretation of this passage). It is an advance over Strauss to note that these verses may belong to covert haggadic/homiletical midrash ("midrash" is a scriptural exposition; "haggadic" means characterized by narrative exposition; and "covert" indicates that the Scripture texts need not be cited). Jews sometimes interpreted their foundation documents by telling a story that explained the relevance of their sources of identity. As already seen throughout the passion narrative, Matthew often does not specify the scriptural text. It is assumed and functions as an allusion. The author(s) of Matthew may very well have used this haggadic (narrative) type of exposition to explain the significance of Jesus's resurrection in the messianists' foundation document.

---

evangelist placed here because of the covert allusion to Ezek. 37:12–14. "The narrator (author) has intruded into the story to offer theological commentary" (Carroll and Green 1995, 49). "The text is to be understood only as a theological concept portrayed as an event" (Schnackenburg 2002, 290). It is "a piece of theology set forth as history" (Hagner 1995, 2:851). The theological concept is that Jesus's resurrection is the beginning of the general resurrection. He is the firstfruits of those who have fallen asleep (1 Cor. 15:20). This, then, is the fulfillment of Ezek. 37's prophecy of the eschatological age, when graves are opened and a raised people are returned to their land (Gurtner 2007, 178–79). The Matthean emphasis on the raised saints appearing to many may also reflect a view like that in *2 Bar.* 50.3–4: when the righteous are raised up for the wicked to see, it will be a sign of judgment's having come.

(B′) **27:54.** Section B′ provides a group of confessors to balance the groups of mockers in 27:39–44. **The centurion and those with him watching over Jesus, when they saw the earthquake and the things that happened, were exceedingly fearful, saying, "Truly this one was son of God."** What would be seen besides the earthquake? The soldiers would not see the veil of the temple split in two. Given where Jesus was likely crucified, not even the outer curtain would be visible to them, much less the inner curtain. Nor would they have witnessed bodies of saints coming out of their tombs after Jesus's resurrection. They have witnessed the earthquake and the rocks splitting. As a result they make a confession about the one who has just died.

Christ's Descent into Hell

By the second century some early Christians associated Christ's descent into hell with Matt. 27:52–53. In the second-century *Gospel of Peter* (10.41–42), the soldiers see three figures emerge from the tomb, Jesus and two angels sustaining him. A voice that comes out of heaven asks if he (Jesus) has preached to the dead. The cross says yes. In the fourth-century (or later) *Acts of Pilate* (17–26), Simeon and his sons, who have been raised from their open tombs, give a sworn, written statement to the Jewish authorities about the miracles Jesus did while in hades. A case may possibly be made for Jesus's saving work associated with his descent into hades, but it cannot be made on the basis of explicit NT texts, including this one from Matthew.

Whereas Mark (15:39) and Luke (23:47) have only a single centurion, Matthew adds **and those with him.** This enables a group of witnesses here to match the multiple mockers earlier. In the plot of the First Gospel, gentiles here, as in Matt. 2, make a discerning confession while the Jewish authorities only mock. In Matthew's narrative world, this is likely a foreshadowing of the gentiles' conversion to Christ (cf. Ps. 22:27–28), not a foreshadowing of the attitude of the wicked on the day of judgment (as Sim 1993a).

(A′) **27:55–61.** Section A′ ends scene 6 with a report of Jesus's burial, framed by notices of disciples watching. Who watches? Matthew mentions not the Eleven but a group of women who watch at a distance as Jesus is crucified and dies. They have **followed him from Galilee, to serve him** (27:55b; cf. Luke 8:1–3). They are disciples (Mattila 2002, 136, 139; Shin 2007; Baby 2003, 127–33). Among them are Mary Magdalene, Mary the mother of James and Joseph (Is this Mary the mother of Jesus? cf. 13:55; John 19:25), and the mother of the

Portents and Professions

In Plutarch's life of *Cleomenes* (39), one whose life was a pattern for all was betrayed by a supposed friend, met a tragic death, and was hung up for the birds to devour. A portent occurred (in this case, a serpent of great size coiled itself about Cleomenes' head so no ravening bird of prey could light on it). As a result of the portent, those who were keeping watch over the body took it to mean that Cleomenes was beloved of the gods and a child of the gods. That a profession of Jesus as son of God by those keeping watch over the body of Jesus followed a portent associated with his death would, therefore, have been easily understood by ancient Mediterranean auditors of the Gospel. Portents functioned as a heavenly vindication of Jesus.

Ignoble Deaths of Noble Figures

Sometimes the accounts of ignoble deaths of noble figures function to defame the character of the enemy who has failed to recognize and appreciate the true worth of the victim. Two examples show the pattern.

First, Herodotus (*Hist.* 3.124–25) tells of the murder of Polycrates (ruler of Samos) by Oroetes (satrap of Sardis). Having killed him, Oroetes then crucified him. Herodotus says such an end to the life of a magnificent ruler is totally incongruous. It reflects on the character of his killer.

Second, Silius Italicus (*Pun.* 1.151–54) relates the death of Tagus, a man of ancient race, remarkable for beauty, and of proven valor, at the hands of the cruel Carthaginian general Hasdrubal. Hasdrubal fastened Tagus high on a wooden cross so their king could be seen by his sorrowing subjects. The story functions as evidence of the base character of the general who did such a thing. In Matthew's narrative, for Jesus to be treated as he was by Jews and Romans functions as a reflection on the character of his accusers and his murderers.

---

sons of Zebedee (20:20). Who has buried Jesus? The evangelist says it is not the Eleven (contrast 14:12) but a rich man, Joseph of Arimathea, **a disciple of Jesus** (27:57b; Acts 13:29 says the ones who were responsible for Jesus's demise took him down from the cross and laid him in a tomb; Luke 23:50 says Joseph was a member of the council). Roman preference was to leave the bodies of criminals to rot on their crosses (Petronius, *Sat.* 112). On occasion, however, they did give a corpse to friends or relatives if they asked permission to bury it (Philo, *Flacc.* 83–84). Jewish custom demanded burial even of criminals by sunset (Deut. 21:23), but usually in a common grave specifically for such people (*m. Sanh.* 6.5; *t. Sanh.* 9.8). Josephus (*J.W.* 4.317) says, "The Jews used to take so much care of the burial of men, that they took down those that were condemned and crucified, and buried them before the going down of the sun" (trans. Thackeray 1927–38). In *Ant.* 4.202, Josephus says, however, that a blasphemer should be buried ignominiously and in obscurity.

When Pilate grants Joseph's request for the body of Jesus, this rich man wraps the corpse in a clean linen shroud (part of burial for the righteous, cf. *T. Ab.* 20A; *L.A.E.* 48.1) and buries the corpse **in his new tomb that he had hewn in the rock. And rolling a large stone in the door of the tomb, he went away** (27:60; Isa. 53:9 RSV: "They made his grave . . . with a rich man"). Jesus's burial, then, was far from being ignominious. (Plutarch [*Alc.* 39.4; *Cor.* 39.5–6] emphasizes the importance of honorable burial.) Notice is again paid to the women. **Now Mary Magdalene and the other Mary were sitting there in front of the tomb** (27:61). As the women have witnessed Jesus's death, they now are witnesses of his burial. They are guarantors of the first part of early

© Stephen von Wyrick

Figure 18. An example of a tomb that would be closed by a rolling stone.

Christian proclamation (1 Cor. 15:3b–4a: "Christ died; . . . he was buried"). Scene 6 is now at its end.

Scene 7: Resurrection (27:62–28:20)

Scene 7 follows an ABA'B' pattern. A and A' deal with the guards at the tomb; B and B' offer appearances and commissions.

A The setting of the guard (27:62–66)
  B Angelic and resurrection appearances and commissions (28:1–10)
A' The bribing of the guard (28:11–15)
  B' A resurrection appearance and commission (28:16–20)

(A) **27:62–66.** In section A (material unique to Matthew), events are located **on the next day, the one after the Day of Preparation** (the Sabbath, Nisan 16; 27:62). The Day of Preparation refers to Friday, when Jews normally prepared for the Sabbath rest (cf. Mark 15:42: the day of preparation, that is, the day before the Sabbath, which is an explanation for gentile readers of Mark). The chief priests and Pharisees ask Pilate for a guard at the tomb to prevent theft of Jesus's body by his disciples and their claim that he has risen from the dead. Pilate responded, **You have guards. Go seal it** (27:65). This they do by sealing the stone and setting a guard. Justin Martyr (*Dial.* 108) says that in his day Jews claimed that the disciples stole the body by night from the tomb and deceived people by saying he had risen from the dead and ascended to heaven. Matthew 27:62–66 and what follows in 28:2–4 and 28:11–15 seem to be a defense against such a charge. (A similar telling of the story, but with elaborations and with quite a different slant, is found in *Gos. Pet.* 28–33.)

(B) **28:1–10.** Section B is set early on the day after the Sabbath (Sunday, Nisan 17). It involves a third reference to women (they watch Jesus die on the cross [27:55–56]; they see Jesus buried in Joseph's tomb [27:61]; they witness the empty tomb and experience a resurrection appearance [28:1–8, 9–10]). Two mentioned by name are in all three episodes: Mary Magdalene and the other Mary (the mother of James and Joseph [27:56] or perhaps Jesus's mother [cf. 13:55]). Although Mark 16:1 says they have come to anoint the body, Matt. 28:1 notes only that they have come to see the tomb. In Matt. 26:12, proleptically Jesus's body has already been anointed for burial. (Plutarch, *Cor.* 39.5–6, says women mourned for Coriolanus for ten months.) An awesome angel of the Lord descends from heaven, rolls the stone away from the tomb's entrance, and sits upon it. The descending angel comes not to raise Jesus but rather to make the empty tomb visible to the women and to tell them what has happened (Schnackenburg 2002, 293). The effect upon the soldiers is typical for an angelophany. **And for fear of him, those guarding the tomb shook and became as dead men** (28:4; cf. *Gos. Pet.* 35–42 for an elaborated account). The effect for the women is different. The angel preaches to them: **I know that you are seeking Jesus who was crucified. He is not here, for he was raised, as he said** (16:21; 17:9, 23; 20:19). **Come, see the place where he lay** (28:5–6). Then he gives the women a commission: **Quickly go and say to his disciples that he has been raised from the dead, and behold, he goes before you (pl.) into Galilee. There you will see him** (28:7).

As the women go to fulfill the angel's commission, **Jesus met them, saying, "Greetings"** (28:9a). They take hold of his feet (showing that he is corporeal; cf. John 20:17) and worship him. Then the risen Jesus gives them a repeat of the angel's commission: **Go and tell my disciples that when they go to Galilee, they will see me there** (28:10). The women are again obedient. They go (28:11a). Now the women (two of them, to guarantee true testimony [Deut. 19:15]) have become guarantors of the second part of the earliest Christian proclamation ("he was raised; . . . he appeared").

(A') **28:11–15.** Section A' returns to the soldiers who have been stationed as guards at the tomb. As the women go to announce to the disciples the good news, the soldiers go into the city and **announce to the chief priests all that had transpired. After getting together with the elders and taking counsel, they gave money to the soldiers, saying, "You say, 'His disciples came by night and stole him while we were sleeping.' And if this should be heard by**

The Worship of Jesus

Outside of Matthew, the Synoptics contain only three references to the worship of Jesus (Mark 5:6; 15:19 is mock worship; Luke 4:15). In the First Gospel there are at least nine references. Two are after the resurrection (28:9, 17); the rest come prior to Jesus's being raised (2:11; 8:2; 9:18; 14:33; 15:25; 20:20; 21:16).

Only the KJV translates *proskyneō* consistently as "worship." Matthew 4:10 raises a question about this practice. Jesus says that only God is to be worshiped. The inference that must be drawn is that this Gospel regards Jesus as son of God and hence worthy of worship (cf. Rev. 5:13–14; Powell 1995b, 28–61).

the governor, we will persuade him, and you will not be held responsible" (28:11b–14; cf. Acts 12:18–19 and Petronius [*Sat.* 112] for the consequences of soldiers' sleeping on guard duty). So the soldiers take the money and do as they were instructed. **And this account has circulated among the Jews until this day** (28:15b). (Aelius Theon, *Progym.* 95, offers direction about effective argumentation: one needs not only to refute but also to show how such a distorted story originated. This Matthew does.)

(B′) **28:16–20.** Section B′ offers another resurrection appearance and commission to disciples. Although numerous attempts have been made to classify this pericope's *Gattung* (e.g., coronation hymn, cult legend, a form that is sui generis), it for the most part reflects a traditional commissioning form (Hubbard 1974; Carter 2000, 549). *Introduction* (28:16): the women's mission has been successful. **The eleven disciples went to Galilee to the mountain to which Jesus had directed them.** *Confrontation* (28:17a): there they see the risen Jesus. *Reaction* (28:17b–c): their reactions are twofold: **they worshiped** and they (*hoi de*) **doubted.** It is the latter that produces a problem. Who doubts? (Do the Eleven worship and others doubt? Do the Eleven worship but some of them doubt? Do the Eleven worship and the Eleven doubt?) In Matthew, the particular phrase (*hoi de* + a verbal construction) always refers to the entire group of people mentioned previously or their spokesman (e.g., 2:9; 8:32; 9:31; 20:4–5; 22:5; 28:9; 28:15; etc.). The point of view of a subgroup is never set against the point of view of the whole body. In Matt. 28:17, therefore, **they doubted** refers to the whole group of the Eleven.

What then does that doubt mean? In the NT, the verb "to doubt" occurs only in Matt. 28:17 and 14:31. In the latter, it means to be a person of little faith, faith that wavers in the face of trial. So here one should translate, **The Eleven worshiped him but with little faith.** *Commission* (28:18–20a): **All authority in heaven and on earth has been given to me** (Dan. 7:13–14; cf. Phil. 2:9–11). **As you go, therefore, make disciples of all the nations, baptizing them in the** name of the Father and the Son and the Holy Spirit, teaching them to observe everything I have commanded you. *Protest* (not present here). *Reassurance* (28:20b): And behold, I am with you all the days until the end of the age. *Obedience to the commission* (not here, but the entire Gospel presupposes the disciples' obedience; cf. 24:14).

This brief commission in 28:18–20 is laden with problems, four in particular. First, how is **all nations** to be understood? Does it refer to "all gentiles" (Hare and Harrington 1975) or "all nations, including Jews" (Meier 1977)? If the gospel is to be preached to all nations before the parousia (24:14), then it will touch both gentiles and Jews who live in those places. The mission to the Jews continues after the resurrection as part of the larger task of evangelization (Kvalbein 1998).

Second, what is to be made of the triad of Father, Son, and Holy Spirit that is an integral part of the First Gospel? There are similar triads in ancient Judaism (e.g., *1 En.* 49.2–3 and *1 En.* 62.1–2 speak of an Elect One, Lord of Spirits, and the Spirit, where the imagery of the heavenly court is evoked). Among NT documents one finds a triad of Father, Jesus, and angels (e.g., Matt. 16:27; 24:36; 25:31–46; 2 Thess. 1:6–7; cf. Rev. 1:4–7; 5:6–7). One also finds in the NT a triad of Father, Son, and Spirit (e.g., Matt. 3:13–17; 10:20–23; Gal. 4:4–6; 1 Cor. 12:4–6; 2 Cor. 13:13; Rom. 8:15–17; Eph. 1:17; 2:13–18; 4:4–6; Titus 3:4–6; Rev. 3:5–6; John 14:16–17, 26; Acts 2:32–33; 10:38; 1 Pet. 1:2). Matthew 28:19 is part of the larger picture of triads in the First Gospel and elsewhere. A connection between the triad (Father, Son, and Holy Spirit) and baptism is also found, near the time of Matthew, in *Did.* 7.1–3 (cf. also baptism in the name of the Lord [Christ] in *Did.* 9.5) and Justin Martyr (*1 Apol.* 61). The Christians of NT times did not have a developed doctrine of the Trinity. They were unable, however, to state fully the meaning of their distinctive experience of God without using together "Father, Son, and Holy Spirit" as God's name (Argyle 1966, 173–84).

Third, how is the task of evangelization conceived? There is an initial general statement: **Make disciples.** Then there follow two dimensions of this task: **baptizing them** is the initial step, and **teaching them to observe everything I have commanded** is the subsequent process. This is to be done **as you go.** There is an event and a process in the making of disciples.

Fourth, what is the function of this appearance? It is a mission-inaugurating experience. In 1 Cor. 15:5, by contrast, the appearance to the Twelve functions as a church-founding experience (Fuller 1980, 80).

Functions of the Unit as a Whole

The passion and resurrection narratives of Matt. 26–28 continue the encomiastic emphasis of the Gospel. Cicero (*Inv.* 1.24.34–35) says that among the items that characterize a person, if that one is no longer alive, is the nature of his death. Aelius Theon presents three main categories from which arguments

Revelation of the Divine Name

Revelation of the divine name was associated with divine deliverance and the making of a covenant. In Exod. 6:2–3, 6–7, God says to Moses, "'I am the LORD [Yahweh]. I appeared to Abraham, Isaac, and Jacob as God Almighty [El Shaddai], but by my name 'The LORD' [Yahweh] I did not make myself known to them. . . . Say therefore to the Israelites, 'I am the LORD [Yahweh], and I will free you . . . and deliver you. . . . I will take you as my people, and I will be your God. You shall know that I am the LORD [Yahweh] your God, who has freed you from the . . . Egyptians.'" Just as Exodus regards the revelation of the divine name as appropriate on the occasion of a deliverance and the establishment of a covenant, so the First Gospel assumes that in connection with the establishment of a new covenant, participants were made to know the name of the God to whom they are now related: Father, Son, and Holy Spirit.

may be developed in an encomium; "things external to us" constitutes the third category. In this category external goods include "first, good birth, and that is twofold, either from the goodness of (a man's) city and tribe and constitution, or from ancestors and other relatives. Then there is education, friendship, reputation, official position, wealth, good children, and a good death" (*Progym.* 110.1–8, trans. Kennedy 2003). Aelius Theon also says that one's manner of death and what followed his death contribute to the characterization of a person (*Progym.* 78.26–27). A person's death might convey either honor or dishonor. Hermogenes (*Progym.* 16), in his discussion of encomium, also includes the manner of one's death as a desired topic. The ancient populace found encomiastic accounts of deaths of important men to be of great interest (Tacitus, *Ann.* 4.33). The Jewish world shared the Greco-Roman perspective. Sirach 11:28 says, "Call no one happy before his death; by how he ends, a person becomes known."

In addition to the encomiastic tendency, the First Evangelist continues his defense of Jesus against attack (e.g., 3:14–15; 5:17). The two episodes of Matt. 27:62–66 and 28:11–15 (the sealing of the tomb and the bribery of the soldiers) defend against the charge that Jesus did not really rise from the dead; rather, his disciples stole his body from the tomb.

That Jesus died by crucifixion on the charge of claiming to be a king created difficulties for his followers. Paul put it this way: "Christ crucified, a stumbling block to Jews and foolishness to Gentiles" (1 Cor. 1:23). The First Evangelist uses at least two major tactics to reverse the usual reading of such a death.

In the first place, he portrays Jesus's suffering and death as integral to the redemptive plan of God (cf. Senior 1972). This is done in part by the overwhelming use of biblical allusions in connection with the events of Jesus's passion. There are only a few explicit references to fulfillment of the Scriptures in Matt. 26–28 (e.g., 26:31b [Zech. 13:7]; 26:56 [?]; 27:9–10 [Zech. 11:12–13; Jer. 18:1–3; 32:6–15?]). Most links are via allusion:

Table 12
Old Testament Fulfillment Texts in Matthew 26–28

Matthew	Old Testament
26:15	Zech. 11:12
26:24	Ps. 41:9
26:63	Isa. 53:7
27:14	Isa. 52:15
27:30–31	Isa. 50:6
27:33–34	Ps. 69:21
27:35–37	Ps. 22:18–19
27:38	Isa. 53:3, 9, 12
27:39–40	Ps. 22:7
27:43	Ps. 22:8
27:46	Ps. 22:1
27:48	Ps. 69:21
27:51	Zech. 14:4–5
27:52–53	Ezek. 37:12–13
27:57, 60	Isa. 53:9

These allusions are typological. What is happening to Jesus is a fulfillment of this type of experience spoken of in the Scriptures. In part also, Matthew uses a prophecy-fulfillment motif to depict Jesus's willing participation in the events that transpire.

Jesus's prophecy of 26:2 is fulfilled in 27:2, 26;
26:21 is fulfilled in 26:47–49;
26:31 is fulfilled in 26:56;
26:32 is fulfilled in 28:16;
26:34 is fulfilled in 26:75;
26:45b is fulfilled in 26:50.

Jesus knows what is to happen and is a willing participant in the events. He does so because his death is part of the divine plan (16:21; *dei*) and will benefit many (20:28). When he is on trial, moreover, he remains silent, impressing Pilate (27:14). His death is that of a righteous man (27:19). The portents that accompany his crucifixion and death attest heaven's witness to his significance (27:45, 51–53).

Typological Interpretation

"The New Testament's use of the Old Testament lies at the heart of its theology, and it is primarily expressed within the framework of a typological exposition" (E. Ellis 1991, 156). New Testament typological interpretation relates the past to the present by means of a historical correspondence and escalation in which the divinely ordered prefigurement finds a complement in the subsequent and greater event. In such covenant typology, various persons, events, and institutions of ancient Israel are viewed as prophetic prefigurements of NT realities. Of course, an OT type may stand in a positive correspondence to the NT reality or in contrast to it.

In the second place, Jesus's resurrection signals God's vindication of his Son. By virtue of his exaltation, Jesus now possesses all authority in heaven and on earth (28:18). Viewed from the perspective of his resurrection, Jesus's death and resurrection constitute his enthronement as king of the Jews (and the cosmos). The entire section, Matt. 26–28, then, is an ironic depiction. Irony occurs when a speaker says exactly the opposite of what is actually thought (Cicero, *De or.* 3.53.203; Quintilian, *Inst.* 6.2.15–16). The Gospel narrates a story of a Jew executed as an insurrectionist by the Romans. The evangelist tells the story with irony. The man who was executed was indeed the king of the Jews, and his crucifixion and resurrection signal his enthronement as the one with all authority in heaven and on earth, fulfilling God's redemptive plan for the ages. Matthew 26–28, then, is the culmination of the encomium that began in chapters 1–2.

Theological Issues

How Christians Have Interpreted the Cross

"The Church, convinced of the great reality of the fact of Atonement, has never found it necessary or desirable to set her seal to any special theory for the explanation of that fact" (Grensted 1962, 2). A variety of models for understanding the meaning of the cross may be found in Christian history. Four stand out:

1. The Christus victor view was the customary doctrine of the atonement for nearly one thousand years. The assumption was that the devil had the right and the power to punish humans with death once their sin had laid them open to that fate. God and Jesus were engaged in some kind of transaction with the devil in order to purchase the freedom of humans. In this model, the problem that the cross dealt with was human

bondage to the devil (e.g., Origen, *Comm. Rom.* 2.13; *Comm. Matt.* 16.8; Gregory of Nyssa, *Or. cat.* 22).

2. The satisfaction theory of Anselm (*Cur Deus Homo?*) is based on the legal assumption of his time, that satisfaction was an alternative to punishment in the case of private offenses. Human sin had violated God's honor. Unless there was satisfaction for that violation, punishment must fall. Satisfaction could only be offered to God by one who was of equal status; satisfaction, however, had to be offered by a human. That is why the incarnation took place. Christ the God-man could do both things required to offer satisfaction to God, whose honor had been violated. The problem that the cross dealt with, therefore, was God's wounded honor.

3. The penal theory gained predominance with the Protestant Reformers (before the Reformers, only a few hints of a penal theory can be found). In this theory, the law demands punishment, and that punishment must be inflicted and endured. Satisfaction is not an alternative. As the Augsburg Confession (pt. 1, art. 3) puts it, Christ "truly suffered, was crucified, dead, and buried, that he might reconcile the Father unto us, and might be a sacrifice, not only for original guilt, but also for all actual sins of men" (Schaff 1931, 3:9). If the penalty is on Christ, then humans are free. The problem dealt with here is abstract justice.

4. According to the moral influence theory of Abelard, the cross was the manifestation of God's love. This love revealed to humans in the cross draws human minds away from the will to sin, breaks the slavery to sin, gives humans true freedom, and inclines them to the fullest love of God (*Comm. Rom.* 4.25; 3.26; 5.5). The problem dealt with by this model is the cold, hard hearts of sinful humans.

Matthew's depiction of Jesus's death, however, does not correspond to any of these four models. While Matthew's view of the meaning of Jesus's death does not exhaust the perspectives of the whole of the NT, the First Gospel's view must be allowed its own integrity and must not be subverted by views coming from outside this Gospel.

Apotheosis and Matthew's Depiction of Jesus's Resurrection

Matthew 26–28 provides the reader with the final piece that enables a correct understanding of Matthew's Christology. In his book *The Foundations of New Testament Christology* (1965), R. H. Fuller argues that there were three different christological patterns to be found in the period before Paul: a two-foci Christology, an exaltation model, and an epiphany pattern. (1) The two focal points of the two-foci Christology are the authoritative word and work of Jesus during his public ministry, on the one hand, and his parousia as end-time judge, on the other. During his ministry Jesus called for repentance. His

Two Types of Mediterranean Deities

As early as Herodotus, a distinction was drawn between two types of deities: those who were eternal and those who had a beginning to their existence; Dionysius and Hercules were examples of the latter (*Hist.* 2.43; 2.145–46). Diodorus Siculus articulates the typology:

> "As regards the gods, . . . men of ancient times have handed down to later generations two different conceptions: certain of the gods, they say, are eternal and imperishable. . . . But the other gods, we are told, were terrestrial beings who attained to immortal honor and fame because of their benefactions to mankind, such as Heracles, Dionysius, Aristaeus, and the others who were like them." (*Bib. hist.* 6.1; cf. 1.13, trans. C. Oldfather et al. 1933–67)

Plutarch reflects the same typology: Apollo is not "from among those deities who were changed from mortals into immortals, like Heracles and Dionysius, whose virtues enabled them to cast off mortality and suffering; but he is one of those deities who are unbegotten and eternal" (*Pel.* 16, trans. Perrin 1914–26). Philo reflects a knowledge of the typology. In his critique of Caligula (*Legat.* 77–114), he says that Gaius began trying to liken himself to the demigods such as Dionysius and Hercules (78–92), and then claimed he was worthy of the veneration and worship due the supreme deities like Mercury, Apollo, and Mars (93–113). Philo concludes that Gaius ought not to be likened to any god, demigod or eternal (114).

The practice of claiming demigod status for many figures resulted in Lucian's satirical *Parliament of the Gods* and the *Passing of Peregrinus*. In the former, Lucian has Momus complain to Zeus about the large number of gods that have been allowed into heaven such as Dionysius, Asclepius, and Hercules (*Deor. conc.* 7–10, 14). In the latter, Lucian tells of one Peregrinus, who tries to imitate Hercules by burning himself on a pyre at a festival, having manufactured myths about his becoming an immortal (*Peregr.* 33–36). A century earlier, Seneca the Younger had satirized the attempted deification of the deceased emperor Claudius in his *The Pumpkinification of Claudius*. Even Augustus, in Seneca's satire, who had previously been made a god, spoke against the deification of Claudius (*Apoc.* 10–11). Claudius was thus denied deification and sent to hades. So widespread was this typology of eternals and immortals/demigods that auditors of the First Gospel could not escape hearing its presentation of Jesus in such categories.

execution functioned as the human no to that call, a rejection of the message and the messenger. His resurrection manifested the divine yes, a vindication of the message and the messenger. In the meantime, he waits in heaven until he will come as messianic judge (e.g., the Palestinian son-of-man sayings; Acts 3:12–26). (2) The exaltation Christology regarded Jesus's resurrection as his enthronement as son of God with power. He rules from heaven until all his enemies have been subdued (e.g., Rom. 1:3–4; Acts 2:33–36; 1 Cor. 15:20–28). (3) The epiphany Christology envisioned a preexistent One who descended at the incarnation, performed his saving work, and then ascended back into the heaven from whence he had come (e.g., 1 Tim. 3:16). Matthew's resurrection narratives place the First Gospel's Christology within the exaltation pattern.

Exaltation Christology represents the attempt by some early Christians to understand Jesus's resurrection in the categories of apotheosis. Apotheosis refers to a human hero's elevation to immortal life among the gods after his or her death. (For what follows, cf. Cotter 2001; Talbert 1975.) Stories of such happenings circulated widely in Mediterranean circles, pagan and Jewish (e.g., Romulus, Aristeas, Cleomenes, Alcmene, Apollonius of Tyana, Peregrinus, Demainete). An apotheosis myth was used on occasion to interpret the lives of historical figures (e.g., Augustus, Moses). Traditions about Romulus may serve as an example of the pattern (Plutarch, *Rom.* 27.7–28.3; Ovid, *Metam.* 14.804–51; Dionysius of Halicarnassus, *Ant. rom.* 2.56.2), which are then compared with traditions about Augustus and details from the First Gospel about Jesus.

Table 13
Parallels between Romulus, Augustus, and Jesus

Romulus	Augustus	Jesus
a good king produced by a miraculous birth	the product of a miraculous birth	produced by a miraculous birth
	a righteous jurist who promoted the laws by his own good example	messiah designate, a benevolent son of David and righteous teacher
killed		killed unjustly
caught up to heaven	ascent to heaven attested by a credible witness	raised from the dead and ascended to heaven
became a benevolent god for his subjects	was declared to be a god and was decreed a temple with worship	
His appearance to a friend included instruction for the Roman people and a promise made to them.		His appearances, witnessed by multiple credible people, provided instruction for his disciples and a promise to them of his ongoing presence.
The people prayed to Quirinus (his new divine name) and honored him as a god.		His exaltation involved his being given all authority in heaven and on earth and his reception of worship.

The story of Jesus has its distinctives, of course. For example, he was raised from the dead by the Jewish God (1 Cor. 15:3–5); his reign began with his exaltation; it included heaven and earth; and it was for all time. The similarities in the overall pattern, however, would have given a Mediterranean auditor every reason to hear Matthew's distinctive story as the exaltation christological pattern with affinities to the apotheosis tradition of antiquity. Matthew was not the only early Christian Gospel to tell the story of Jesus in such terms. Luke-Acts is an even clearer example of the pattern.

Later Christian Interpretations of Jesus's Resurrection

The proclamation of the resurrection of Jesus has rightly been the object of intense intellectual scrutiny. The various interpretations in its reception history, however, fall into a few distinct categories. What follows is a brief survey of representative interpretations from the past two or more centuries. There are two main categories.

On the one hand are those who say that the resurrection of Jesus was a historical event. Two distinguishable camps fall under this heading: the claims of orthodoxy and those of the rationalists. We begin with the claims of orthodoxy. Let us take Merrill Tenney as an example:

> Admittedly Christ's resurrection is a unique phenomenon, for it differs even from the instances of resuscitation accomplished by the prophets and by Jesus. . . . Whether or not one can believe that such an event actually occurred will be determined by his presuppositions rather than by the historical record. The written accounts are as valid as any history can be. (1963, 196)

Here the uniqueness of the resurrection is conceded. Nevertheless, it is understood as an event that can be established by historical research. The problem with this position for most scholars of the last two centuries is well put by Pfleiderer:

> At this decisive point [the resurrection of Jesus], the historical method has least right to withdraw from a critical examination of the traditional stories.

A Christian Use of the Romulus Tradition

In his *Seven Books against the Heathen*, Arnobius compares Romulus and Jesus:

"Father Romulus himself, who was torn to pieces by the hands of a hundred senators, do you not call Quirinus Martius, and do you not honour him with priests and with gorgeous couches, and do you not worship him in most spacious temples; and in addition to all this, do you not affirm that he has ascended into heaven? Either, therefore, you too are to be laughed at, who regard as gods men slain by the most cruel tortures; or if there is sure ground for your thinking that you should do so, allow us too to feel assured for what causes and on what grounds we do this." (1.41, ANF 6:424)

... More cannot be expected of historical research, than such an explanation ... as comports with the analogy of other human experience and is therefore thinkable and probable. (1906, 133)

For Pfleiderer and those like him since his day, the very uniqueness of the event removes it from the category of a historical event (i.e., an event that can be established by the historical method). An event that can be established by the historical method is one for which there is reliable source material and that has analogies in general human experience. Without the latter, by definition, it cannot be a historical event.

The second camp that treats the resurrection of Jesus as a historical event consists of the rationalists. H. E. G. Paulus (1828) is the classic example of those who regard the resurrection of Jesus as a historical event because it has analogies in human experience. Jesus, he says, was taken down from the cross in a deathlike trance. The cool grave and the aromatic spices contributed to his resuscitation. The earthquake brought Jesus to full consciousness and rolled the stone away from the entrance. Jesus found a gardener's clothes and put them on. He lived for forty days with his disciples in Jerusalem and Galilee. Sensing his end was near, he met with his disciples one last time on the Mount of Olives. Two secret disciples, mistaken as angels, removed him. Where he died, the disciples never knew. They came to describe the last meeting as an ascension. Josephus (*Life* 75) provides an analogy. He says that on one occasion he found several Jewish prisoners crucified. He asked Titus to let him take down three whom he knew. He did so and carefully attended them. One lived. Rationalists therefore argue that Jesus's resurrection was historical because it was a natural event with analogies in human experience.

The problem with this reading is twofold. First, the NT authors do not regard Jesus's resurrection as a natural event. They regard it as unique, without any human analogies. Second, the rationalists' explanation cannot account for what happened to the disciples. D. F. Strauss critiques the rationalists this way:

It is impossible that a being who had stolen half-dead out of the sepulcher, who crept about weak and ill, wanting medical treatment, who required bandaging, strengthening and indulgence, and who still at last yielded to his sufferings, could have given to the disciples the impression that he was a Conqueror over death and the grave, the Prince of Life, an impression that lay at the bottom of their future ministry. Such a resuscitation could only have weakened the impression which he had made on them in life and in death . . . but could by no possibility have changed their sorrow into enthusiasm, have elevated their reverence into worship. (1879, 1:412)

On the other hand, there are those who say that the resurrection of Jesus was not a historical event. There are two varieties of scholars who espouse this position. First, there are those who say that Jesus's resurrection was/is a subjective event. Johannes Weiss is representative:

> For those . . . who take account of the modern scientific doctrine of the un-broken sequence of causality, there is scarcely any alternative to the view that these experiences of the disciples were simply "visions." The scientific meaning of this term is that an apparent act of vision takes place for which there is no corresponding external object. . . . At the same time the sense-impression of sight is accepted by the one who experiences the vision as completely as if it were wholly objective. (1959, 1:28–29)

A more recent adaptation of this subjective view is that of Rudolf Bultmann (1961), who sees the meaning of Jesus's resurrection for the disciples (and for us) as the rise of faith in them (and us). R. H. Fuller's response is representa-tive of critics of this hypothesis:

> If . . . by "historical" we mean "verifiable" or "demonstrable by historical criti-cism" the resurrection itself, apart from the rise of the Easter faith, is not his-torical. . . . (Yet) the New Testament understands the resurrection not merely as a mythological statement of the saving significance of the cross, but as an occurrence between God and Jesus. . . . It must be insisted that the resurrection of Christ does not occur first, or exclusively, in my existence, in my rising with Christ. . . . His resurrection . . . is prior to all other resurrections, including existential ones. (Fuller 1962, 23–24)

Second, some contend that Jesus's resurrection was a trans-subjective event. What is meant here is that the resurrection happened ontically to Jesus. God transformed him from mortal into immortal, an absolutely unique event. The facticity of the resurrection of Jesus is guaranteed, even if it cannot be called a historical event. The historical method cannot establish the facticity of the event. It can, however, show the inadequacy of alternative explanations. The historical method can also show how the first disciples came to believe in the resurrection of Jesus through the appearances. For a modern person, the process taken by the first disciples is prototypical. They started with their contact with the life, suffering, and death of Jesus. We also start with Jesus's life and teachings, suffering and death. Our faith develops by analogy with the prototypical faith of the disciples. Eventually, however, we, like they, en-counter that which is outside every analogy: the resurrection of Jesus. Helmut Thielicke (1964) is representative of this view.

While this view does come closer than the other options surveyed so far to what the NT obviously means by Jesus's resurrection, it does not satisfactorily explain how the noetic process reaches faith in Jesus's resurrection. Having begun with Jesus's life and teaching, suffering and death, how does one make the leap to resurrection faith? What in the encounter with such an event, an event without analogies, brings one to credible belief? Perhaps it is the shaping of one's worldview by participation in a community of two-thousand-years' duration that began out of the conviction of Jesus's resurrection; by the experience of transcendence that answers to the name Jesus; and by the experience of this presence in events that affect the physical world (e.g., healings). With *hints* derived from such shaping forces as these, the disciple's worldview may be shaped to the point where the Easter kerygma evokes belief, belief that the living God does intervene in this world even in ways that are visible only to eyes of faith.

Bibliography

Albright, W. F., and C. S. Mann. 1971. *Matthew*. Anchor Bible. Garden City, NY: Doubleday.

Allison, Dale, Jr. 1983. "Matthew 23:39 = Luke 13:35b as a Conditional Prophecy." *Journal for the Study of the New Testament* 18:75–84.

———. 1988. "Two Notes on a Key Text: Matthew 11:25–30." *Journal of Theological Studies* 39:477–84.

———. 1993. *The New Moses: A Matthean Typology*. Minneapolis: Fortress.

Alston, William P. 1991. *Perceiving God: The Epistemology of Religious Experience*. Ithaca, NY: Cornell University Press.

Arens, Eduardo. 1976. *The Ēlthon-Sayings in the Synoptic Tradition*. Orbis biblicus et orientalis 10. Göttingen: Vandenhoeck & Ruprecht.

Argyle, A. W. 1966. *God in the New Testament*. New York: Lippincott.

Ariarajah, Wesley. 1985. *The Bible and People of Other Faiths*. Geneva: World Council of Churches.

Ascough, Richard S. 2001. "Matthew and Community Formation." In *The Gospel of Matthew in Current Study*, edited by D. E. Aune, 96–126. Grand Rapids: Eerdmans.

Aus, Roger David. 2004. *Matthew 1–2 and the Virginal Conception*. New York: University Press of America.

Austin, J. L. 1962. *How to Do Things with Words*. Cambridge, MA: Harvard University Press.

Baby, Parambi. 2003. *The Discipleship of Women in the Gospel according to Matthew*. Testi gregoriana, Serie teologia 94. Rome: Editrice Pontificia Universita Gregoriana.

Bacon, B. W. 1930. *Studies in Matthew*. New York: Holt.

Balabanski, Vicky. 2002. "Opening the Closed Door: A Feminist Rereading of the Wise and Foolish Virgins (Matthew 25:1–13)." In *The Lost Coin: Parables of Women, Work and Wisdom*, edited by Mary Ann Beavis, 71–97. Biblical Seminar 86. London: Sheffield Academic Press.

Balch, David, ed. 1991. *Social History of the Matthean Community*. Minneapolis: Fortress.

Barrett, C. K. 1987. *The New Testament Background: Selected Documents*. Rev. and expanded ed. San Francisco: HarperSanFrancisco.

Bauckham, Richard. 1985. "The Son of Man: 'A Man in My Position' or 'Someone.'" *Journal for the Study of the New Testament* 23:23–33.

———. 1998. *The Gospel for All Christians: Rethinking the Gospel Audiences*. Edinburgh: T&T Clark.

Bauer, David R. 1988. *The Structure of Matthew's Gospel*. Journal for the Study of the New Testament: Supplement Series 31. Sheffield: Almond.

———. 1990. "The Literary Function of the Genealogy in Matthew's Gospel." In *SBL 1990 Seminar Papers*, edited by D. J. Lull, 451–68. Atlanta: Scholars Press.

———. 1995. "The Kingship of Jesus in the Matthean Infancy Narrative: A Literary Analysis." *Catholic Biblical Quarterly* 57:306–23.

Baxter, W. S. 2006. "Healing and the Son of David: Matthew's Warrant." *Novum Testamentum* 48:36–50.

Betz, Hans Dieter. 1995. *The Sermon on the Mount*. Hermeneia. Minneapolis: Fortress.

Betz, Otto. 1992. "Jesus and the Temple Scroll." In *Jesus and the Dead Sea Scrolls*, edited by J. H. Charlesworth, 75–103. Anchor Bible Reference Library. New York: Doubleday.

Bietenhard, H. 1967. "*Onoma*." In *Theological Dictionary of the New Testament*, edited by G. Kittel and G. Friedrich, translated by G. W. Bromiley, 5:242–81. Grand Rapids: Eerdmans.

Birch, Bruce, and Larry Rasmussen. 1976. *Bible and Ethics in the Christian Life*. Minneapolis: Augsburg.

Blackburn, Barry. 1991. *Theios Anēr and the Markan Miracle Traditions*. Wissenschaftliche Untersuchungen zum Neuen Testament 2/40. Tübingen: Mohr Siebeck.

Blair, E. P. 1960. *Jesus in the Gospel of Matthew*. Nashville: Abingdon.

Blinzler, Josef. 1969. *Der Prozess Jesu*. 4th ed. Regensburg: Pustet.

Bloch, Ernst. 1986. *The Principle of Hope*. Part 5. Oxford: Blackwell.

Blomberg, Craig L. 1986. "The Miracles as Parables." In *Gospel Perspectives*, edited by David Wenham and Craig Blomberg, 6:327–60. Sheffield: JSOT Press.

———. 1992. *Matthew*. New American Commentary 22. Nashville: Broadman.

Boccaccini, Gabriele. 1991. *Middle Judaism*. Minneapolis: Fortress.

Bock, Darrell. 1998. *Blasphemy and Exaltation in Judaism and the Final Examination of Jesus*. Wissenschaftliche Untersuchungen zum Neuen Testament 2/106. Tübingen: Mohr Siebeck.

Boer, M. C. de. 1988. "Ten Thousand Talents? Matthew's Interpretation and Redaction of the Parable of the Unforgiving Servant (Matthew 18:23–35)." *Catholic Biblical Quarterly* 50:214–32.

Boerman, Daniel. 2005. "The Chiastic Structure of Matthew 11–12." *Calvin Theological Journal* 40:313–25.

Bohler, D. 1998. "Jesus als Davidssohn bei Lukas und Micha." *Biblica* 79:532–38.

Bonnard, Pierre. 1963. *L'Évangile selon Saint Matthieu*. Commentaire du Nouveau Testament 1. Neuchâtel: Delachaux & Niestlé.

Boring, Eugene. 1995. "Matthew." In *The New Interpreter's Bible*, 8:87–506. Nashville: Abingdon.

Branden, Robert C. 2006. *Satanic Conflict and the Plot of Matthew*. Studies in Biblical Literature 89. New York: Peter Lang.

Bratcher, Robert G. 1958. "A Study of Isaiah 7:14." *The Bible Translator* 9:97–126.

Braude, William G. 1959. *The Midrash on Psalms*. 2 vols. Yale Judaica Series 13. New Haven: Yale University Press.

———. 1968. *Pesikta Rabbati*. 2 vols. New Haven: Yale University Press.

Brenton, L. C. L. 1906. *The Septuagint Version of the Old Testament: With an English Translation; and with Various Readings and Critical Notes*. London: S. Bagster and Sons; New York: James Pott.

Brown, Raymond E. 1977. *The Birth of the Messiah*. Garden City, NY: Doubleday.

———. 1994. *The Death of the Messiah*. 2 vols. New York: Doubleday.

Bruner, Frederick Dale. 2004. *Matthew: A Commentary*. Rev. ed. 2 vols. Grand Rapids: Eerdmans.

Bultmann, Rudolf. 1961. "New Testament and Mythology." In *Kerygma and Myth*, edited by H. W. Bartsch, 1–44. New York: Harper & Brothers.

———. 2007. *Theology of the New Testament*. New ed. 2 vols. in 1. Waco: Baylor University Press.

Burger, Christoph. 1973. "Jesu Taten nach Matthäus 8 und 9." *Zeitschrift für Theologie und Kirche* 70:272–87.

Burgess, Joseph A. 1976. *A History of the Exegesis of Matthew 16:17–19 from 1781 to 1965*. Ann Arbor, MI: Edwards Brothers.

Burnett, Fred W. 1979. *The Testament of Jesus-Sophia: A Redaction-Critical Study of the Eschatological Discourse in Matthew*. Washington, DC: University Press of America.

Burridge, Richard. 1992. *What Are the Gospels?* Society for New Testament Studies Monograph Series 70. Cambridge, UK: Cambridge University Press.

Callon, Callie. 2006. "Pilate the Villain: An Alternative Reading of Matthew's Portrayal of Pilate." *Biblical Theology Bulletin* 36:62–71.

Calvin, John. 1972. *The Harmony of the Gospels: Matthew, Mark, and Luke*. Edinburgh: St. Andrews Press.

Cameron, Peter S. 1984. *Violence and the Kingdom: The Interpretation of Matthew 11:12*. Arbeiten zum Neuen Testament und Judentum 5. Frankfurt am Main: Peter Lang.

Caragounis, Chrys. 1990. *Peter and the Rock*. Beihefte zur Zeitschrift für die neutestamentliche Wissenschaft 58. Berlin: de Gruyter.

Cargal, Timothy. 1991. "His Blood Be upon Us and upon Our Children: A Matthean Double Entendre?" *New Testament Studies* 37:101–12.

Carroll, John T., and Joel Green. 1995. *The Death of Jesus in Early Christianity*. Peabody, MA: Hendrickson.

Carter, Warren. 1992. "Kernels and Narrative Blocks: The Structure of Matthew's Gospel." *Catholic Biblical Quarterly* 54:463–81.

———. 1994. *Households and Discipleship: A Study of Matthew 19–20*. Journal for the Study of the New Testament: Supplement Series 103. Sheffield: JSOT Press.

———. 1998. "Toward an Imperial-Critical Reading of Matthew's Gospel." In *SBL 1998 Seminar Papers*, 1:296–324. Atlanta: Scholars Press.

———. 2000. *Matthew and the Margins*. Journal for the Study of the New Testament: Supplement Series 204. Sheffield: Sheffield Academic Press.

———. 2005. "Matthean Christology in Roman Imperial Key: Matthew 1:1." In *The Gospel of Matthew in Its Roman Imperial Context*, edited by John Riches and D. C. Sim, 143–65. London: T&T Clark.

Carter, Warren, and John Paul Heil. 1998. *Matthew's Parables: Audience-Oriented Perspectives*. Catholic Biblical Quarterly Monograph Series 30. Washington, DC: CBA.

Cartlidge, D. R., and David Dungan, eds. 1980. *Documents for the Study of the Gospels*. New York: Collins.

Cassidy, Richard J. 2007. *Four Times Peter: Portrayals of Peter in the Four Gospels and at Philippi*. Interfaces. Collegeville, MN: Liturgical Press.

Catchpole, D. R. 1971. "The Answer of Jesus to Caiaphas (Matt. 26:64)." *New Testament Studies* 17:213–26.

———. 1979. "The Poor on Earth and the Son of Man in Heaven: A Reappraisal of Matthew 25:31–46." *Bulletin of John Rylands Library* 61:355–97.

Chae, Young Sam. 2006. *Jesus as the Eschatological Davidic Shepherd*. Wissenschaftliche Untersuchungen zum Neuen Testament 2/116. Tübingen: Mohr Siebeck.

Chamberlain, W. D. 1957. *An Exegetical Grammar of the Greek New Testament*. New York: Macmillan.

Charlesworth, James H. 1993. "Has the Name 'Peter' Been Found among the Dead Sea Scrolls?" *Qumran Chronicle* 2:105–6.

———. 1996. "Solomon and Jesus: The Son of David in the Ante-Markan Traditions." In *Biblical and Humane: A Festschrift for John Priest*, edited by L. Bennett Elder et al., 125–51. Atlanta: Scholars Press.

Cheney, Emily R. 1986. "The Instructing Function of Selected Accounts of the Miraculous in Matthew." MA thesis, Wake Forest University.

Christ, Felix. 1970. *Jesus-Sophia: Die Sophia-Christologie bei den Synoptikern*. Abhandlungen zur Theologie des Alten und Neuen Testaments 57. Zurich: Zwingli-Verlag.

Christian, Paul. 1975. *Jesu und seine geringsten Brüder: Matthäus 25:31–46 redaktionsgeschichtlich untersucht*. Leipzig: St. Benno.

Collins, A. Y. 1994. "Rulers, Divine Men, and Walking on the Water (Mark 6:45–52)." In *Religious Propaganda and Missionary Competition in the New Testament World*, edited by Lukas Bormann et al., 207–27. Leiden: Brill.

Collins, John J. 1993. "A Pre-Christian 'Son of God' among the Dead Sea Scrolls." *Bible Review* 9:34–38, 57.

———. 1995. "A Throne in the Heavens: Apotheosis in Pre-Christian Judaism." In *Death, Ecstasy, and Other Worldly Journeys*, edited by J. J. Collins and Michael Fishbane, 41–56. Albany: SUNY.

Colson, F. H., et al., trans. 1929–62. *Philo*. 12 vols. Loeb Classical Library. Cambridge, MA: Harvard University Press.

Combrink, H. J. B. 1980. "Structural Analysis of Matthew 9:35–11:1." *Neotestamentica* 11:98–114.

Conybeare, F. C., trans. 1912. *Philostratus: Life of Apollonius of Tyana*. 2 vols. Loeb Classical Library. Cambridge, MA: Harvard University Press.

Cotter, Wendy. 2001. "Greco-Roman Apotheosis Traditions and the Resurrection Appearances in Matthew." In *The Gospel of Matthew in Current Study*, edited by D. E. Aune, 127–53. Grand Rapids: Eerdmans.

Crosby, H. Lamar, trans. 1951. *Dio Chrysostom: Discourses 61–80; Fragments; Letters*. Loeb Classical Library. Cambridge, MA: Harvard University Press.

Crosby, Michael H. 2008. "Rethinking a Key Biblical Text and Catholic Church Governance." *Biblical Theology Bulletin* 38:37–43.

Crossan, John D. 1975. "Jesus and Pacifism." In *No Famine in the Land*, edited by James W. Flanagan and Anita W. Robinson, 195–208. Missoula, MT: Scholars Press.

———. 1992. "Parable." In *Anchor Bible Dictionary*, edited by D. N. Freedman, 5:146–52. New York: Doubleday.

Cullmann, Oscar. 1948. *Le retour du Christ: Espérance de l'Église selon le Nouveau Testament*. Cahiers Théologiques 1. Paris: Delachaux & Niestlé.

Danby, Herbert. 1933. *The Mishnah*. Oxford: Clarendon.

Danker, Frederick W. 1982. *Benefactor*. St. Louis: Clayton.

Daube, David. 1972. *Civil Disobedience in Antiquity*. Edinburgh: Edinburgh University Press.

Davies, W. D. 1966. *The Setting of the Sermon on the Mount*. Cambridge, UK: Cambridge University Press.

Davies, W. D., and Dale Allison Jr. 1988, 1991, 1997. *A Critical and Exegetical Commentary on the Gospel according to Saint Matthew*. 3 vols. International Critical Commentary. Edinburgh: T&T Clark.

Deutsch, C. 1996. *Lady Wisdom, Jesus, and the Sages: Metaphor and Social Context in Matthew's Gospel*. Valley Forge, PA: Trinity.

Dobbeler, Axel von. 2000. "Die Restitution Israels und die Bekehrung der Heiden: Das Verhältnis von Matt. 10:5b–6 und Matt. 28:16–20." *Zeitschrift für neutestamentliche Wissenschaft* 91:18–44.

Dodson, Derek. 2002. "Dreams, the Ancient Novel, and the Gospel of Matthew: An Intertextual Study." *Perspectives in Religious Studies* 29:39–52.

———. 2006. "Reading Dreams: An Audience-Critical Approach to the Dreams in the Gospel of Matthew." PhD diss., Baylor University.

Doyle, B. R. 1994. "The Place of the Parable of the Laborers in the Vineyard in Matthew 20:1–16." *Australian Biblical Review* 42:39–58.

Draper, Jonathan A. 1993. "The Development of 'the Sign of the Son of Man' in the Jesus Tradition." *New Testament Studies* 39:1–21.

Drewermann, Eugen. 1992. *Tiefenpsychologie und Exegese*. 2 vols. Alten: Walter-Verlag.

Duling, Dennis. 1978. "The Therapeutic Son of David: An Element in Matthew's Christological Apologetic." *New Testament Studies* 24:392–410.

Dupont, Jacques. 1958. "Vous n'aurez pas achevé les villes d'Israel avant que le Fils de l'Homme ne vienne." *Novum Testamentum* 2:230–44.

Edwards, James R. 2005. *Is Jesus the Only Savior?* Grand Rapids: Eerdmans.

329

Edwards, Richard A. 1997. *Matthew's Narrative Portrait of Disciples*. Harrisburg, PA: Trinity.

Ellis, E. Earle. 1991. *The Old Testament in Early Christianity*. Wissenschaftliche Untersuchungen zum Neuen Testament 54. Tübingen: Mohr Siebeck.

Ellis, Peter F. 1985. *Matthew: His Mind and Message*. Collegeville, MN: Liturgical Press.

Eloff, Mervyn. 2008. "*Apo . . . heōs* and Salvation History in Matthew's Gospel." In *Built upon the Rock: Studies in the Gospel of Matthew*, edited by D. M. Gurtner and J. Nolland, 85–107. Grand Rapids: Eerdmans.

Epstein, I. 1948. *The Babylonian Talmud*. 24 vols. London: Soncino.

Eskola, Timo. 1997. "Paul, Predestination and Covenantal Nomism: Reassessing Paul and Palestinian Judaism." *Journal for the Study of Judaism* 28:390–412.

Evans, Craig. A. 1989. *To See and Not Perceive: Isaiah 6:9–10 in Early Jewish and Christian Interpretation*. Journal for the Study of the Old Testament: Supplement Series 64. Sheffield: JSOT Press.

———. 1992. *Noncanonical Writings and New Testament Interpretation*. Peabody, MA: Hendrickson.

Ewherido, Anthony O. 2006. *Matthew's Gospel and Judaism in the Late First Century C.E.: The Evidence from Matthew's Chapter on the Parables*. Studies in Biblical Literature 91. New York: Peter Lang.

Faierstein, M. M. 1981. "Why Do the Scribes Say That Elijah Must Come First?" *Journal of Biblical Literature* 100:75–86.

Falcetta, Alessandro. 2003. "The Logion of Matthew 11:5–6 par. from Qumran to Abgar." *Revue biblique* 110:222–48.

Falconer, W. A. 1923. *Cicero: De Senectute; De Amicitia; De Divinatione*. Loeb Classical Library. Cambridge, MA: Harvard University Press.

Falls, Thomas B. 1948. *Justin Martyr: The First Apology; The Second Apology; Dialogue with Trypho; Exhortation to the Greeks; Discourse to the Greeks; The Monarchy, or the Rule of God*. Fathers of the Church 6. Washington, DC: Catholic University of America Press.

Feldman, Louis H. 2002. "Philo's View of Moses' Birth and Upbringing." *Catholic Biblical Quarterly* 64:258–81.

Fenton, J. C. 1959. "Inclusio and Chiasmus in Matthew." In *Studia Evangelica*, vol. 1, edited by F. L. Cross, 174–79. Texte und Untersuchungen zur Geschichte der altchristlichen Literatur 73. Berlin: Akademie-Verlag.

———. 1978. *The Gospel of Saint Matthew*. Westminster Pelican Commentaries. Philadelphia: Westminster.

Feuillet, André. 1961. "Les Origines et la Signification de Matthieu 10:23b." *Catholic Biblical Quarterly* 23:182–98.

Fiedler, Peter. 1991. "Die Passion des Christus." In *Salz der Erde, Licht der Welt: Exegetische Studien zum Matthäusevangelium*, edited by L. Oberlinner and P. Fiedler, 299–319. Stuttgart: Katholisches Bibelwerk.

———. 2006. *Das Matthäusevangelium*. Theologischer Kommentar zum Neuen Testament 1. Stuttgart: Kohlhammer.

Filson, Floyd. 1960. *The Gospel according to St. Matthew*. Black's New Testament Commentaries. New York: Harper.

Fitzmyer, J. A. 1959. "The Aramaic Qorban Inscription from Jebel Hallet et-Turi and Mark 7:11//Matthew 15:51." *Journal of Biblical Literature* 78:60–65.

———. 1993. "4Q246: The 'Son of God' Document from Qumran." *Biblica* 74:53–74.

Forkman, G. 1972. *The Limits of Religious Community: Expulsion from the Religious Community within the Qumran Sect, within Rabbinic Judaism, and within Primitive Christianity*. Coniectanea biblica: New Testament Series 5. Lund: Gleerup.

Frankemölle, Hubert. 1974. *Jahwehbund und Kirche Christi*. Neutestamentliche Abhandlungen 10. Münster: Aschendorf.

———. 1997. *Matthäus*. 2 vols. Düsseldorf: Benziger.

Freedman, H., and Maurice Simon. 1939. *Midrash Rabbah*. 10 vols. London: Soncino.

Freese, J. H., trans. 1975. *Aristotle: The Art of Rhetoric*. Loeb Classical Library. Cambridge, MA: Harvard University Press.

Fuller, R. H. 1962. *The New Tesament in Current Study*. Scribner Studies in Biblical Interpretation. New York: Scribner.

———. 1963. *Interpreting the Miracles*. London: SCM.

———. 1965. *The Foundations of New Testament Christology*. New York: Scribner.

———. 1980. *The Formation of the Resurrection Narratives*. 2nd ed. Philadelphia: Fortress.

Gaechter, Paul. 1963. *Das Matthäus-Evangelium*. Innsbruck: Tyrolia.

———. 1965. *Die literarische Kunst im Matthäus-Evangelium*. Stuttgarter Bibelstudien 7. Stuttgart: Katholisches Bibelwerk.

Gager, John G. 1983. *The Origins of Anti-Semitism*. New York: Oxford University Press.

———. 1990. "Re-inventing Paul: Was the Apostle to the Gentiles the Father of Christian Anti-Judaism?" In *A Multiform Heritage: Studies on Early Judaism and Christianity*, edited by B. G. Wright, 49–63. Atlanta: Scholars Press.

Gale, Aaron. 2005. *Redefining Ancient Boundaries: The Jewish Scribal Framework of Matthew's Gospel*. New York: T&T Clark.

Gamba, G. G. 1998. *Vangelo di San Matteo: Una proposta di lettura*. Vol. 1, *Matteo 1:1–4:16: Chi è Gésu Christo*. Rome: LAS.

García Martínez, Florentino. 1996. *The Dead Sea Scrolls Translated*. 2nd ed. Grand Rapids: Eerdmans.

Garland, David E. 1979. *The Intention of Matthew 23*. Novum Testamentum Supplements 52. Leiden: Brill.

———. 2001. *Reading Matthew: A Literary and Theological Commentary on the First Gospel*. Reading the New Testament Series. Macon, GA: Smyth & Helwys.

Gaster, Moses. 1971. *Studies and Texts in Folklore, Magic, Mediaeval Romance, Hebrew Apocrypha and Samaritan Archaeology*. 3 vols. New York: KTAV.

Gaston, Lloyd. 1987. *Paul and the Torah*. Vancouver: University of British Columbia Press.

Gench, Frances Taylor. 1997. *Wisdom in the Christology of Matthew*. New York: University Press of America.

Genette, Gerad. 1982. *Palimpsestes: La literature au second degree.* Paris: Seuil.

Gerhardsson, Birger. 1966. *The Testing of God's Son.* Coniectanea biblica: New Testament Series 2.1. Lund: Gleerup.

————. 1981. *The Ethos of the Bible.* Philadelphia: Fortress.

————. 1991. "If We Do Not Cut the Parables out of Their Frames." *New Testament Studies* 37:321–35.

Gibbs, Jeffrey A. 2000. *Jerusalem and Parousia: Jesus's Eschatological Discourse in Matthew's Gospel.* St. Louis: Concordia Academic Press.

Giblin, C. H. 1968. "Theological Perspective and Matthew 10:23b." *Theological Studies* 29:637–61.

Gibson, Jeffrey B. 1995. *The Temptations of Jesus in Early Christianity.* Journal for the Study of the New Testament: Supplement Series 112. Sheffield: Sheffield Academic Press.

Gifford, E. H., trans. 1981. *Eusebius: Preparation for the Gospel.* Twin Brooks Series. Repr., Grand Rapids: Baker.

Gnilka, Joachim. 1986–88. *Das Matthäusevangelium.* 2 vols. Herders theologischer Kommentar zum Neuen Testament 1. Freiburg: Herder.

Goldin, Judah. 1955. *The Fathers according to Rabbi Nathan.* Yale Judaica Series 10. New Haven: Yale University Press.

Goodenough, E. R. 1953–68. *Jewish Symbols in the Greco-Roman Period.* 13 vols. New York: Pantheon Books.

Gooding, D. W. 1978. "Structure littéraire de Matthieu 13:53–18:35." *Revue biblique* 85:227–52.

Goulder, M. D. 1974. *Midrash and Lection in Matthew.* London: SPCK.

Gowler, David B. 2000. *What Are They Saying about the Parables?* New York: Paulist Press.

Grant, Robert M. 1978. "The Sermon on the Mount in Early Christianity." *Semeia* 12:215–31.

Gray, Sherman W. 1989. *The Least of My Brothers: Matthew 25:31–46; A History of Interpretation.* Society of Biblical Literature Dissertation Series 114. Atlanta: Scholars Press.

Grensted, L. W. 1962. *A Short History of the Doctrine of the Atonement.* Manchester, UK: Manchester University Press.

Grundmann, W. 1971. *Das Evangelium nach Matthäus.* 2nd ed. Theologischer Handkommentar zum Neuen Testament 1. Berlin: Evangelische Verlagsanstalt.

Gummere, Richard M., trans. 1970–79. *Seneca: Ad Lucilium Epistulae Morales.* Loeb Classical Library. Cambridge, MA: Harvard University Press.

Gundry, Robert H. 1982. *Matthew: A Commentary on His Literary and Theological Art.* Grand Rapids: Eerdmans.

Gurtner, David M. 2007. *The Torn Veil: Matthew's Exposition of the Death of Jesus.* Society for New Testament Studies Monograph Series 139. Cambridge, UK: Cambridge University Press.

Haenchen, Ernst. 1951. "Matthäus 23." *Zeitschrift für Theologie und Kirche* 48:38–63.

Hagner, Donald A. 1993–95. *Matthew*. 2 vols. Word Biblical Commentary 33A–B. Dallas: Word.

———. 1997. "Ethics and the Sermon on the Mount." *Studia theologica* 51:44–59.

———. 2000. "Matthew's Parables of the Kingdom (Matthew 13:1–52)." In *The Challenge of Jesus's Parables*, edited by R. N. Longenecker, 102–24. Grand Rapids: Eerdmans.

Hahn, Ferdinand. 1965. *Mission in the New Testament*. London: SCM.

Hamilton, James M., Jr. 2008. "The Virgin Will Conceive: Typological Fulfillment in Matthew 1:18–23." In *Built upon the Rock: Studies in the Gospel of Matthew*, edited by D. M. Gurtner and J. Nolland, 228–47. Grand Rapids: Eerdmans.

Hanson, John S. 1980. "Dreams and Visions in the Graeco-Roman World and Early Christianity." In *Aufstieg und Niedergang der römischen Welt*, edited by H. Temporini and W. Haase, 23.2:1395–1427. Berlin: de Gruyter.

Hanson, R. P. C. 1966. "A Note on Origen's Self-Mutilation." *Vigiliae christianae* 20:81–82.

Hare, D. R. A. 1967. *The Theme of Jewish Persecution of Christians in the Gospel according to St. Matthew*. Society for New Testament Studies Monograph Series 6. Cambridge, UK: Cambridge University Press.

———. 1993. *Matthew*. Interpretation. Louisville: John Knox.

Hare, D. R. A., and D. J. Harrington. 1975. "Make Disciples of All the Gentiles (Matthew 28:19)." *Catholic Biblical Quarterly* 37:359–69.

Harrington, Daniel. 1991. *The Gospel according to Matthew*. Sacra Pagina. Collegeville, MN: Liturgical Press.

———. 1998. "The Sermon on the Mount: What Is It?" *Bible Today* 36:280–86.

Harrington, Daniel, and James Keenan. 2002. *Jesus and Virtue Ethics*. Lanham, MD: Sheed & Ward.

Heil, John Paul. 1991a. *The Death and Resurrection of Jesus: A Narrative-Critical Reading of Matthew 26–28*. Minneapolis: Fortress.

———. 1991b. "The Narrative Roles of the Women in Matthew's Genealogy." *Biblica* 72:538–45.

———. 1993. "Ezekiel 34 and the Narrative Strategy of the Shepherd and Sheep Metaphor in Matthew." *Catholic Biblical Quarterly* 55:698–708.

Heitmüller, W. 1903. *In Namen Jesu*. Forschungen zur Religion und Literatur des Alten und Neuen Testaments 2. Göttingen: Vandenhoeck & Ruprecht.

Held, Heinz J. 1963. "Matthew as Interpreter of the Miracle Stories." In *Tradition and Interpretation in Matthew*, edited by G. Bornkamm, G. Barth, and H. J. Held, translated by Percy Scott, 165–229. London: SCM.

Hengel, Martin. 1981. *The Charismatic Leader and His Followers*. New York: Crossroad.

Hermant, Dominique. 1996. "Structure littéraire du 'Discours communautaire' de Matthieu 18." *Revue biblique* 103:76–90.

Herzog, William R. 1994. *Parable as Subversive Speech*. Louisville: Westminster John Knox.

Hicks, John. 1984. "The Sabbath Controversy in Matthew: An Exegesis of Matt. 12:1–14." *Restoration Quarterly* 27:79–91.

Hicks, R. D., trans. 1925. *Diogenes Laertius: Lives of the Eminent Philosophers*. 2 vols. Loeb Classical Library. Cambridge, MA: Harvard University Press.

Hill, D. 1980. "Son and Servant: An Essay on Matthean Christology." *Journal for the Study of the New Testament* 6:2–16.

Höistad, Ragnar. 1948. *Cynic Hero and Cynic King*. Lund: Carl Bloms Boktryckeri.

Horsley, Richard A. 1984. "Popular Messianic Movements around the Time of Jesus." *Catholic Biblical Quarterly* 46:471–95.

Horst, Pieter W. van der. 2002. "Celibacy in Early Judaism." *Revue biblique* 109:390–402.

Hubbard, B. J. 1974. *The Matthean Redaction of a Primitive Christian Commissioning: An Exegesis of Matthew 28:16–20*. Society of Biblical Literature Dissertation Series 19. Missoula, MT: Scholars Press.

Huizenga, Leroy A. 2005. "The Incarnation of the Servant: The Suffering Servant and Matthean Christology." *Horizons in Biblical Theology* 27:25–58.

Hultgren, Arland. 2000. *The Parables of Jesus*. Grand Rapids: Eerdmans.

Hunter, A. M. 1950. *The Work and Words of Jesus*. Philadelphia: Westminster.

Jackson, Glenna. 2002. *Have Mercy on Me: The Story of the Canaanite Woman in Matthew 15:21–28*. Journal for the Study of the New Testament: Supplement Series 228. Sheffield: Sheffield Academic Press.

James, M. R. 1924. *The Apocryphal New Testament*. Oxford: Clarendon.

Jeremias, Joachim. 1955. *The Parables of Jesus*. New York: Scribner.

———. 1958. *Jesus's Promise to the Nations*. Studies in Biblical Theology 24. Naperville, IL: Allenson.

Johnson, Luke T. 1989. "The New Testament's Anti-Jewish Slander and the Conventions of Ancient Polemic." *Journal of Biblical Literature* 108:419–41.

Kallas, James. 1968. *Jesus and the Power of Satan*. Philadelphia: Westminster.

Karris, Robert J. 1977. *Invitation to Luke*. Garden City, NY: Image Books.

Käsemann, Ernst. 1964. *Essays on New Testament Themes*. Studies in Biblical Theology 41. London: SCM.

Keck, L. E. 1986. "Toward the Renewal of New Testament Christology." *New Testament Studies* 32:362–77.

Keener, Craig. 1999. *A Commentary on the Gospel of Matthew*. Grand Rapids: Eerdmans.

Kennedy, George A. 2003. *Progymnasmata: Greek Textbooks of Prose Composition and Rhetoric*. Writings from the Greco-Roman World 10. Atlanta: Society of Biblical Literature.

Keyes, Clinton W., trans. 1928. *Cicero: De Republica; De Legibus*. Loeb Classical Library. Cambridge, MA: Harvard University Press.

Kim, Seyoon. 1985. *The Son of Man as the Son of God*. Grand Rapids: Eerdmans.

King, J. E., trans. 1945. *Cicero: Tusculan Disputations*. Rev. ed. Loeb Classical Library. Cambridge, MA: Harvard University Press.

Kingsbury, Jack D. 1969. *The Parables of Jesus in Matthew 13*. Richmond, VA: John Knox.

———. 1978. "Observations on the 'Miracle Chapters' of Matthew 8–9." *Catholic Biblical Quarterly* 40:559–73.

———. 1979. "The Figure of Peter in Matthew's Gospel as a Theological Problem." *Journal of Biblical Literature* 98:67–83.

———. 1986. *Matthew as Story*. Philadelphia: Fortress.

———. 1987. "The Place, Structure, and Meaning of the Sermon on the Mount within Matthew." *Interpretation* 41:131–43.

———. 1988. "On Following Jesus: The 'Eager' Scribe and the 'Reluctant' Disciple (Matthew 8:18–22)." *New Testament Studies* 34:45–59.

———. 1989. *Matthew: Structure, Christology, Kingdom*. 2nd ed. Minneapolis: Fortress.

———. 1992. "The Plot of Matthew's Story." *Interpretation* 46:347–56.

———. 1993. "The Significance of the Cross within the Plot of Matthew's Gospel." In *The Synoptic Gospels*, edited by Camille Focant, 263–80. Bibliotheca ephemeridum theologicarum lovaniensium 110. Louvain: Leuven University Press.

———. 2001. "The Birth Narrative of Matthew." In *The Gospel of Matthew in Current Study*, edited by D. E. Aune, 154–65. Grand Rapids: Eerdmans.

Kloppenborg, John S. 2005. "Evocatio Deorum and the Date of Mark." *Journal of Biblical Literature* 124:419–50.

Klostermann, Eric. 1927. *Das Matthäusevangelium*. Handbuch zum Neuen Testament 4. Tübingen: Mohr.

Knowles, Michael. 1993. *Jeremiah in Matthew's Gospel: The Rejected-Prophet Motif in Matthean Redaction*. Journal for the Study of the New Testament: Supplement Series 68. Sheffield: Sheffield Academic Press.

Kolenkow, Anitra B. 1976. "A Problem of Power: How Miracle Doers Counter Charges of Magic in the Hellenistic World." In *SBL 1976 Seminar Papers*, edited by George MacRae, 105–10. Missoula, MT: Scholars Press.

Kollmann, Bernd. 2006. "Images of Hope: Towards an Understanding of New Testament Miracle Stories." In *Wonders Never Cease: The Purpose of Narrating Miracle Stories in the New Testament and Its Religious Environment*, edited by M. Labahn and B. J. Lietaert Peerbolte, 244–64. Library of New Testament Studies 288. London: T&T Clark.

Korte, A.-M., ed. 2001. *Women and Miracle Stories: A Multidisciplinary Exploration*. Studies in the History of Religions 88. Leiden: Brill.

Krentz, E. 1964. "The Extent of Matthew's Prologue." *Journal of Biblical Literature* 83:401–14.

Küng, Hans. 1963. *The Council in Action*. New York: Sheed & Ward.

———. 1976. *On Being a Christian*. Garden City, NY: Doubleday.

Kupp, David. 1996. *Matthew's Emmanuel: Divine Presence and God's People in the First Gospel*. Society for New Testament Studies Monograph Series 90. Cambridge, UK: Cambridge University Press.

Kvalbein, Hans. 1998. "Hat Matthäus die Juden aufgegeben? Bemerkungen zu Ulrich Luz' Matthäus-Deutung." *Theologische Beiträge* 29:301–14.

Laato, Timo. 1995. *Paul and Judaism: An Anthropological Approach*. South Florida Studies in the History of Judaism 115. Atlanta: Scholars Press.

Lake, Kirsopp, trans. 1975. *Apostolic Fathers*. 2 vols. Loeb Classical Library. Cambridge, MA: Harvard University Press.

Lambrecht, Jan. 1972. "The Parousia Discourse: Composition and Content in Matthew 24–25." In *L'Évangile selon Matthieu*, edited by M. Didier, 309–42. Gembloux: Duculot.

———. 1981. *Once More Astonished: The Parables of Jesus*. New York: Crossroad.

———. 1985. *The Sermon on the Mount*. Good News Studies 14. Wilmington, DE: Michael Glazier.

———. 1991. *Out of the Treasure: The Parables in the Gospel of Matthew*. Grand Rapids: Eerdmans.

Lampe, G. W. H. 1984. "AD 70 in Christian Reflection." In *Jesus and the Politics of His Day*, edited by E. Bammel and C. F. D. Moule, 153–71. Cambridge, UK: Cambridge University Press.

Lauterbach, Jacob Z., trans. 1961. *Mekilta de-Rabbi Ishmael: A Critical Edition on the Basis of the Manuscripts and Early Editions*. Philadelphia: Jewish Publication Society of America.

Léon-Dufour, X. 1965. "Vers l'annonce de l'Église: Matthieu 14:1–16:20." In *Études d'évangile*, 231–54. Parole de Dieu. Paris: Seuil.

Linton, Otto. 1976. "The Parable of the Children's Game: Matthew 11:16–19." *New Testament Studies* 22:159–79.

Lohr, C. H. 1961. "Oral Techniques in the Gospel of Matthew." *Catholic Biblical Quarterly* 23:403–35.

Lohse, E. 1961. "Der Prozess Jesu Christi." In *Ecclesia und Res Publica*, edited by G. Kretschmar and B. Lohse, 24–39. Göttingen: Vandenhoeck & Ruprecht.

Lowe, Malcolm. 1982. "From the Parable of the Vineyard to a Pre-Synoptic Source." *New Testament Studies* 28:257–63.

Luomanen, Petri. 1998a. "Corpus Mixtum—An Appropriate Description of Matthew's Community?" *Journal of Biblical Literature* 117:469–80.

———. 1998b. *Entering the Kingdom of Heaven: A Study on the Structure of Matthew's View of Salvation*. Wissenschaftliche Untersuchungen zum Neuen Testament 2/101. Tübingen: Mohr Siebeck.

Lutz, Cora E. 1947. *Musonius Rufus, "The Roman Socrates."* Yale Classical Studies 10. New Haven: Yale University Press.

Luz, Ulrich. 1992. "The Son of Man in Matthew: Heavenly Judge or Human Christ." *Journal for the Study of the New Testament* 48:3–21.

———. 1994. *Matthew in History*. Minneapolis: Fortress.

———. 1995. "The Disciples in the Gospel according to Matthew." In *The Interpretation of Matthew*, edited by G. Stanton, 115–48. Studies in New Testament Interpretation. Edinburgh: T&T Clark.

———. 1989–2005. *Matthew: A Commentary*. 3 vols. Minneapolis: Augsburg Fortress.

Macaskill, Grant. 2007. *Revealed Wisdom and Inaugurated Eschatology in Ancient Judaism and Early Christianity*. Supplements to the Journal for the Study of Judaism 115. Leiden: Brill.

Maher, M. 1975. "Take My Yoke upon You (Matthew 11:29)." *New Testament Studies* 22:97–103.

Malherbe, A. J., ed. 1977. *The Cynic Epistles: A Study Edition.* Society of Biblical Literature Sources for Biblical Study 12. Missoula, MT: Scholars Press.

Marchant, E. C., and O. J. Todd, trans. 1979. *Xenophon: Memorabilia and Oeconomicus; Symposium and Apologia.* Loeb Classical Library. Cambridge, MA: Harvard University Press.

Marcus, Joel. 2006. "Crucifixion as Parodic Exaltation." *Journal of Biblical Literature* 125:73–87.

Marguerat, Daniel. 1995. *Le jugement dans l'Évangile de Matthieu.* Le Monde de la Bible. 6th ed. rev. Geneva: Labor et Fides.

Marguerat, Daniel, and Yvan Bourquin. 1999. *How to Read Bible Stories: An Introduction to Narrative Criticism.* London: SCM.

Martens, Allan W. 2000. "Produce Fruit Worthy of Repentance: Parables of Judgment against the Jewish Religious Leaders and the Nation (Matthew 21:28–22:14)." In *The Challenge of Jesus's Parables,* edited by R. N. Longenecker, 151–76. Grand Rapids: Eerdmans.

Marxsen, Willi. 1993. *New Testament Foundations for Christian Ethics.* Minneapolis: Fortress.

Mason, Steve. 1990. "Pharisaic Dominance before 70 C.E. and the Gospels' Hypocrisy Charge (Matthew 23:2–3)." *Harvard Theological Review* 83:363–81.

Matera, Frank. 1986. *Passion Narratives and Gospel Theologies.* New York: Paulist Press.

———. 1987. "The Plot of Matthew's Gospel." *Catholic Biblical Quarterly* 49:233–53.

Mattila, Talvikka. 2002. *Citizens of the Kingdom: Followers in Matthew from a Feminist Perspective.* Finnish Exegetical Society in Helsinki 83. Göttingen: Vandenhoeck & Ruprecht.

McArthur, Harvey. 1960. *Understanding the Sermon on the Mount.* New York: Harper & Brothers.

McDermott, John M. 1984. "Matt 10:23 in Context." *Biblische Zeitschrift* 28:230–39.

McGing, Brian. 1991. "Pontius Pilate and the Sources." *Catholic Biblical Quarterly* 53:416–38.

Meier, John P. 1977. "Nations or Gentiles in Matthew 28:19?" *Catholic Biblical Quarterly* 39:94–102.

———. 1979. *The Vision of Matthew.* Theological Inquiries. New York: Paulist Press.

———. 1980. "John the Baptist in Matthew's Gospel." *Journal of Biblical Literature* 99:383–405.

———. 1992. "The Brothers and Sisters of Jesus in Ecumenical Perspective." *Catholic Biblical Quarterly* 54:1–28.

Merenlahti, Petri. 2002. *Poetics for the Gospels? Rethinking Narrative Criticism.* Studies of the New Testament and Its World. London: T&T Clark.

Meyer, Ben F. 1994. *Five Speeches That Changed the World.* Collegeville, MN: Liturgical Press.

Michaels, J. R. 1965. "Apostolic Hardships and Righteous Gentiles: A Study of Matthew 25:31–46." *Journal of Biblical Literature* 84:27–37.

Milavec, Aaron A. 1989. "A Fresh Analysis of the Parable of the Wicked Husbandmen in the Light of Jewish-Catholic Dialogue." In *Parable and Story in Judaism and Christianity*, edited by Clemens Thoma and M. Wyschogrod, 81–117. New York: Paulist Press.

Miller, Walter, trans. 1914. *Xenophon: Cyropaedia*. 2 vols. Loeb Classical Library. Cambridge, MA: Harvard University Press.

Mohrlang, R. 1984. *Matthew and Paul*. Society for New Testament Studies Monograph Series 48. Cambridge, UK: Cambridge University Press.

Moiser, Jeremy. 1985. "The Structure of Matthew 8–9: A Suggestion." *Zeitschrift für neutestamentliche Wissenschaft* 76:117–18.

Moore, Clifford H., trans. 1925–31. *Tacitus: Histories*. 2 vols. Loeb Classical Library. Cambridge, MA: Harvard University Press.

Moore, George F. 1927–30. *Judaism in the First Centuries of the Christian Era*. 3 vols. Cambridge, MA: Harvard University Press.

Morosco, Robert E. 1984. "Matthew's Formation of a Commissioning Type-Scene out of the Story of Jesus's Commissioning of the Twelve." *Journal of Biblical Literature* 103:539–56.

Morris, Leon. 1992. *The Gospel according to Matthew*. Grand Rapids: Eerdmans.

Münch, Christian. 2004. *Die Gleichnisse Jesu im Matthäusevangelium*. Wissenschaftliche Monographien zum Alten und Neuen Testament 104. Neukirchen-Vluyn: Neukirchener Verlag.

Murphy-O'Connor, Jerome. 1975. "The Structure of Matthew 14–17." *Revue biblique* 82:360–84.

Murray, A. T., trans. 1924–25. *Homer: Iliad*. 2 vols. Loeb Classical Library. Cambridge, MA: Harvard University Press.

Mussies, Gerard. 1988. "Joseph's Dream (Matt. 1:18–23) and Comparable Stories." In *Text and Testimony: Essays on New Testament and Apocryphal Literature in Honour of A. F. J. Klijn*, edited by T. J. Baarda, 177–86. Kampen: Kok.

Nau, Arlo J. 1983. "A Redaction-Critical Analysis of the Role of Peter in the Gospel of Matthew." DTheol diss., University of Toronto.

Neirynck, F. 1967. "La rédaction Matthéenne et la structure du premier évangile." *Ephemerides theologicae lovanienses* 43:41–73.

———. 1988. "*Apo Tote Erxatō* and the Structure of Matthew." *Ephemerides theologicae lovanienses* 64:21–59.

Neirynck, F., J. Verheyden, and R. Corstjens. 1998. *The Gospel of Matthew and the Sayings Source Q: A Cumulative Bibliography 1950–95*. Louvain: Leuven University Press and Peeters.

Nepper-Christensen, P. 1954. *Das Matthäusevangelium: Ein judenchristliches Evangelium?* Aarhus: Universitetsforlaget.

Neusner, Jacob. 1973. *From Politics to Piety*. Englewood Cliffs, NJ: Prentice-Hall.

———, trans. 1982–94. *The Talmud of the Land of Israel*. Chicago: University of Chicago Press.

———, trans. 1985. *Genesis Rabbah: The Judaic Commentary to the Book of Genesis; A New American Translation*. Brown Judaic Studies 104. Atlanta: Scholars Press.

———, trans. 1988. *Mekhilta according to Rabbi Ishmael: An Analytical Translation*. Brown Judaic Studies 148. Atlanta: Scholars Press.

———. 2000. *A Rabbi Talks with Jesus*. Rev. ed. Montreal: McGill-Queens University Press.

———, trans. 2002. *The Tosefta: Translated from the Hebrew with a New Introduction*. Peabody, MA: Hendrickson.

Neusner, Jacob, and Richard S. Sarason, eds. 1977–86. *The Tosefta*. New York: Ktav.

Newport, Kenneth G. C. 1995. *The Sources and Sitz im Leben of Matthew 23*. Journal for the Study of the New Testament: Supplement Series 117. Sheffield: Sheffield Academic Press.

Neyrey, Jerome. 1980. "The Apologetic Use of the Transfiguration in 2 Peter 1:16–21." *Catholic Biblical Quarterly* 42:504–19.

———. 1982. "The Thematic Use of Isaiah 42:1–4 in Matthew 12." *Biblica* 63:457–73.

———. 1998. *Honor and Shame in the Gospel of Matthew*. Louisville: Westminster John Knox.

Nicholls, Rachel. 2008. *Walking on the Water: Reading Mt 14:22–33 in the Light of Its Wirkungsgeschichte*. Biblical Interpretation Series 90. Leiden: Brill.

Nickelsburg, George W. E. 2006. "First and Second Enoch: A Cry against Oppression and the Promise of Deliverance." In *The Historical Jesus in Context*, edited by A. J. Levine et al., 87–109. Princeton Readings in Religion. Princeton: Princeton University Press.

Nock, A. D. 1998. *Conversion*. Baltimore: Johns Hopkins University Press.

Nolan, Brian M. 1979. *The Royal Son of God*. Orbis biblicus et orientalis 23. Göttingen: Vandenhoeck & Ruprecht.

Nolland, John. 1993. *Luke 9:21–18:34*. Word Biblical Commentary 35B. Dallas: Word.

———. 2005. *The Gospel of Matthew*. New International Greek Testament Commentary. Grand Rapids: Eerdmans.

Novakovic, Lidija. 2003. *Messiah, the Healer of the Sick: A Study of Jesus as the Son of David in the Gospel of Matthew*. Wissenschaftliche Untersuchungen zum Neuen Testament 2/170. Tübingen: Mohr Siebeck.

Nowell, Irene. 2008. "Jesus's Great-Grandmothers: Matthew's Four and More." *Catholic Biblical Quarterly* 70:1–15.

Oldfather, C. H., et al., trans. 1933–67. *Diodorus Siculus: Library of History*. 12 vols. Loeb Classical Library. Cambridge, MA: Harvard University Press.

Oldfather, W. A., trans. 1925–28. *Epictetus*. 2 vols. Loeb Classical Library. Cambridge, MA: Harvard University Press.

Olmstead, Wesley G. 2003. *Matthew's Trilogy of Parables: The Nation, the Nations and the Reader in Matthew 21:28–22:14*. Society for New Testament Studies Monograph Series 127. Cambridge, UK: Cambridge University Press.

Orton, David. 1989. *The Understanding Scribe: Matthew and the Apocalyptic Ideal*. Journal for the Study of the New Testament: Supplement Series 25. Sheffield: Sheffield Academic Press.

Ostmeyer, Karl-Heinrich. 2004. "Jesus's Acceptance of Children (Matthew 19:13–15)." *Theology Digest* 51:125–28.

Paley, William. 1794. *A View of the Evidences of Christianity*. London: Faulder.

Park, Eung Chun. 1995. *The Mission Discourse in Matthew's Interpretation*. Wissenschaftliche Untersuchungen zum Neuen Testament 2/81. Tübingen: Mohr Siebeck.

Patte, Daniel. 1987. *The Gospel according to Matthew*. Philadelphia: Fortress.

Paulus, H. E. G. 1828. *Das Leben Jesu als Grundlage einer reinen Geschichte des Urchristentums*. 2 vols. Heidelberg: Winter.

Penney, D. L., and M. O. Wise. 1994. "By the Power of Beelzebub: An Aramaic Incantation Formula from Qumran." *Journal of Biblical Literature* 113:627–50.

Pennington, Jonathan. 2007. *Heaven and Earth in the Gospel of Matthew*. Novum Testamentum Supplements 126. Leiden: Brill. Repr., Grand Rapids: Baker Academic, 2009.

Perrin, Bernadotte, trans. 1914–26. *Plutarch: The Parallel Lives*. 11 vols. Loeb Classical Library. Cambridge, MA: Harvard University Press.

Pfleiderer, Otto. 1906. *Christian Origins*. New York: Huebsch.

Pilch, John. 1995. "The Transfiguration of Jesus: An Experience of Alternate Reality." In *Modeling Early Christianity*, edited by Philip Esler, 47–64. New York: Routledge.

Porter, Stanley. 1989. *Verbal Aspect in the Greek of the New Testament*. New York: Peter Lang.

Powell, Mark A. 1992. "The Plot and Subplots of Matthew." *New Testament Studies* 38:187–204.

———. 1995a. "Do and Keep What Moses Says (Matthew 23:2–7)." *Journal of Biblical Literature* 114:419–35.

———. 1995b. *God with Us: A Pastoral Theology of Matthew's Gospel*. Minneapolis: Fortress.

———. 2003. "Binding and Loosing: A Paradigm for Ethical Discernment from the Gospel of Matthew." *Current Theology of Mission* 30:438–45.

Pregeant, Russell. 1996. "Wisdom Passages in Matthew." In *Treasures New and Old: Contributions to Matthean Studies*, edited by D. R. Bauer and M. A. Powell, 197–232. Society of Biblical Literature Symposium Series 1. Atlanta: Scholars Press.

Pritchard, James B. 1955. *Ancient Near Eastern Texts Relating to the Old Testament*. 2nd ed. Princeton: Princeton University Press.

Rabinowitz, Peter J. 1977. "Truth in Fiction: A Reexamination of Audiences." *Critical Inquiry* 4:121–41.

———. 1987. *Before Reading: Narrative Conventions and the Politics of Interpretation*. Ithaca, NY: Cornell University Press.

———. 1989. "Whirl without End: Audience-Oriented Criticism." In *Contemporary Literary Theory*, edited by G. D. Atkins, 81–100. Amherst: University of Massachusetts Press.

Rackham, H., et al., trans. 1938–63. *Pliny: Natural History*. 10 vols. Loeb Classical Library. Cambridge, MA: Harvard University Press.

Rad, Gerhard von. 1962. *Old Testament Theology*. 2 vols. Edinburgh: T&T Clark.

Ratzinger, Joseph (Pope Benedict XVI). 2007. *Jesus of Nazareth*. New York: Doubleday.

Reinbold, Wolfgang. 1994. *Der älteste Bericht über den Tod Jesu.* Beihefte zur Zeitschrift für die neutestamentliche Wissenschaft 69. Berlin: de Gruyter.

Renberg, Gil H. 2003. "Commanded by the Gods: An Epigraphical Study of Dreams and Visions in Greek and Roman Religious Life." PhD diss., Duke University.

Repschinski, Boris. 2000. *The Controversy Stories in the Gospel of Matthew.* Forschungen zur Religion und Literatur des Alten und Neuen Testaments 189. Göttingen: Vandenhoeck & Ruprecht.

Reuther, Rosemary. 1974. *Faith and Fratricide: The Theological Roots of Anti-Semitism.* New York: Seabury.

Riches, John. 1996. *Matthew.* New Testament Guides. Sheffield: Sheffield Academic Press.

———. 2000. *Conflicting Mythologies: Identity Formation in the Gospels of Mark and Matthew.* Studies of the New Testament and Its World. Edinburgh: T&T Clark.

Riches, John, and David C. Sim, eds. 2005. *The Gospel of Matthew in Its Roman Imperial Context.* Journal for the Study of the New Testament: Supplement Series 276. London: T&T Clark.

Ringe, Sharon. 1985. "A Gentile Woman's Story." In *Feminist Interpretations of the Bible,* edited by Letty Russell, 65–72. Philadelphia: Westminster.

Ringe, Sharon, and H. C. Paul Kim, eds. 2004. *Literary Encounters with the Reign of God.* New York: T&T Clark.

Rivkin, Ellis. 1978. *The Hidden Revolution.* Nashville: Abingdon.

Robbins, Vernon. 1984. *Jesus the Teacher.* Philadelphia: Fortress.

Roberts, W. R., et al., trans. 1965. *Aristotle: The Poetics; Longinus: On the Sublime; Demetrius: On Style.* Loeb Classical Library. Cambridge, MA: Harvard University Press.

Rolfe, John C., trans. 1927. *Gellius: Attic Nights.* 3 vols. Loeb Classical Library. Cambridge, MA: Harvard University Press.

———, trans. 1997–98. *Suetonius: The Lives of the Caesars.* Rev. ed. 2 vols. Loeb Classical Library. Cambridge, MA: Harvard University Press.

Roloff, Jürgen. 2005. *Jesu Gleichnisse im Matthäusevangelium: Ein Kommentar zu Mt 13,1–52.* Edited by Helmut Kreller and Rainer Oechslen. Biblisch-theologische Studien 73. Neukirchen-Vluyn: Neukirchener Verlag.

Rosenzweig, Franz. 1971. *The Star of Redemption.* New York: Holt, Rinehart & Winston.

Sabourin, Leopold. 1977. "You Will Not Have Gone through All the Towns of Israel, Before the Son of Man Comes (Matthew 10:23b)." *Biblical Theology Bulletin* 7:5–11.

Saldarini, Anthony J. 2001. "Reading Matthew without Anti-Semitism." In *The Gospel of Matthew in Current Study,* edited by D. E. Aune, 166–84. Grand Rapids: Eerdmans.

Sanders, E. P. 1983. *Paul and Palestinian Judaism.* Philadelphia: Fortress.

———. 1985. *Paul, the Law, and the Jewish People.* Philadelphia: Fortress.

Sato, M. 2001. "Ist Matthäus wirklich Judenchrist?" *Annual of the Japanese Biblical Institute* 27:155–73.

Schaff, Philip. 1931. *The Creeds of Christendom: With a History and Critical Notes.* Revised by David S. Schaff. 6th ed. 3 vols. New York: Harper & Row. Repr., Grand Rapids: Baker, 1990.

341

Schnackenburg, Rudolf. 2002. *The Gospel of Matthew*. Grand Rapids: Eerdmans.

Schneemelcher, Wilhelm, ed. 1991–92. *New Testament Apocrypha*. English translation edited by R. McL. Wilson. Rev. ed. 2 vols. Cambridge: James Clarke; Louisville: Westminster/John Knox.

Scholem, G. G. 1995. *Major Trends in Jewish Mysticism*. New York: Schocken Books.

Schwartz, Joshua. 1995. "Peter and ben Stada in Lydda." In *The Book of Acts in Its Palestinian Setting*, edited by R. Bauckham, 391–414. Grand Rapids: Eerdmans.

Schweitzer, Albert. 1910. *The Quest of the Historical Jesus*. Cambridge, UK: Black.

———. 1957. *The Mystery of the Kingdom of God*. New York: Macmillan.

Schweizer, Eduard. 1975. *The Good News according to Matthew*. Atlanta: John Knox.

Seeley, David. 1994. *Deconstructing the New Testament*. Biblical Interpretation Series 5. Leiden: Brill.

Segal, Alan F. 1986. *Rebecca's Children*. Cambridge, MA: Harvard University Press.

———. 1990. *Paul the Convert*. New Haven: Yale University Press.

Senior, Donald. 1972. "The Passion Narrative in the Gospel of Matthew." In *L'Évangile selon Matthieu*, edited by M. Didier, 309–42. Bibliotheca ephemeridum theologicarum lovaniensium 29. Gembloux: Duculot.

———. 1990. *The Passion of Jesus in the Gospel of Matthew*. Collegeville, MN: Liturgical Press.

———. 1998. *Matthew*. Abingdon New Testament Commentaries. Nashville: Abingdon.

Shin, In-Cheol. 2007. "Matthew's Designation of the Role of Women as Indirectly Adherent Disciples." *Neotestamentica* 41:399–415.

Shuler, Philip L. 1982. *A Genre for the Gospels*. Philadelphia: Fortress.

Siegman, Henry. 1978. "A Decade of Catholic-Jewish Relations: A Reassessment." *Journal of Ecumenical Studies* 15:243–60.

Sim, D. C. 1993a. "The Confession of the Soldiers in Matthew 27:54." *Heythrop Journal* 34:401–24.

———. 1993b. "The Meaning of *Palingenesia* in Matthew 19:28." *Journal for the Study of the New Testament* 50:3–12.

Smith, David W. 1970. *Wisdom Christology in the Synoptic Gospels*. Rome: Pontificia Studiorum Universitas a S. Thoma Aq. in Urbe.

Smith, Robert H. 1992. "Matthew's Message for Insiders." *Interpretation* 46:229–39.

Snodgrass, Klyne. 1996. "Matthew and the Law." In *Treasures New and Old: Contributions to Matthean Studies,* edited by David Bauer and M. A. Powell, 99–128. Society of Biblical Literature Symposium Series. Atlanta: Scholars Press.

———. 2000. "From Allegorizing to Allegorizing." In *The Challenge of Jesus's Parables*, edited by R. N. Longenecker, 3–29. Grand Rapids: Eerdmans.

———. 2008. *Stories with Intent: A Comprehensive Guide to the Parables of Jesus*. Grand Rapids: Eerdmans.

Soares Prabhu, George M. 1976. *The Formula Quotations in the Infancy Narrative of Matthew*. Analecta biblica 63. Rome: Biblical Institute Press.

Stanley, D. M. 1956. "The Concept of Salvation in the Synoptic Gospels." *Catholic Biblical Quarterly* 18:345–63.

———. 1980. *Jesus in Gethsemane*. New York: Paulist Press.

Stanton, Graham N. 1992. *A Gospel for a New People: Studies in Matthew*. Louisville: Westminster John Knox.

———. 2004. "Jesus of Nazareth: A Magician and a False Prophet Who Deceived God's People." In *Jesus and Gospel*, 127–47. Cambridge, UK: Cambridge University Press.

Stendahl, Krister. 1960. "Quis et Unde? An Analysis of Matthew 1–2." In *Judentum, Urchristentum, Kirche*, edited by W. Eltester, 94–105. Beihefte zur Zeitschrift für die neutestamentliche Wissenschaft 26. Berlin: Töpelmann.

———. 1968. *The School of St. Matthew and Its Use of the Old Testament*. Philadelphia: Fortress.

———. 1976. *Paul among Jews and Gentiles and Other Essays*. Philadelphia: Fortress.

Stern, David. 1989. "Jesus's Parables from the Perspective of Rabbinic Literature: The Example of the Wicked Husbandmen." In *Parable and Story in Judaism and Christianity*, edited by C. Thoma and M. Wyschogrod, 42–50. New York: Paulist Press.

Sternberg, Meir. 1985. *The Poetics of Biblical Narrative*. Bloomington: Indiana University Press.

Stock, Augustine. 1987. "Is Matthew's Presentation of Peter Ironic?" *Biblical Theology Bulletin* 8:24–33.

———. 1994. *The Method and Message of Matthew*. Collegeville, MN: Liturgical Press.

Strauss, David F. 1879. *A New Life of Jesus*. 2nd ed. 2 vols. London: Williams & Norgate. Orig. German edition, 1864.

———. 1972. *The Life of Jesus Critically Examined*. Edited by Peter Hodgson. Lives of Jesus Series. Philadelphia: Fortress. Orig. German edition, 1840.

Strecker, G. 1962. *Der Weg der Gerechtigkeit*. Forschungen zur Religion und Literatur des Alten und Neuen Testaments 82. Göttingen: Vandenhoeck & Ruprecht.

Suggs, M. Jack. 1970. *Wisdom, Christology, and Law in Matthew's Gospel*. Cambridge, MA: Harvard University Press.

Sutton, E. W., and H. Rackham, trans. 1942. *Cicero: De Oratore*. 2 vols. Loeb Classical Library. Cambridge, MA: Harvard University Press.

Tagawa, Kenso. 1966. *Miracles et Évangile, la pensée personelle de l'évangéliste Marc*. Études d'histoire et de philosophie religieuses 62. Paris: Presses universitaires de France.

Talbert, Charles H. 1975. "The Concept of Immortals in Mediterranean Antiquity." *Journal of Biblical Literature* 94:419–36.

———. 1977. *What Is a Gospel?* Philadelphia: Fortress.

———. 1988. "Once Again: Gospel Genre." *Semeia* 43:53–73.

———. 1994. *The Apocalypse: A Reading of the Revelation of John*. Louisville: Westminster John Knox.

———. 2001. "Indicative and Imperative in Matthean Soteriology." *Biblica* 82:515–38.

———. 2002. *Reading Luke*. Rev. ed. Macon, GA: Smyth & Helwys.

———. 2004a. "Is It with Ethics That the Sermon on the Mount Is Concerned?" In *Literary Encounters with the Reign of God*, edited by S. H. Ringe and H. C. P. Kim, 45–63. New York: T&T Clark.

———. 2004b. *Reading the Sermon on the Mount*. Columbia: University of South Carolina Press. Repr., Grand Rapids: Baker Academic, 2006.

———. 2005. *Reading John*. Rev. ed. Macon, GA: Smyth & Helwys.

Tannehill, Robert C. 1975. *The Sword of His Mouth*. Semeia Supplements 1. Missoula, MT: Scholars Press.

Tenney, Merrill. 1963. *The Reality of the Resurrection*. New York: Harper & Row.

Thackeray, H. St. John, trans. 1927–28. *Josephus: The Jewish War*. 3 vols. Loeb Classical Library. Cambridge, MA: Harvard University Press.

Theissen, Gerd. 1991. *The Gospels in Context*. Minneapolis: Fortress.

Thielicke, Helmut. 1964. "The Resurrection Kerygma." In *The Easter Message Today*, edited by Markus Barth, 59–116. New York: Nelson.

Thomas Aquinas. 2009. *Compendium of Theology*. Translated by Richard J. Regan. Oxford: Oxford University Press.

Thompson, M. M. 1982. "The Structure of Matthew: A Survey of Recent Trends." *Studia biblica et theologica* 12:195–238.

Thompson, William G. 1970. *Matthew's Advice to a Divided Community: Matthew 17:22–18:35*. Analecta biblica 44. Rome: Biblical Institute Press.

———. 1971. "Reflections on the Composition of Matthew 8:1–9:34." *Catholic Biblical Quarterly* 33:365–88.

Tisera, Guido. 1993. *Universalism according to the Gospel of Matthew*. Europäische Hochschulschriften XXIII/482. Frankfurt: Peter Lang.

Trilling, Wolfgang. 1959. *Das Wahre Israel*. Leipzig: St. Benno-Verlag.

Tropper, Amram. 2006. "Children and Childhood in Light of the Demographics of the Jewish Family in Late Antiquity." *Journal for the Study of Judaism* 37:299–343.

Turner, David L. 2008. *Matthew*. Baker Exegetical Commentary on the New Testament. Grand Rapids: Baker Academic.

Underdowne, Thomas, trans. 1923. *Heliodorus of Emesa: An Æthiopian Romance*. Revised and partly rewritten by F. A. Wright. New York: Dutton.

Unnik, W. C. van. 1959. "Dominus Vobiscum: The Background of a Liturgical Formula." In *New Testament Essays*, edited by A. J. B. Higgins, 270–305. Manchester, UK: Manchester University Press.

Van Aarde, A. G. 1982. "Matthew's Portrayal of the Disciples and the Structure of Matthew 13:53–17:27." *Neotestamentica* 16:21–34.

Verseput, David. 1986. *The Rejection of the Humble Messianic King: A Study of the Composition of Matthew 11–12*. European University Studies XXIII/291. New York: Peter Lang.

———. 1992. "The Faith of the Reader and the Narrative of Matthew 13:53–16:20." *Journal for the Study of the New Testament* 46:3–24.

Via, Dan O., Jr. 1967. *The Parables: Their Literary and Existential Dimension*. Philadelphia: Fortress.

Viviano, Benedict T. 2007. *Matthew and His World: The Gospel of the Open Jewish Christians; Studies in Biblical Theology*. Novum Testamentum et Orbis Antiquus, Studien zur Umwelt des Neuen Testaments 61. Göttingen: Vandenhoeck & Ruprecht.

Vledder, Evert-Jan. 1997. *Conflict in the Miracle Stories: A Socio-Exegetical Study of Matthew 8 and 9*. Journal for the Study of the New Testament: Supplement Series 152. Sheffield: Sheffield Academic Press.

Wainwright, Elaine. 2001. "The Matthean Jesus and the Healing of Women." In *The Gospel of Matthew in Current Study*, edited by D. E. Aune, 74–95. Grand Rapids: Eerdmans.

Weaver, Dorothy Jean. 1990. *Matthew's Missionary Discourse*. Journal for the Study of the New Testament: Supplement Series 38. Sheffield: Sheffield Academic Press.

Weaver, Joel A. 2007. *Theodoret of Cyrus on Romans 11:26: Recovering an Early Christian Elijah Redivivus Tradition*. American University Studies Series VII/249, Theology and Religion. New York: Peter Lang.

Weiss, Johannes. 1959. *Earliest Christianity*. 2 vols. New York: Harper & Brothers.

Wenham, David. 1984. *The Rediscovery of Jesus's Eschatological Discourse*. Gospel Perspectives 4. Sheffield: JSOT Press.

Wenham, John W. 1981. "When Were the Saints Raised? A Note on the Punctuation of Matthew 27:51–53." *Journal of Theological Studies* 32:150–52.

Weren, W. J. C. 2006. "The Macrostructure of Matthew's Gospel: A New Proposal." *Biblica* 87:171–200.

Westcott, B. F. 1859. *Characteristics of the Gospel Miracles*. Cambridge, UK: Macmillan.

Williams, Benjamin E. 1988. "Miracle-Mission-Competition? Miracle-Working in the Early Christian Mission and Its Cultural Environment." ThD diss., Erlangen.

Willitts, Joel. 2007. *Matthew's Messianic Shepherd-King*. Beihefte zur Zeitschrift für die neutestamentliche Wissenschaft 147. Berlin: de Gruyter.

Wise, M. O., and J. D. Tabor. 1992. "The Messiah at Qumran." *Biblical Archaeology Review* 18.6:60–63, 65.

Witherington, Ben, III. 2006. *Matthew*. Smyth & Helwys Bible Commentary. Macon, GA: Smyth & Helwys.

Wittig, Susan. 1975. "A Theory of Polyvalent Reading." In *SBL 1975 Seminar Papers*, edited by George MacRae, 169–83. Missoula, MT: Scholars Press.

Wright, W. C., trans. 1921. *Philostratus and Eunapius: The Lives of the Sophists*. Loeb Classical Library. Cambridge, MA: Harvard University Press.

Wuellner, Wilhelm. 1967. *The Meaning of Fishers of Men*. New Testament Library. Philadelphia: Westminster.

Yoder, John Howard. 1994. *The Politics of Jesus*. 2nd ed. Grand Rapids: Eerdmans.

Zimmern, Alice, trans. 1986. *Porphyry's Letter to His Wife Marcella: Concerning the Life of Philosophy and the Ascent to the Gods*. With an introduction by David R. Fideler. Repr., Grand Rapids: Phanes.

345

Subject Index

Index of Modern Authors

351

Index of Scripture
and Ancient Sources

375